BE
BOOKS

EXPERTS CHOOSE THEIR FAVOURITES

BEST BOOKS

EXPERTS CHOOSE THEIR FAVOURITES

Helicon

© Helicon Publishing Ltd 1996

First published 1996
Paperback edition 1997

Helicon Publishing Ltd
42 Hythe Bridge St
Oxford OX1 2EP

Set in 9/11 Plantin

Page make-up TechType, Abingdon
Printed and bound in Great Britain by
The Bath Press Ltd, Bath

ISBN 1-85986-195-4

**British Library Cataloguing in
Publication Data**
A catalogue record for this book is
available from the British Library

A 10% royalty on the net receipts of all
sales of this book will be donated to
Oxfam (United Kingdom and Ireland), a
registered charity number 202918.
Oxfam UK and Ireland is a member of
Oxfam International.

Cover illustration and drawings
by Nicolette Castle

Papers used by Helicon Publishing Ltd are
natural recyclable products made from wood
grown in sustainable forests. The
manufacturing processes of both raw
materials and paper conform to the
environmental regulations of the country of
origin.

MANAGING EDITOR
Denise Dresner

EDITOR
Chris Murray

TEXT EDITORS
Ingrid von Essen
Jo Linzey

PREFACE

by Doris Lessing

Into a very large bookshop the other day came two girls of about fifteen, both as excited as if off to a party, but when they saw all those books, shelves upon shelves of them, their faces became apprehensive and they stood very close together, staring around. They were about to turn tail, but I went up to them and asked if they needed help. They were looking for a book, they said. Which book? Well ... they didn't know. Their teacher had told them they must read books and not watch so much television. They had had no idea there were so many books. No, there were no books in either of their homes, their parents did not read books. I stood with them and saw through their eyes a space the size of a warehouse filled with thousands of books, each one an unknown, a challenge, a mystery. So I went with them to this section and that, explaining how the store was laid out, how the divisions represented novels, biography (stories about other people), autobiography (stories by people about themselves), animals, travel, science, and so on. They went out with half a dozen books, and I hope that later they did return to a bookshop.

I think that people whose profession is books, or who have been brought up in a household where books are taken for granted, can have no idea of the confusion, the dismay, the discouragement, that must afflict young people advised to read, when they have no parent or older friend to advise them.

I left that bookstore wishing there were a book of simple – perhaps even oversimplified – suggestions for reading, to help young people. Or, for that matter, older ones, who may suddenly realize that their experience has deprived them of that great pleasure, reading, the adventure of literature, of the pursuit of knowledge, which can begin for the lucky ones when they are very young indeed, and go on through a lifetime, with happy discoveries all the way, when you may take a book down off a shelf – perhaps by chance – and find you have stumbled on a new world whose existence you had never even suspected. Here is that book. The suggestions made by contributors are all because of personal enthusiasm or admiration or love for a book, and that is the most important thing of all: love of literature, of books, of ideas, is communicated by the enthusiasm of a teacher. When one meets some person, young or old, who says, I was so lucky, I had this teacher who influenced me – this is always because the teacher was in love with literature, with science, with an idea, and this lucky pupil absorbed the love through osmosis. A cold way of teaching, analysis, exegesis, does not create readers who experience reading or the pursuit of ideas as a continuing passion.

This book is the equivalent of the enthusiastic teacher whose pupils are fortunate, and who bless them through their lives. It is a book so obviously essential, so necessary, that the question must be, why didn't it come into being before?

And now a personal note. It happened that I left school when I was fourteen, and thereafter educated myself with reading. It took a long time – years – for it to occur to me that after all I was only one in a long tradition of women who for one reason or another (in the old days it was because girls did not go to school, their brothers got the education) educated themselves in their parents' libraries, or with books they begged, borrowed, or stole. Virginia Woolf was one. But there were books in the house where I grew up, where I had parents who saw to it that I had the best that had been written – certainly not only from the English tradition – and where there was an atmosphere that took for granted that books are necessary for the good life. I was fortunate. I had advice. But I know that there are young people everywhere, particularly in what we call the Third World, and even in the fortunate rich part of the world, who dream of an education and cannot have one, who long for books and cannot get them, and who have no one to advise them. I can only too easily put myself into the position of some person – not necessarily a child – who has missed out on an education and dreams of having books to remedy the deficiency and enable him or her to become, after all, an educated person. It is my hope that this most useful book will find its way into the hands of such people. And, too, into the hands of parents, for there is a generation of parents who are trying to help their children but – themselves uneducated – do not know how.

There are also young people who, having taken A-level literature, have found that familiarity with the four set books – that is all that is needed in some places now to claim an education in literature – has given them a thirst for more.

To end with, a tiny tale. In Africa, in an area far from a town, in a bush school, which did not expect to educate its pupils for more than half a dozen years, a boy of ten was found with a stolen book under his bed. It was a tome of advanced physics, of which he could not have understood one word. 'Why did you steal this book?' 'But I want a book. I have no books. I wanted my own book,' said he. 'But why did you steal this difficult book?' 'I want to be a doctor,' he said, most passionately weeping, and clutching the book to him.

CONTENTS

LANGUAGE AND LITERATURE

THE ARTS

SCIENCE AND TECHNOLOGY

ASPECTS OF
SOCIETY

EDUCATION

CONTEMPORARY ISSUES IN EDUCATION
Maureen O'Connor

Education in most countries today finds itself in the front line of the war between ideologies. A utilitarian view conflicts with the liberal notion of education for self-fulfilment more fiercely than ever. The introduction of competition and market forces is resisted by those who hold education as a right which should be equally available to all. Education is variously regarded as a means to social and political liberation and as a weapon in the international battle for economic hegemony. The books I have chosen provide an introduction to these conflicts without necessarily offering solutions because one thing at least is clear: the great education debate will continue.

Education costs money, but then so does ignorance.

CLAUS MOSER

The Pedagogy of the Oppressed (1970) by Paulo Freire. The seminal text on education as empowerment, based on Freire's experience with illiterate Brazilian peasants but equally applicable to those trapped in a 'culture of silence' anywhere. Education as an alternative to revolution.

The Unschooled Mind (1989) by Howard Gardner. Building on his work on multiple intelligences, Gardner argues that teaching and learning must be adapted to the needs of individual children, who may learn in particular ways.

Teach Your Own (1981) by John Holt. A fierce critic of American schooling advises parents to take control of their children's education and educate them at home.

School Matters (1988) by Peter Mortimore, Pamela Sammons, Louise Stoll, David Lewis, and Russell Ecob. The research study which by analysing the progress of children in London primary schools gave the first scientific basis upon which school improvement might be based.

Closely Observed Children (1980) by Michael Armstrong. A fascinating first-hand account of a progressive primary school by a determined advocate of child-centred learning, written in the form of a teacher's diary.

Parents and Schools, Customers, Managers or Partners? (1993) edited by Pamela Munn. A collection of discussion papers on the growing involvement of parents in education.

Education and the Social Order (1991) by Brian Simon. The final volume of Simon's definitive history of British education up to and including the Thatcher revolution which has still not run its course. This and the following book look closely at the impact of radical – or controversial – changes in educational policy of the British government during the 1980s and 1990s.

Take Care Mr Baker! (1988) edited by Julian Haviland. The initiative that brought into the light of day the responses to Kenneth Baker's *Education Reform Bill* from public bodies and individuals. It exposes the strengths and weaknesses of the legislation that still affects British schooling and is still being amended.

MYTHOLOGY

MYTHOLOGY – *Roy Willis*

Although competing theories of myth abound, no single explanation has yet received unanimous scientific endorsement. Probably most of the theories have some truth in them, and the suggested readings represent some of the more significant recent attempts at solving the mystery of why ancient mythical tales continue to fascinate the modern mind.

The kind of logic used by mythical thought is as rigorous as that of modern science.

CLAUDE LÉVI-STRAUSS

The Inner Reaches of Outer Space (1988) by Joseph Campbell. The best-known modern exponent of the meaning of myth argues for the relevance of mythology to the predicament of present-day humankind.

The Sacred Narrative: Readings in the Theory of Myth (1984) edited by Alan Dundes. Wide-ranging survey of theories of myth by experts from different scholarly fields.

The Golden Bough (1890–1915) by James George Frazer. There are several abridged editions of the classic study by the late-Victorian scholar of the widely occurring theme of the Dying King and his ritual sacrifice.

The Myth of the Eternal Return (1949) by Mircea Eliade. This persuasive study sees myths as windows to an underlying sacred and spiritual reality.

Psychological Reflections (1953) by Carl Jung. A master of psychoanalysis explains the heroes and heroines of myth as embodiments of 'archetypes', or permanent underlying features of the human mind.

Myth and Meaning (1979) by Claude Lévi-Strauss. A lucid summary of this famous French anthropologist's view of myth as embodying the basic processes of human thought.

Magic, Science and Religion (1948) by Bronislaw Malinowski. Influential account of primitive myths as 'charters' for existing social orders, written by the founding father of modern anthropology.

MYTHOLOGIES – *Roy Willis*

The 20th century has seen a growing scholarly and popular respect for the wisdom enshrined in the many and varied mythological traditions belonging to the human heritage worldwide. Some of these, like the brilliant mythologies of the eastern Mediterranean, sprang from civilizations long extinct; while others, including those studied by anthropologists working with tribal cultures in Africa, Australia, and the Americas, remain local sources of inspiration and guidance to this day. The following works exemplify something of the rich variety available.

There is a dream dreaming us.

BUSHMAN HUNTER OF THE KALAHARI DESERT
REPORTED BY LAURENS VAN DER POST.

African Mythology (1963) by Geoffrey Parrinder. Readable, well-illustrated introduction to the main mythical themes of black Africa.

Classical Hindu Mythology (1978) by Cornelia Dimmitt and J A B van Buitenen. A selection of texts from one of the richest mythical traditions in the world.

Art and Myth in Ancient Greece (1991) by T H Carpenter. Draws on ancient Greek art to add new meaning to some of the central stories of the classical tradition.

Kingdoms of Jade, Kingdoms of Gold (1991) by Brian Fagan. Lively presentation of mythical themes from the complex civilizations of pre-Columbian Central America.

Polynesian Mythology (1965) by George Grey. Ancient myths from the island peoples of the Pacific.

Celtic Mythology (1970) by Proinsias MacCana. The vivid mythical imagination of the ancient Celts is brought to life in this scholarly and readable collection.

Gods and Myths in Northern Europe (1964) by Hilda Davidson. The mythical tales of the Nordic peoples, replete with the doings and epic conflicts of gods, goddesses, and monsters.

Middle Eastern Mythology (1963) by S H Hooke. An authoritative account of the mythical themes that arose in the great civilizations of the ancient Middle East.

RELIGION

INTRODUCTION TO RELIGION

Elizabeth Breuilly (and members of ICOREC)

Whether we are aware of it or not, each of us builds our life and actions on belief and ritual, be they religious or secular. Much of the study of religion has been as psychology, philosophy, anthropology, or Christian theology. There are many works dealing with religion from these viewpoints, but this book list is intended to serve as an introduction to the study of religion in general, as well as giving reference information about the world's faiths, their beliefs, practices, and distribution. The study of religion as a human phenomenon is different from the study of any one particular religion, but each study feeds the other. The more we know of the details of how a religion is lived and celebrated, and how it colours and shapes the lives of its adherents, the more we can recognize similar dynamics at work in another faith. Conversely, the more we have studied how different religions approach a particular aspect of life (the problem of suffering, for example, or what happens at death), the greater insight we can have into the traditions of one particular faith.

In these our days it is almost impossible to speak of religion without giving offence either on the right or on the left. With some, religion seems too sacred a subject for scientific treatment; with others it stands on a level with alchemy and astrology, as a mere tissue of errors or hallucinations, far beneath the notice of the man of science.

F MAX MÜLLER

Sainsbury's Religions of the World (1993) by Elizabeth Breuilly and Martin Palmer. Although written for readers aged 10 upwards, this is of interest to anyone wanting a brief summary of the beliefs and practices of the major world religions. Fully illustrated.

From Primitives to Zen (1967) by Mircea Eliade. A fascinating thematic source-book of religious writings, compiled by a recognized pioneer of the systematic study of the world's religions. As the title implies, the material ranges from accounts of preliterate religions, through historic religions, to the major world faiths. However, Christianity and Judaism are omitted, since biblical material in English is readily available elsewhere.

Contemporary Religions: a World Guide (1992) edited by Ian Harris, Stuart Mews, Paul Morris, and John Shepherd. Part I contains essays on the history, beliefs, and current trends of five major religious traditions – Christianity, Islam, Judaism, Buddhism, Hinduism – and new religious movements, together with a general survey, 'Religions in the Contemporary World'. Part II is an alphabetical dictionary of religious groups and movements, and Part III is a country-by-country summary.

A Handbook of Living Religions (1984) edited by John Hinnells. Detailed articles on the history, beliefs, and practices of religion worldwide, including indigenous faiths and new religious movements as well as established religions.

Who's Who of World Religions (1991) edited by John Hinnells. An impressive and very readable A–Z reference to 1,500 religious figures, both contemporary and historical.

The Study of Religions (1977) by Jean Holm. A clear and readable introduction to the whole field of religious studies, what it is, and what problems it presents, written for students.

Themes in Religious Studies Series: *Worship, Sacred Writings, Making Moral Decisions, Attitudes to Nature, Myth and History, Human Nature and Destiny, Picturing God, Rites of Passage, Women in Religion, Sacred Place* (all 1994) edited by Jean Holm and John Bowker. Each book takes a central theme which touches on a wide range of religions, and has an introductory essay, followed by chapters from authorities on different religions.

The State of Religion Atlas (1993) by Joanne O'Brien and Martin Palmer. Thirty-four maps with notes illustrate the history, distribution and present activities of world religions.

The World's Religions: Old Traditions and Modern Transformations (1989) by Ninian Smart. A richly illustrated exploration of all the major religions of the world – their beliefs and practices, and how they have shaped the history of the world. The arrangement is by areas of the world, which gives a clearer picture than many books of the interaction and development of religions in varying contexts.

BUDDHISM – *Michael Carrithers*

Buddhism is a system of spiritual practice and thought which arose 2,500 years ago in N India. The founder of Buddhism is known as the Buddha, meaning 'awakened one', and this notion of awakening is central to Buddhism. It was a widely held understanding in the Buddha's India that the experience of ordinary life is shot through with unsatisfactoriness and suffering. The Buddha's solution to this problem stressed that a right understanding of human experience, combined with wisely guided behaviour and meditation, allows one to wake up to the real character of experience and, in awakening, to escape its painful character. By attending minutely to the nature of experience as it occurs moment by moment, the successful Buddhist meditator learns that the fruits of our desires are transient and hence painful – that is the bad news – but also that the ultimate subject of our desires, namely our self, is quite insubstantial and transient as well, and so is not pinned helplessly and eternally to a world of pain. That is the good news, and leads to the cessation of suffering and to release.

Although Buddhism may seem to be a matter of thought, its realizations are in fact based on practice and the transformation of oneself through practice. Buddhism now has a robust presence throughout the world and is making its way confidently in the West. In the two and a half millennia since the Buddha taught, Buddhism has shown itself to be adaptable to almost any cultural and social setting, and Buddhists have created a wealth of widely varying systems of thought and practice. Some Buddhists come close to a Christian style of spirituality in their stress on sin and salvation, whereas others have taken a more austerely intellectual path. The Buddha and many of his disciples down the ages were celibate monks, but Buddhists have also developed forms of behaviour consistent with ordinary life in the world. And though the Buddha's teaching seems to stress thought over feeling and contemplation over morality, in fact Buddhist ethics have proven to be a powerful and compelling feature of Buddhist life wherever it is found.

As a cart wheel follows the step of the ox, so suffering follows him who speaks or acts with a blemished mind.

FROM THE *DHAMMAPADA*

The World of Buddhism (1984) edited by Heinz Bechert and Richard Gombrich. This handsome volume contains articles by some of the world's leading scholars of Buddhism, and covers nearly every aspect of the religion, both in the past and present. The illustrations are excellent, conveying a vivid impression of the variety of Buddhist art, architecture, and practice.

The Buddha (1983) by Michael Carrithers. This is a brief, clearly written, and accessible explanation of the Buddha, his times, and his thought and practice, which can easily be read in bed.

The Forest Monks of Sri Lanka (1983) by Michael Carrithers. This is the most extensive and intimate account available concerning the meditating monks of S and SE Asia who represent the living tradition that is closest to the Buddha's original way of life. It has been used by Buddhists in the West as a basis for criticizing and commenting on their own practices.

Theravada Buddhism: A Social History from Ancient Benares to Modern Colombo (1988) by Richard Gombrich. This well-written book demonstrates one strand in the complex and sometimes ironic fate that awaited Buddhism as it developed into a widespread religion involved with ordinary affairs of the world.

An Introduction to Buddhism: Teaching, History and Practices (1990) by Peter B Harvey. This is a wide-ranging introduction which includes an excellent list of further readings.

The Heart of Buddhist Meditation (1962) by Thera Nyanaponika. This is a classical account of the nature of meditation, the central practice in Buddhism, from the perspective of southern Buddhism.

The Buddha (1979) by M Pye. This biography of the Buddha is written from a very different viewpoint than that of Carrithers above. It shows how Buddhists themselves thought, and told stories, of the Buddha and how they preserved and expanded their sense of who he was.

What the Buddha Thought (1967) by Walpola Rahula. This frequently reprinted volume conveys a sense of the Buddha's teaching by weaving together admirably plain writing with quotations from the original scriptures. The overall effect is very powerful.

The Buddhist Handbook: A Complete Guide to Buddhist Teaching and Practice (1987) by John Snelling. This book is written by a committed British Buddhist who conveys a practical, no-nonsense flavour of Buddhism, both in the past and in the West today. It is full of useful advice for those becoming personally committed to Buddhist practice and thought.

The Buddhist Religion: A Historical Introduction (1982) by Richard Robinson and Willard Johnson. This is a quite superb slender introduction to Buddhism, which can be recommended for its ability to convey in a graspable form some of the complexities of Buddhist history.

Zen Training: Methods and Philosophy (1975) by Katsuki Sekida. Sekida conveys vividly and with unforgettable imagery the approach to Buddhist practice taken by the Zen school. Contrast this with Nyanaponika's work.

The Practice of Chinese Buddhism 1900–1950 (1967) by Holmes Welch. This book could be read as a contrast to the book on Sri Lankan monks by Carrithers, above, since it presents an alternative development which grew out of Buddhism.

CHRISTIANITY – *Andrew Linzey*

The Christian tradition is so multiform and so multifaceted that any attempt to represent it in a few volumes must appear partisan, even eccentric. Almost everything we experience in Western culture has been influenced – for good or ill – by its Judaeo-Christian roots. Despite the appearance of secularization, Christian forms of life still flourish and prosper in a wide variety of guises: in art, literature, sculpture, poetry; in all forms of music from classical to gospel rock; in visual communications, specifically Christian ideas and images still retain a powerful hold on our imagination, and in intellectual life generally, especially the humanities: literature, philosophy, politics, and, of course, theology, specifically Christian notions of goodness, truth, and beauty still undergird and inform common notions even in their reactive anti-Christian forms. The truth is that even, and especially, in its pluralist forms, Christianity still remains the dominant ideology of the West. This does not mean, of course, that Christianity remains unchanged or immutable; precisely the reverse. One of the great strengths of the Christian tradition is the way in which it merges, collides, incorporates, sometimes even wholly assimilates, elements or thoughts originally alien to itself. The line attributed to T S Eliot that Christianity is always adapting itself to what is credible is ever more true of contemporary Christianity. I have selected a handful of the major accessible works that describe some of the main features of this tradition and also some works that provide an insight into how this tradition is remoulding itself in the light of contemporary challenges.

Christianity is an anvil that has worn out many hammers.

SYDNEY EVANS

A Dictionary of Judaism and Christianity (1991) edited by Dan Cohn-Sherbok. The first dictionary to explain and compare the key concepts, beliefs, and practices of both Judaism and Christianity. In a single volume the wealth of the Judaeo-Christian heritage is uncovered – and in direct and simple language. Specifically, it shows how Christianity is vastly indebted to Jewish ideas and how it made use of them. An invaluable guide for the general reader.

Encyclopedia of Modern Christian Thought (1993) edited by Alister E McGrath. A wide-ranging 'state of the art' introduction to contemporary Christian thinking in its very diverse forms. Contains detailed consideration of main ideas and issues as well as brief introductions to key thinkers. All admirably concise and – for the most part – well written and accessible for the general reader.

Dictionary of Ethics, Theology and Society (1995) edited by P A B Clarke and Andrew Linzey. It is often suggested that Western society has no coherent ideology left and that utter pluralism in faith and practice is now inevitable. But this view fails to recognize the continuing indebtedness of Western society to the Judaeo-Christian tradition and the resultant synthesis with political and social thought. This pioneering dictionary maps out the ethical, theological, and social influences which have formed Western society. More than 250 contributions explore theoretical and practical topics from abortion to worship. Appropriate for the student rather than the general reader, but indispensable as a work of reference.

The Wound of Knowledge: Christian Spirituality from the New Testament to St John of the Cross (1979) by Rowan Williams. A much needed and much valued history of Christian spirituality. Takes the reader through the giants of the tradition: Paul, John, Ignatius, Irenaeus, Clement of Alexandria, Origen, Athanasius, Basil, Gregory of Nyssa, Gregory of Nazianzen, Augustine, Maximus, Eckhart, and finally to Luther and St John of the Cross. Impressively illustrates the coherence of Christian spirituality: 'Christianity is born out of struggle because it is born from men and women faced with the paradox of God's purpose made flesh in a dead and condemned man.' Not always an easy read, but compelling and inspiring.

Perfect Fools: Folly for Christ's Sake in Catholic and Orthodox Spirituality (1980) by John Saward. In many ways the natural counterpart to Williams's book. Saward recounts and explains the long tradition of 'folly for Christ' found within Catholic and Orthodox spirituality. 'This is the story of those who have taken the Lord and his apostle [Paul] at their word and received from God the rare and terrible charism of holy folly.' The 'fools for Christ' described here range from the slightly dotty to the classable insane who speak words of prophetic insight against the 'wisdom of the age'. An audacious work on a very serious subject but written with an enviable lightness of touch. A delight to read.

True God: An Exploration in Spiritual Theology (1985) by Kenneth Leech. The third in a series following his best-selling *Soul Friend* (1977) and *True Prayer* (1980). Leech's starting point is the spiritual deprivation and impoverishment of the West. This, according to Leech, is due to a false and inadequate picture of God as an intellectual abstraction unconcerned with, or uninvolved in, the affairs of the world. Leech argues that orthodox belief requires a God intimately involved in human suffering and determined to secure social justice. 'The message of the crucified God includes the amazing truth that God allows us to share in his passion and death. Made in his image, we are signed with his cross, healed by his wounds, set free by his strange work of love.' Breathtakingly impressive vision of Christian spirituality and its relevance to contemporary philosophy, politics, ecology, and feminism. A modern classic.

The New Oxford Book of Christian Verse (1981) edited by Donald Davie. The notion of 'Christian' verse is problematical – not only because most of the major poets have been religious but also because 'good verse' is 'good verse' no matter how much – or how little – 'Christian' it may be. Nevertheless, Davie insists that the content of some verse is explicitly Christian in that it is concerned with the central narratives (creation, fall, incarnation, redemption) of the Christian faith. Davie assembles an astonishingly wide range of poets (including John Donne, John Bunyan, Thomas Traherne, Isaac Watts, Wesley, William Cowper, T S Eliot, Stevie Smith, W H Auden, and R S Thomas) who have made Christian themes their own and have done so in a way that harmonizes both Christian faith and poetic insight. The result is not just an inspiring collection but also one that introduces and illuminates the main Christian doctrines.

The Body and Society: Men, Women and Sexual Renunciation in Early Christianity (1988) by Peter Brown. A masterful and brilliant history of the development of Christian thinking about sexuality. Illustrates with unsparing detail the full depths and heights of Christian preoccupation with sexuality – from apparent promiscuity to a horror of carnality. 'If my book gives back to the Christian men and women of the first five centuries a little of the disturbing strangeness of their most central preoccupation, I will consider that I have achieved my purpose in writing it.' Indispensable to understanding the Augustinian legacy which has so damaged Christian attitudes to sexuality. A great work of historical scholarship: lucid, imaginative, and compassionate.

Heaven: A History (1990) by Colleen McDannell and Bernard Lang. In case this may seem a rather unlikely subject for historical study, the authors explain: 'We study heaven because it reflects a deep and profound longing in Christianity to move beyond this life and to experience more fully the divine', and the 'ways in which people imagine heaven tells us how they understand themselves, their families, their society, and their God'. The result is an ambitious and fascinating social history which illustrates how the imagination of heaven has influenced art, politics, literature, and philosophy as well as Christian thinking throughout the ages. The book is copiously illustrated and easy to read.

The Foolishness of God (1970) by John Austin Baker. One of the major works of contemporary apologetics offering a unified vision of the Christian faith. Baker argues that the case for Christianity is essentially a moral one – for or against love as the ruling principle in one's life. God creates a world which is truly contingent and free. The offering of sacrificial love is the moral heart of the universe and is revealed to be the very nature of God: 'The crucified Jesus is the only accurate picture of God the world has ever seen.' Its impressive biblical scholarship, wide-ranging sympathy and disarmingly simple style have made it a contemporary classic.

HINDUISM – *Veronica Voiels*

The great variety of belief and practice expressed within Hinduism sometimes defies any attempts to reduce it to a simple formula. The distinguishing features of this great world religion are its great antiquity; its cyclic view of existence incorporating a belief in reincarnation not just of human beings but the whole created universe; its understanding of the nature of the ultimate reality as Brahman in the abstract symbol 'Om'; its acceptance of the manifestation of god in many different forms; its understanding of dharma as the moral law governing all aspects of social behaviour and cultural traditions. The depth and sophistication of its religious philosophy is as fascinating as its rich variety of symbolism, ritual, and mythology. So in order to appreciate fully the various dimensions of this religion it is necessary to explore its philosophy, history, anthropology, and sacred art and mythology.

Half the world moves on the independent foundations which Hinduism supplied. China, Japan, Tibet and Siam, Burma and Ceylon look to India as their spiritual home. Its historic records date back for over four thousand years and even then it has continued its unbroken, though at times slow and almost static course, until the present day. It has stood the stress and strain of more than four or five millennia of spiritual thought and experience.

RADHAKRISHNAN

The Hindu World (1982) by Patricia Bahree. A good introduction intended for the general reader and young people. It provides a very good insight and appreciation of the cultural context of Hinduism in India, with an easy-to-read text and wonderful colour photography.

Teach Yourself Hinduism (1995) by Mel Thompson. This is suitable for the general reader as well as A-level and undergraduate studies. It is part of a series on Teach Yourself World Faiths which provide good reference books to promote understanding of world faiths in a multicultural society.

The Sacred Thread: Hinduism in its Continuity and Diversity (1981) by J L Brockington. This is a historical approach to Hinduism and suitable for A-level and undergraduate study. It is a very readable text and very comprehensive and detailed in its treatment of various developments in Hinduism in relation to the circumstances of the time.

The Upanishads (this edition 1989) translated by Alistair Shearer and Peter Russell (there are several other good translations available). Part of the Hindu sacred writings of the Vedas, the Upanishads contain some of the most profound insights into the ultimate questions of life. This edition selects various passages and presents them with some commentary and carefully selected photographs to contribute to the meaning of the text. A delightful experience to read.

Hinduism: An Introduction (1989) by Shakunthala Jagannathan. A book intended for the general reader and written by a Hindu woman to communicate the central teachings of Hinduism to both Hindus and non-Hindus. It provides a good insight into Hinduism from a Hindu perspective, rather than a Western scholar's interpretation. The illustrations, photographs, and colour plates contribute to one's understanding of this intriguing religion.

Hindus: Their Religious Beliefs and Practices (1994) by Julius J Lipner. This book provides a wealth of knowledge about both the philosophical traditions and popular religion. It approaches an understanding of Hinduism through some central themes, including scripture, tradition, experience, time, space, and eternity.

The Camphor Flame: Popular Hinduism and Society in India (1992) by C J Fuller. An anthropological study which explores in considerable detail the various aspects of village Hinduism. It gives some fascinating insights into the practice of Hinduism in rural India, in the home and in the temples. It is very detailed in some of its accounts but unlike many anthropological studies it is accessible to the general reader.

The Essential Teachings of Hinduism (1989) edited by Kerry Brown. This book collects together passages from various Hindu scriptures related to key concepts of Hinduism, such as Brahman, the self, consciousness, and yoga. This is a valuable resource for gaining an appreciation of Hindu teachings from their original source in scripture.

The Hindu Vision: Forms of the Formless (1993) by Alistair Shearer. An attempt to appreciate Hinduism through its sacred art in the images of the deities and shrines and temples. The photography is splendid and provides a visual understanding of Hinduism and the text is readable and of special interest to those who regard the visual image as the best medium for understanding.

Indian Mythology (1967) by Veronica Ions. It is impossible to appreciate the Hindu world-view without reading some of its mythology, and this book provides a good overview of the stories of the gods and the Mahabharata. It is well illustrated and easy to read.

ISLAM – *Mawil Izzi-Dien*

The following brief selection of books tries to reflect the broad diversity of Islamic thought and experience. Diversity in any religion can be one of the essences of the faith. In Islam, diversity is a key to understanding not only the books written about Islam but also the culture that stems from it. Islam, as the youngest divinely inspired religion, offered all cultures a firm ground from which they can present themselves without being lost within the main Arabic culture which was the original cradle of Islam. When Muhammad started the call for Islam, the notion of 'submitting to God' represented a new and effective ground upon which human life and society was to be established. Submitting to God took the place of race, wealth, or any other social underpinning. Yet, despite this ideal vision of life, the history of Islamic culture contains examples of how distant theory can be from practice. Muslims, like the rest of the human race, seem to have ignored Islamic instructions in many stages of history, raising the very interesting question of why man has always been a rebel, even against what he appears to believe in.

God is the Light of the heavens and the earth; the likeness of His Light is as a niche wherein is a lamp (the lamp in a glass, the glass as it were a glittering star) kindled from a Blessed Tree, an olive that is neither of the East nor of the West whose oil wellnigh would shine, even if no fire touched it; Light upon Light (God guides to His Light whom he will).

A J ARBERRY, KORAN TRANSLATION

What Everyone Should Know About Islam and Muslims (1979) by S Haneef. A well-written quick reference to Islam. Written by an American Muslim, it is a comprehensive survey of the basic teaching of Islam for the Western reader with emphasis on the significance of Islam's central concept, faith, and submission to the divine. The author is active in the field of Islamic education and has travelled widely in the Muslim world.

Islam the Straight Path (1988) by John L Esposito. Combining the best of Western scholarship with an insider's understanding of the Muslim world, the author has produced a well-written introduction to Islam from its origin in the 7th century to the contemporary resurgence. The book has the added advantage of a large number of excerpts from a wide range of original sources.

The Legacy of Islam (1979) by Joseph Shacht and C E Bosworth. One of the classic analyses of the achievements of Islamic civilization. The relationship of Islam to the rest of the world is examined with accuracy and scholarship. This includes a large area of interests written by renounced Western scholars like the famous French scholar Maxim Rodenson, and the Indian Aziz Ahmad.

Islamic Art (1989) by David Talbot Rice. A valuable book, describing and portraying Islamic art as a supreme triumph of pattern and colour. These qualities of Islamic art are colourfully and elegantly presented in an academic and historical manner that makes the book worthwhile reading.

A Popular Dictionary of Islam (1992) by Ian R Netton. This work is a unique dictionary and glossary of Islamic terms. It provides a key general source on the popular area of Islam. A well-written, comprehensive, cross-referenced book intended for the student, scholar, and general reader, whether Muslim or non-Muslim.

Islam: Its Meaning and Message (1976) by Khurshid Ahmad and others. A good general introductory book to Islam with a pinch of specialized flavour written by a reputable range of Muslim academics and modern scholars. The editor is an internationally established Islamic scholar who occupied academic ministerial posts in Pakistan and other parts of the Muslim world. The book is divided into four parts covering the Islamic outlook to life, the prophet and the Koran, the Islamic system, and Islam and the world.

The Eternal Message of Muhammad (1979) by 'Abd ar-Rahman Azzam. This book discusses Islam through the life of the prophet of the faith. He also offers a good account of Islam as a social religion that does not recognize either nationalism or racism. The author was founder and first secretary general of the Arab League 1945–52.

Morals and Manners in Islam (1986) by M I al-Kaysi. A concise account of the unique area of Islamic culture that is often unknown by the West. The book covers a large range of patterns of behaviour regulating Islamic conduct at personal, family, and social levels. The book contents are derived mainly from Islamic legal sources. The author is a Jordanian university professor and scholar who has travelled extensively in the Muslim world.

Shari'ah: The Islamic Law (1984) by A R I Doi. One of the few comprehensive standard books on Islamic law available in English. Despite some topographical errors, the book offers an excellent detailed overview of Islamic law in general and in relation to family, crime and punishment, inheritance and disposal of property, economics and external relationships.

An Introduction to Islamic Law (1964) by Joseph Shacht. This book is considered one of the best accounts of the history of Islamic law. A fascinating book with its accuracy and detailed knowledge. Although the book is described by the author as not intended for the specialists, many specialists find it extremely useful as a starting point within the complex phenomena of Islamic law. The author, who died in 1969, was professor of Arabic and Islamic studies at Columbia University, New York.

JUDAISM – *Julia Neuberger*

The books that follow are my absolute favourites. A complete reading list would have to include the Hebrew Bible (the Old Testament), the main rabbinic works such as the Mishnah and Talmud, and a huge corpus of historical and philosophical works. So what follows is an idiosyncratic selection, which I hope will give the reader some of the flavour of what Judaism is, and what being Jewish might be like.

Being a Jew is like walking in the wind or swimming: you are touched at all points and conscious everywhere.

LIONEL TRILLING

A Rabbinic Anthology (1938) edited by C G Montefiore and H Loewe. A collection of writings from the rabbis, with a brilliant introduction. One of my favourites is from the Jerusalem Talmud: 'The Holy Spirit only rests on someone who has a joyous heart.'

Atlas of the Jewish World (1984) by Nicholas de Lange. The best of the atlases of Jewish history and modern existence, by far. You get a feel for where Jews were, where they are, and why it is they moved from one country to another.

World of our Fathers: The Journey of the East European Jews to America and the Life They Found and Made (1976) by Irving Howe. Just what it says it is, but brilliantly expressed as a journey from one world to another, with a great deal of the atmosphere of eastern Europe included.

The Jewish People: Their History and Religion (1987) by David J Goldberg and John D Rayner. Clear, concise, helpful. A good one-volume treasury of information about who Jews are, what they practise, and what the varieties of Judaism are.

The Holocaust: The Jewish Tragedy (1986) by Martin Gilbert. The authoritative book on the history of the Holocaust. Painful reading, but essential to understanding present-day Jews.

Benevolence and Betrayal: Five Italian Jewish Families under Fascism (1991) by Alexander Stille. A strange choice, but it tells the tale so well of Italian Jews who had lived a peaceful life, very happily, utterly integrated into Italian life, and then were betrayed. It raises lots of questions, and is beautifully written.

Konin: A Quest (1995) by Theo Richmond. Richmond researched and recreated in words the small town in Poland from which his family came, and where the Jews were completely destroyed during World War II. It is a remarkable achievement, and people long dead live again, as does a vanished world.

If This Is a Man (1960) by Primo Levi. Records what it means to be a Jew, and to experience the concentration camps. Anything else by Levi is also recommended.

WESTERN PHILOSOPHY

INTRODUCTION – *PAUL ROWNTREE*

There is no agreed definition of philosophy. The question 'What is philosophy?' is itself a philosophical question. However, broadly speaking, philosophy is the systematic analysis of our concepts of – and the construction of theories about the nature of – mind, reality, language, logic, the self, free will, perception, causation, science, God, morality, rationality, time, space, and so on. Philosophy includes logic (the study of valid inference), epistemology (the theory of knowledge), and metaphysics (the study of the nature of existence), as well as ethics, aesthetics, political theory, the philosophy of science, and the philosophy of religion. General readers can begin the study of philosophy either with books about the history of philosophy or with books about certain topics within philosophy. They should then move on without delay to reading some of the works of the great philosophers.

Philosophy begins in wonder.

PLATO

Philosophy Made Simple (1993) by Richard H Popkin and Avrum Stroll. Revised edition of a readable and very useful introduction to philosophy with chapters on ethics, political philosophy, metaphysics, philosophy of religion, the theory of knowledge, logic, and contemporary philosophy. Each chapter contains critical summaries of the theories of the great philosophers. Highly recommended for the beginner.

A Dictionary of Philosophy (1990) by G Vesey and P Foulkes. A valuable dictionary of philosophical terms and theories. The major topic entries and the entries on individual philosophers can be read as an introduction to philosophy for the general reader.

Modern Philosophy: An Introduction and Survey (1994) by Roger Scruton. A remarkably wide-ranging survey of contemporary developments in both European and Anglo-Saxon philosophy. Readable and stimulating, but some chapters are quite technical.

Body, Mind and Death (1964) edited by Anthony Flew. A fascinating anthology of readings on the question 'What is consciousness?' Contains extracts from the works of Plato, Aristotle, Thomas Aquinas, Thomas Hobbes, René Descartes, Benedict Spinoza, Gottfried Leibniz, John Locke, David Hume, and many others.

Free Will (1972) by D J O'Connor. The best introduction to this classic philosophical problem. Examines a selection of arguments for and against the view that some human actions are freely chosen. Short and lucid.

A Short History of Ethics: A History of Moral Philosophy from the Homeric Age to the Twentieth Century (1966) by Alasdair MacIntyre. An early work by arguably the most original of contemporary moral philosophers. Here, he argues that moral concepts cannot be understood apart from their history. A challenging historical survey, covering many thinkers not usually regarded as moral philosophers.

The Problems of Philosophy (1912) by Bertrand Russell. A short, classic introduction to philosophical analysis by one of this century's great philosophers. Topics covered include the nature and existence of matter, appearance and reality, and the value of philosophy.

Philosophy and the Meaning of Life (1971) by Karl Britton. Written for the general reader concerned about philosophical questions such as 'Why does the universe exist?' and 'Why do I exist?'. The author asks what these questions mean, what could count as answers, and what methods can be used to find answers. Highly recommended for the beginner.

A History of Western Philosophy (1946) by Bertrand Russell. An entertaining history of philosophy in one volume. Weak on the medieval period and occasionally rather misleading, it nevertheless provides a useful historical survey for the beginner.

ANCIENT PHILOSOPHY – *Paul Rowntree*

Ancient philosophy covers a period of a thousand years – from about 650 BC to about AD 350. It helps to divide ancient philosophy into three subsidiary periods. 1. Pre-Socratic philosophy covers those speculative cosmologists (such as Democritus and Pythagoras) who flourished in the period *c.* 650–*c.* 450 BC. 2. Classical Greek philosophy begins with Socrates (469–399 BC), covers Plato (*c.* 428–347 BC), and ends with Aristotle (384–322 BC). 3. Hellenistic philosophy covers the period from the death of Aristotle until the fall of the Roman Empire, and it includes Plotinus and the neo-Platonists, Epicurus, and the Stoics. The Hellenistic philosophers were influenced by Greek culture, but often lived outside Greece.

> *The history of Western philosophy is, after all, no more than a series of footnotes to Plato's philosophy.*
>
> A N WHITEHEAD

Before and After Socrates (1932) by F M Cornford. A classic account of the pre-Socratics, Plato and Aristotle. Short and very readable.

The Last Days of Socrates (4th century BC) by Plato (translated 1993 by Hugh Tredennick and Harold Tarrant). A collection of four of Plato's works in which he displayed the methods and teaching of Socrates. Contains the *Apology* (Socrates's speech at his trial) and the *Phaedo* (Plato's account of Socrates last conversation). Readable and short. Newcomers to Plato are recommended to start here.

The Republic (4th century BC) by Plato (translated 1974 by Desmond Lee). Plato's philosophical and literary masterpiece in which he expounds his most important theories. Books VI and VII and particularly interesting. A fluent and elegant translation.

The Nicomachean Ethics (4th century BC) by Aristotle (translated 1976 by J A K Thomson, revised by Hugh Tredennick, and introduced by Jonathan Barnes). Aristotle's *Ethics* is one of the most influential books in history, and a standard text in moral philosophy. Addresses the issue of how to live well, and is important as much for its analytical methods as for its conclusions. A book that will repay a lifetime's study. A readable translation.

Aristotle (1982) by Jonathan Barnes. A short, elegant, and comprehensive introduction to Aristotle for the general reader by a leading philosopher and classical scholar.

The Neo-Platonists (1991) translated by John Gregory. A useful anthology mainly devoted to Plotinus, but containing pieces by Porphyry, Iambilichus, and Proclus.

Meditations (2nd century AD) by Marcus Aurelius (translated 1964 by Maxwell Staniforth). A classic statement of the stoic philosophy of life by a famous Roman emperor. A very influential and inspiring work by a sensitive and humble mind. Short and readable.

Hellenistic Philosophy (1974) by A A Long. An excellent survey and general appraisal. The best introduction to the subject. Scholarly but still suitable for the general reader.

MEDIEVAL PHILOSOPHY IN EUROPE
Paul Rowntree

Historians will always dispute when the Middle Ages began and ended. The Renaissance and the Middle Ages overlapped; and much of the medieval philosophical outlook survived into the late 17th century and even later. For philosophical purposes, the Middle Ages can be divided into: 1. The early Middle Ages (5th–11th centuries), beginning with St Augustine of Hippo (AD 354–430) and Boethius (AD 480–524) and ending with St Anselm (1033–1109). 2. The high Middle Ages (12th–13th centuries) in which scholastics such as St Thomas Aquinas (*c.* 1225–1274) flourished. 3. The later Middle Ages (14th–15th centuries) in which the greatest philosopher was probably William of Occam (*c.* 1285–1349). Undoubtedly, Aquinas has been the most influential of all medieval philosophers.

Examine carefully what has been said, and if possible, reconcile faith and reason.

ANICIUS MANILUS SEVERINUS BOETHIUS

A History of Medieval Philosophy (1972) by F C Copleston. An interesting and useful survey of the entire period, including medieval Islamic and Jewish philosophy. The author draws attention to the similarities between particular medieval philosophers and philosophers of later periods. Contains good bibliographies.

Medieval Thought: St Augustine to Ockham (1958) by Gordon Leff. A brisk, brilliant, and brief introduction by an historian. Contains plenty of short quotations from the works of the medieval philosophers.

Renaissance Thought: The Classic, Scholastic and Humanist Strains (1961) by Paul O Kristeller. A short, brilliant account of philosophy in the transitional period of the 15th and 16th centuries. Suitable for the beginner and the expert alike.

The Confessions of St Augustine (4th century) translated 1961 by R S Pine-Coffin. St Augustine's spiritual autobiography. Contains some notable philosophical reflections on the nature of time in Book XI, and communicates his highly influential outlook as well. A readable translation of a masterpiece.

The Consolation of Philosophy (524 AD) by Anicius Manilus Severinus Boethius (translated 1969 by V E Watts). A very beautiful and influential work in verse and prose, written while the author awaited execution. Boethius was a Christian philosopher who drew extensively on Plato, Aristotle, and the Stoics. He and St Augustine shaped medieval philosophy. Contains his famous definitions of eternity and of Providence, which were adopted by Aquinas. A masterpiece.

The Prayers and Meditations of St Anselm (11th century) translated 1973 by Sister Benedicta Ward. Mainly devotional, but the book contains the *Prologion* in which appears Anselm's brilliant version of the ontological argument for the existence of God. The ontological argument fascinates philosophers, and it has generated a vast literature.

Summa Theologicae by St Thomas Aquinas: A Concise Translation (1989) edited by Timothy McDermott. The most readable translation of selections from Aquinas's great synthesis of St Augustine and Aristotle. Omits the conventions of medieval debate used in the original in favour of the modern format of continuous paragraphs. Therefore, to appreciate Aquinas's methods and style, it should be read in conjunction with another anthology of his writings.

Aquinas (1955) by F C Copleston. Good introduction for those who have no previous knowledge of this great but difficult philosopher.

The Five Ways (1969) by Anthony Kenny. A lucid philosophical analysis of Aquinas's five proofs of the existence of God by a former Roman Catholic priest turned agnostic Oxford philosopher. Quite technical in places, but very rewarding.

A History of Political Thought: The Middle Ages (1965) by Walter Ullman. Valuable historical introduction to medieval political philosophy. Traces the emergence of the concepts of sovereignty, parliament, citizenship, the rule of law, and the state.

PHILOSOPHY IN 17TH-CENTURY EUROPE
Paul Rowntree

Philosophy in the 17th century was emerging from its subjection to theology; and the physical sciences began to separate from philosophy. Increasingly, the God of medieval philosophy was no longer seen as the guarantee and foundation of all knowledge. Accordingly, some of the leading philosophers sought a foundation for knowledge in mathematical reasoning, while others sought a foundation for knowledge in the experience of the senses and the inductive reasoning of the physical senses. The former are known as rationalists – René Descartes (1596–1650), Benedict Spinoza (1632–1677), and Gottfried Leibniz (1646–1716). The latter are known as empiricists – Francis Bacon (1561–1626), John Locke (1632–1704), and (arguably) Thomas Hobbes (1588–1679). Empiricism became the dominant trend in the next century, and it remains an important trend to this day.

As regards any subject we propose to investigate, we must inquire not what other people have thought, or what we ourselves conjecture, but what we can clearly and manifestly perceive by intuition or deduce with certainty. For there is no other way of acquiring knowledge.

RENÉ DESCARTES

Descartes: Philosophical Writings (1954) selected and translated by Elizabeth Anscombe and P T Geach. One of several very useful selections of the most important works. Includes *The Meditations* – one of the most readable (though deceptively simple) philosophical classics.

Descartes: The Project of Pure Enquiry (1978) by Bernard Williams. Probably the best commentary by a leading modern philosopher. Quite a difficult book in places, but it repays the effort.

Ethics (1677) by Benedict Spinoza (translated by A Boyle and revised by G H R Parkinson 1993). The best of the easily accessible translations. Fascinating, remarkable, and beautiful. This most impressive work of speculative metaphysics is modelled on Euclid's geometrical demonstrations. Read Spinoza's prefaces and notes before attempting the work as a whole. Demanding but highly recommended.

Spinoza (1988) by Stuart Hampshire. Revised edition of the best of the basic introductions. Covers not only the monistic metaphysics but the political philosophy and biblical criticism as well. Lucid and concise.

Leibniz: Philosophical Writings (1973) edited by G H R Parkinson and translated by Mary Morris and G H R Parkinson. The best selection of Leibniz's shorter works. Includes the very concise and readable *Monadology*.

Leibniz (1954) by Ruth L Saw. Good introduction, which pieces together Leibniz's doctrines in metaphysics and formal logic. Avoids undue technicalities and is useful for anyone new to Leibniz.

An Essay Concerning Human Understanding (1690) by John Locke (edited by A S Pringle-Pattison 1924). One of several editions of this long but important work. Begin by reading only selected passages on substance, personal identity, and the distinction between primary and secondary qualities. Locke's conception of substance as a completely featureless substratum is important.

John Locke (1952) by D J O'Connor. Covers Locke's highly influential political philosophy as well as his metaphysics and epistemology. A very readable introduction.

Leviathan (1651) by Thomas Hobbes (edited by M Oakeshott 1946). One of many editions of Hobbes's masterpiece, written in his magnificently pithy style. Commentators still argue about this most important work of political theory. Was Hobbes an authoritarian pessimist and atheist, or not?

Hobbes (1956) by R S Peters. A good introduction to a remarkably original, important, and rather neglected philosopher – the first great philosopher to write in English. Considers Hobbes's achievement as a whole, and not just the *Leviathan*. Very helpful.

The Seventeenth-Century Background (1953) by Basil Willey. A masterly exercise in the history of ideas by a professor of English literature. Very readable and highly recommended.

PHILOSOPHY IN 18TH-CENTURY EUROPE
Paul Rowntree

In 18th-century philosophy, the dominant trend in metaphysics and epistemology was empiricism, while the dominant trend in political philosophy was liberal individualism. The Irish philosopher and bishop George Berkeley (1685–1753) devised a form of empiricism now known as subjective idealism. The Scottish philosopher David Hume (1711–1774) arrived at generally sceptical views about reason, causation, the self, and religion. The German philosopher Immanuel Kant (1724–1804), claiming that Hume had woken him from his 'dogmatic slumbers', developed a synthesis of British empiricism and continental rationalism known as critical philosophy. In France, Jean-Jacques Rousseau (1712–1778) argued for direct rather than representative democracy. In England, Jeremy Bentham (1748–1832), the founder of utilitarianism, held that the essence of morality was 'the greatest happiness of the greatest number'.

If we take in our hand any volume; of divinity or school metaphysics, for instance; let us ask, 'Does it contain any abstract reasoning concerning quantity or number? No. Does it contain any experimental reasoning concerning matter of fact and existence? No.' Commit it then to the flames: for it can contain nothing but sophistry and illusion.

DAVID HUME

Principles of Human Knowledge/Three Dialogues (1710–1734) by George Berkeley (edited by Roger Woolhouse 1988). For Berkeley, the existence of objects depends on their being perceived: objects have continuous existence only because God perceives them all the time. May sound bizarre, but highly influential. The *Three Dialogues* are short and entertaining.

Berkeley (1953) by Geoffrey J Warnock. An excellent account of Berkeley's philosophy. Explains very clearly how Berkeley came to such extraordinary conclusions as a result of rejecting, in the name of common sense, Locke's conception of substance as a featureless substratum.

Fifteen Sermons (1914) by Bishop Joseph Butler (edited by W R Matthews). Great, if underestimated, work of moral philosophy. Butler, the leading conscience theorist, holds that conscience governs and limits both our benevolence and our selfishness. Subtle in content, solemn in tone. Highly recommended.

Dialogues Concerning Natural Religion (1779) by David Hume (edited by Martin Bell 1990). Of all Hume's philosophical works, this is the shortest and most accessible to the general reader. A work by a master of English prose. Never a dull moment. A masterpiece.

Hume (1980) by Alfred J Ayer. A short and stylish account of the main themes in Hume's philosophy by a modern empiricist. Tends to assume that Hume's philosophical intentions are not in dispute, but nevertheless very valuable.

Prolegomena to any Future Metaphysics (1783) by Immanuel Kant (translated by P G Lucas 1953). The shortest and most accessible of the main works of one of the greatest and most difficult philosophers. Dense and technical, so read a general commentary on Kant first.

The Philosophy of Kant (1968) by John Kemp. Kant is probably the most influential philosopher in the post-Enlightenment period. This is a classic account of Kant's critical philosophy. Lucid, short, and readable.

Kant's Moral Philosophy (1970) by Harry B Acton. An excellent and very short account of Kant's ethics and the categorical imperative. Essential preparation for reading Kant's influential moral philosophy.

Utilitarianism: For and Against (1975) by J J C Smart and Bernard Williams. Two essays on utilitarian ethics. J J C Smart refines Bentham's classical utilitarianism. Bernard Williams opposes this view. A good introduction to the ethics that influences so much social policy. Highly recommended.

The Social Contract: Essays by Locke, Hume, and Rousseau (1946) introduced by Ernest Barker. Brings together three great works of political philosophy – Locke's *Second Treatise on Government*, Hume's *Of the Original Contract*, and Rousseau's *Social Contract*. A very valuable volume for anyone interested in contractarianism in political theory. Rousseau's work has been variously interpreted as a blueprint for totalitarianism and a defence of individual liberty. It is more important as a source of ideas than as a system of philosophical arguments.

19TH-CENTURY PHILOSOPHY – *Robert C Solomon*

The 19th century displayed a remarkably rich and exciting explosion of philosophical energy and talent, perhaps even comparable to the generation that gave birth to Socrates, Plato, and Aristotle. The scale of the revolution set off in philosophy by Immanuel Kant was comparable, by Kant's own estimation, to the Copernican revolution that ended the Middle Ages. Following Kant were some of the most imaginative philosophers of modern times, including G W F Hegel and Arthur Schopenhauer as well as the philosophers he inspired in opposition to him, notably Soren Kierkegaard, Karl Marx, and Friedrich Nietzsche. Unfortunately, the 19th century on the European continent was not known for the clarity of its writing style, an unfortunate aspect of the Kantian inheritance. (One might compare the writing of John Stuart Mill and William James, their English and American contemporaries.) Hegel and Schopenhauer quite consciously employed a formidable Kantian jargon, although Schopenhauer's cutting wit often shines through. Kierkegaard used this same jargon ironically to mock Hegel. The later part of the century – which Virginia Woolf described as the passing of a dark cloud – showed a few signs of clearing. Although Marx's later economic writings are indeed difficult, his earlier philosophical writings are quite bold and accessible. Nietzsche's writing is among the best one can find in German, although his style is misleadingly facile, often hyperbolic and intentionally polemical. Easy (if sometimes offensive) to read, he is a master of subtlety and irony. My choice of books, accordingly, is confined to original texts (and collections of texts) that, nevertheless, are approachable by the intelligent general reader. More difficult texts are merely suggested.

It is not difficult to see that ours is a birth-time and a period of transition to a new era. Spirit has broken with the world it has hitherto inhabited and imagined, ... Spirit is never at rest but always engaged in moving forward. But just as the first breath drawn by a child after its long, quiet nourishment breaks the gradualness of merely quantitative growth, ... so likewise the Spirit in its formation matures slowly and quietly into its new shape, dissolving bit by bit the structure of its previous world.

G W F HEGEL

Reason in History (1820s; 1953), *The Philosophy of Right* (1821; translated 1967), and *The Phenomenology of Spirit* (1807; translated 1977) by G W F Hegel. The first is actually the introduction to a series of lectures Hegel delivered to his students in Berlin. Although it is difficult, what clearly emerges is an optimistic vision of a rational, progressive view of history, in which individual freedom emerges from 'the slaughter bench of history' but whose significance is to be found not in individuals (even the 'greatest' individuals) but in the development of spiritual consciousness as a whole. *The Phenomenology of Spirit* is an earlier, much more detailed and ambitious work, in which Hegel develops the concept of an emerging world-spirit. (It is not unimportant that he wrote the book just as Napoleon was reaching the full extent of his European conquests, including the western German states.) The reading is enormously difficult, but I encourage courageous readers to ascertain the general movement – or 'dialectic' – of the text. The most famous (and readable) sections: on 'Master and Slave' (in part B) and his discussion of *Antigone* and the conflict between divine law and civil society (in part C).

Parerga and Paralipomena (1851; translated 1974) and *The World as Will and Idea* (1818; translated 1948–50) by Arthur Schopenhauer. Although Schopenhauer certainly earned his self-styled reputation as the most 'pessimistic' of all modern philosophers, he is arguably one of the wittiest and most humorous of all modern philosophers as well. Despite the morbid message ('life is meaningless'), reading Schopenhauer is almost always an unexpected pleasure.

Journals (1839; translated from Danish by A Dru 1938), *Concluding Unscientific Postscript* (1846; translated by D Swenson and W Lowrie 1944), *Either/Or* (1843; translated by D Swenson, W Lowrie, and H Johnston 1954) by Soren Kierkegaard. Kierkegaard was fundamentally a religious writer and the first 'existentialist' (often misunderstood as a purely atheist movement). He defended the personal, passionate existence and commitments of the individual (for example, against Hegel's global notion of world-spirit) and defended a view of Christianity – 'becoming a Christian' – which was first of all a passionate personal commitment, a 'leap of faith'.

Early Writings (1843–4; translated and edited by Thomas Bottomore 1963) by Karl Marx; *The Communist Manifesto* (1848; edited by A Taylor 1967) by Karl Marx and Friedrich Engels. Karl Marx is best known as the economist and polemicist who inspired worldwide revolutions. He is less well known for his humanistic and philosophical writings.

The Gay Science (1881–82; translated by W Kaufmann 1974), *Beyond Good and Evil* (1886; translated by W Kaufmann 1966), *The Viking Portable Nietzsche* (translated and edited by W Kaufmann 1954), *Thus Spake Zarathustra* (1883–85), and *Twilight of the Idols* (1889; translated 1954) by Friedrich Nietzsche. Nietzsche died in 1900, in many ways bringing to an end the philosophical idealism of the 19th century and anticipating the moral confusion and violence of the 20th. He rejected glib notions of 'objectivity', especially in philosophy. He was, above all, a moralist, who (in the name of 'immorality') attempted to reinvent a morality of nobility in place of what he perceived as the 'decadent' and decaying values of the Judaeo-Christian tradition.

20TH-CENTURY PHILOSOPHY – *Richard Rorty*

In the early decades of this century, philosophers thought a lot about the impact of Charles Darwin's theory of evolution on traditional conceptions of man's place in the universe. Bergson, James, and Dewey all tried to rearrange old philosophical notions so as to make room for evolutionary thought. Later on, philosophy split down the middle into the 'analytic' and the 'continental' schools. The analysts (Ayer, Danto, Dennett, Rawls) are mostly anglophone. They think of philosophy as argumentative problem-solving. The 'continentals' (Heidegger, Foucault, Jacques Derrida) typically view philosophy as reflection on our contemporary historical situation. These two philosophical schools rarely interact, but both have produced first-rate books. By now, they have so little in common that the use of the term 'philosophy' for both tells one little more than that both kinds of philosophers trace some of their concern back to Plato, Aristotle, David Hume, and Immanuel Kant.

When it is acknowledged that under disguise of dealing with ultimate reality, philosophy has been occupied with the precious values embedded in social traditions, that it has sprung from a clash of social ends and from a conflict of inherited institutions with incompatible contemporary tendencies, it will be seen that the task of future philosophy is to clarify men's ideas as to the social and moral strifes of their own day.

JOHN DEWEY

Introduction to Metaphysics (1903) by Henri Bergson. A short, lucid presentation of Bergson's central idea: that ultimate reality is an evolutionary flux, and that material objects and minds are merely abstractions from that flux.

Pragmatism (1907) by William James. Argues that true ideas are ideas that get us what we want, that the search for truth is therefore part of the pursuit of happiness, and that the human mind is an organ for coping with reality rather than copying it.

Reconstruction in Philosophy (1920) by John Dewey. Debunks the idea that philosophy gives you an understanding of the true nature of reality, or mind, or anything else. Dewey's alternative conception of philosophy is illustrated by the quotation above.

Language, Truth and Logic (1936) by A J Ayer. A brilliantly clear and persuasive presentation of logical empiricism, the doctrine that all knowledge of the world is a matter of predicting the occurrence of sense experiences.

Connections to the World: The Basic Concepts of Philosophy (1989) by Arthur C Danto. An introduction to philosophy by one of the leading contemporary analytic philosophers. Presupposes no previous acquaintance with the subject.

Political Liberalism (1993) by John Rawls. A defence of the institutions of the liberal democracies, arguing that they do not need metaphysical or religious foundations, but only the informed consent of citizens to procedures for resolving conflicts.

Darwin's Dangerous Idea: Evolution and the Meanings of Life (1995) by Daniel Dennett. A brilliant defence of the claim that the entire history of the universe, from the Big Bang to the primeval slime, and from there to us, can be explained as the chance product of the movements of matter.

Basic Writings of Martin Heidegger (1993) edited by D F Krell. A good sampling from the writings of the most original of 20th-century philosophers. Heidegger was a Nazi, and is often denounced as an irrationalist obscurantist. But his influence has been enormous.

A Foucault Reader (1984) edited by Paul Rabinow. A selection from the work of Michel Foucault, a brilliant historian of ideas and political radical. His books have almost replaced Marx's as manuals for leftist intellectuals.

A Derrida Reader: Between the Blinds (1991) edited by Peggy Kamuf. Selections from the voluminous works of the most original French thinker of his day, the inventor of 'deconstruction' and a philosopher who tries to bring Heidegger together with Sigmund Freud.

GOVERNMENT AND POLITICS

THEORY – *Denis Derbyshire*

Whatever our views about the way we are governed and the people who occupy positions of power, the business of government is something we cannot avoid: it is all-pervading. Despite this, there is an alarming degree of ignorance and apathy about the institutions and workings of government and the political process itself. The teaching of government in schools is generally not well done, apart from some notable exceptions. The dilemma facing teachers and educational authorities is that of achieving impartiality and balance. They feel they must lean over backwards to avoid charges of political bias and yet, in truth, to try to understand government without considering the dynamic political process is like studying the human body by visiting a mortuary. There are many books about government in Britain and other individual countries but relatively few that attempt to cover a wider canvas. The dearth of books on politics as an activity is also evident.

I ... could not help reflecting in my way upon the singular ill-luck of this my dear country, which, as long as I can ever remember it, and as far back as I have read, has always been governed by the only two or three people, out of two or three millions, totally incapable of governing, and unfit to be trusted.

4TH EARL OF CHESTERFIELD

In Defence of Politics (1982) by Bernard Crick. The most perceptive, and readable, description of the political process.

The Nature of Politics (1965) by J D B Miller. Covering much the same ground as Crick but less of a polemic, and hence, not quite as readable.

The English Constitution (1867) by Walter Bagehot. The definitive account of the British system of government in the 19th century, which became the model for parliamentary democracy all over the world. The Fontana edition 1988 has a perceptive foreword by R H S Crossman.

The Penguin Dictionary of Politics (1985) by David Robertson. A useful compilation of contemporary political ideas and institutions.

World Political Systems: An Introduction to Comparative Government (1991) by J Denis Derbyshire and Ian Derbyshire. An assessment of the political systems and political ideologies of all the world's nation states, assuming no prior knowledge.

Comparative Government and Politics: An Introduction (1987) by Rod Hague and Martin Harrop. A useful introduction to comparative government, again assuming little or no prior knowledge.

Comparative Government (1986) by Roger Charlton. Another introduction to comparative government. Designed primarily for school sixth-formers or first-year non-specialist undergraduates, but also suitable for the general reader.

BRITISH POLITICS: 20TH CENTURY
Ian D Derbyshire

Unique in Western Europe in being free from invasion for more than 900 years and having escaped violent revolution during the last three centuries, Britain is unusual in having an unwritten constitution or external 'supreme court' watchdog, a hereditary monarch as head of state, an unelected, substantially hereditary, upper chamber, and a 'winner-takes- all' first-past-the-post, rather than proportionally based, electoral system. As a consequence, the political executive, when backed by a clear party majority in the House of Commons, has unrestrained authority to make considerable changes to the direction of national life. This was seen in the cases of the Liberal administration 1906–14, the Attlee Labour government of 1945–51, and the Conservative Thatcher administration of 1979–90, which carried out sweeping programmes of constitutional, social, and economic reforms. During other periods, although the Conservatives have dominated a predominantly two-party system, a largely centrist consensus had been adhered to.

I'm sure I was wrong on a number of occasions, but I cannot think of anything immediately.

MARGARET THATCHER

The British Polity (1994) by Philip Norton. An excellent, lucid, and accessible text on the institutions and processes of contemporary British politics, written by one of the country's foremost political scientists. Norton, in his coverage of the political culture, the constitution, Parliament, the monarchy, the electoral and party systems, and the roles of interest groups and the mass media, draws attention to elements of continuity and change, and makes insightful comparisons to the US political system.

The British Prime Minister (1985) edited by Anthony King. An outstanding collection of essays by leading political scientists analysing the changing role of the key office in the British political system, that of prime minister. With the growing influence of the mass media and the development of a sophisticated 'Number Ten' private office, the position has become almost presidential, with power being notably concentrated by Margaret Thatcher.

Britain since 1945: A Political History (1992) by David Childs. A popular, readable, and reliable overview of political developments in Britain, covering the period from the election of Clement Attlee's Labour administration in the July 1945 postwar general election to the re-election of John Major's Conservative Party in April 1992. Organized in chronological chapters, based around the 11 postwar administrations, the book also includes useful information on the changing social backcloth.

Ruling Performance: British Government from Attlee to Thatcher (1987) edited by Peter Henessy and Anthony Seldon. This fine work contains eight separate chapters, written by distinguished political scientists and historians, analysing the records of the Labour and Conservative administrations that held office between 1945 and 1987, as well as two general background and overview chapters. Particular attention is given to differing cabinet styles, interministerial relations, the degree to which manifesto pledges were redeemed, and the treatment of public expenditure.

Churchill (1993) edited by Robert Blake and William Roger Louis. This volume complements the multivolume official biography by Martin Gilbert of Britain's greatest 20th-century statesman, its outstanding war leader, and one of its most colourful politicians, who held ministerial office as first a Liberal and then a Conservative. 29 chapters, contributed by leading political scientists and historians, analyse various aspects of Churchill's career, ideology, and record.

Labour in Power 1945–1951 (1985) by Kenneth O Morgan. An outstanding account of the achievements and failures of Clement Attlee's Labour administration of 1945–51, which, with its welfare state and nationalization initiatives, set the agenda for the postwar era until a Thatcherite 'counter-revolution' was launched from 1979. Morgan provides expert analysis of the policies, programmes, and personalities of the administration.

One of Us: A Biography of Margaret Thatcher (1991) by Hugo Young. A towering figure in the postwar political landscape, Margaret Thatcher, the century's longest-serving prime minister (1979–90), shattered the centrist 'Butskellite' consensus that had prevailed between the 1950s and 1970s and sought to impose a new free-market, individualist, and nationalistic right-of-centre consensus. A controversial figure, Thatcher has been the subject of numerous biographies and has also written her own lengthy account, *The Downing Street Years* (1993), of her terms in office. This is the definitive biography.

Conservative Century: the Conservative Party since 1900 (1994) edited by Anthony Seldon and Stuart Ball. Alone or in coalition, the Conservative Party has held power for almost two-thirds of the period since 1900, establishing itself as the 'dominant party' in a somewhat skewed two-and-a-half-party system. This edited volume provides a comprehensive analysis of the structure of the Conservative Party, its support base, social and regional, its internal factional and ideological divisions, its public image, its leaders, and its record in power.

A Short History of the Labour Party (1993) by Henry Pelling. An excellent, succinct account of the Labour Party, from its founding at its February 1900 conference to its defeat in the April 1992 general election and the appointment of John Smith as leader, heralding a revival in the party's fortunes. Pelling, a social historian, discusses the role of trade unions within the party, the relationship of the rank and file with the parliamentary leadership, the record of Labour administrations, and the ideological divisions that, periodically, have led to electorally crippling splits.

A Short History of the Liberal Party 1900–92 (1993) by Chris Cook. An engaging analysis of the changing fortunes of the country's 'third force'. Up to the close of World War I, the Liberal Party, under the leadership of Asquith and Lloyd George, was the country's leading progressive, centre-left force and the predominant party of government. Subsequently eclipsed by the rise of Labour, as the franchise was extended, the Liberals regressed into third-party oblivion until the 1962 by-election triumph in Orpington signalled something of a revival, and in the 1983 general election the Liberal-led Lib-SDP Alliance attracted a quarter of the national vote.

US POLITICS: 20TH CENTURY – *Ian D Derbyshire*

The US political system, with its distinct separation of executive, legislative, and judicial powers and its strong federal system, has been copied by a number of newly emergent states, but remains in many ways unique. It is characterized by a classic two-party system, but one in which party discipline is notoriously weak, as is ideological cohesion. Instead, the political process is highly atomized, with politicians acting largely as 'freelances', raising their own finance to fight hugely expensive election contests and working in Congress to promote the interests of their own constituencies. At the apex of the political system stands the president, who, as both the constitutional head of state and the chief executive, provides unity, vision, and direction to the political process. Strong presidents, through force of personality and empathy with changing national sentiment, have been able to transform the direction of US politics. This was true of F D Roosevelt, who launched the New Deal during the 1930s, John F Kennedy and Lyndon B Johnson, who oversaw the Great Society reforms of the 1960s, and Ronald Reagan, who re-established the Republicans as the dominant force in the 1980s. At other times of weak presidential leadership, Congress has asserted itself, resulting in a gridlocked political process.

In the absence of institutions and education by which the environment is so successfully reported that the realities of public life stand out very sharply against self-centred opinion, the common interests very largely elude public opinion entirely, and can be managed only by a specialized class whose personal interests reach beyond the locality.

WALTER LIPPMANN

The Government and Politics of the United States (1993) by Nigel Bowles. A broad-ranging textbook introduction to American political institutions and processes, set in their historical context. The particular focus is on the evolving constitutional framework and the federal government system.

The Uncertain Power: A Political History of the United States since 1929 (1990) by Robert Garson and Christopher J Bailey. A succinct history of American political developments, economic social changes, and the country's role in international affairs between the Great Depression and the Bush presidency.

Presidential Power and the Modern Presidents: The Politics of Leadership from Roosevelt to Reagan (1990) by Richard Elliott Neustadt. A classic, subtle study of the modern presidency. Neustadt, a Harvard professor, notes that the USA has a 'government of separated institutions sharing powers' and shows, consequently, president and Congress to be locked in a complex relationship of mutual dependence. The underlying theme of the work is presidential weakness – that is, the gap between what is expected of presidents and their capacity to deliver – and the attempts by such strong presidents as Roosevelt, Truman, Kennedy, and Reagan to bridge this gap through their personalities.

The New American Political System (1990) edited by Anthony King. This excellent work, comprising analytical chapters written by leading American political scientists, explains the key changes which have taken place in the US political system during recent decades, in the post-Watergate era. There are chapters on the presidency,

Congress, the Supreme Court of Warren Burger and William Rehnquist, political parties, the electorate, the media, interest groups, federalism, and ideology.

The US Congress (1989) by Christopher J Bailey. A clear, analytical description of the organization and procedures of the US Senate and House of Representatives, which treats Congress as a dynamic institution whose structure has varied over time. Bailey focuses on membership and leadership of Congress, the role of parties, and the constitutional framework, and explains why the committee system is so powerful and how it works.

The Power Game: How Washington Works (1988) by Hedrick Smith. A fascinating, vivid account which takes the reader deep into the corridors of power in Washington and shows how Washington really works, describing the pressures exerted by lobbyists, the 'constant campaign', the influence of money from political action committees, the emphasis on image and presentation, and the weakening of party discipline.

Franklin D Roosevelt and the New Deal, 1932–1940 (1963) by William E Leuchtenburg. A classic account of the transformation brought about in American politics and society by the Democratic president F D Roosevelt, who responded to the challenge of the Great Depression by instituting an interventionist programme of federal government support for farmers, the unemployed, and the aged. In the process, Roosevelt achieved an electoral coalition that established the Democrats as the majority party in the country for five decades.

President Kennedy: Profile of Power (1993) by Richard Reeves. A detailed narrative account of the 'thousand days' presidency of the charismatic Democrat John F Kennedy between 1961 and 1963. Reeves reveals Kennedy, the first Roman Catholic to become president, to have been an enormously ambitious, charming, and risk-taking politician, but one who lacked a clear vision from the outset of what he sought to achieve during his administration.

Nixon (1987–91) by Stephen E Ambrose. A definitive account in three volumes of the dramatic political career of the Republican professional politician Richard M Nixon, the only US president to be forced to resign from office. Volume 1 covers the period 1913–62, when Nixon's career seemed to have been finished by defeats in challenges for the US presidency and governorship of California. Volume 2, 1962–72, encompasses Nixon's two victories in the presidential elections of 1968 and 1972. Volume 3, 1973–90, covers the Watergate scandal, which brought about his fall from power, and his later recovery in the 1980s as an 'elder statesman' and a prolific writer.

President Reagan: The Role of a Lifetime (1991) by Lou Cannon. A detailed biographical account of the career and presidency of Ronald Reagan, the movie star turned politician, by a political correspondent for the *Washington Post*, who had earlier 'tracked' Reagan when he was governor of California. Cannon believes the major contribution of Reagan, the 'Great Communicator', to have been a revival of national confidence, but criticizes him for taking his role as president 'too lightly'.

INTERNATIONAL RELATIONS – *Ian D Derbyshire*

International relations is a term used to cover all interactions between state-based actors across state boundaries. The subject is multidisciplinary, encompassing international politics and history, military and strategic studies, transnational economic relationships, and international law. During recent centuries the focus has been on

Great Power relationships, the balance of power, and the art of diplomacy. Between 1945 and 1991, during what became known as the Cold War era, international relations were dominated by the global ideological, political, and military battle between communism and liberal democratic free-market capitalism. More recently, particularly following the collapse of the Soviet empire, the focus has shifted to international interdependencies, as regional economic and political power blocs have become more developed, and the attention of the 'developed world' has been redirected towards the policing of relatively localized national and ethnic conflicts within the periphery and semiperiphery.

There can be no greater error than to expect, or calculate, upon real favours from nation to nation. It is an illusion which experience must cure, which a just pride ought to discard.

GEORGE WASHINGTON

An Introduction to International Relations (1994) by P A Reynolds. This popular text explores the nature and structure of international relations. Reynolds examines both 'microinternational relations' – that is, individual national objectives and motivations – and 'macrointernational relations', or international state systems and behavioural systems. The author emphasizes the increasing complexity of international relations as non-state actors, notably multinational corporations, have grown in importance and interdependencies have developed.

The Structure of International Society (1995) by Geoffrey Stern. An up-to-date multidisciplinary historical analysis of the origins, development, and early networks of international relations, and exposition of the diverse ways in which modern 'international society' has been defined and interpreted. Such key concepts as sovereignty, nationalism, balance of power, national interest, and interdependence are expertly addressed.

Classic Readings of International Relations (1994) edited by Phil Williams, Donald M Goldstein, and Jay M Shafritz. A collection of extracts from classic books and articles by major political thinkers, statesmen, and academics. The 58 readings include pieces by Sun Tzu, written in the 4th century BC, Machiavelli from the early 16th century, von Clausewitz from the 18th century, Hobson and Lenin from the early 20th century, and Immanuel Wallerstein and Paul Kennedy in the late 20th century.

Diplomacy (1994) by Henry Kissinger. A magisterial overview of the history of diplomacy over the course of three centuries, from Cardinal Richelieu, the founder of the modern state system, to the contemporary 'New World Order', by one of the 20th century's greatest exponents of the art. Kissinger, secretary of state under the US Republican presidents Nixon and Ford and an adherent to pragmatic realpolitik, based on a hard headed analysis of the balance of regional and global power, argues that America, protected by its own idealistic streak, has, in other times, pursued a unique, transformatory foreign policy.

The Struggle for Mastery in Europe (1954) by A J P Taylor. A classic account, by one of Britain's greatest historians, of Great Power rivalries in Europe between the failed revolutions of 1848 and the close of World War I, with the associated collapse of the Austrian Habsburg, Russian tsarist, and Turkish Ottoman ancien régimes. Taylor analyses the material, military, and ideological motivations behind the shifting alliances of this period, and sketches the characters of the leading personalities, notably Otto von Bismarck.

The Rise and Fall of the Great Powers: Economic Change and Military Conflict from 1500 to 2000 (1988) by Paul Kennedy. A hugely popular and influential work which, based on an analysis of five centuries of world history, argues that the rise and fall of great military powers is ultimately determined by the material resources at their disposal. Seized upon at the time as a critique of the adverse economic consequences of 'imperial America's' high defence burden, it can be seen, in retrospect, as providing a compelling explanation for the sudden collapse of the Soviet empire between 1989 and 1991.

The World that Came in from the Cold (1993) by Gabriel Partos. A very readable account of the Cold War era, between 1945 and 1991, based on around 200 interviews for a BBC World Service radio series. The major themes and events of the decades after World War II are surveyed, encompassing the spread of the Soviet Union's global influence into Africa and W Asia to the late 1970s, the détente era and the disbanding of the Warsaw Pact in July 1991. Participants from both East and West tell their own stories.

The Grand Failure: The Birth and Death of Communism in the Twentieth Century (1989) by Zbigniew Brzezinski. An influential and prophetic book by one of the USA's leading strategic thinkers, secretary of state during the Democrat Carter administration. Completed in 1988, this work anticipated the collapse of communism in the Soviet Union, as a result of its economic failures, and the dangerous resurgence of nationalism in Eastern Europe. Characterized as 'the twentieth century's most extraordinary political and intellectual aberration', communism has been one of the century's most influential ideologies, leading to an exaltation of the state and the division of the world into two contending blocs.

International Politics: States, Power and Conflict since 1945 (1992) by G R Berridge. This introductory text focuses on states, the conflicts that divide them, the instruments they employ to pursue their ideals and secure their interests, and the system of rules and institutions through which conflicts are worked out. There are chapters on United Nations peacekeeping and welfare works, secret intelligence, propaganda, the world economy, and economic statecraft.

World Conflicts: Why and Where They Are Happening (1992) by Patrick Brogan. A regionally arranged historical account of the genesis and development of international and ethnic conflicts in more than 40 states and disrupted territories in the world. The work includes coverage of the collapse of the Soviet empire 1989–91, the Gulf War of 1990–91, and the outbreak of civil war in 1991 in the former states of Yugoslavia. Valuable, informative, and readable.

HUMAN RIGHTS

Nigel Wright

It is an impossibly difficult task to select the best books on human rights. I could have drawn up dozens of lists of 'must-read' books. From Martin Luther King to Gandhi and Mandela, prison has inspired some of the world's best minds to produce some of the world's best literature. It is an unfortunate fact that good literature, by its power, makes its authors a target of tyrannical regimes. With almost painful reluctance I was forced to discard some truly great works. Much of my inspiration for human-rights work comes not only from accounts of the terrible ordeals that people suffer, but also from fiction that depicts the strength and individuality of human beings. My list includes the relatively obscure *Hanging Tree*, and a comic novel to help you get through some of the others. The dazzling flashes of humour from Sachs assured his inclusion, and Keenan's account of his ordeal as a hostage is simply among the best-written work to be produced in the 1990s.

Words like 'freedom', 'justice', 'democracy' are not common concepts;
on the contrary, they are rare. People are not born knowing what
these are. It takes enormous and, above all, individual effort to arrive
at the respect for other people that these words imply.

JAMES BALDWIN

The Hanging Tree (1994) by Vic Gatrell. Compelling study which explodes the myth of the mob, revealing what the British people really thought about executions in the 18th and 19th centuries.

I, Rigoberta Menchú: Indian Woman in Guatemala (1983) by Rigoberta Menchú. The riveting story of the Guatemalan Nobel Peace laureate.

A Boy's Own Story (1982) by Edmund White. A beautifully written story of how a young boy tries to grow and develop in his own way and, as often happens, his family and society cannot cope with anything that is 'different'.

The Jail Diary of Albie Sachs (1978) by Albie Sachs. A brilliant account of his ordeal in solitary confinement in South Africa.

An Evil Cradling (1992) by Brian Keenan. The pick of the Lebanese hostage books.

The Periodic Table (1975; translated 1984) by Primo Levi. Marvellously written novel from someone who experienced at first hand life and near death in a Nazi concentration camp.

Darkness at Noon (1940) by Arthur Koestler. A grim, but compelling, account of how a totalitarian system is not satisfied with imprisoning or executing dissent, but tries to destroy an individual's will to live.

The Unbearable Lightness of Being (1984) by Milan Kundera. A novel that vividly portrays totalitarian society.

The Songlines (1991) by Bruce Chatwin. A moving description of a people and their culture and what happens when others, who do not understand them, persecute and try to destroy them instead.

Brrm! Brrm! (1991) by Clive James. Not an obvious human-rights choice, but very funny. It shows how much can be misunderstood between different cultures. It also represents the author's desire to understand and appreciate a culture that has caused his family great suffering as a result of the war against Japan.

FEMINISM

Gloria Steinem

Feminism, women's liberation, the women's movement, women's rights, woman-ism, and feminisms in the plural – all these and more are terms to describe the current transformative movement for female *equality* as human beings. This wave follows the 19th- and early-20th-century wave known as suffrage or female emancipation, in which women succeeded in winning an *identity*. Previously they had been chattels with a legal status that provided the model for slavery. Indeed, there have been successive waves of rebellion in every part of the world, in public and in private, for the last few thousand years since patriarchy replaced ways of life in which power seems to have been more balanced.

By now, the feminist argument for equal status for females of all races, classes, ages, ethnicities, abilities, and sexualities has begun to sound reasonable and to have majority support in public opinion polls, but it is still opposed by forces that range from religious fundamentalists to multinational companies, from right-wing patriarchs to left-wing nationalists. After all, equal pay and equal access to land, credit, and inheritance would constitute a massive redistribution of wealth; women's sexual and reproductive freedom would take away control of the means of reproduction from family, religion, and state; redefining and revaluing work to include the unpaid or underpaid production and reproduction now done by 'women who don't work', whether homemakers in overdeveloped countries or food producers in underdeveloped ones, would eliminate the world's largest source of cheap labour; challenging the division of human nature into 'masculine' and 'feminine' would uproot the passive/dominant paradigm on which race, class, and other hierarchies are based; shifting from religions in which God looks like the ruling class to spiritualities in which god is present in women and all living things would delegitimize man's domination of women and nature; and nurturing the full range of human qualities in both males and females would eliminate the violence implicit in having to prove 'masculinity', and transform our ideas about human nature itself.

Whether we are working towards each person's empowerment in ways large or small, we are part of the feminist movement.

Most of these books come from North America and Europe, but many include references to movements on other continents. In general, each book will lead you to many more.

I myself have never been able to find out precisely what feminism is. I only know that people call me a feminist whenever I express sentiments that differentiate me from a doormat.

REBECCA WEST

Beyond Power: On Women, Men, and Morals (1985) by Marilyn French. A well-documented and mind-changing argument that current power systems are neither inevitable nor natural.

The Great Cosmic Mother: Rediscovering the Religion of the Earth (1987) by Monica Sjoo and Barbara Mor. Starting in Africa, where human beings first developed

– and with the 95% of human history that preceded patriarchy, monotheism, and nationalism – this fills in some of the knowledge dismissed as 'prehistory'.

The Mermaid and the Minotaur: Sexual Arrangements and Human Malaise (1976) by Dorothy Dinnerstein. By exploring why women have such unequal responsibility for child-rearing – and the far-reaching impact of men raising children as much as women do – Dinnerstein creates a starting place for changing everything from women's double role to the roots of male violence.

Feminism: The Essential Historical Writings (1972, 1992, and 1994) and ***Feminism in Our Time: The Essential Writings, World War II to the Present*** (1994) edited with an introduction and commentaries by Miriam Schneir. These are excerpts from essays, fiction, memoirs, letters, and political theory by major feminist writers, from pre-suffrage through Simone de Beauvoir, Betty Friedan, Kate Millett, Susan Brownmiller, Audre Lorde, Adrienne Rich, and other modern pioneers (though its commentary misunderstands Carol Gilligan, Andrea Dworkin, and others). You can browse and see which ones you want to read in their entirety.

Sisterhood Is Powerful (1970) edited by Robin Morgan; ***Radical Feminism*** (1973) edited by Anne Koedt, Ellen Levine, and Anita Rapone; and ***This Bridge Called My Back: Writings by Radical Women of Color*** (1983) edited by Charrie Moraga and Gloria Anzaldua. Any of these three anthologies will take you from the personal to the political and back again. Consciousness-raising, rap groups, revolutionary cells: whatever you want to call this process of learning from each other's lives and sharing insights, it is made portable here.

Sisterhood Is Global: The International Women's Movement Anthology (1984) edited by Robin Morgan. An unmatched overview of female history and status in almost every country, from Afghanistan to Zimbabwe, with a modern feminist also writing a personal essay from each one.

If Women Counted: A New Feminist Economics (1988) by Marilyn Waring. A practical, visionary, international plan for attributing value to women's unpaid labour and to the environment.

The New Our Bodies Ourselves: A Book by and for Women (revised edition 1995) by the Boston Women's Health Collective. This premier self-help book of the women's health movement has been updated periodically over more than 20 years, and translated into most of the world's major languages. (See also *Ourselves Growing Older*.)

Writing a Woman's Life (1988) by Carolyn Heilbrun. A slender volume full of insight into the current cultural differences between male and female life patterns that mean many women become ourselves after 50.

Outlaw Culture: Resisting Representations (1994) by Bell Hooks. An astute and passionate black feminist critic's essays on contemporary culture, from sex and movies to love and freedom.

Trauma and Recovery: The Aftermath of Violence, from Domestic Abuse to Political Terror (1992) by Judith Lewis Herman. A brilliant analysis of the parallels between the mostly female survivors of child sexual abuse and domestic violence. By exposing the similar political and spirit-breaking results of trauma, she offers ways of healing.

Staying Alive: Women, Ecology and Development (1988) by Vandana Shiva. Linkage among these mega-issues of our time by an Indian philosopher of science and activist.

The Anatomy of Freedom: Feminism in Four Dimensions (1982; second edition 1994) by Robin Morgan. How feminism and the new physics are breaking down hierarchy and creating holographic ways of perceiving reality.

For men – all of the above, plus:

Against the Tide: Pro-feminist Men in the United States, 1776–1990, a Documentary History (1992) edited by Michael S Kimmel and Thomas E Mosmiller.

DEVELOPMENT STUDIES

Deborah Eade

Strengthening people's capacity to determine their own values and priorities, and to organize themselves to act on these, is the basis of development. It is about women and men becoming empowered to bring about positive changes in their lives; about personal growth together with public action; about both the process and the outcome of challenging poverty, oppression, and discrimination; and about the realization of human potential through social and economic justice. Above all, it is about the process of transforming lives, and transforming societies.

The right to development is the right of individuals, groups, and peoples to participate in, contribute to, and enjoy continuous economic, social, cultural, and political development, in which all human rights and fundamental freedoms can be fully realized ... Development is not only a fundamental right but a basic human need, which fulfils the aspiration of all people to achieve the greatest possible freedom and dignity both as individuals and as members of the societies in which they live ... A development strategy that disregards or interferes with human rights is the very negation of development.

UNITED NATIONS

The Open Veins of Latin America (1971) by Eduardo Galeano. A compelling account of colonialism in Latin America, and its contemporary repercussions. Although the historical detail varies from one region to another, the legacy of deepening poverty and an ever-widening gap between rich and poor lives on today throughout Latin America, Africa, and Asia, and also distorts human development within the industrialized nations.

Where There Is No Doctor (1977) by David Werner. First written in Spanish for peasant farmers in the mountains of Mexico, this influential manual is inspired by the belief that 'health care is not only everyone's right, but everyone's responsibility'. Its lasting message is that even the poorest and most oppressed people can take control of their lives when given the means to do so, and is a classic depiction of primary health care in practice.

A Quiet Violence: View from a Bangladesh Village (1983) by Betsy Hartmann and James Boyce. A powerful case study demonstrating how global, national, local, and household forces combine to consign millions to hunger and deprivation in a world of plenty. Written from a grass-roots perspective, this study shows that in the context of skewed power relations, aid may be part of the problem rather than part of the solution.

Woman at Point Zero (1975) by Nawal El Saadawi. This novel explores the real human suffering caused by class and gender oppression. It is a terrible indictment of intolerance and the abuse of power as it affects all human development.

The Universal Declaration of Human Rights (1948) by theUnited Nations. This comprehensive document remains touchstone against which to measure the distance separating humankind from development. Stressing the universal and indivisible nature of human rights, the Declaration underlines that all development is undermined as long as there is one woman, man, or child whose rights are not fully realized.

Hunger and Public Action (1989) by Jean Drèze and Amartya Sen. A ground-breaking examination of the role of governments and of social actions by the public in eradicating famines and eliminating deprivations. It stresses how discrimination against women creates a 'sex bias in famine'. A free press is critical in ensuring that governments are exposed to public scrutiny; and may be 'the most effective early-warning system a famine-prone country can rely on'.

Rising from the Ashes: Development Strategies in Times of Disaster (1989) by Mary B Anderson and Peter J Woodrow. Building on several case studies, this book shows that relief programmes are never neutral in their developmental impact. It presents a deceptively simple framework for understanding the dynamic relationship between different people's needs, vulnerabilities, and capacities. Criticizing most current relief practice, the authors show various ways in which it might be improved.

Women and Development Series (1989–95). Prepared under the direction of the UN liaison service for nongovernmental organizations. Consisting of ten volumes on topics including human rights, empowerment, employment, literacy, and refugees, the series provides a detailed overview of women's exclusion from development, and of ways in which women's and other organizations around the world, as well as the UN system itself, have attempted to 'mainstream' women's rights.

Rural Development: Putting the Last First (1983) by Robert Chambers. A major work that has influenced recent development thinking and practice, contending that poor people are themselves the best sources of information about their poverty. 'Experts' have only a limited role to play, helping to articulate and give shape to the actions of the poor.

The Pedagogy of the Oppressed (1973) by Paolo Freire. In this seminal book demonstrating the political nature of education, Freire explicitly links literacy to popular empowerment and social mobilization. His work in Brazil has had an irrevocable impact on adult education and social development work in Latin America and elsewhere.

ECONOMICS

ECONOMICS – *Alain Anderton*

Modern economics is often said to date from the publication of Adam Smith's book *The Wealth of Nations*. Adam Smith was the first writer to describe a market economy as we might recognize it today. Since 1776, economic thought has developed considerably against a backdrop of ever more complex economies. David

Ricardo, an economist working in the early 19th century, predicted that eventually economies would cease to grow and that workers' wages would settle down at a subsistence level while landowners and capitalists would reap huge rewards. His prediction led to economics being dubbed 'the dismal science'. We know today that Ricardo's thinking was flawed and that workers in the rich industrialized countries of the world enjoy a prosperity undreamed of in Ricardo's time. However, economics has always been controversial because it is used by individuals, businesses, and governments to make decisions. Economic agents all too often look around for an economic theory that confirms their prejudices rather than accepting that our understanding of how a system as complex as a market economy works is often imperfect. The ever changing nature of economics and the potential for entering a debate about causes, effects, and policy implications are just some of the factors that make economics so fascinating.

The theory of economics does not furnish a body of settled conclusions immediately applicable to policy. It is a method rather than a doctrine, an apparatus of the mind, a technique for thinking, which helps its possessor draw correct conclusions.

JOHN MAYNARD KEYNES

History of Economic Thought (1991) by William J Barber. Like any discipline, economics and its concerns have changed over time. This book is one of the most readable and authoritative guides to these changes in economic thought which in turn have influenced the way governments have run their economies.

An Inquiry into the Nature and Causes of the Wealth of Nations (1776; many later editions) by Adam Smith. Adam Smith is often considered to be the founder of modern-day economics because he was the first writer to outline and appraise the workings of a free-market economy. The workings of the 'invisible hand' of the marketplace, which allocated resources according to the self-interest of both producers and consumers, led to the promotion of the social good. Limiting competition, for instance through monopolies, raised prices and led to less being produced. His story of the pin factory, which he used to illustrate the benefits of the division of labour, is particularly memorable.

Capital (1867–95; many editions) by Karl Marx. This is definitely one of those books to take to your desert island. Widely bought but rarely read, it is a seminal work which had a profound influence on the 20th century. For those who lack the time or the patience to read this large tome, some extracts, or *The Communist Manifesto* (1849), will give the reader the flavour and an insight into the abstract nature of Marxian analysis but also the very real social problems that Marx attempted to address.

The General Theory of Employment, Interest and Money (1936) by John Maynard Keynes. This book was the starting point for our modern-day understanding of macroeconomics, the study of how the economy works as a whole. It is very much a book written by an economist to other economists about the great issue of the day – why could economies stay in deep depression over a long period of time, and how could governments get economies out of the depression? In it, Keynes argues that governments have a responsibility to kick-start an economy in deep depression by spending money, and then allowing private businesses and consumers to take over with more investment expenditure and consumption expenditure as the recovery proceeds.

Keynes and After (1991) by Michael Stewart. This book, which has been regularly updated over time, provides the lay person's guide to the Keynesian revolution in economic thinking. Stewart explains Keynes's thinking and sets it in its historical context. He then considers the monetarist counterattack to Keynesian thought mounted from the late 1960s which rapidly became a counter-orthodoxy.

The Affluent Society (1958) by J K Galbraith. J K Galbraith has been the great popularizer of left-wing liberal economics in the USA since the mid-1950s. This, his first seminal work, was an attack on the failure of government to provide a social infrastructure that matched the growing affluence of private spending. He coined the phrase 'private affluence, public squalor' to encapsulate his main theme. Galbraith has since written a number of important works, including the highly readable *The Great Depression* and *The Liberal Hour*.

Free to Choose (1980) by Milton Friedman (with A J Schwartz). In the 1950s and 1960s, belief in the importance of state intervention to correct a market system that was prone to failure became increasingly dominant. The tide was turned by Milton Friedman, who became a great popularizer of right-wing economics. In *Free to Choose*, he outlined the benefits of allowing markets to decide what is to be produced and how it is to be produced. Individuals should be allowed to control their own destinies, whereas government power and control in the economic sphere should be reduced to its barest minimum. For Friedman, governments usually made far worse decisions than the individuals whose lives were being affected by those decisions.

Small Is Beautiful: A Study of Economics as if People Mattered (1973) by E F Schumacher. Traditional economics, whether of the right or of the left, is not without its critics. There are those who argue that we need completely new economic structures if the planet is to survive and human beings are to be allowed to be fully human. This seminal work provided such an alternative vision. Schumacher argues that we need to go back to small structures in society and that the trend towards the large – the large firm, large production, global consumption – is self-defeating and unsustainable.

The State We're In (1995) by Will Hutton. A surprise best seller of 1995, this left-wing analysis of the state of the British economy paints a gloomy picture of today's Britain. It vigorously attacks Thatcherite economic policies and argues the case for more state intervention both to increase the efficiency of the economy and to reduce growing inequalities.

The Death of Economics (1994) by Paul Ormerod. A very readable critical appraisal of current thinking on economics and how that thinking has influenced government policy. It is particularly harsh in its judgement on the way mathematics and statistics have been used within the discipline and tries to suggest a way forward that is more concerned with the dynamics and institutions of the economy.

BUSINESS – *Alain Anderton*

The study of business is relatively young. It is also changing so fast that what seems important today is of only historical interest in the business climate of tomorrow. As John Harvey Smith writes in an introduction to the Penguin edition of Igor Ansoff's *Corporate Strategy*: 'Despite the fact that the world of business prides itself on its self-analytical and ordered approach to things, businessmen are no less prone than the next man to fashion and crazes. As the ground of what constitutes business success is ploughed over again and again 'new discoveries' are made, new methodology is produced and new panaceas for success are recommended, and as eagerly sought.' Any airport bookshop will contain a wide selection of the latest books from today's fashionable gurus, testament to the ephemeral nature of the subject. Nevertheless, there are some classics in the field and the very fact that business is so changeable makes it one of the most compelling and exciting areas for reading today.

The best class of scientific mind is the same as the best class of business mind. The great desideratum in either case is to know how much evidence is enough to warrant action. It is as unbusiness-like to want too much evidence before buying and selling as to be content with too little.

SAMUEL BUTLER

The Principles of Scientific Management (1911) by Frederick W Taylor. A business classic in which the US author analyses how work can be organized under scientific principles to maximize output per labourer. For Taylor, labourers are motivated only by money, so they need to be scientifically motivated and controlled by management.

The Practice of Management (1994) by Peter Drucker. A management classic by the father of American business gurus. In this seminal book, he laid down many of the ideas about how managers should manage by setting objectives which were taken up and reworked by others, such as Charles Handy and Tom Peters.

The Human Side of Enterprise (1960) by Douglas McGregor. In a counterblast to Frederick Taylor, Douglas McGregor outlined a complex theory of what motivates workers. For McGregor, pay is just one of many factors that are important in determining motivation. He placed stress on the positive side of human nature and saw labour as a resource to be released rather than controlled. McGregor was one of a number of people who helped develop our modern understanding of workplace motivation.

Strategic Management (1979) by Igor Ansoff. *Strategic Management* is a heavyweight classic by an author who has specialized in writing about how businesses should operate within the business environment in which they find themselves. Ansoff discusses, for instance, how businesses should decide what to produce, how to sell, what size to be, and how to respond to competitors.

When Giants Learn to Dance (1992) by Rosabeth Moss Kantor. This is book aimed at those interested in the giants of the business world – the IBMs, the Fords, and the Shells. Kantor discusses how big can mean cumbersome, bureaucratic, and inefficient. To remain like this is to die. To survive in today's climate, giant companies need to learn how to be responsive, nimble, flexible, and efficient.

In Search of Excellence (1982) by Tom Peters and Robert H Waterman. The case-study approach is at the root of business education. In this seminal work, Peters and Waterman look at a number of American companies which, in their opinion, have been immensely successful. They then focus on the management of these companies and explore why particular managers and management cultures stand above the rest.

Competitive Advantage of Nations (1990) by Michael Porter. Some countries have been immensely successful economically. The economic performance of other countries has been mediocre, and some very poor. Michael Porter explores why this has been the case, and in particular discusses what it is about businesses and the business environment that has contributed to nations such as Japan being so successfully competitive.

The Age of Unreason (1989) by Charles Handy. In an information age, structures within businesses and within society will be far more flexible than before. To survive, organizations will have to be in a continuous process of learning. To create this environment, workers will be constantly changing their roles. Those employed within organizations will have a number of temporary briefs. A large number of workers, however, will work on the periphery, accumulating a portfolio of jobs subcontracted from organizations. Inevitably, the number of workers employed permanently by an organization will diminish. Education will be a constant feature of the worker's life, and many will choose to work part-time in retirement. Handy predicts that fewer and fewer workers will have a 'job for life'.

Troubleshooter (1991) by John Harvey Jones. The former chair of ICI, famous for his loud ties, is constantly providing a stream of light, easy-to-read but penetrating books. This book, based on a BBC television series, has John Harvey Jones reporting on a number of businesses that faced problems. He identifies those problems and suggests solutions. A fun read!

Body and Soul: How to Succeed in Business and Change the World (1992) by Anita Roddick. This is a book for those who want an alternative perspective on the business world. In this book, Anita Roddick describes how she founded the Body Shop and discusses the ethics and values – including spirituality – upon which the Body Shop has been built.

EXPLORATION

Chris Murray

E xploration is an inevitable consequence of man's success as a species: as groups thrive, habitats are exhausted and new ones have to be sought: having spread from the savannas of Africa to exploit every inhabitable corner of the Earth, man is now on the point of exploring space. This need to explore is, consequently, a central theme in the early literature of most societies, the search for new lands and the fascination of the unknown acquiring a mythic dimension; Homer's *Odyssey* is one of the best-known examples. Books on exploration can be roughly divided into those that aim to convey its adventure and those that seek to explain its social, economic, and cultural aspects.

... towards the North, as it were thick Cloudes, which did put us in some hope of Land; knowing how that part of the South Sea was utterly unknowne; and might have Islands, or Continents, that hitherto were not come to light.

FRANCIS BACON

Travels (many editions) by Marco Polo. Recounting his travels (1260–95) across Asia and a 17-year stay in China as guest of the Mongol emperor Kublai Khan, this book remains one of the most colourful and fascinating accounts of exploration. It is all the more remarkable for being – unlike so many early accounts of travel – largely true and accurate. Polo's account stimulated an interest in the Far East that led eventually to the voyage of Columbus, and until the early 19th century it remained (astonishingly) Europe's prime source of information about the Far East.

Mandeville's Travels (late 14th century; several modern editions available). The authorship of these travels is unclear; they have their origins in several 14th-century French books based on much misinterpreted reports of the Crusades. This is largely exploration in the mind, to worlds full of fantastical beasts; one of the ancestors of the Italian novelist Italo Calvino's *Invisible Cities*.

Principal Navigations, Voyages and Discoveries of the English Nation (1589; several modern editions) by Richard Hakluyt. Brings together salty accounts of early English exploration by such contemporaries as Francis Drake, Walter Raleigh, Martin Frobisher, and Jacques Cartier. Exploration now goes hand in hand not only with trade, but also with piracy and colonization.

Age of Reconnaissance (1970) by John Parry. The economic, political, and religious aspects of the 'Age of Exploration' are described in this scholarly but highly readable account of exploration, trade, and settlement beyond Europe from the 15th to the 17th century. The same period – the age of Ferdinand Magellan, Christopher Columbus, Vasco da Gama, Amerigo Vespucci, Francis Drake, Henry Hudson, Francisco Pizarro, and others – is covered in the lavishly illustrated Time-Life *Age of Discovery* (1966).

Christopher Columbus: The Dream and the Obsession (1986) by Gianni Canzotto. The story of the discovery of the 'New World'. Canzotto gives a vivid account of Columbus's many adventures, concentrating on what drove him on against all odds.

The True History of the Conquest of Spain (1632; several modern translations) by Bernal Díaz. An eye-witness account of the Spanish in South America by Díaz, who accompanied Cortés on his fateful and bloody journey through Mexico.

In the Wake of Cook: Exploration, Science and Empire 1780–1801 (1985) by David Mackay. Looks at the broad context of 18th-century exploration and its close links with the rapid development of science, the growth of industry, and the economics of empire.

Missionary Travels and Researches in South Africa (1857; modern edition available) by David Livingstone. A classic of African exploration. It is still fascinating both as a vivid first-hand account and (for the modern reader) as a revelation of 19th-century cultural imperialism.

Heart of Darkness (1902) by Joseph Conrad. The moral bankruptcy of the 'opening-up' of Africa is exposed in this short novel based on personal experience of the Congo. Here again exploration has taken on a mythic quality as exploration of the *terra incognita* of the modern psyche.

Scott and Amundsen (1979) by Roland Huntford. A controversial account of Robert Falcon Scott's polar exploration, which deflates the heroic image built up by largely uncritical earlier biographies.

The Myth of the Explorers (1993) by Beau Riffenburgh. The heroic role of 19th-century and early-20th-century explorers in popular culture is examined in this book.

For the armchair explorer who wants to sample a wide range of the literature, the best selection is the *Oxford Book of Exploration* (1993) edited by Robin Hanbury-Tenison.

For those who want a broad view of exploration, there is *Discovery and Exploration: A Concise History* (1982) by Alan Reid and *The Discoverers: An Encyclopedia of Exploration* (1980), edited by Hellen.

SPORT

Andrew Ward

Sport is a worldwide phenomenon that bonds nations by its rules and yet provides a basis for competition. Major sporting events, such as Olympic Games and World Cups, attract record television audiences and generate enormous interest. But sport also gives people fun and friendship at the grass-roots level, and it is a great source of stories. This reading list concentrates on nonfiction books, but there is also a vast amount of fictional work that provides an emotional feel for sport; in particular, see the work of P G Wodehouse (golf), Bernard Malamud and W P Kinsella (baseball), Frederick Exley (American football), David Storey (rugby league), Jack London (boxing), and Dick Francis (horse racing). In recent years, as sport gains more credence as a subject of serious study, it has become a fertile ground for sociologists, philosophers, psychologists, and historians, who have all shown that sport can teach us a lot about society and relationships.

Sport may have to be explained in terms of things beyond itself but it has also to be enjoyed for its own sake.

RICHARD HOLT

Homo Ludens: A Study of the Play Element in Culture (1938; translated from Dutch 1949) by Johan Huizinga. A classic study of the philosophy of play.

The Football Man: Passions and People in Soccer (1968) by Arthur Hopcraft. Hopcraft provides a highly readable overview of the traditional roles of soccer people. Concentrating on Britain, where soccer has its roots, he captures what the game means to all participants, from players to spectators.

The Boys of Summer (1971) by Roger Kahn. A journalist tells of his love affair with the Brooklyn Dodgers baseball team of the 1950s. Kahn not only describes the players, interviewed 20 years on, but also explains how he was captivated by sport through his father's interest.

Sports in America (1976) by James Michener. A sports enthusiast and best-selling novelist, Michener reviews the pains and pleasures of sport in the late 20th century.

The Oxford Companion to Sports and Games (1976) edited by John Arlott. A comprehensive paperback which documents the history of every sport and has entries on key people and venues.

Sport and the British (1989) by Richard Holt. Holt's book examines sport as part of the general history of Britain. He describes the origins of fair play and amateurism, and traces the development of gambling and professionalism.

Muhammad Ali: His Life and Times (1990) by Thomas Hauser. A wonderfully researched book which reconstructs the life of the world's greatest ever boxer in the words of those who knew him during his career.

Information Sources in Sport and Leisure (1992) edited by Michele Shoebridge. A book for serious students researching specific aspects of sport.

The Complete Book of the Olympics (1992) by David Wallechinsky. A massive compendium which gives the result of every Olympic final event since 1896 and documents the most fascinating stories of the Games.

LANGUAGE AND LITERATURE

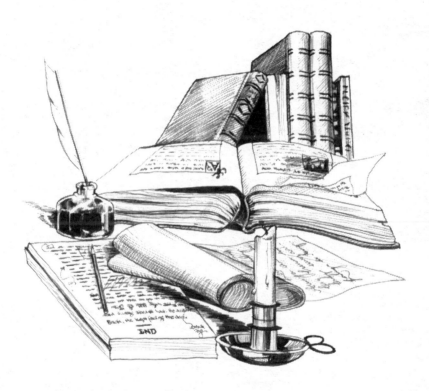

LANGUAGE

ENGLISH LANGUAGE – *David Crystal*

The unprecedented growth in the English language since the 1960s presents authors with a new agenda, if they are to provide a balanced account of the subject. With over a thousand million people using English to native or near-native levels of fluency, distributed throughout the world, the traditional accounts of the language – focusing just on Britain or on America – are no longer persuasive. Alongside the books dealing with traditional topics of interest, therefore – pronunciation, spelling, grammar, and vocabulary – there is increasing attention being paid to the diversity of uses which can be encountered within the English-speaking communities around the world, and to the speed at which the language is changing as it spreads. Each region presents fresh trends and norms. And even within one country, there is unprecedented variety and change, especially in relation to the media and electronic communication. How we cope with this diversity, so that we can preserve standards of mutual intelligibility without losing our local identity, in both spoken and written English, is one of the more intriguing questions which many authors are now attempting to answer.

Words will not lie down. Even if we left them alone, they would not, for vocabulary grows, changes, and dies without anyone being in charge. There is no Minister for the Lexicon, and in countries which do have an Academy with responsibility for the language, vocabulary rules with a bland disregard for the pronouncements of academics, politicians, and pedants. It is the most anarchic area of language. But we do not leave words alone. We do not even let them rest in peace. There are linguistic resurrectionists, who try to revive words that have been dead for centuries – such as the Anglo-Saxon enthusiasts. There are reincarnationists, who recall the previous existence of a word, and let it influence their lives. There are revolutionaries, who are trying to change the lexical world today, and even that is too late. There are resuscitators, who assail the letter-columns of publications with pleas to preserve past usage; redeemers, who believe that all words can be saved; and retributionists, who believe that, for some words, hanging's too good for 'em. A few, well-intentioned souls think that the government should legalize lexical euthanasia.

DAVID CRYSTAL

English in Use (1990) by Randolph Quirk and Gabriele Stein. This is the book which replaces *The Use of English*, Quirk's introductory account of English variety and style that motivated students of the language over 25 years. The new book provides somewhat greater depth in its approach to contemporary issues of structure and usage.

The Cambridge Encyclopedia of the English Language (1995) by David Crystal. A full-colour, illustrated guide to the history, structure, and range of uses of the language, with particular reference to the regional variety of English around the world.

Words in Time: A Social History of the English Vocabulary (1988) by Geoffrey Hughes. An account of the way words have changed their meaning in association with the changes which have taken place in society, in such fields as economics, journalism, politics, and advertising. Detailed word-histories are provided, using the files of the *Oxford English Dictionary*.

Rhetoric: The Wit of Persuasion (1989) by Walter Nash. A book which shows that this ancient and most respected of subjects has just as much relevance today as it had to Classical authors. Rhetoric is seen as a framework for argument and as a technique for presenting point of view, important as much for the study of everyday conversation as for the study of literature.

The Dialects of England (1990) by Peter Trudgill. An account of the history and geography of the chief regional dialects of England, including their pronunciation as well as their grammar and vocabulary. Lots of local examples are presented in a friendly transcription.

The Oxford Guide to Word Games (1984) by Tony Augarde. An account of the extraordinary things that people do to English (and other languages) when they begin to play with it. The many topics include anagrams, crosswords, alphabet games, tongue-twisters, puns, consequences, and spoonerisms.

LINGUISTICS – *Frederick J Newmeyer*

Linguistics is a field that bridges the humanities, the natural sciences, and the social sciences. Studies of metrical patterning in Old English verse, of the physics of speech sounds, and of turn-taking conventions in conversation all fall within its domain. Today, the dominant – and most productive – orientation of the field focuses on the cognitive aspects of language; that is, on the properties of linguistic representations in the mind and on the degree to which these properties point to an innately specified language faculty.

There are several reasons why language has been and will continue to be of particular significance for the study of human nature. One is that language appears to be a true species property, unique to the human species in its essentials and a common part of our shared biological endowment. Furthermore, language enters in a crucial way into thought, action, and social relations. Finally, language is relatively accessible to study. In this respect the topic is quite different from others that we would hope to address: problem solving, artistic creativity, and other aspects of human life and activity.

NOAM CHOMSKY

The Language Instinct: How the Mind Creates Language (1994) by Steven Pinker. A brilliantly elegant and readable book that introduces the concerns and results of modern linguistics to the lay reader. This should be everybody's introduction to the field.

Patterns in the Mind: Language and Human Nature (1994) by Ray Jackendoff. Another good introduction to linguistics, this one focusing especially on the relationship between the language faculty and other cognitive faculties.

The Chomsky Update: Linguistics and Politics (1990) by Raphael Salkie. The next best thing to reading Chomsky himself – the latter a task not for the faint of heart. Chomsky's approach to language is explained in clear detail as well as, for those who are interested, how his linguistic theories relate to his radical politics.

Language and Problems of Knowledge: The Managua Lectures (1988) by Noam Chomsky. This is probably Chomsky's most accessible recent book. It records his lectures on the fundamentals of linguistic theory to students and teachers in Nicaragua. The transcription of the discussion session at the end is especially useful.

The Politics of Linguistics (1986) by Frederick J Newmeyer. A nontechnical history of the past two centuries of linguistic theorizing. Special attention is given to the ways in which the social context has influenced the directions that the field has taken.

The Linguistics Wars (1993) by Randy Allen Harris. A rollicking account of the debates among theoretical linguists in the 1970s over the analysis of the interaction of form and meaning. A little technical in places, but it gives one a feel for how linguists go about the formal analysis of language.

Language and Society: An Introduction to Sociolinguistics (1994) by Suzanne Romaine. A very readable introduction to those aspects of language study that fall under the social sciences.

Endangered Languages (1991) edited by R H Robins and E M Uhlenbeck. The sad account of the threat of extinction to more than half of the languages in the world. The contributors spell out in detail both the human and the scientific cost of minority languages giving way to socially dominant ones.

You Just Don't Understand: Women and Men in Conversation (1990) by Deborah Tannen. On how and why men and women have difficulty communicating with each other. Lots of references to more technical work in the subfield of conversation analysis.

Language (1921) by Edward Sapir. The fact that this book is still in print after three quarters of a century testifies to its timelessness. Written by one of the greatest linguist-anthropologists of history, this was the first introduction to the scientific study of language for several generations of scholars. Fun to read as well.

AMERICAN ENGLISH – *Bill Bryson*

If you *park* a car, *fly off the handle, stay put, paint the town red* or even *keep a stiff upper lip*, you are using an Americanism. America has played a more vital and central role in the growth and development of the English language in the last three centuries than most people, inside or outside America, realize. Because it is such a neglected and finite topic, not all of the following are expressly about American words, but all shed considerable light on American speech and culture.

The American was good natured, generous, hospitable and sociable, and he reversed the whole history of language to make the term stranger *one of welcome.*

HENRY STEELE COMMAGER

The American Language: An Inquiry into the Development of English in the United States (1989) by H L Mencken. This is the classic and still definitive work. Originally issued in three volumes, it has been condensed into a single volume with the addition of much new and updated material, but Mencken's crusty and endearingly irascible tone still shines through.

The Barnhart Dictionary of Etymology (1988) by Robert K Barnhart. First of a series of a surprisingly fascinating and browsable books on new words and where they come from.

The Americans: The Colonial Experience, The Americans: The Democratic Experience, The Americans: The National Experience (1974) by Daniel Boorstin. Outstanding and accessible social history of the USA, full of interesting sidelights on the stories behind American inventions and the words they spawned.

The American Mind: An Interpretation of American Thought and Character Since the 1880s (1950) by Henry Steele Commager. Only indirectly pertaining to American speech, this is none the less an essential work for anyone wishing to understand the American character.

Our Own Words (1974) by Mary Helen Dohan. An engaging and always readable survey of the development of American speech over three centuries.

Democratic Eloquence: The Fight over Popular Speech in Nineteenth Century America (1990) by Kenneth Cmiel. Earnest but comprehensive look at American speech during a century that saw the USA go from being an agrarian nation on the periphery of world affairs to an economic and military colossus.

CLASSICAL LITERATURE

Graham Ley

Classical literature now commands greater attention than ever before, with good-quality translations of a large number of ancient authors prompting a wide readership to explore the origins of a European tradition. Recent approaches to epic, drama, lyric poetry, the novel, and the prose genres of historiography and rhetoric have drawn on developments in contemporary literary criticism and theory, and have tended to integrate social with purely formal considerations. Partly as a result of this expansion in interest, it is now easier to find accessible works on individual authors than the kind of broad introduction that was popular a generation or so ago. But most translations now include an up-to-date introduction and some useful suggestions for further, critical reading.

A poet is a light, winged, holy creature, and cannot compose until he is possessed and out of his mind, and his reason is no longer in him; no man can compose or prophesy so long as he has his reason.

PLATO ION

The Cambridge History of Classical Literature (1983) edited by E J Kenney and W V Clauseh. A series of introductions by literary specialists to the full range of Greek and Latin literature in antiquity. Available in sections devoted to particular genres and subjects.

The Oxford History of the Classical World (1988) edited by John Boardman. An illustrated compendium of introductions to ancient literature, art, history, and culture by specialist authors, with each chapter carrying suggestions for further reading.

The Pelican History of Greek Literature (1985) by Peter Levi. A good general introduction by a Greek scholar who is also a poet.

A Short History of Greek Literature (1985) by Jacqueline de Romilly. A translation of an introduction by one of the most sensitive critics of Greek tragedy.

Ancient Greek Literature (1981) edited by Kenneth Dover. A selection of helpful introductions to major genres and authors.

Roman Literature and Society (1980) by Robert Ogilvie. A good, contextual introduction for the student or general reader.

The Latin Love Poets from Catullus to Ovid (1980) by R Lyne. An outstanding study of a major tradition in Latin poetry of the later republic and early principate.

Virgil (1986) by Jasper Griffin. An accessible introduction to the leading national and ideological poet of the Augustan era.

The series of translations in Penguin Classics offers many of the ancient authors in separate volumes. Two anthologies of translated selections, *Greek Literature* (1977) and *Latin Literature* (1979), both prepared by Michael Grant, may be helpful in providing an impression of the range available.

ENGLISH LITERATURE

INTRODUCTION – *Brenda Richardson*

What are the defining boundaries of English literature? Can we use Milton's assertion to distinguish 'literature' from 'writing', suggesting that 'literature' contains some essence of the writer, 'treasured up on purpose' for the use of posterity? Even if we do there remains the problem of defining 'English'. Is it a matter of location or language? Simply to define English literature as British literature in English is too arbitrary. Should Northern Irish or all Anglo-Irish writing be included? Is literature written in English in Wales or Scotland part of a Wales-wide or Scotland-wide Welsh or Scottish literature regardless of medium? If we include the work of resident black or Asian writers in English are we denying their distinctiveness or recognizing their Britishness? What is English? Are dialect or patois poems in English? I would like to include all interesting writing in English in Britain or Ireland under this heading, but readers will find that many of the books suggested are more conservative.

A good book is the precious life-blood of a master spirit: embalmed and treasured up on purpose to a life beyond life.

JOHN MILTON

The Oxford Companion to English Literature (1985) edited by Margaret Drabble. A comprehensive guide to facts and dates, with good cross- referencing.

The Oxford Literary Guide to the British Isles (1977) edited by Dorothy Eagle and Hilary Carnell. English literature from the other end: look up Dorchester and find out about its literary connections beyond Thomas Hardy.

The Oxford Book of Literary Anecdotes (1975) edited by James Sutherland. A rich mine of bits and pieces of literary information and sidelights on literary figures, giving a flavour of literary life in different ages, in different regions, for both sexes and all classes.

Literary Theory: An Introduction (1983) by Terry Eagleton. Lucid, entertaining, comprehensive, a good way in to the sophisticated way of talking about literature in the 1990s.

A History of English Literature: Forms and Kinds from the Middle Ages to the Present Day (1987) by Alistair Fowler. The most accessible of the current one-volume histories: clear and concise but rather conservative in its scope.

The Short Oxford History of English Literature (1994) by Andrew Sanders. This may seem a bit stodgy but it is the history most aware of the problems of creating a canon of English literature in 1994. The result is a survey generously revisionist where women's writing is concerned, and offering pointers to the possibilities for multi-culturalism in the English literature of recent decades.

The Oxford Dictionary of Quotations (1953) edited by Angela Partington. With generous samplings of major authors and titillating glimpses of lesser-known ones, this offers a conspectus of a wide range of writing in English, literary, philosophical, and historical.

The New Pelican Guide to English Literature: A Guide for Readers (1991) edited by Boris Ford. A compendious and regularly updated guide that will enable the reader to find more information about almost any aspect of the field desired.

THE BRITISH NOVEL – *Brenda Richardson*

This entry involves problems of both definition and ideology. Down to about 1970 there is no perceived problem. Studies of 'the English novel' abound, and a selection is offered in the reading list below. But after this the scope for alternative definitions widens as Anglo-Irish novels become arguably a separate genre and practitioners of Indian or Caribbean origin reside wholly or partly in England and produce novels from their own distinctive cultural matrices. At the same time concepts of gender or racial identity become prominent, and it becomes tendentious to appropriate either feminist or Afro-Caribbean writing to a genre that is seen in some quarters as a part of Victorian and post-Victorian cultural imperialism, reinforcing gender stereotypes and imposing white, middle-class, male-centred narrative patterns. So the list also includes a couple of collections of essays which explore these problems of racial, national, and gender identity, and their relation to narrative fiction, whether or not we call the result a novel.

'Oh! it is only a novel!' replies the young lady: ... 'It is only Cecilia, or Camilla or Belinda' or in short, only some work in which the most thorough knowledge of human nature, the happiest delineation of its varieties, the liveliest effusions of wit and humour are conveyed to the world in the best chosen language.

JANE AUSTEN

The Rise of the Novel: Studies in Defoe, Richardson and Fielding (1957) by Ian Watt. The classic study of the origins of the novel conceived as a product of middle-class economic individualism.

The English Novel: Form and Function (1953) by Dorothy Van Ghent. Contains a mixture of studies in the interpretation of a wide range of individual works and studies of problems of form.

The Rhetoric of Fiction (1983) by Wayne C Booth. A classic American study dealing with British and other fiction. Here we see the rise of literary theory: concepts of the meaning of form, the importance of point of view, of reader-theory.

Mothers of the Novel: 100 Good Women Writers before Jane Austen (1986) by Dale Spender. A corrective to Ian Watt and other less carefully nuanced versions of the great male line of English novelists from Defoe to Dickens and Conrad. Dare a feminist say that the definition of 'good' may seem to need a bit of stretching?

The Modern British Novel (1993) by Malcolm Bradbury. All studies date quickly at the recent end of their period. This very new and comprehensive book covers the wide range of subgenres and cultural subsets into which the novel tradition may be seen to have fragmented as well as doing a good job on the 'mainstreams'.

The Bloomsbury Guide to English Literature: The Novel: A Guide to the Novel from its Origins to the Present Day (1993) edited by Andrew Michael Roberts. A work of reference in which authors, genres, and technical terms can alike be checked.

Reading Women: Essays in Feminist Criticism (1986) by Mary Jacobus. This collection has a European and international focus, indicating this aspect as well as the gender aspect of the shifting focus of literary and especially novelistic criticism in Britain.

Nation and Narration (1990) edited by H K Bhabha. Essays on various aspects of cultural identity and cultural imperialism, some more and some less relevant to the particular matter of the British novel, but indicating by its very existence the way in which the study of the novel has been problematized and politicized in the present decade.

ENGLISH PROSE – *Brenda Richardson*

The selection, it will be seen, contains no identified writer more recent than Lytton Strachey, though the letters and diaries come down well into the present century. Where more formal writing is concerned the defining examples do belong in earlier periods. Nonfictional prose is not one genre but many. There are essays, biographies, history, criticism, topography, humour, satire, pastoral, some separable, some not or barely so. The examples are chosen partly for style, partly for content, partly to give a taste of different periods and different contexts. The pleasures are many and diverse, and virtually impossible to summarize.

Prose can never be too truthful or too wise.

WILLIAM WATSON

Essays (1597–1625; several recent editions) by Francis Bacon. Like *Hamlet* they turn out to be full of quotations! They also provide a good sense of what life was like under Elizabeth I and James I and an illustration of the terse and plain style of writing.

The Compleat Angler (1653; several recent editions) by Izaak Walton. A favourite of mine, and a lovely example of a very minor genre, the pastoral idyll in English. Should you wish to cook pike, it can also serve as a recipe book!

Selections from the Tatler and Spectator (1988) edited by Angus Ross. 18th-century fashionable journalism, well selected, and offering a range of interests to do with both the style and diction and the content.

The Natural History and Antiquities of Selborne (1789; several recent editions) by Gilbert White. An evocation of rural life and an example of scientific and descriptive and yet eminently readable prose.

Reflections on the Revolution in France (1790; several recent editions) by Edmund Burke. An elegiac celebration of traditional aristocratic society incorporated in vigorous counter-revolutionary propaganda.

The Life of Charlotte Brontë (1857; several recent editions) by Elizabeth Gaskell. The life of a woman by a woman from a very paternalistic age. It offers social history and detail of the distinctive character of the West Riding of Yorkshire, as well as chronicling Brontë's struggle to achieve self-expression and self-fulfilment.

Studies in the History of the Renaissance (1873) by Walter Pater. Romantically impressionistic essays in art history which encouraged subjective responses to beauty.

Eminent Victorians (1918) by Lytton Strachey. Funny, irreverent, often desperately unfair, these studies offer a debunking, ironic corrective to uncritical treatments of Victorian piety and heroism.

The Englishwoman's Diary: An Anthology (1992) edited by Harriet Blodgett. A wide-ranging sampling of the regional, domestic, and personal writing which is characteristic of the female writer and fills in the blanks around the public life featured in the formal essays of London male culture.

The Oxford Book of Letters (1995) edited by Frank and Alice Kermode. An anthology stretching from the 16th to the 20th century, offering an insight into the life of different periods and the function of the letter in each.

THE 18TH-CENTURY BRITISH NOVEL
Chris Murray

It was during the 18th century that the prose tale underwent the subtle and profound transformation into the novel, for many the supreme literary form of the modern world. Its origins were modest. Though novels were soon to acquire the social graces of the drawing room, the earliest were redolent of the tavern, the brothel, and the debtors' prison, their language spiced with the racy vernacular of pimps, harlots, drunks, thugs, cardsharps, cutthroats, penniless fops, corrupt politicians, and scheming lawyers. In other words, early novels (strongly influenced by such writers as Cervantes) were essentially picaresques, a form for which the burgeoning ranks of the urban middle classes had a huge appetite. Young heroes and heroines, beset by a seemingly endless series of farcical trials and tribulations, finally, often by a totally unexpected twist of fate, achieve wealth and happiness. The following includes a few precursors of the true novel.

The novel is practically a Protestant form of art; it is a product of the free mind, of the autonomous individual.

GEORGE ORWELL

Oroonoko (about 1688) by Aphra Behn. A remarkable woman whose eventful life included working as a spy for Charles II, a spell in a debtors' prison, and a busy career as a translator, dramatist, and novelist – she was probably the first Englishwoman to earn her living by writing. A long prose romance influenced by continental writers, *Oroonoko*, with its attack on the slave trade, anticipates the much later concept of the 'noble savage'.

Robinson Crusoe (1719) by Daniel Defoe. Tradesman turned literary jack of all trades and polemicist who was thrown into prison several times, Defoe, freely combining fiction and fact, brought a new imaginative scope and vigour to storytelling. *Robinson* is his masterpiece, though his vividness of characterization, sure sense of everyday reality, and his narrative drive make *Moll Flanders* (1722) and *The Journal of the Plague Year* (1722) highly readable.

Gulliver's Travels (1726) by Jonathan Swift. Not a novel, quite, but a bitter, and at times obscene, satire in prose (the satires of John Dryden and Alexander Pope had set a very high standard in verse). By curious irony that might well have given its author a good deal of sardonic pleasure, *Gulliver's Travels* became a children's classic (parts of it, at least).

Pamela: Or Virtue Rewarded (1740–42) by Samuel Richardson. Generally considered to be the first English novel. Told in a long, long series of letters, it recounts the seduction of a young woman who, virtuous and true, brings about the moral transformation of her vile seducer, though both of them die in the process. A successful printer by trade, Richardson had a shrewd sense of what people wanted: a good story that ended with 'an useful moral'. His sensitivity to the psychology of his characters had a huge impact on the development of the novel, and in his lifetime he was feted throughout Europe: Dr Johnson as well as the French philosopher Rousseau wept for Pamela.

Tom Jones (1749) by Henry Fielding. A long picaresque romp through 18th-century England, probably the greatest novel of its age. Fielding detested what he regarded as the prissy and hypocritical morality of Richardson (he wrote a parody called *Shamela*), and his own novels combine a shrewd intelligence and an earthy frankness about human nature (the character Tom Jones is far from being a model of snowy-white virtue). His work as a dramatist gave his novels a sureness of structure absent in many works of the period. Essential reading.

The Expedition of Humphrey Clinker (1771) by Tobias Smollett. An account of a family on their travels through England and Scotland, told in a series of letters by each member of the family, this is probably Smollett's finest work. Smollett hasn't Fielding's sense of form, but the countless comic escapades of his vividly drawn characters show him to be ceaselessly inventive, his satire on human folly relentless, though just a little mellower here than in earlier works.

The Vicar of Wakefield (1766) by Oliver Goldsmith. A vicar and his family fall on hard times: he loses his position and is finally thrown into debtors' prison, his daughter elopes with a scoundrel. But it all turns out happily in the end. A neglected work (a little tame perhaps after Fielding and Smollett) which deserves more attention. The German poet Goethe, who dubbed it a 'prose idyll', was deeply moved.

The Life and Opinions of Tristam Shandy (1760) by Laurence Sterne. A unique work, this is one of the strangest books of the century. To use modern jargon, it 'deconstructs' the novel form, and far more amusingly than many 20th-century attempts. It has long mock-philosophical authorial asides, blank pages, a few squiggles to illustrate the rambling and inconsequential narrative, a mixture of styles high and (very) low, including stream-of-consciousness, and a gallery of colourful eccentrics – like one of its more recent relatives, James Joyce's *Ulysses*, it is either a sheer delight or an insufferable irritation. Despite its oddity it was extremely popular in his own day.

The Castle of Otranto (1764) by Horace Walpole. This is another queer fish. Disdaining the 'vulgar' realistic novels of his day, Walpole turned to medieval stories of chivalry and high romance. The result was a surrealistic novel of the supernatural – statues that bleed, ghosts, a giant helmet that falls from the sky killing a man, murder, rattling chains, and ruined castles. A rejection of the down-to-earth good sense of much 18th-century fiction, *The Castle of Otranto*, the first 'Gothic novel', is one of the earliest expressions of Romanticism and the ancestor of the modern horror novel.

THE 19TH-CENTURY BRITISH NOVEL
Roz Kaveney

There is a tendency on the part of critics of the novel to talk as if Romanticism was something that only happened in poetry, or abroad. In fact, the 19th-century British novel crucially concerns itself with key issues of Romanticism – the conflict between the individual striving to be entirely themselves and the community that has rights and in which the individual has to some extent to live. Often this conflict is posed in terms of a struggle between shadow selves or with a landscape; often also multiple narrative strands make possible the exploration of more than one point of view, more than one possible way of existing.

Dead, your Majesty. Dead, my lords and gentlemen. Dead, Right Reverends and Wrong Reverends of every order. Dead, men and women, born with Heavenly Compassion in your hearts. And dying thus around us every day.

CHARLES DICKENS

Emma (1816) by Jane Austen. Has the poise and elegant malice that we expect of Austen, but is surprisingly perceptive about the dangers of intelligence and talent. Emma makes mischief and manipulates almost everybody around her; she has a novelist's instincts and puts them to work in real life.

The Confessions of a Justified Sinner (1824) by James Hogg. Brilliantly originates a whole school of psychological horror stories. Its hero, persuaded of his elect status as one of the saved, comes to believe he can dispose of everyone in his way and serve God thereby; is his companion and adviser a delusion, the incognito Russian tsar, or the Prince of Lies?

A Christmas Carol (1843) by Charles Dickens. A moral lecture on charity that escapes mere preachiness because of the fertility of Dickens' fantastic imagination. It denounces not only miserliness and politics which stifles humanity in the affluent by denying it to an underclass; in the process, it crystallizes the manners of a particular time as the authentic way of celebrating Christmas. Mythopoeia is an underrated function of the novel and the tale.

Vanity Fair (1847) by William Makepeace Thackeray. Has a heart of unforgiving flint beneath the flip cynicism and sentimentality of its surface. Thackeray does not let even his virtuous characters get away with anything – by the time worthy Dobbin wins the widowed, dim Amelia, he has seen how little she is worth. Becky Sharp starts with our sympathy – she has, after all, her way to make in a cruel world – but forfeits it by gratuitous acts of petty cruelty.

Wuthering Heights (1847) by Emily Brontë. The most Romantic of great British novels, with its blasted landscapes and hopeless love. Based as it is on some crudely conceived dualisms like the opposition of calm and storm in the make-up of its characters, there is considerable subtlety in its execution; the distanced narrative turns up the heat on the emotional material by pretending to recollect it in tranquillity.

Bleak House (1852–53) by Charles Dickens. Perhaps his most comprehensive denunciation of a society in which the letter of the law is allowed to kill the spirit. The Chancery case of Jarndyce and Jarndyce becomes indistinguishable from the London fog; spontaneous combustion, smallpox, madness, and murder strike indiscriminately and the orphan Esther, the illiterate crossing sweeper Jo, and the snobbish Lady Deadlock have more to do with each other than we can imagine.

The Ring and the Book (1869) by Robert Browning. A great poem now most usefully read as if a novel; verse is its means of expression, rather than its soul. A classic Roman murder case is retold time after time from different viewpoints, becoming a meditation on truth and how truth is used within a society, and a touchstone for our perception of the characters who discuss it.

Daniel Deronda (1876) by George Eliot. Demonstrates that the 19th-century novel could be about ideas as well as plots and emotional extremes; the critic F R Leavis disapproved of the subplots about Zionism and music and wanted to edit it down to the story of Gwendolen Harlech, which demonstrates how little F R Leavis understood about story.

The Mayor of Casterbridge (1886) by Thomas Hardy. Reminds us usefully that the England of the 19th century started off as a rural economy, but that things changed ... Turned sober after selling his wife at a fair, Henchard becomes a model of Victorian energy, but secrets will out, and the assistant he fostered becomes his rival. Hardy at his best combined a sense of society as a whole with the most complete tragic sense of the century.

The Master of Ballantrae (1889) by Robert Louis Stevenson. Uses the last British civil war, the Jacobite rebellion of 1745, and its conflicts of loyalty to dramatize the clash of the two sorts of man. Observed by a narrator alienated from both, two brothers struggle for estate, wife, and ascendancy; often underrated as a children's adventure story, Stevenson's best book is endlessly inventive and emotionally subtle.

20TH-CENTURY BRITISH FICTION – *Roz Kaveney*

The 20th-century British novel hardly exists as a single concept – nor is this just a result of nearness in time and failures of perspective. For one thing, there was no longer any one idea of Great Britain to which to assent or dissent; a sense of marginalization was common not only to those who had been marginalized, but also to many writers whom most would see as at the centre of things as they were. Society is an antagonist in most of the good novels of the century, not a medium through which protagonists move. Exploration of technique was another crucial factor, of course, but looks less of one at century's end than it seemed in the middle; technical innovation was consistently recruited back into the mainstream so that James Joyce's *Ulysses*, for example, looks greater than ever, but far less radical a departure.

Yes – oh dear, yes – the novel tells a story.

E M FORSTER

The Secret Agent (1907) by Joseph Conrad. Conrad brought a European sophistication about motive and the political cast of mind to the British novel. This tale about the domesticity of the suburbs, the idiot games of high politics, and the tragedy of the mundane was a farsighted view of how the century was going to work. What also characterizes, perhaps, the 20th-century British novel is a sense of the weirdness of life which derives from Dickens and makes for real quirkiness; if the British novel of the second half of the century is for the most part distinctly minor, it is because there are in it so many goodish writers who wrote strange books.

The Good Soldier (1915) by Ford Madox Ford. This is, as the book's opening tells us, the saddest story ever told, largely because its quite trivial story of adultery, deceit, suicide, and madness is made to stand for a whole dying world of middle-class security. What seemed sensible arrangements had bad faith at the roots and destroyed everyone – the narrator gradually learns all that had been kept from him. Ford finished the book, and then went off to the war that the book never mentions, directly.

Mrs Dalloway (1925) by Virginia Woolf. Woolf despised Joyce's work for its grubby realism, but successfully appropriated the stream of consciousness in several of her books. Clarissa Dalloway is a social parasite, but she has a set of tasks to get through in a day and becomes admirable for doing them in spite of the endless distractions of her thoughts and senses. This is a slight book in many ways, but achieves grandeur through its sense of human solidarity.

Brighton Rock (1938) by Graham Greene. Greene's decision to divide his work into serious novels and 'entertainments' cost us, for the most part, a sense of him as a whole writer. This novel of gangsterism and damnation combines a nasty wit with a real sense of the complexity of quite ordinary lives; it is one of the best of thrillers because it is perhaps the best novel about criminals and their power struggles. Nemesis comes in the shape of a barmaid with a grievance and the worst horror of all is a short-play record.

Brideshead Revisited (1945) by Evelyn Waugh. This great, rich, purple convolvulus of a book was Waugh's reactionary farewell to the sweetness of life as he believed it to have been lived by a Catholic aristocracy he turned into myth as he worked. It is one of the great novels of regret partly because it is so clearly set in the imagination; it is also full of great comic moments and brilliant observation of a social climbing that was part of the artificial paradise that Waugh thought was dying.

Anglo-Saxon Attitudes (1956) by Angus Wilson. If tragedy is the nonfulfilment of promise, then this is one of the best and most pregnant tragic works of the century; Wilson's sense of Englishness is quietly unhappy, and full of chickens coming home to roost. A complicated affair of intellectual fraud and misunderstanding comes back to haunt Gerald and triggers every booby trap his bad faith has created.

The Fountain Overflows (1956) by Rebecca West. It is perhaps the sheer difficulty of her personality, and her longevity, that has led to the underrating of West as a novelist. This novel of an Edwardian childhood, the only completed volume of a trilogy, is one of the best descriptions of a child's fierce loyalties and incomplete understanding of the world; the heroine's personally unreliable gallant crusader of a father is a subtly conceived feminist comment on politics as Boys' Game still worth playing.

The Wide Sargasso Sea (1966) by Jean Rhys. Jean Rhys's early novels dealt with her rackety life and affairs with Ford Madox Ford and others with a slightly masochistic wit and sense of the randomness of life that makes them starkly depressing. Even more bracingly bleak, paradoxically, because of the richness of its prose is this late book, the story of a mad wife in Charlotte Brontë's *Jane Eyre*; Rhys made Woman as Victim the subject of great prose poetry.

When My Girl Comes Home (1961) and **The Camberwell Beauty** (1974) by V S Pritchett; both in **Collected Stories** (1982–83). The novella is a form often left out of the accounting and Pritchett, probably the greatest short story writer in the language his century, wrote two great novellas and no novels of real importance. These two tales show us private worlds and the way that privacy skews a sense of the real world or of ordinary morality; they are at the same time quietly nightmarish and hysterically funny.

The Infernal Desire Machines of Doctor Hoffman (1972) by Angela Carter. There had to be a great British surreal novel and the only odd thing about it is that it took until the 1970s. Carter's journey from rationality to a dream landscape and betrayals that leave ambiguities in the mouth is perhaps the most satisfactory foreshadowing of our ambivalence to their legacy.

Ulysses (1922) by James Joyce. Much prosecuted, much damned, much discussed, this is a novel about a day in the life of three Dubliners in 1905. The battery of technical devices – stream of consciousness, parody, abstracted musicalized dialogue – are not there to replace realism, but to enhance it; even the underlying and determining structure, the analogies between each episode and a book of the *Odyssey*, is a creation of limits in which the representation of the real can be pressurized. It is the most universal and the most particular of novels; it lets you know a time and a place and some people better than almost any other. And it includes within it a great meditation on mortality – proscribed and atheist, nonetheless Joyce is a Catholic writer.

At Swim-Two-Birds (1939) by Flann O'Brien. One of the other great 20th-century novels by an Irishman, this combines a sense of shabby-genteel debauchery with endless recursions into a world of cowboy novellas, heroic myths, and doggerel about stout. There are few books as funny – but the underlying sense of sadness comes out time and time again in the bleak side stories. A joke is a tragedy that happened to someone else.

POETRY ANTHOLOGIES – *Anthony Thwaite*

Some people affect to despise anthologies of poetry; but for readers just starting out they are a good way of sampling and sniffing and tasting. The first anthology I bought was Arthur Quiller-Couch's *Oxford Book of English Verse*. I was 15 and had just begun to read poems voluntarily, and to try to write them. Quiller-Couch published this book in 1900; and then in 1939, just before World War II, revised it. It was the revised edition I bought in 1945. The preface was weirdly old-fashioned ('it were profane to misdoubt the Nine as having forsaken these so long favoured islands'), and so were some of Quiller-Couch's choices; but the book still has a lot of undisputedly good things in it. However, I don't think I'd recommend it today. I list below a few anthologies I do recommend.

The New Oxford Book of English Verse (1972) edited by Helen Gardner. This is a full, wide ranging, reliable collection, from medieval anonymous songs to Dylan Thomas.

Six Centuries of Verse (1984) by Anthony Thwaite. This is a mixture of anthology and comment, historical and critical, which I put together as a companion to a Thames Television series I was asked to write. It can be read without any knowledge of the television programmes, and tries to be a sort of guided tour of poetry in English from Chaucer to Philip Larkin and Ted Hughes, including some Americans, from Poe to Robert Lowell and Sylvia Plath.

The Rattle Bag (1982) edited by Seamus Heaney and Ted Hughes. Intended for 'young people', this is a deliberate mix of old and new poems, arbitrary and jumbled, much as the title suggests. It 'is also for those who may feel they have missed their first chance with poetry and are ready to give it – and themselves – a second chance'.

The Oxford Book of Comic Verse (1994) edited by John Gross. I think this is the best and funniest of the many anthologies of 'comic' (or sometimes 'light') verse, particularly brilliant on the 19th and 20th centuries, in which John Gross has found some little-known gems.

Poets of the English Language (1952) edited by W H Auden and Norman Holmes Pearson. If you ever see a second-hand set of this five-volume collection, snap it up. This is a majestic full-scale gathering, from Langland to Yeats, much the best overall anthology. I wish it was still in print.

As for anthologies of contemporary poetry, I don't think there is a single wholly satisfactory one. But it wouldn't be expensive to buy three Penguins (*Contemporary Verse*, edited by Kenneth Allott; *British Poetry Since 1945*, edited by Edward Lucie-Smith; *Contemporary British Poetry*, edited by Blake Morrison and Andrew Motion), and then throw in a Bloodaxe paperback, *The New Poetry* (1993). These four between them pretty well cover the ground.

INDIVIDUAL POETS – *Anthony Thwaite*

My choice of 12 individual poets is personal without (I hope) being completely eccentric. People who read these lists will make their own discoveries in the anthologies I've recommended. I have omitted the great quartet (Chaucer, Shakespeare, Milton, Wordsworth), because I take it for granted that anyone who wants to read poems will have to tackle them some time. The editions I list are big ones, but all these poets are mostly easily available in a variety of selections as well.

The Poet takes note of nothing that he cannot feel emotionally. My opinion is that a poet should express the emotion of all the ages and the thought of his own. To find beauty in ugliness is the province of the poet.

THOMAS HARDY

John Donne (1592–1631): The Complete English Poems (1982) edited by A J Smith Dramatic, immediate, sometimes difficult, Donne is full of ingenious arguments, whether he is writing about seducing a woman or about God, and he grabs your attention from the start with his opening words: 'Busy old fool, unruly Sun', 'Death, be not proud', 'What if this present were the world's last night?'

George Herbert (1593–1633): English Poems (1990) edited by C A Patrides. All the poems he wrote in his maturity, towards the end of his short life, are religious, specifically Christian. But one doesn't need to share his faith to find Herbert beautifully convincing in his plain strengths, his ability to think aloud with subtlety and delicacy.

John Wilmot, Earl of Rochester (1647–1680): The Complete Works (1994) edited by Frank H Ellis. This 'wicked' aristocrat was not only one of the most notorious libertines at Charles II's court but a passionate and witty writer of lyrics and satires. I don't recommend Rochester to those easily shocked.

George Gordon, Lord Byron (1788–1824): The Poems (1963) edited by G Pocock, revised by V de Sola Pinto. I much prefer the Byron of such poems as *Don Juan* and *Beppo* to the high Romantic of *Childe Harold's Pilgrimage*: in other words, the cynical, exuberant, sardonic, mocking, and self-mocking poet. He was as famous for his life as for his works, and it's amazing how much of both he crowded into his 36 years.

Robert Browning (1812–1889): The Poems (1982) edited by J Pettigrew and T J Collins. The ones to begin with are the dramatic monologues, such as those in *Men and Women*, which are like strangely self-contained incidents from lost plays. Poems like 'My Last Duchess' are as gripping as any short story, and at the same time a speaking likeness from the past come to life.

Alfred Tennyson (1809–1892): The Poems (1989) edited by Christopher Ricks. There's so much variety in Tennyson that it's hard to know where to begin: the greatest extended elegy in English, *In Memoriam*; wonderfully musical lyrics ('Tears, idle tears'); brooding monologues; epic Arthurian stuff; and those jaunty poems in Lincolnshire dialect.

Emily Dickinson (1830–1886): The Complete Poems (1976) edited by Thomas H Johnson. The greatest woman poet writing in English, and in my opinion the greatest American writer. She had no success in her lifetime, but the thousands of tiny poems she left behind in a box in her New England home include some of the most extraordinary riddling masterpieces about death and immortality and eternity. The best of them take the top off your head.

Thomas Hardy (1840–1928): Complete Poems (1995) edited by James Gibson. Though he earned his living as a novelist, and wrote some great novels, Hardy the poet is the writer I prefer. Often a storyteller in his verse, he was also someone who could catch a moment of truth, of vision, of regret, of lost love, preserving for ever some chilling revelation or one of 'life's little ironies'.

A E Housman (1859–1936): Collected Poems (1939) edited by John Carter. He published only two slim volumes in his lifetime, and the whole of this collected volume isn't a large one. On the face of it, his poems are simple and repetitive – love is fleeting, lovers fickle, youth decays into age, death is final. What makes them utterly memorable is their seductive, instantly recognizable music: 'Tell me not here, it needs not saying', 'The troubles of our proud and angry dust', 'In valleys green and still'.

T S Eliot (1888–1965): Complete Poems and Plays (1969) by T S Eliot. Eliot was the first 'modern' poet who really caught my attention, soon after I read that Quiller-Couch anthology (in which he does not appear). And it was *The Waste Land* that did it. I don't think that at 16 I understood anything about it – but it seemed to me the most intoxicating thing I had ever read. After 50 years, I can talk fairly learnedly about it; but what remains is the excitement, and indeed the memorable mystery.

W H Auden (1907–1973): Collected Poems (1976, revised edition 1994) edited by Edward Mendelson.. Auden was the great virtuoso of our century, capable of writing every kind of poem from the intricate intellectual argument to the popular song ('Stop all the clocks, cut off the telephone'). I admire that variety, and his energy, restlessness, verbal and rhythmical skills. Reading Auden often makes you want to write a poem yourself, because (you think for a wild moment) you can do it too.

Philip Larkin (1922–1985): Collected Poems (1988) edited by A Thwaite. I became besotted with Larkin from the moment I first properly read him in 1955. Sad, observant, exact, funny, most of his poems work themselves into your memory as if, somehow, they had always been there – something that is seldom true of most poems at most times.

BIOGRAPHY – *Claire Tomalin*

Biographies are on the whole ephemeral. Nothing seems so old-fashioned as the biographies of the 1920s, gathering dust on library shelves. The exceptions are those that are fired by passion and understanding of their subject and period, and written with as much art as good fiction. A biography cannot put you inside someone else's skin, as fiction tries to, but it can (and should) immerse you in another world. The biographer draws on many disciplines – history, geography, sociology, medicine, psychology, art history among them – and has to be a scholarly jackdaw, picking up bits of information wherever they can be found. There may also be an intention to establish or restore a reputation, reveal a social problem, or do justice where it has not hitherto been done. Among the earliest English-language biographies are William Roper's of his father-in-law Thomas More (1626) and Izaac Walton's of the poet John Donne (1641); biography has been much more popular with the English and the Americans than with other nations.

A true delineation of the smallest man, and his scene of pilgrimage through life, is capable of interesting the greatest man; ... all men are to an unspeakable degree brothers, each man's life a strange emblem of every man's; and ... Human Portraits, faithfully drawn, are of all pictures the welcomest on human walls.

THOMAS CARLYLE

The Life of Samuel Johnson (1791) by James Boswell. By general consent one of the greatest books in the language, for its first-hand portrait of the man and rendering of his conversation, and for the art with which Boswell put his material together after the death of his friend.

Memoirs of the Author of A Vindication of the Rights of Woman (1798) by William Godwin. Written immediately after the death of Godwin's wife, Mary Wollstonecraft, in childbirth. Its frankness about her private life, extraordinary for the time, made it a cause of scandal, but it is a deeply affecting short account in which the characters of both author and subject emerge with striking force.

Life of John Sterling (1851) by Thomas Carlyle. Sterling was a minor literary figure, poet, and friend of the poet and critic S T Coleridge, and a political idealist who in his youth planned to assist in the overthrow of Ferdinand VII of Spain, only failing to join the disastrous expedition at the last minute, remaining behind to get married instead. He died in his thirties of tuberculosis, mourned by his many devoted friends, but he would scarcely be remembered were it not for Carlyle's affectionate tribute.

The Life of Charlotte Brontë (1857) by Elizabeth Gaskell. Another scandalous book when it first appeared, it is the tribute of a friend and a finely judged account of the almost overwhelming difficulties facing a woman of genius attempting to work in a society that preferred women to be purely domestic creatures. It remains brilliantly readable, and can profitably be followed up by Jenny Uglow's excellent *Elizabeth Gaskell* 1993.

John Keats (1968) by Robert Gittings. Casts new light on the process of composition as well as the life of the poet; a masterly study.

Henry James (1953–1972) by Leon Edel. A five-volume study, totally absorbing to admirers of James's work. It is the product of immense labour, feelingly written, and still the best available. (There is an abridged version, but what Jamesian would want that?)

Disraeli (1966) by Robert Blake. A classic political biography, magisterial in pace and tone, and enthralling.

The Rise and Fall of the Man of Letters (1969) by John Gross. Could be called a group biography, one of the most entertaining, original, and informative ever written.

Alan Turing: The Enigma of Intelligence (1983) by Andrew Hodge. This gave many readers their first insight into the development of computer technology, and at the same time an appalling revelation about officially sanctioned persecution of homosexuals, for Turing ended his life in suicide.

Mrs Humphry Ward (1990) by John Sutherland. Minor subject, major biography of a best-selling niece of Matthew Arnold and aunt of Aldous Huxley, indomitable charity worker, hypochondriac, and anti-suffragette: a witty, marvellous book.

Coleridge: Early Visions (1989) by Richard Holmes. A finely wrought account which takes the reader out walking the fells with the poet as well as into his intricate and sometimes disordered mind; the narrative rises to a wonderful climax.

AMERICAN LITERATURE

INTRODUCTION – *Malcolm Bradbury*

American literature really emerged from the sheer novelty of the New World. The wonders of landscape, the vast tracts of the continent, the ancient settlements, civilizations, and myths that were mistakenly thought of as 'Indian', the mythological expectations that were then brought over the Atlantic by settlers from Europe, and the new lives and experiences they encountered – all these combined to make the narratives told on the continent very different from those elsewhere. Then, in the 20th century, America became a world emblem of the spirit of modernity itself, and this too became part of the great American myth. American writing became dominant, American writers became world-famous, and American stories and narratives became part of the experience of people right across the globe. Though the phrase 'American literature' generally applies to the writings of the USA, it could and should, in these multicultural times, fairly include the 'other' American literatures. That means Canadian and Latin American literature, Native American literature, and African-American literature. Here is a list of some of the most useful, informative, and classic general studies.

Two bodies of modern literature seem to me to come to the real verge: the Russian and the American ... The furtherest frenzies of French modernism or futurism have not yet reached the pitch of extreme consciousness that Poe, Melville, Hawthorne, Whitman reached. The Europeans were all trying to be extreme. The great Americans I mentioned just were it.

D H LAWRENCE

The Literature of the United States (1954) by Marcus Cunliffe. A straightforward and excellently told narrative history for the general reader, with a strong sense of the historical importance of American experience and culture, written for Penguin books by a leading British historian and critic.

The Continuity of American Poetry (1961) by Roy Harvey. Pearce Outstanding analysis of the development of American verse from the Puritan poets through to the era of Wallace Stevens, Ezra Pound, and the 'Beat' movement.

Frontier: American Literature and the American West (1965) by Edwin Fussell. A powerful study reminding us how central the American West was to the formation of the classic American literary imagination.

Modern Latin American Literature (1973) by D P Gallagher. A fine general survey of literature in Latin America, with special emphasis on the writers of the 20th century, when Latin American writing was seen to be of world importance.

A Homemade World: The American Modernist Writers (1975) by Hugh Kenner. A lively and idiosyncratic portrait of the power of the Modern movement in American literature, including the work of Gertrude Stein, Pound, Stevens, Faulkner, and Hemingway, by an enthusiastic and deeply informed American critic.

Harvard Guide to Contemporary American Writing (1979) edited by Daniel Hoffman. Essays by leading critics on American literature from the end of World War II to the end of the 1970s, showing the wide variety of trends and movements in fiction, poetry, and drama.

The Cambridge Handbook of American Literature (1986) by Jack Salzman. An invaluable reference work on American literature, with detailed and informative entries.

Columbia Literary History of the United States (1988) edited by Emory Elliott. A collection of modern and up-to-date essays by many expert contributors, following the history of American literature from the prehistoric cave narratives to the literary trends and movements of the present.

Literature in America: An Illustrated History (1989) by Peter Conn. A lively and learned history of American literature from early days to the present, told in narrative form, with good social background and plentiful illustrations.

From Puritanism to Postmodernism: A History of American Literature (1991) by Richard Ruland and Malcolm Bradbury. An up-to-date narrative history, in Penguin paperback, of American literature from the 17th century to the immediate present, co-written by an American and a British critic. Including detailed study of many major texts, it shows the ways American literature has always been seen as distinctively 'modern', and also sees it in the context of world literature.

THE AMERICAN NOVEL – *Malcolm Bradbury*

Though the novel started off late in America (the Puritans disapproved of it), it began to flourish after the American Revolution, and became one of the most powerful forms of American narrative. To this day its nature seems shaped by its early subject matter: the encounter with nature, the wilderness, and the vast scale of the American continent; the meeting of cultures and races; the ever-shifting nature of society and civilization; the Gothic strangeness of American experience. In the 19th century, writers like James Fenimore Cooper, Edgar Allan Poe, Herman Melville, and Nathaniel Hawthorne established the distinctive flavour of American fiction. Henry James, Mark Twain, Stephen Crane, Theodore Dreiser, and Edith Wharton followed. By the 20th century, the American novel was to enter a major period, and play a dominant part in the future of fiction, under the influence of Ernest Hemingway, William Faulkner, John Dos Passos, and many more. Today, among the novelists who have won the Nobel Prize for Literature, the dominant number are Americans, and include Saul Bellow and Toni Morrison. These are some of the basic studies dealing with the history and development of American fiction.

Between the novel and America there are peculiar and intimate connections. A new literary form and a new society, their beginnings coincide with the beginnings of the modern era and, indeed, help to define it. We are living not only in the Age of America but also in the Age of the Novel, at a moment when the literature of a country without a first-rate epic or a memorable verse tragedy has become the model of half the world.

LESLIE FIEDLER

The American Novel and Its Tradition (1957) by Richard Chase. This is a classic study, establishing the difference between the traditions of the European 'novel' and the American 'romance', and giving some excellent readings of major authors from Cooper through to Faulkner.

Love and Death in the American Novel (1960) by Leslie Fiedler. Brilliant, very thorough study of the rise and development of the novel in North America, from its beginnings after the Revolution through to the period after World War II. It distils the distinctive themes and 'Gothic' qualities that made it so different from European writing.

On Native Grounds: A Study of American Prose Literature from 1890 to the Present (1942) by Alfred Kazin. This is another classic (and very influential) study, a little dated now, looking at the development of the realistic and social aspects of American fiction and its treatment of American life 'on native grounds'.

Radical Innocence: Studies in the Contemporary American Novel (1971) by Ihab Hassan. An important, analytical interpretation of the development of American fiction after World War II, emphasizing its concern with innocence and extremity, and its sense of experiment. By a noted critic.

City of Words: American Fiction 1935–1970 (1971) by Tony Tanner. A wonderful study of the experiments, in form and language, of American fiction in one of its most exciting and innovative periods, by a British critic who has been a major interpreter of American literature.

In Search of Our Mothers' Gardens (1983) by Alice Walker. This strongly personal book – by the author of *The Color Purple* – emphasizes and explores her double inheritance, black and female, as a novelist, and shows the importance of both traditions to the contemporary American novel.

American Fiction, 1865–1940 (1987) by Brian Lee. A fine general survey of the overall development of American fiction by a British critic, writing with a strong sense of the social developments taking place at the time.

Columbia History of the American Novel (1991) edited by Emory Elliott. A thorough, large-scale historical study of American fiction from the beginnings to the present by various experts with a contemporary standpoint.

Odd Jobs: Essays and Criticism (1992) by John Updike. Not all these highly readable essays – 160 of them, by a major writer who is also a warm and wonderful critic – are about American fiction. But the many that are illuminate it with a vivid humanity and understanding.

The Modern American Novel (1995) by Malcolm Bradbury. An extended survey of the American novel from the time of Henry James, Mark Twain, and William Dean Howells through to the immediate present, covering the many movements and trends – including modernism, postmodernism, 'dirty realism', and black and feminist fiction. Extensive bibliography.

THE 19TH-CENTURY AMERICAN NOVEL
Malcolm Bradbury

Nineteenth-century American fiction followed a very different course from that of the novel in Europe at the same time. The wonder of American nature, the drama of exploring and settling the great continent, and the fascination of recent American history took its writers into new and original materials. And then, between 1861 and 1865, came the Civil War, which threatened to break up the Union. American fought American in a period of national agony, changing the nature of American culture. After 1865, the USA set out on a period of massive modernization – partly helped by the industrialization the war had required. Its railroads spanned the continent, its cities rose high, and immigration multiplied. By the end of the century America was no longer a 'virgin land' but a great modern industrial power. American fiction changed to respond to these new conditions: romance and stories of history and nature gave way to a new spirit of reportage and literary naturalism. This is the story that lies behind some of the great American novels of the 19th century; here are my ten favourites – five from each half of America's divided century.

Our civilization is still in a middle stage, scarcely beast, in that it is no longer wholly guided by instinct, scarcely human, in that it is not yet wholly guided by reason.

THEODORE DREISER

The Prairie (1827) by James Fenimore Cooper. Cooper was the first real novelist of the American wilderness, and in *The Prairie* he takes his famous hero of the five novels of the Leatherstocking saga, Natty Bumppo, to the flat prairies west of the Mississippi River. He's now an old man, and America is quickly expanding west, away from the New York frontier where Leatherstocking started his adventures. Again he meets Indians, and makes his final peace with nature. A classic work of the American imagination.

The Narrative of Arthur Gordon Pym of Nantucket (1837) by Edgar Allan Poe. This is Poe's one novel (most of his work was in short story and poetry), and shows his famous, Gothic extremity of imagination. It's about a shipboard mutiny which ends in a formidable journey to the Antarctic, and the blank whiteness of experience, and is written with all Poe's sense of poetry – and horror.

The Scarlet Letter (1850) by Nathaniel Hawthorne. Set in Puritan Boston in the 1650s, this is the story of a woman, Hester Prynne, who affronts the 'iron law' of church and state by committing adultery with a minister. She is forced to wear a badge of shame, the scarlet letter A, but insists on the 'natural' law of her actions. Hawthorne called the novel a 'romance', meaning not just that it is a story of adulterous love but of the conflict between the claims of fact and imagination.

Moby Dick, or The Whale (1851) by Herman Melville. Melville said he wrote this book 'in the name of the devil', and it is a classic tragedy, the story of the obsessed Captain Ahab, who, sailing on the whaler *Pequod*, determines to avenge himself against the 'diabolic' white whale that has injured him. The book, filled with learning and parody, is a vivid, moving seaborne adventure, but also a profound work of modern experiment.

Uncle Tom's Cabin (1852) by Harriet Beecher Stowe. For the 19th century, this was America's most famous novel, a world best seller. Abraham Lincoln once suggested it started the Civil War. Sentimentally written, it still remains nonetheless a remarkable portrait of slave experience, portraying the cruelties and sufferings inflicted on the black slaves on the Southern plantations, and their basic humanity.

The Portrait of a Lady (1881) by Henry James. It's hard to have a preference among the novels of James; not only do his novels mark the refinement of the modern art of fiction, but they change and develop decade by decade, through to the great last works of the early 20th century. But this is his first great novel, displaying his mature art. And the story of Isabel Archer, the strong, free, young American girl come to her 'wondrous' Europe to encounter experience, and finding it grimly in her unhappy marriage to Gilbert Osmond, is one of the most remarkable character portrayals James ever achieved.

The Adventures of Huckleberry Finn (1884) by Mark Twain. This was the book with which, Ernest Hemingway said, all American literature began. And if James is the novelist of modern fictional artistry, Twain was the novelist of the modern vernacular voice. Huck Finn, the poor boy from Hannibal, Mississippi, who sets out on a raft down a great river with his black friend, Nigger Jim, each of them looking for freedom, tells his own story, with childish truth, innocence, and clarity. Like the river, the book seemed to take charge of Twain as he wrote it, producing his most profound as well as vivid novel.

The Red Badge of Courage (1895) by Stephen Crane. This short novel about a young man, Henry Fleming, as he goes into battle during the American Civil War, was a *tour de force*. Crane was too young to have known the Civil War; he said he imagined it from the football field. What makes the book so remarkable is that it is a portrait of instantaneous consciousness. We are not concerned with why the war is fought, or how Henry got there, just with every moment of experience in the line or in flight from it. Henry wants to win his red badge of courage, and in the end he does so, in one of the great stories of initiation.

McTeague, A Story of San Francisco (1899) by Frank Norris. Later filmed as *Greed*, Norris's remarkable story of an untrained, brutish San Francisco dentist who lives for his beer and his concertina until he falls in love with Trina, the greedy Swiss girl whom he finally murders, is a classic work of naturalism and the *bête humaine*, the human animal. Norris brilliantly, and fatalistically, captures the urban atmosphere of San Francisco and its ordinary lives, and contrasts it with the life in nature and the desert beyond.

Sister Carrie (1900) by Theodore Dreiser. By the end of the 19th century, America was becoming an urban society, and the typical 'shock-city' was Chicago, which had turned from village to second city in 50 years, its skyscrapers, stockyards and department stores typifying modern America. Carrie Meeber, the poor girl who goes to Chicago and becomes rich by any means to hand, shocked the first readers, just as Dreiser's method – naturalism again – dismayed them by its apparent lack of morality. But Dreiser, a writer from German immigrant stock, brought raw new America to the page, and told its story unsparingly.

THE 20TH-CENTURY AMERICAN NOVEL
Malcolm Bradbury

At the start of the 20th century, American fiction was still thought of as a provincial relation of European, especially British fiction. By the 1930s the balance was changing, thanks to the emergence of novelists like Ernest Hemingway, Scott Fitzgerald, William Faulkner, and Sinclair Lewis. And by the 1950s it had become clear that the American writers of the next generation – Saul Bellow, Norman Mailer, John Updike, and many more – were among the leading novelists of the world. The change came from many things: the vast development of the nation, in its industrial capacity, economic strength, and influence; the powerful energies of modernity, which changed American lives and made them seem among the most advanced in the world; the American fascination with style and personal consciousness; and eventually the emergence of America, after World War II, as a global superpower, affecting the lives and shaping the cultural experience of people right across the world. But it also came from the cultural complexity of American experience. American writers came from many places – from recent European immigrant stock, and from the established American tradition; from great skyscraper cities and distant regions; from varied ethnic mixtures and origins. Jewish-American fiction, African- American fiction, Native American fiction, and feminist fiction all added to the cultural variety and the scale of the drama that unfolded in the American novel. With such riches, choice is almost impossible, and major omissions inevitable. But here are my ten favourite works of modern American fiction.

How does one in the novel (the novel which is a work of art and not a disguised piece of sociology) persuade the American reader to identify that which is basic in man beyond all differences of class, race, wealth, or formal education?

RALPH ELLISON

The Custom of the Country (1913) by Edith Wharton. Wharton was very much a social novelist, who lived much of her life in Paris. Her novels possess a vigorous irony about the collapse of social relations, and none is more ironic than this. The 'custom' in question is the American habit of social self-advancement through divorce. The book's heroine, Undine Spragg, is essentially an opportunist who uses sexuality for advantage, and both succeeds and morally fails in the end.

The Great Gatsby (1925) by F Scott Fitzgerald. Not all Fitzgerald's books are carefully written, but *The Great Gatsby* is the masterpiece, a classic modern American novel. Jay Gatz, the poor boy who becomes rich and is known as the 'great Gatsby', still retains an American innocence amid the glitter, corruption and waste of the 1920s. His love for Daisy Buchanan leads to disaster, but it remains a version of the American dream – carefully observed by the narrator Nick Carraway.

The Sound and the Fury (1929) by William Faulkner. Faulkner is the great novelist of the American South, and with this book he broke loose from the form of historical fiction to try a complex experiment with history, time, and language. The book contains four stories and several time-schemes; part of the story is indeed a tale of sound and fury, told by an 'idiot'. The book's theme is the stained, incestuous, corrupted world of the American South, and the agony of its modern survivors. Hard to read, it's worth it, as a work of cunning modernism.

A Farewell to Arms (1929) by Ernest Hemingway. Hemingway had been wounded on the Italian front in World War I, and this story of Lt Frederic Henry, who is similarly wounded while serving with the Italian forces, and falls in love with the English nurse, Catherine Barkley, who looks after him, has a strong autobiographical quality. But this is a classic tragedy of wartime experience. Henry leaves the war to make a 'separate peace', and tries to create a life of his own with Catherine. But she dies in childbirth, and the sense of a universal modern tragedy pervades the book, told in Hemingway's tight, tough, economical style.

Invisible Man (1952) by Ralph Ellison. One of the founding novels of African-American fiction, this work about a black man rendered invisible by his colour in the chaos and white exclusiveness of American life is a story of mental and then actual revolt. It's a serious exploration of the moral price that is paid when identity is revoked, and hence a work of great existential power.

Lolita (1955) by Vladimir Nabokov. Nabokov was an émigré for most of his life, displaced from Russia by the Bolshevik Revolution. This is his one true American novel, the story of another émigré, Humbert Humbert, whose sexual taste is for 'nymphets', young girls on the cusp of puberty. The erotic aspects of the book made it sensational at the time; but it is fundamentally a myth about the supposedly 'experienced' European observing the supposedly 'innocent' America, and finding the tables constantly turned: an ironic love affair with America and with the English language, which in Nabokov's hands turns into a formidable instrument.

Catch-22 (1961) by Joseph Heller. If *A Farewell to Arms* was the decisive war novel to emerge from World War I, *Catch-22* was the book that captured for its generation the ironic and bitter implications of World War II. Set among flyers on the Italian front, it's an epic of extreme absurdity. The military machine is a system of illogical orders; so is the disaster that is being created for humanity. A work of black humour, a great modern comic classic, the novel also evidently applied to Heller's contemporary America, as it developed ever more absurd systems of human management and new forms of Cold War fever.

V (1963) by Thomas Pynchon. Perhaps the ultimate work of what became known at the time as 'postmodern fiction' or 'metafiction', *V* is the wonderfully elaborate story of a quest into history conducted in a time of late modern chaos, where no order falls into place and information is in excess of human comprehension. Herbert Stencil is engaged in a quest for a mysterious figure, V, who seems to have some significant role in the making of modern history, though her story dissolves each time it's approached. Meantime a contemporary figure, Benny Profane, is seen attempting to surf the modern chaos. A work of dense historical research as well as technical cunning, it's no easy read, but is of undoubted importance.

Herzog (1964) by Saul Bellow. Bellow, a Jewish-American writer, has been the conscience and consciousness of much in American fiction after World War II, as was acknowledged when he won the Nobel prize in 1976. Moses Herzog, a 'suffering joker', is an intellectual who attempts to come to terms with the heritage of romantic expectation in modern life, addressing letters to the illustrious dead of modern thought; at the same time he has great trouble in living one. As in other Bellow novels, it's the mixture of high intellectual energy with superb social observation of life in modern Chicago and New York that makes this a work of formidable wit and power.

Beloved (1987) by Toni Morrison. By another Nobel prizewinner, the African-American author of *Song of Solomon* 1977 and *Tar Baby* 1981. *Beloved* is about an escaped former slave who has killed her baby girl in the age of slavery, to protect it from being returned to the plantation, and then is haunted by its ghost in the time of freedom after the Civil War. A powerful and poetic myth, written in a lyrical prose, it is a work both of haunting realism and strange fantasy, revealing the current strength of African-American fiction.

AMERICAN POETRY – *Oliver Harris*

All American poetry comes from one book by Walt Whitman called *Leaves of Grass* 1855. With this extraordinary, exuberant epic, America – the poem – found its first true poet; or rather, it was Whitman who answered the nation's call for an independent cultural voice. His work was made to match America in scale, energy, democracy, above all in its unlimited sense of possibility, both material and mystical, sensual and spiritual. His legacy has been twofold. On the one hand, national history betrayed his bright vision; from the Civil War onwards, the grand rhetoric of America and often the grim reality of it have moved ever further apart. On the other hand, rebuffed in his own day, considered too 'American' to be 'poetic', Whitman's time did eventually come, a century late: Richard Gray's *American Poetry of the Twentieth Century* (1990) has an entry three times longer for Whitman than for any other poet. Modernist American poetry, directed by the expatriates Ezra Pound and T S Eliot, and by the 'home-made' William Carlos Williams, did its 'carving' on, as well as with, language. Poetry demanded new, more active, more demanding, roles from its readers – and this tended to build on the experimentalism of Whitman, at the expense of his populism.

But is the revolutionary idea of America that has most inspired its poetry to inspire its people. When the 'Beat' poet Allen Ginsberg writes 'America, I'm putting my queer shoulder to the wheel', or the black feminist poet Nikki Giovanni writes 'i wish i knew how it would feel / to be free', you are listening to the poetic voice of America.

I make a pact with you, Walt Whitman – I have detested you long enough ... It was you that broke the new wood, Now is a time for carving.

EZRA POUND

Leaves of Grass (1855) by Walt Whitman. Includes his great *Song of Myself*, a unique work which shouts, whispers, sings, rants, and absolutely insists on being alive.

The Complete Poems (1955) by Emily Dickinson. All but unpublished in her own lifetime, her poetry is remarkable for its consistent brevity and density. Utterly idiosyncratic, darkly witty.

The Weary Blues (1926) by Langston Hughes. Best of the 1920s Harlem Renaissance poets, perhaps the first to make poetry sing with a black voice.

Collected Poems (1963) by T S Eliot. Brilliant, yet hard to enjoy, especially given the too great influence of his heavily allusive poetic style and his conservative criticism.

Collected Poems (1954) by Wallace Stevens. Lyrical, philosophical poetry, at times exquisitely simple, at others obscure, always wrestling with the imagination.

Howl and Other Poems (1960) by Allen Ginsberg. Very uneven as a poet (his credo the opposite of Eliot's craftsmanship), but always valuable for his provoking, radical energies.

AMERICAN PROSE (NONFICTION) – *Ian F A Bell*

While American poetry and prose have been acknowledged and celebrated as arguably the most innovative and experimental of all Western cultures (the modern novel begins with Henry James, while modern poetry derives its impetus from Ezra Pound), American nonfiction has tended to remain in the shadow of these more glamorous colleagues. To leave it thus is to lose out on a remarkable body of donatively energetic writing. Founded by a declaration of opposition to British colonial rule, the American nation has found in the voices of its essayists a persistent polemical strain which maintains the world as open to debate: founded on invention, the nation has held true to a discourse of change where constructivity and alterability are the key notes. Openness, a resistance to closure, a constant interrogation of the seeming given of things – these are the hallmarks of a tradition of writing from the 18th century onwards which refuses settlement and finish of all kinds and which testifies to existence itself, both national and personal, as a process of becoming, never merely the stasis of being.

Existing likes and powers are to be treated as possibilities, as starting-points, that are absolutely necessary for any healthy development. But development involves a point towards which as well as one from which; it involves constant movement in a given direction. Then when the point that is for the time being the goal and end is reached, it is in its turn but the starting-point for further reconstruction.

JOHN DEWEY

The Adams–Jefferson Letters (1959) edited by Lester J Cappon. A marvellously wide-ranging discussion of politics, culture, and science between two of the leading formers of the early republic. As Ezra Pound acknowledged in the 20th century, 'nothing surpasses the evidence that CIVILISATION WAS in America, than the series of letters exchanged between Thomas Jefferson and John Adams'.

Selected Writings of Emerson (1981) edited by Donald McQuade. Ralph Waldo Emerson was the major American thinker of the 19th century whose essays on just about everything not only had a profound influence upon contemporaries such as Henry David Thoreau and Walt Whitman, but also remained a vital imaginative resource for the cultural activities of the 20th century, ranging from the architect Frank Lloyd Wright to the poetry of the Beat Generation.

Abraham Lincoln, Speeches and Letters (1993) edited by Peter Parish. Unlike the prose of Jefferson or Adams, coloured and structured by great learning, that of Lincoln is relatively untutored and stands as a wonderful example of the kind of voice always applauded in America – straight, simple, uncluttered, and direct.

The Gentle Art of Making Enemies (1890) by James McNeill Whistler. Witty, iconoclastic, and abrasive, Whistler here inaugurates Modernism in painting and diagnoses the responsibilities and fate of art in a commercial and philistine age.

The Education of Henry Adams (1973) by Henry Adams. First published privately in 1906, and subtitled *A Study of Twentieth-Century Multiplicity*, this remarkable cojoining of genres (part history, part autobiography, and taking as its models the *Confessions* of St Augustine and Jean-Jacques Rousseau) attempts to work through the crisis of preparing for life in the new century.

The Theory of the Leisure Class (1970) by Thorstein Veblen. Written at the turn of the century, Veblen's brilliant analysis of America's new bourgeoisie presents an encyclopedia of the signs whereby status was to be measured, most notably through the tokens of what he called 'conspicuous consumption'.

Look at Me Now and Here I Am – Writings and Lectures 1911–45 (1967) by Gertrude Stein. 'Why don't you read the way I write?' was a question posed by this most radical of modern linguistic experimenters, and her efforts to teach new freshness and new ways of reading are more appropriately found in this diverse collection on diverse subjects than in the more familiar single-lensed projects such as *The Making of Americans* (1906–08) and *The Autobiography of Alice B Toklas* (1932).

Guide to Kulchur (1938) by Ezra Pound. Analogous to the project of his epic poem *The Cantos*, Pound's 'Guide' offers an inflammatory curriculum for civilization at midcentury: eccentric, wise, foolish, and eclectic, his Baedeker to cultural mores achieves the true pedagogical aim of annoyance into action.

Advertisements for Myself (1961) by Norman Mailer. How to be hip while not writing the Great American Novel.

The Electric Kool-Aid Acid Test (1968) by Tom Wolfe. How to be cool while attempting to go *further*.

THIRD WORLD LITERATURE

FICTION – *Kadiatu Kanneh*

The rubric 'Third World literature' immediately ushers in a range of difficulties. To designate the field already involves a range of political questions around the term 'Third World'. Other alternatives are 'postcolonial' or 'black'. To write an introduction to this vast field is necessarily limiting and will involve a biased and individual choice. I include here texts that allow for insights into major preoccupations of the 'field' (such as colonialism, nationalism, racial identities, feminist issues, and independence). The texts chosen have great literary and imaginative value, and can be seen as classics.

He had done nothing shameful, it was the way they had forced him to live, forced all of them to live, which was shameful. Their intrigues and hatreds and vengeful acquisitiveness had forced even simple virtues into tokens of exchange and barter.

ABDULRAZAK GURNAH

Things Fall Apart (1958) by Chinua Achebe. A classic of African literatures, depicting the advent of colonialism on a Nigerian Ibo community. Its analysis of the transforming and traumatizing effects of colonialism, as well as its moving portrayal of family relationships, honour, love, and death, make it an enduring and often witty novel.

Petals of Blood (1977) by Ngugi wa Thiong'o. A novel from independent Kenya, again depicting the transformation of a community. Its weaving together of lives, narratives, and histories into a geography of modern African sensibility make it an illuminating and unforgettable novel.

Our Sister Killjoy (1977) by Ama Ata Aidoo. A novel which beautifully satirizes Joseph Conrad's *Heart of Darkness*. Set in Ghana and Europe, the novel blends narrative with poetry, confronting the choices available to African women, and dealing with histories of racism and oppression.

Idu (1970) by Flora Nwapa. A novel set in Ghana and centred on the life of one woman. The narrative is about love, fertility, communal life, and joy.

A Bend in the River (1979) by V S Naipaul. This novel is set in postcolonial central Africa (Zaire), written by an Indo-Caribbean author, and narrated by an East Indian African. A fascinating evocation of Conrad's *Heart of Darkness*, revealing the complexities of racial and national identity, the constant insurgence of history, and the problems of cultural dialogue.

Love in the Time of Cholera (1985) by Gabriel Garcia Marquez. A novel set in Latin America using magic realist techniques. It engages with the powers of time, memory, love, and pain and uses language as a poetic tool. Translated from Spanish.

The Arrivants (1973) by Edward Kamau Brathwaite. Set in Africa, the Caribbean, Europe, and the USA, this trilogy of poetic volumes traces a modern understanding of black migrant identities. Written by a Barbadian poet, this collection of powerfully connected poems covers an imagining of black consciousness and histories to create a poem of the diaspora.

Song of Lawino (1966) and *Song of Ocol* (1967) by Okot p'Bitek. Written by a Ugandan poet, these two long poems represent a dialogue between a traditional African woman and a man with modern, western tastes. Brilliantly witty and metaphoric poetry, pitting the values of traditional and modern Africa against each other, with female anger winning the day.

Season of Migration to the North (1969) by Tayeb Salih. Translated from the Arabic, this novel, set in Sudan, Cairo, and England, presents a humorous, traumatic, and complex illustration of inter-racial sexual desire, exploring the psychopathology of colonialism and migration.

Nervous Conditions (1988) by Tsitsi Dangarembga. This novel, set in Zimbabwe, discusses the effects of language loss, exile, and cultural dislocation on the body and psyche of a young African woman.

BOOKS ON THIRD WORLD LITERATURE
Kadiatu Kanneh

This collection of texts problematizes and engages with the category of 'Third World' writing, allowing for an informed critical focus. The texts vary from a direct analysis of a range of Third World literatures to a more theoretical or political discussion of prevalent themes, issues, histories. The texts examine debates around language, history, gender, often exploring how issues of self-determination and independence affect the analyses of literary criticism.

Night after night my mother would talk-story until we fell asleep. I couldn't tell where the stories left off and the dreams began, her voice the voice of the heroines in my sleep.

MAXINE HONG KINGSTON

Myth, Literature and the African World (1976) by Wole Soyinka. This text interrogates the definition, both of African literature and of Africa, engaging directly with a range of literary texts from Africa and contextualizing their meanings and aesthetic value within a conception of Africa as a distinct mythic and philosophical whole.

Decolonising the Mind (1986) by Ngugi wa Thiong'o. This text presents a polemic against colonial domination and the prevalence of colonial languages in African literatures. A major touchstone for political readings of African literatures.

The Empire Writes Back (1989) by Ashcroft, Griffiths, and Tiffin. This text defines the field of 'Third World literature' as 'postcolonial', and presents a survey of the major issues and complexities which currently dominate literary critical analysis in this area.

The Wretched of the Earth (1961; translated 1963) by Frantz Fanon. This French text is rightly called an enduring classic. Dealing with the effects of colonialism on the identity and economics of the Third World, Fanon's argument insists on the relevance of political resistance to literature and its criticism.

African Literature and African Critics (1988) by Rand Bishop. This text discusses a history of African literary criticism, dealing with contested issues of cultural appropriation, linguistic determination, and literary value.

Chinua Achebe (1990) by C L Innes. This careful analysis of Achebe's novels and their significance usefully contextualizes his work and provides thorough readings of the narratives.

Reading the African Novel (1987) by Simon Gikandi. A very useful reading of African literatures, both anglophone and francophone, with close analysis, comparative work, and insightful argument.

Manichean Aesthetics (1983) by Abdul R Janmohamed. A well-argued and interesting polemic on the theory and analysis of African literatures, examining a range of African literatures and literatures about Africa.

Motherlands (1991) edited by Nasta Susheila. A collection of essays on women's writing from the Caribbean, Africa, and S Asia.

Colonial Discourse and Post-Colonial Theory (1993) edited by Patrick Williams and Laura Chrismas. This collection of critical essays designates the field as 'postcolonial'. The introduction addresses the politics of this designation, and the text provides a very useful collection of major essays.

Resistance and Caribbean Literature (1980) by Selwyn R Cudjoe. A critical survey of Caribbean novels, drawing from the English-, French-, and Spanish-speaking traditions in the Caribbean.

GENRE FICTION

SCIENCE FICTION - *Brian Aldiss*

Since the days of Jules Verne and H G Wells, whose books have been translated into most of the languages on Earth, science fiction has been perennially popular. Its zenith of popularity may have been reached in the 1960s and early 1970s, when investigation of alternative lifestyles was at its height. As the blithe 19th-century belief in Progress with a capital P has dwindled, so sections of science fiction have appeared to merge at least temporarily with fantasy, essentially a more conservative mode of fiction. This shift can be seen in movies, computer games, and similar, as well as in the written word. An invaluable reference work to the entire field is *The Encyclopedia of Science Fiction* (1979, revised 1993) edited by John Clute and Peter Nicholls.

Almost any novel set in the future is classifiable as science fiction. Tomorrow is the plimsoll line between science fiction and the ordinary novel.

MARTIN SEYMOUR-SMITH

The Foundation Trilogy (1951–53) by Isaac Asimov. Despite wafer-thin characterization, this trilogy remains the most enduring of the popular SF works. Its theory of 'psychohistory', worked out against a panorama of a long galactic future, remains compelling. Later 'Foundation' novels have less to recommend them.

The Drowned World (1962) by J G Ballard. This was the first of Ballard's apocalyptic novels, depicting London under flood, and a hero who finds disaster not unwelcome, in an elegant holistic prose. Published in the early 1960s, when London was under the flood of New Wave SF, *The Drowned World* established Ballard as a major stylist, and contained many themes to which he was later to revert.

Blood Music (1985) by Greg Bear. A startling example of hard SF by a writer who rose to eminence in the mid-1980s. His central character creates microchip computers from biological material and, in smuggling them from the laboratory in his body, creates conditions in which the new intelligences overwhelm the world. A strongly poetic legend.

Mission of Gravity (1954) by Hal Clement. This wonderful story, dating from the 1950s, is archetypal SF, set on a radically strange world. Human explorers, landing on the planet Mesklin, must cooperate with the local centipede-like inhabitants to effect a rescue. Mesklin is a heavy-gravity world with a rapid rotation. Physical details well worked out, characters engaging, scenery compulsive.

Martian Time-Slip (1964) by Philip K Dick. Dick is a kind of model Californian SF writer, into the 1960s drug culture, mentally strange, dying fairly young. *Martian Time-Slip*, set on a desolate world occupied by the United Nations, contains anguishing flaws of consciousness involving several characters, including an autistic boy. As in many of Dick's excellently eccentric novels, the real and unreal are confused.

Neuromancer (1984) by William Gibson. When this book appeared Gibson was hailed as the apostle of cyberpunk. Fast action accounts in part for its wide popularity, and for the young computer generation it was irresistible; all longed to negotiate Gibson's grey, nonphysical cyberspace, despite its perils. Grim but amusing.

Mythago Wood (1981) by Robert Holdstock. This remarkable novel, together with its sequel, *Lavondyss*, forms a unique saga of great beauty and darkness, poised between fantasy and SF. A rich prose style informs a tale of an ancient English wood wherein archetypes or 'mythagoes' exist, acting out primordial roles upon those who venture into their thickets. That rare thing: new subject matter, highly metaphorical and – as the well-wrought prose reveals – deeply felt.

Frankenstein, or The Modern Prometheus (1818) by Mary Shelley. This profound novel has been badly treated as mere horror by the movie industry. It is a penetrating study of pained human relationships, transfused by wonder and melancholy. Written by a young woman still in her teens, it is the first novel to employ the theme of man usurping nature by scientific means, and thus may be regarded as the first – and in many ways most famous – SF novel.

Star Maker (1937) by Olaf Stapledon. Of all SF novels, this is the grandest and most austere. A human soul ventures out into the galaxy and eventually meets the Supreme Being, conjuror of universes. Philosophical in intent – Stapledon was a philosopher – *Star Maker* is full of poetry and wonder. Its sheer scale outclasses even Stapledon's earlier and better known *Last and First Men*

The Time Machine (1895) by H G Wells. 'The Great General of Dreamland', as Wells styled himself, wrote many famous scientific romances, but none more grand and enduring than this, his first. The time traveller ventures into a near future, the world of Eloi and Morlocks, and then into the distant future, where the Sun has cooled and Earth is empty of all life. Evolutionary; and astronomical theories fuel a mood which is mainly of tender regret.

HORROR – *Roz Kaveney*

The great precursors of the modern horror genre are mythopoeic novels of the 19th century, whose principal direct influence on culture was to be through

Hollywood. There is a sense in which Boris Karloff's Monster or Bela Lugosi's Dracula are far more the thing conceived than any passage in Mary Shelley's *Frankenstein* or Bram Stoker's *Dracula* ever manages quite to be. The genre horror fiction that came to fruition in the last two decades deals in the first place with sheer sensation and surprise; the best horror also deals, usually, in human emotion, not least, but not only, because we have been made to care who gets eaten. Horror fiction speaks to our condition, which is a worrying statement about the state we are in; there has been a tendency to underrate good writing in the genre as a way of avoiding noticing that that writing tells us some uncomfortable truths about ourselves.

Every body is a book of blood. Wherever you open us, we're red.

CLIVE BARKER

The Collected Ghost Stories of M R James (1931) by Montague Rhodes James. *A Warning to the Curious*, the title of one of the earlier collections of these tales, might serve as a useful summary for all of them; James specialized in the antiquarian back story that lends authority to his horrors. Later genre horror learned from him the art of explanation, which is not the same thing as explaining away.

The Outsiders and Others (1939) by H P Lovecraft. Lovecraft is a special case, a recluse obsessed with maggoty theories of racial degeneration and class hatred, who created, most unseriously, an elaborate mythos of sinister gods and other beings to whom humanity were no more than prey. The intermittent awfulness of his overwriting should not blind us to the sheer passion of his best work and its sense of the abysses of deep time that surround our fragile lives; Jorge Luis Borges admired him.

The Shining (1977) by Stephen King. King's sense of the small-town life and perpetual empathy with children are the light side of what has made him the richest horror writer in history; his empathy with men on the brink of madness, led by their own faults and a little supernatural prompting, into acts unforgivable even by themselves is what makes him, at his best, remarkable. *The Shining* has perhaps the best of these damned-viewpoint characters and, in the Overlook Hotel, one of the most concretely imagined Bad Places in fiction.

The Land of Laughs (1980) by Jonathan Carroll. Carroll's gloomy tales of prayers answered in ways not dreamed of find their most typical example in his first ingenious book. What could be more innocent than the desire to write a biography of one's favourite children's author? The odd metamorphosis of the dead writer's fellow townspeople into the phantasmagoric creatures he based on them is surely just an illusion, not a cause for concern? And so it goes, on to hell through good intentions, to perhaps the best last-line logical plot twist in modern fiction.

The Arabian Nightmare (1983) by Robert Irwin. There are few good, and many bad, books about dreams and dreamers, and Irwin's endless chamber of mirrored horrors is one of the very best. An expert on *The Thousand and One Nights* and author of the best study of it in English, he takes medieval Cairo and turns it into a hell of repetition from which his protagonist is trying to awake; he also, in passing, makes some elegant comments on the myth of Orientalism and the bad faith in which the West has dreamed it.

The Books of Blood (1984–85) by Clive Barker. These six slim volumes of short stories kick started a whole approach to the job of terror and disgust; they finished for ever the convention that you don't show the monster or the blood, but rely on delicate suggestions. Barker's strong visual sense dictated that fiction was a stepping stone from his paintings to his films and his novels have been disappointing; the imagery of the body and its vulnerability to distortion and destruction which pervades these books haunts the mind like a stain.

Hawksmoor (1985) by Peter Ackroyd. Biographer and novelist Ackroyd wrote by far his best novel under the joint influence of James and Lovecraft, as well as of the poems of Ian Sinclair and various strange theories about the occult geography of London. An architect and occultist of the early 18th century creates towers and crypts which write the script for murders in the late 20th century; the investigating detective comes to feel merely a puppet. This is one of the most atmospheric of books about London's near East End, a gloomily splendid recreation of a real place as a malign geography.

Koko (1988) by Peter Straub. A cultural obsession with serial killers and child abuse and Vietnam found one of its headier results in this dreamlike thriller from Straub, author of several of the most poetic of horror and ghost novels, but here perhaps at his best. The horror here is partly the horror of atrocity, but partly too an almost Calvinist sense of consequences – those to whom evil is done, do things in return that it is almost impossible to imagine.

The Stress of Her Regard (1989) by Tim Powers. Powers is obsessed with fantasies of history, with explanations; here we learn why the Romantic poets were obsessed with mountains and vampires and why Keats and Shelley died young. His doctor hero, on the run after his wife dies horribly on their wedding night, finds out more than he wishes to know and suffers for his knowledge; his sister-in-law nemesis is dragged into madness and self mutilation and out the other side. This is an inventive book full of the shabbiness in which the horrid manifests itself.

Use of Weapons (1990) by Ian M Banks. Banks, in his pseudonymous space-operatic mode, managed to combine a technical *tour de force* of narrative structure, a galaxy-spanning tale of intrigue and mayhem, and perhaps one of the grimmest studies of brutality and guilt in recent fiction. Some books are genre horror by endless playing with its tropes; this belongs to a list because it works so insidiously to the awful revelation at the heart of darkness.

Lost Souls (1992) by Poppy Z Brite. The absence of women from this list partly reflects the boys in the dark obsessions of the genre, partly the extent to which women writers tended to be off at a tangent to genre horror, writing Gothic romances in which vampires were the ultimately good, or the ultimately dangerous, version of male sexuality. For Brite, whose interest in male subjects is so all con-suming as to leave women out of her books almost altogether, vampires are cool and hip and deadly, and a threat to her nice young male lovers in peril; this is tosh, in a sense, but tosh with a generational sensibility that makes it a key text of 1990s subcultures.

FANTASY – *Roz Kaveney*

Strictly speaking, of course, fantasy is a term that includes both horror and science fiction in that both are ultimately non-realistic genres whose refusal of more than surface mimesis is a conscious choice. There is a large body of work, most of it overtly generic, which falls into neither category; much of it is set in a medieval-cum-archaic-cum-Oriental Fantasyland with diction to match; some of it is set in our own time and place into which incursions are made from Outside. Some of it deals with cures for the world's pain, or the reconciliation of the mundane and faerie, or with ultimate apocalypses of good versus evil – but some of it is just about people making their way in trying circumstances. As with other genre literature, any list has to include forgotten works from the mainstream that only the genre has kept alive and works which only devotees have read, to the loss of the average reader.

Fairy stories may invent monsters that fly the air or dwell in the deep, but at least they do not try to escape from heaven or the sea.

J R R TOLKIEN

Jurgen (1919) by James Branch Cabell. This almost forgotten satire on human aspiration was, in its time, both frighteningly hip and the subject of a major obscenity trial. Its mild bawdy has not dated well, but its sense of the absurd and its touches of the wildly romantic have lasted better. Jurgen, poet turns pawnbroker, searches for his lost youth, and the women of his ideals and finds neither Elysium, Hell, nor the Heaven of his grandmother remotely to his satisfaction.

Lud-in-the-Mist (1926) by Hope Mirrlees. A small bourgeois town which has sat comprehensively on its dark history of mad dukes and wild rebellion find that what goes out one door will come in at another; the world of faerie finds that intervention in human affairs has its consequences in the bringing of human law. This neglected, warm, humane book is perhaps still the best fantasy of finding balance.

The Lord of the Rings (1954–55) by J R R Tolkien. The one genre fantasy that most people have actually read, this created most of the preconceptions that dominate readers and writers of fantasy. To read it again, forget all that has followed on from it, and think of it as a book about Tolkien's experiences in World War I or about the needs for limits as a creator of ethical context; it is a book of real invention, high romance, grimness, wit, and charm, and what more needs be said for anything?

The Swords of Lankhmar (1968) by Fritz Leiber. There was always a pulp genre of capers and mayhem in Fantasyland, much of which can be forgotten. Leiber's template series about the sensitive barbarian hunk Fafhrd and the streetwise vain urchin Gray Mouser ran for decades, and brought wit and sophistication and irony to the whole enterprise. One of its culminations was this novel of conspiracy, urban depravity, and sword-wielding rats, which demonstrated that Leiber could not only write action adventure, he could also write sexually charged farce.

A Wizard of Earthsea (1968) by Ursula K LeGuin. This first of the trilogy, later expanded into a quartet, which made LeGuin a children's cult as well as the writer of SF and fantasy for people who don't usually like that sort of thing, is still one of the most intellectually satisfying of explorations of magic. Ged, apprenticed as a wizard, tests limits and nearly destroys himself and those around him; this is a book about the getting of wisdom, and, appropriately, is itself wise.

Peace (1975) by Gene Wolfe. An early novel by the trickster writer of *The Book of the New Sun*, this is complicatedly not what it seems. An old man muses on mortality and his family history and on stories, none of which ever quite manages to reach completion ... This is a novel, but it is also a riddle to which there are no wholly satisfactory answers; it is a book which stretches form and comprehension to breaking point without ever raising its voice or doing anything radical with prose.

Little, Big (1981) by John Crowley. This and two other novels by Crowley are the only genre fantasies to make it into Harold Bloom's Canon. *Little, Big*, a novel where even the comma in the title is important, takes the sleeper under the hill, the conditions imposed on a lover, the animal adviser, the quest for a lost love, and the place that is bigger than it seems, and mixes them into a story of change and transfiguration, where what seemed twee becomes almost unbearably moving with a change of perspective.

The Anubis Gates (1983) by Tim Powers .Brendan Doyle, a widower and Coleridge expert, thinks he knows about the Regency London in which he is marooned. He knows only rumours, though, about the body- jumping werewolf, the Egyptian magicians, and the malignant clown, and vivisectionist Horrabin ... Powers is remorselessly inventive here, but Doyle's predicament, and those of the lives he touches, is emotionally real even when the events surrounding it are at their most bizarre.

Rats and Gargoyles (1990) by Mary Gentle. A city where anything is possible, particularly the nastier things; a city sustained by the imagination of its gods, yet constantly undermined by memories of its past incarnations – Mary Gentle took ideas from Gnosticism and elsewhere in the mystical tradition and made of them an adventure playground. Swashbuckling and metaphysics go oddly well together here – and a problem is solved according to the rules in whose language it has been set.

Waking the Moon (1994) by Elizabeth Hand. We almost think we know where we are here, as crabbed old patriarchal conspirators use magic to blast out of life a feminist archaeologist and a young disciple takes up her work ... Restoring the rule of the Goddess is not a task without its own moral implications, though, and this vividly peopled book turns a lot of clichés on their head as its central characters find themselves rejecting the human consequences of things to which in abstract they might assent. Fantasy is never allegory, at its best, but it is often a device for representing, in heightened phantasmagorical form, genuine moral choices.

ROMANTIC FICTION – *Marina Oliver*

Almost any novel that contains a strong love story and has a happy or optimistic ending can be described as a romantic novel. That encompasses a lot, from Jane Austen to the Brontës, the present-day short genre romance, through historical settings including fictionalized biographies and rip-roaring adventure, the popular family sagas, Aga sagas, glitz, modern problem novels, and literary prizewinners. Serious critical analysis is meagre, and what there is tends to be American. The *Twentieth Century Romance and Historical Writers* (third edition 1994) is the most comprehensive reference book for details of writers, lists of their books, and a critical view of each author's work.

As the world becomes increasingly ugly, callous and materialistic, it needs to be reminded that the old fairy stories are rooted in truth, that imagination is of value, that happy endings do, in fact, occur, and that the blue spring mist that can make an ugly street look beautiful is just as real a thing as the street itself.

ELIZABETH GOUDGE

Advances (1992) by Anita Burgh. This is a wickedly funny look at the world of publishing, by a writer with the ability to carry along her readers by the sheer power of her storytelling, whether set in the present day or past times.

The Lymond Series (1961–75) by Dorothy Dunnett. Six huge books with an attractive hero and an unlikely heroine, set against a masterly, vast panorama of 16th-century Europe. These books are full of detailed knowledge, totally absorbing, intense, and brilliant.

The Unknown Ajax (1959) by Georgette Heyer. The Regency novel was 'invented' by Georgette Heyer, and the deliciously frothy, eminently easy-to-read style conceals formidable research and superb technical skill. This title has a serious theme of smuggling, combined with wit, humour, and deep emotion.

A Better World than This (1986) by Marie Joseph. The heroine is searching for a dream, away from the tedium of a Lancashire mill town. This heartwarming novel won the Major Award of the Romantic Novelists' Association in 1987.

The Suffolk Trilogy (1959–62) by Norah Lofts. Set, like many of her novels, in East Anglia, these books feature one house through several centuries. She can convey time and place impeccably, and her characters are intensely real.

The Chatelaine (1981) by Claire Lorrimer. A family novel, set in the 1900s, it is a powerful story of a girl's early love, disillusionment, and final triumph over adversity. It is superbly plotted and compelling.

Mango Walk (1981) by Rhona Martin. She won the first Georgette Heyer Prize with *Gallows Wedding*, a historical novel, but this is set in the 20th century, equally uncompromising and powerful, the story of an unlikely love that endures despite almost unbearable pressures.

Csardas (1975) by Diane Pearson. Both editor and author, Pearson is president of the Romantic Novelists' Association. She achieved immense acclaim with this epic story of Hungary during half a century of travail.

Nine Coaches Waiting (1958) by Mary Stewart. This book can be called a Gothic novel or a suspense novel, but is above all a compelling story involving hard decisions and firm values.

The Native Air (1990) by Sarah Woodhouse. The author can take unlikely characters and charm her readers into utter fascination. This is the last in a trilogy set around 1800, where love eventually triumphs. The writing is delightful, almost fey, but conveys with a sure touch the sometimes bleak realities of Norfolk life.

CRIME FICTION – *Colin Dexter*

More people read crime and detection novels than any other form of fiction. It cuts across differences of age, culture, gender, and class, combining the fascination of crime with the reassurance of order restored, a mystery solved. It began in the 19th century with the works of Wilkie Collins and Edgar Allan Poe, and soon became a genre with many (very different) forms – such as the very English 'murder in the vicarage' of Agatha Christie, the hardboiled American writing of Hammett and Chandler, the psychological analysis of Patricia Highsmith. It can be pulp fiction, sophisticated entertainment, and (in the hands of writers such as Jorge Luis Borges and Umberto Eco) philosophical speculation. One of the best introductions to crime and detection fiction is Julian Symons's *Bloody Murder* (1972), a history of the genre. The following list includes representative works from each of the main genres ('whodunnit', 'whydunnit', 'howdunnit', 'thriller', 'spy story', 'historical reconstruction').

*Tremendous enjoyment underlies the superficially tragic
subject-matter of most crime fiction.*

DIOGENES SMALL

The Murder of Roger Ackroyd (1926) by Agatha Christie. The most brilliant thing she ever wrote. A hugely imaginative woman, today sometimes sadly underrated.

The Hollow Man (1935) by John Dickson Carr. Most implausible plot ever but the most staggeringly ingenious of all his books. Excellent.

The Glass Key (1931) by Dashiell Hammett. Probably one of the best detective novels ever written. Balance between plot, characterization, and tension is superb.

Farewell, My Lovely (1940) by Raymond Chandler. Almost everyone would have him on their list. Any book would do. This is Chandler at his very best.

The Spy Who Came in from the Cold (1963) by John Le Carré. Perhaps the finest and most poignant of all spy stories. Haunting atmosphere, superb plot.

Malice Aforethought (1931) by Frances Iles. One of the most important crime books ever written. Frances Iles is a pseudonym of Anthony Berkeley.

The Daughter of Time (1951) by Josephine Tey. Historical crime fiction – was Richard III a murderer? Not an easy read, but wonderfully worth it.

A Fatal Inversion (1987) by Barbara Vine. Barbara Vine is a pseudonym of Ruth Rendell. This superb psychological thriller displays her incredible talents to the full.

The Day of the Jackal (1971) by Frederick Forsyth. Probably the best thriller written since World War II. Everyone knows there will be no assassination, but the ingenuity is breathtaking, and the pace splendidly maintained.

The False Inspector Dew (1982) by Peter Lovesy. Extremely clever, interesting, and so easy to read. Based on the transatlantic liner route and the Crippen murder story. A very fine present-day writer.

CHILDREN'S LITERATURE

Alison Lurie

Until about 20 years ago children's literature was the Cinderella of literary studies. Everyone read fairy tales and books like *Tom Sawyer*, *The Wizard of Oz*, and *Winnie-the-Pooh* when they were young, but almost no one thought about them seriously later. This meant that some of the most original and influential works of all time were overlooked by critics and scholars. Today the situation is much improved. Many universities in America now offer courses in children's literature, and there are several first-rate periodicals in the field, including *Children's Literature*, *Children's Literature Quarterly*, and *The Lion and the Unicorn*. And good books about the subject, including those listed below, continue to appear.

*Nothing you do for children is ever wasted. They seem
not to notice us, hovering, averting our eyes, and they seldom
offer thanks, but what we do for them is never wasted.*

GARRISON KEILLOR

*Childhood's Pattern: A Study of the Heroes and Heroines of Children's Fiction
1770–1950* (1975) by Gillian Avery. A very well-informed, interesting, and thoughtful
study by a recognized British authority, who is also the author of many much- admired
historical novels for children. It is especially good on England and on the 18th and early
19th centuries.

The Seed and the Vision: On the Writing and Appreciation of Children's Books
(1993) by Eleanor Cameron. A collection of sensitive and wide-ranging essays by the
American critic, author of many popular children's books, and winner of the
Commonwealth Award. The focus is meditative and personal rather than analytic.

Secret Gardens: A Study of the Golden Age of Children's Literature (1985) by
Humphrey Carpenter. Brilliant, original, and knowledgeable discussion of the most
famous writers for children by a well-known British biographer who is also the
coeditor of the *Oxford Companion to Children's Literature*.

Audacious Kids: Coming of Age in America's Classic Children's Books (1992)
by Jerry Griswold. This is a lively, intelligent, and much needed study of American fiction for children from a cultural-history point of view. It includes and analyses some
immensely popular books like *Toby Tyler* and *Pollyanna*, which have often been overlooked by other writers.

Fairy Tales and After: From Snow White to E B White (1978) by Roger Sale. An
unusual and well-written collection of essays on works of children's literature and folklore, and what they have meant to the author, addressed to the general reader as well as
the expert. Professor Sale's earlier book, *Man Reading and Child Reading: Oz, Babar, and
Pooh* is also interesting.

Breaking the Magic Spell: Radical Theories of Folk and Fairy Tales (1979) by
Jack Zipes. Professor Zipes, a world-class expert on the folk tale, is also one of the most
interesting and original writers on modern fairy tales. As the title suggests, his approach
is radical, with an emphasis on social and political history. His recent *Don't Bet on the
Prince: Contemporary Feminist Fairy Tales in North America and England* (1986) combines
the best examples of the genre with a first-rate analysis.

WOMEN AND LITERATURE

Kadiatu Kanneh

Women's literature has become a wide and varied field, with the range of texts,
collections of essays, and criticism about women's literature reflecting this. The
following, necessarily truncated list provides an introduction to the range of writing
that women's literature represents, writing from a variety of cultures, countries,

historical periods. The following provide an overview of different feminist perspectives on the literature, different contextualizing strategies, and often conflicting arguments.

To be a woman and a writer is / double mischief, for / the world will slight her who slights 'the servile house,' and who would rather / make odes than beds.

DILYS LAING

Political Gender (1994) edited by Sally Ledger et al. This collection of essays by a range of academics with different critical viewpoints approaches the issue of gender and its significance in literature. The essays discuss both historical and more contemporary literatures.

New Feminist Discourses (1992) edited by Isobel Armstrong. A collection of essays that provides contemporary critical analyses of women's texts from various feminist viewpoints.

Black Women Writers (1985) edited by Mari Evans. This text brings together a range of interviews with African-American women writers, including excerpts from their poetry and prose.

Home Girls: A Black Feminist Anthology (1983) edited by Barbara Smith. This is a collection of critical and creative writing by contemporary African-American women writers, allowing theory, politics, and analysis to be read together.

Black Women Novelists and the Nationalist Aesthetic (1994) by Madhu Dubey. Using black feminist theory, this text reads writing by authors such as Toni Morrison and Alice Walker to challenge traditional notions of black female identity.

Contemporary African Literature and the Politics of Gender (1994) by Florence Stratton. Studies the influence of colonialism and race on African literatures, especially those by women.

Francophone African Women Writers (1994) by Irene Assiba D'Almeida. A survey of writing by French-speaking African women that discusses the issue of silence in women's texts.

Sexual/Textual Politics (1985) by Toril Moi. Ground-breaking critical analysis of women's writing and its relation to sexual politics.

A Literature of Their Own (1977) by Elaine Showalter. More traditional feminist analyses from a less theoretical perspective. Lacks the range of attention to differences between women, but remains useful as an introduction to the field.

THE ARTS

PAINTING AND SCULPTURE

CLASSICAL ART – *Graham Ley*

It is inevitable that the lavishly illustrated coffee-table book will attract most attention in this as in other artistic subjects, and most libraries have a good stock of volumes of this sort. But in this extremely short reading list I have also included more modest books which provide a clear discussion of the artefacts, and offer helpful critical guidelines on an introductory level. So readers are advised to 'move about' between the different books for illustrations and commentary, and to be aware that each particular selection of objects or pictures is always (and inevitably) going to give a rather limited impression of what is available. The more recent books can take advantage of any discoveries that have been made, and most contain suggestions for further reading.

Yet Greek art is not only the first entirely self-conscious art that we know of; it stands apart from all other traditions in its almost exclusive search for beauty, and in particular the beauty of the human form ...

ROGER FRY

Oxford History of Classical Art (1993) edited by John Boardman. An excellent, new survey of both Greek and Roman art in a relatively large format, with good illustrations and up-to-date suggestions for reading in specialist areas.

Minoan and Mycenean Art (1981) by R Higgins. The art of the societies of Bronze Age Crete (Minoan) and mainland Greece (Mycenaean) presented in the second edition of a popular introduction.

Greek Art (1985) by John Boardman. The most comprehensive, and consequently also the most concise, of a series of illustrated handbooks by a distinguished commentator.

Art and Experience in Classical Greece (1972), ***Art in the Hellenistic Age*** (1986) by Jerry Pollitt. These two books offer stimulating interpretations of Greek art in major periods. The latter considers Greek art from the time of Alexander the Great until the domination of Rome.

Archaic Greek Art (1971) ***Classical Greek Art*** (1973) ***Hellenistic Art*** (1973) by J Charbonneaux and others. These three volumes provide superb illustrations.

Art of the Etruscans (1970) by M Moretti and G Maetzke. An illustrated guide to the art of the culture dominant in central Italy before the Romans.

Roman Art (1991) by Susan Walker. A short, well-illustrated introduction to the subject, which draws on the artefacts in the British Museum in London.

Roman Art (1976) by Donald Strong. One of the best and most reliable introductions.

Handbook of Roman Art (1983) edited by Martin Henig. A careful, collective survey of major aspects, which also includes a helpful chapter on 'Late Antiquity'.

Roman Painting (1953) by A Maiuri. Extremely valuable for its excellent illustrations of the remarkable survivals.

MEDIEVAL ART – *Chris Murray*

A very elastic term, 'medieval' changes its scope according to context. Here it is being used in its widest sense: the period from the end of the Roman Empire (4th century AD) to the beginning of the Renaissance (15th century). This vast stretch of time, far from being an artistic Dark Age – first barbaric and then dominated by monkish virtues, stern and life-denying – was a period of extraordinary variety and richness. In varying degrees, the styles of the collapsed Roman civilization blended with those of such 'barbaric' peoples as the Celts and the Anglo-Saxons to produce styles expressing the complex and dynamic character of a new civilization – Christendom. In Byzantium in particular, where the Roman legacy was strongest, the need to express a spiritual sense of the world produced a style of great grandeur and power. The masterpieces of medieval art include stained glass, metalwork, manuscript illumination, sculpture (in stone, metal, wood, and ivory), frescoes, and panel paintings. The main artistic divisions are: early Christian, Byzantine, Romanesque, and Gothic.

The contrast between suffering and joy, between adversity and happiness, appeared more striking. All experience had yet to the minds of men the directness and absoluteness of the pleasure and pain of child-life. Every event, every action, was still embodied in expressive and solemn forms, which raised them to the dignity of a ritual.

JOHAN HUIZINGA

Early Christian and Byzantine Art (1970) by John Beckwith. A scholarly yet quite accessible account. This covers the very earliest part of the Middle Ages. Most of the book looks at Byzantine art, but the section on early Christian art, tracing how Roman styles were gradually transformed by the need to find a Christian form of expression, is welcome as this is a much neglected period.

A Concise History of Painting from Prehistory to the 13th Century (1967) by David Talbot Rice. The title is somewhat misleading, for art until the Christian era is covered in 60 pages, the rest of the book (another 200 pages) being devoted to medieval art. Brief text (many illustrations) by one of the leading scholars of early art.

Medieval Art (1989) by James Snyder. A clear, perceptive, and enthusiastic account of the period from the 4th century to the 14th, covering all the arts. Nearly 700 beautiful illustrations, giving a strong impression of the range and vitality of the medieval arts.

Byzantine Style and Civilization (1975) by Steven Runciman. A short, classic study, beautifully illustrated. Byzantine art, which has a history of over 900 years, forms the richest and stylistically most consistent expression of medieval art.

Early Medieval Art (1969) by John Beckwith. A standard work that looks at the period from the coronation of Charlemagne (800 AD) to the 12th century – that is, the styles known as Carolingian, Ottonian, and Romanesque. A European art is forming out of the many tribal divisions of Europe.

Gothic Art (1967) by Andrew Martindale. This can be seen as a companion to Beckwith (published in the same series). It covers the period from the 12th century to the 14th. For many, Gothic art is the quintessential art of the Middle Ages.

Cambridge Introductions to the History of Art: The Middle Ages (1982) by Anne Shaver-Crandell. Although this looks mostly at architecture, it is the best short introduction. The author covers the period from the 11th century to the 14th.

Gothic (1967) by George Henderson. A stimulating complement to Martindale, this examines Gothic art in terms of the ideas, and the political and social order, of the late Middle Ages.

The Rise of the Artist (1972) by Andrew Martindale. A short but fascinating account of the changing role of the artist (and therefore art and society) in the late Middle Ages, when courts were becoming increasingly important sources of patronage.

RENAISSANCE AND BAROQUE
Francesca M Speight

The Renaissance (French for 'rebirth') was a relatively brief but vital period in the history of Western European culture in which inspiration came from the antique remains of ancient Greece and Rome. It reflects both the continuation of the Christian beliefs found in the preceding Middle Ages and the revival of humanist thought, resulting in an increasing emphasis on the individual and on secular concerns. The Renaissance, which is usually seen as extending approximately from 1400 to 1600, includes the approach known as Mannerist, which was subsequently viewed as a falling-away of the achievements of the High Renaissance period, but is now recognized as a valid and important style in its own right.

With the commencement of the 17th century, the dominant style was that of Baroque, which echoed a time of renewed Catholic fervour and confidence in the church, and this is clearly seen in the dramatic and turbulent approach which incorporates illusionism on a grand scale combined with sumptuous decoration and the merging of all three art forms – painting, sculpture, and architecture. Interiors were especially lavishly conceived, with decorated ceilings particularly revered at this time. The Baroque in Germany and eastern Europe became even more lavish and exuberant; in France and England, on the other hand, it was tempered by a preference for Classical restraint.

The deity which invests the science of the painter functions in such a way that the mind of the painter is transformed into a copy of the divine mind, since it operates freely in creating many kinds of animals, plants, fruits, landscapes, countrysides, ruins, and awe-inspiring places.

LEONARDO DA VINCI

History of Italian Renaissance Art (1970) by Frederick Hartt. Considered for over 20 years to be the best book written on this period, it is packed with information on individual painters, sculptors, and architects, all placed within a historical context.

The Art of the Renaissance (1963) by Peter and Linda Murray. Covers the early Renaissance, commencing with Giotto and culminating in the High Renaissance giants of painting and sculpture – Leonardo, Michelangelo, and Raphael.

The Late Renaissance and Mannerism (1967) by Linda Murray. A companion to *The Art of the Renaissance*, this begins with the late works of the major High Renaissance artists and continues to the close of the 16th century and Mannerism, ending with an appraisal of the art of El Greco.

Baroque and Rococo (1964) by Germain Bazin. Bazin explores the richness and complexity of the Baroque and Rococo, taking into account the persistence of earlier styles, and studies in depth the 'Baroque' and 'Realist' approaches to art, both of these considered to be the two 'new styles' of this period. The 'Romanticism' of Rococo is also analysed.

Painting and Experience in 15th Century Italy (1972) by Michael Baxandall. This book serves as an introduction to painting in Italy during the early Renaissance, and also introduces the reader to the technique of reading social history from the style of the pictures produced. For Baxandall, Renaissance painting is closely 'related to such activities as preaching, dancing, and gauging barrels'.

The Medici (1980) by Marcel Brion. A history of this famous dynastic family of 15th- and 16th-century Florence, with emphasis placed on their role as influential patrons of the arts. This book also gives clear insights into the social conditions, intellectual climate, and artistic ideas that prevailed during this period.

Encyclopedia of the Italian Renaissance (1981) edited by J R Hale. An invaluable guide to every aspect of the Italian Renaissance.

Patronage in Renaissance Italy (1994) by Mary Hollingsworth. Perhaps a little demanding for the uninitiated, but worth the effort, for patronage was a vitally important factor in the development of Renaissance art.

Baroque (1977) by John Rupert Martin. Still one of the best introductions to the Baroque. Instead of looking at the Baroque in Italy, the Baroque in France, and so on (the standard approach), Martin looks at the whole broad range of 17th-century art in terms of such concepts as space, light, allegory, 'passions of the soul'. A delight.

NEO-CLASSICISM AND ROMANTICISM
Francesca M Speight

Neo-Classicism was a style of the late 18th and early 19th centuries strongly influenced by Classical art from the ancient Greek and Roman empires – even to the point of some painters and sculptors taking their subject matter from ancient history and the antique. This is seen especially in the works of the French artist Jacques Louis David. Neo-Classicism places great emphasis on draughtsmanship, on pure, clean contours, on idealized and noble subjects treated in a solid, three-dimensional way. David's *The Death of Socrates* is a key example.

The Romantic style of the 19th century arose as a direct reaction against the intellectual conceptions of the Neo-Classicists. The clearly defined forms and cool tones of Neo-Classicism gives way to indefinite shapes, warm tones, and atmospheric effects. In the French school of Romanticism, led by Eugène Delacroix, a love of the Oriental and exotic is seen; J M W Turner and William Blake are considered to be the leading English Romantics.

> *How awful is the silence of the waste, / Where nature lifts her*
> *mountains to the sky. / Majestic solitude, behold the tower /*
> *Where hopeless Owen, long imprisoned, pined /*
> *And wrung his hands for liberty, in vain.*
>
> J M W TURNER

Neo-Classicism (1968) by Hugh Honour. Short standard work. Honour's achievement lies in showing that Neo-Classicism, far from being a conservative movement supporting establishment values, was the culmination of Enlightenment radicalism, high-minded, idealistic, revolutionary. Artistically and politically it was the avant-garde of its day.

Civilisation (1969) by Kenneth Clark. This book is a classic portrayal of how western Europe evolved after the collapse of the Roman Empire, and provides a very readable account of the major art produced within each age, a particularly good section covering the time of both Neo-Classical and Romantic works of the 18th and early 19th centuries.

The Romantic Rebellion (1973) by Kenneth Clark. Here Clark gives a far more detailed account of Romanticism. Lucid and authoritative, his account is of particular value because it focuses on the constant interplay between Romanticism and Classicism.

The Story of Art (1950) by E H Gombrich. The classic, standard textbook for all those interested in the arts as a total picture of human endeavour from prehistoric times to the experimental art of the first half of the 20th century. The Age of Reason and the subsequent break in tradition are clearly and interestingly set out by the author.

Rococo to Revolution (1966) by Michael Levey. This book covers the major trends in 18th-century painting, and is based on a series of lectures given at Cambridge during the author's tenure there as Slade professor of art.

The Arts and Crafts Movement (1991) Elizabeth Cumming and Wendy Kaplan. Surveys all aspects of design within the movement, including architecture, furniture, glass, ceramics, textiles, and books.

The Art of J M W Turner (1990) by David Blayney Brown. This is a comprehensive coverage of all aspects of the artist's work, is beautifully illustrated, and avoids an academic approach in favour of using revealing analysis which vividly brings the subject to life. Incorporating many original sources of information, such as letters, critics' reviews, and political records, the author gives a complete background to Turner's life and times.

Art of the Romantic Era (1966) by Marcel Brion. Superbly illustrated history of Romantic art. This very accessible account is particularly interesting because it looks not only at the many major figures, but also at a host of fascinating minor ones.

IMPRESSIONISM TO POST-IMPRESSIONISM
Francesca M Speight

This period includes the school of Realism, headed by the French artist Gustave Courbet, which turned its back on the ennobling subject matter beloved by the official Academy, and focused instead on everyday contemporary scenes depicted in an accurate manner rather than idealized or transformed into 'picturesque' works. Another form of Realism is found in the French Impressionist movement's output, but they saw their motifs in terms of the analysis of light, which produced a new way of observing reality and has earned them the accolade of 'the first modern movement' in the history of art.

Working through Impressionism and developing their own distinctive individuality where the Post-Impressionists, including Georges Seurat (Neo-Impressionism), Paul

Gauguin (a form of Symbolism), Vincent van Gogh (early Expressionism), and Paul Cézanne (combining Realism and Classicism).

This period also includes the Pre-Raphaelite Brotherhood, an English group of idealistic young men drawn to medieval legends and romantic literary sources as subject matter, but using a technique of microscopically detailed analysis, in which truth to nature was uncompromisingly observed.

Show me an angel and I'll paint one.

GUSTAVE COURBET

Impressionism (1967) by Phoebe Pool. A good basic textbook on the movement, ideal as an introduction.

The History of Impressionism (1973) by John Rewald. A detailed, extensively researched history of the movement by one of the leading authorities. It was works like this that rescued Impressionism from chocolate-box sentimentality and gave it (after decades of critical neglect) a firm intellectual and aesthetic foundation. Essential reading.

A History of Modern Art (1969) by H H Arnason. A comprehensive guide, commencing with the prehistory of modern painting and continuing through all the major movements and individual figures up to Conceptualism.

The Victorian Treasure House (1973) by Peter Conrad. A wide-ranging study of Victorian art, with excellent coverage of the history and artistic output of the Pre-Raphaelites.

The New Painting: Impressionism 1847–1886 (1986) by Charles S Moffet. A scholarly presentation of the history of the movement, with each of the Impressionist exhibitions dealt with in detail.

Impressionism and Post-Impressionism 1874–1904 (1966) by Linda Nochlin. A collection of sources and documents in the History of Art series, containing the critics' views of the movement at that time, accounts of the individual major masters, and source material concerning Cézanne and the Neo-Impressionists, van Gogh, Gauguin, and the Symbolists.

Cézanne (1989) by Hajo Duchting. This monograph critically analyses the successive stages of Cézanne's art in both subject matter and style, culminating in the late, great paintings which earned him the name of the father of Modernism.

Realism (1971) by Linda Nochlin. A standard work, lucid and scholarly, which sets the many expressions of Realism within the political and social upheavals of the second half of the 19th century.

20TH-CENTURY ART – *Francesca M Speight*

This period commences with Cubism, a movement considered to be the source of all subsequent abstract art. Pablo Picasso and Georges Braque were the leading exponents of this new, intellectual approach to perception. Cubism produced many offshoots, including such styles as Neo-Plasticism, represented by Piet Mondrian, and also the geometric reliefs of Britain's Ben Nicholson. Concurrently a representational and intensely romantic stance in art continued alongside abstraction, as seen in Fauvism in France and Expressionism in Germany.

Other major movements to emerge in the 20th century include Surrealism, with Salvador Dali and René Magritte perhaps the best-known exponents; American Abstract Expressionism exemplified by such artists as Jackson Pollock and Willem de Kooning; and Pop art, which began in England but was taken up on a bigger and brasher scale by such Americans as Andy Warhol and Roy Lichtenstein.

Subsequent developments include Land art, Conceptual art, Installation art, Op art, and many variations on past styles. The *enfant terrible* and darling of the art world at present is Damien Hirst, with his installations of animal corpses displayed in tanks of formaldehyde. The shock element has always been associated with the avant-garde since Courbet produced his unidealized peasant scenes, and it seems destined to stay.

Sometimes I think that extreme beauty must be absolutely humourless.
But then I think of Marilyn Monroe and she had the best fun lines.

ANDY WARHOL

The Story of Modern Art (1980) by Norbert Lynton. The author states his intention of not only helping readers towards a confident relationship with modern art through providing information, but also actively encouraging the reader to combine this information of historical facts and knowledge of the works themselves with his or her experience of modern life and thought.

Painting in the Twentieth Century (1961) by Werner Haftmann. Two invaluable volumes of material of modern art. Volume 1 is solely text and sources information; volume 2 consists mainly of illustrations to complement volume 1. However, the second volume contains an excellent commentary throughout.

Art Today (1977) by Edward Lucie-Smith. Informative and lavishly illustrated, this book takes the reader through the birth of Modernism in both painting and sculpture and continues to Post-Modernism and the revival of Classicism.

The Bride and the Bachelors (1965) by Calvin Tomkins. The eyewitness description of the Swiss sculptor Jean Tinguely creating a self-destructing sculpture, complete with tooting horns and smoke bombs, is enough to make this book worth seeking out. The essay on Marcel Duchamp is a good introduction to this seminal figure. Tomkins also writes about Robert Rauschenberg and the composer John Cage.

The Shock of the New (1980) by Robert Hughes. One of the most lucid and authoritative histories of 20th-century art. Hughes has broad sympathies, but is not shy about expressing his own preferences. Lavishly illustrated.

Warhol: The Biography (1989) by Victor Bockris. Warhol's life encompassed the heyday of the New York art scene, from 1950s Abstract Expressionism to the gallery graffiti of the 1980s. This acclaimed biography shows the interaction between the artist's life and work. The films, freaks, drugs, and rock and roll are amply covered. An insider's view.

David Hockney (1976) by David Hockney. Britain's best-known living artist is also one of the best and least pretentious communicators on the subject. This book has hundreds of pictures with his explanations.

How to Look at Modern Art (1991) by Philip Yenawine. A stimulating introduction to a broad range of modern artists. The author (director of education at the Museum of Modern Art in New York) is less concerned with exploring the many complex theories that underlie modern art than with encouraging readers/viewers to explore their own reactions to specific works.

What Is Post-Modernism? (1986) by Charles Jencks. Short, surprisingly lucid account of a very complex and still controversial subject. A good starting point, wherever your sympathies may lie.

ARCHITECTURE

INTRODUCTION – *Joe Staines*

Architecture is unique among the arts, in as much as it is impossible to avoid. From birth to death, the spaces that surround us are largely defined by structures – walls, doors, windows, corridors – that have been consciously designed and built, albeit with varying degrees of finesse. The very ubiquity of architecture leads most people to take it for granted. It usually enters our awareness only for the most negative reasons: the destruction of something familiar and well loved, or the arrival of something else that seems incongruous or out of scale. The experience of architecture can be much more rewarding than this, and the following books have been chosen because all the authors, in their varying ways, have the ability to make the act of looking at the built environment seem like an active and creative process, an act of interpretation as much as one of contemplation.

All fine architectural values are human values, else not valuable.

FRANK LLOYD WRIGHT

The Seven Lamps of Architecture (1849) by John Ruskin. A highly idiosyncratic look at the fundamentals of architecture. Ruskin's high moral tone and sometimes eccentric opinions will not appeal to everyone but, after nearly 150 years, he is still worth reading for the poetic vigour of his prose style and the brilliance of his observations.

Experiencing Architecture (1959) by Steen Eiler Rasmussen. A refreshingly clear and unpretentious approach that concentrates on the many different ways of perceiving architectural forms: as an interplay of solids and voids, as a succession of rhythmic patterns, and even in terms of the acoustical character of buildings.

An Outline of European Architecture (1963) by Nikolaus Pevsner. A confident sweep through Western (including American) architecture: Pevsner's slightly awkward prose style persuades through its passion and its directness.

A Cartoon History of Architecture (1975) by Osbert Lancaster. Lancaster was a famous cartoonist who also wrote for the *Architectural Review* for many years. His eye for detail and dry wit make this a both amusing and highly insightful guide to the vagaries of taste.

Illustrated History of Architecture 800–1914 (1993) by Jill Lever and John Harris. First published in 1966 as the *Illustrated Glossary of Architecture*. The effectiveness of this dictionary derives from the way the authors have combined clearly written definitions of key terms with a remarkable collection of photographs with which to illustrate them.

The Classical Language of Architecture (1963) by John Summerson. Originally a series of radio talks, this is an elegantly phrased and lucid account of the way in which the essential elements of Classical Greek and Roman architecture have been used and reinterpreted by succeeding generations of architects from Bramante to Le Corbusier.

Masterpieces of Architectural Design (1982) edited by Helen Powell and David Leatherbarrow. Architects have used drawing in a variety of ways over the centuries: as a conceptual tool, as a means of communicating with builders, and as a way of impressing clients. This book presents over 100 fascinating examples accompanied by short but apposite commentaries.

GOTHIC ARCHITECTURE – *Joe Staines*

The rebuilding of the east end of the abbey church of St Denis, just north of Paris, was begun in 1140. It took just four years and is widely regarded as the first consistent manifestation of Gothic architecture. It was rapidly followed by similar building and rebuilding programmes across the Isle de France, then in England, and eventually throughout Europe. The vital elements of Gothic building – the pointed arch, the rib vault, and the flying buttress – all enabled the medieval master builder to replace the solid but earthbound architecture of the Romanesque with something more dynamic and transcendent. Walls, no longer load-bearing, could be filled with windows of coloured glass, creating – as at Chartres – a jewel-like glow within the often vast interiors. The Gothic cathedral dominated the surrounding landscape and the lives of those within it, so it is hardly surprising that subsequent architectural history has concentrated on ecclesiastical buildings almost entirely at the expense of secular ones.

Gothic is not only the best, but the only rational architecture, as being that which can fit itself most easily to all services, vulgar or noble ... it can shrink into a turret, expand into a hall, coil into a staircase, or spring into a spire, with undegraded grace and unexhausted energy.

JOHN RUSKIN

Cathedral (1974) by David Macaulay. The story of the construction of an imaginary, but typical, French cathedral is told for children using vivid explanatory drawings and a minimum of text. Much essential information is imparted in the most painless of ways.

The Cathedral Builders (1980) by Jean Gimpel. The perfect compliment to Macaulay's book, written by an enthusiast. A stimulating text gives us the political and religious background to the 'cathedral crusade', and provides a detailed view into the lives of the various itinerant craftsmen responsible for its realization.

Gothic (1967) by George Henderson. Henderson sees the Gothic as rather more than a revolution in architectural construction. His short book provides an overview of all the medieval visual arts, concentrating on their stylistic unity and emphasizing both their human quality and their ornamental daring.

Gothic Architecture (1962) by Paul Frank. A wide-ranging history of Gothic architecture that stresses the importance of structural developments. This is a classic account written by one of the subject's greatest scholars in a style that is thoroughly readable and enjoyable. Includes a brief survey of secular architecture.

The Gothic Cathedral (1956) by Otto von Simson. For Simson, the symbolic function of the great cathedrals – as an image of the City of God – is their greatest importance. Using contemporary texts, especially the writings of Abbot Suger of St Denis, he tries to show the true significance of these buildings for medieval man.

Medieval Architecture, Medieval Learning (1992) by Charles M Radding and William W Clark. In this challenging book a historian and an art historian attempt to unravel the connections and shared approaches between architecture and scholasticism in the 11th and 12th centuries. Not an easy read but worth the effort.

The Nature of Gothic (1853) by John Ruskin. This chapter from *The Stones of Venice* was so admired by William Morris that he printed it as a separate work. It is not difficult to understand Morris's enthusiasm, for here is Ruskin at his most rhapsodic: confidently defining the essentials of Gothic architecture, extolling its superiority – both aesthetic and moral – to all other architectural styles, and linking this superiority to the independent character of those from northern climes.

RENAISSANCE AND BAROQUE ARCHITECTURE
Francesca M Speight

The study of architecture reflects, perhaps more than any other art form, the prevailing aesthetic tastes of a period. The Renaissance is no exception, the rebirth of Classical ideas on form, proportion, and decoration, as found in the remains of ancient Greece and Rome, providing inspiration for such major architectural masters as Leon Battista Alberti, Filippo Brunelleschi, and Michelangelo. Baroque architecture, however, reflects the penchant of the time towards lavish decorative schemes on a grand scale, the simplicity and clarity of the Classical giving way to the love of complexity and dramatic effects.

He departed not a little from the work regulated by measure, order and rule which other men did according to a common use and after Vitruvius and the antiquities, to which he would not conform ...

GIORGIO VASARI ON THE ARCHITECTURE OF MICHELANGELO

Introduction to Architecture (1983) by Stephen Gardiner. A valuable textbook which looks at the origins and development of each style, followed by important examples of each type being examined, and concluding with a review of the international impact and national variations of the style in question.

The Architecture of the Italian Renaissance (1969) by Peter Murray. Clear, beautifully illustrated account, ideal for the beginner.

The Penguin Dictionary of Architecture (1966) by John Fleming, Hugh Honour, and Nikolaus Pevsner. An invaluable aid for the newcomer to the many terms used within this discipline.

History of Italian Renaissance Art (1970) by Frederick Hartt. Packed with information on all major and minor painters, sculptors, and architects, all placed within a broad historical context. For over 20 years this has been considered to be the best book written on this period.

Architectural Principles in the Age of Humanism (1949) by Rudolf Wittkower. A seminal work, lucid and stimulating. Relating Renaissance architecture to Renaissance music, philosophy, and science, Wittkower argues that its aesthetic principles were grounded not in a secular view of the world, but a deeply religious one – that it was, fundamentally, a 'sacred' architecture.

An Outline of European Architecture (1943) by Nikolaus Pevsner. Reprinted many times, this remains a standard reference book of exceptional quality. It is scholarly in approach, but the reader's perseverance is well rewarded in the wealth of information it contains.

Baroque and Rococo (1964) by Germain Bazin. The author explores the richness and complexity of this period, and takes into account the persistence of earlier styles. A scholarly but accessible study of the architecture as well as painting and sculpture of the Baroque and Rococo.

WESTERN ARCHITECTURE 1750–1900
Rosamund Diamond

From the middle of the 18th century, as much as the other aspects of culture, architecture was affected by ideas of the Enlightenment and significant changes that were taking place in the political structures of certain nations, the most significant of these being the French and American Revolutions. Architecture became influenced by contemporary philosophy, in its ideas about nature and society, and the conflict between empiricism and rationalism. Change in conceptions of history, and archaeological expeditions to cultivate the examination of Roman and Greek architecture, led to the questioning of Vitruvius' Classical precepts and the singular route presented by Renaissance and Baroque. It also resulted in the development of Neo-Classicism.

In the 19th century, the Industrial Revolution presented architecture with new approaches to development, as a result of both mass increases in production and technological innovation. Enlarged urban development and, in the densely occupied cities, the need to install comprehensive servicing systems, such as the provision of drainage and water, as well as advances in mobility and communication, led to strategic planning, which produced both structured urban designs and, in the latter part of the century, suburbanization. The rise of the new bourgeois classes in cities generated places of leisure and consumption: new parks marked the urbanization of landscape, and technological advancement made possible the construction of the arcade.

Technical innovation from the middle of the 18th century, which included the development of iron as a structural material and the birth of the steam engine, encouraged a division in the roles of the engineer and the architect. The new materials and techniques of construction presented multiple rather than singular solutions to design projects. This presaged 20th-century diversity. Advances in the production of power, leading, for example, to the invention of the lift and the electric light, resulted not only in more ambitious constructions, but in architecture as a more sophisticated means of tempering the environment, which might respond to individual need while expressing changes in society.

Unremittingly science enriches itself and life with newly discovered useful materials and natural powers that work miracles, with new methods and techniques, with new tools and machines. It is already evident that inventions no longer are, as they had been in earlier times, means for warding off want and for helping consumption; instead, want and consumption are the means to market the inventions. The order of things has been reversed.

GOTTFRIED SEMPER

Neo-Classical and Nineteenth Century Architecture (1979) by Robin Middleton and David Watkin. (The paperback version is in two volumes: *The Enlightenment in France and England* and *The Diffusion and Development of Classicism and the Gothic Revival.*) This is one of the most useful and readable studies of the period 1750–1850, covering its major themes, which include the influence of the antique, visionary architecture, Neo-Classicism, and the Gothic revival. It includes an invaluable list of the main architectural protagonists and a comprehensive bibliography.

The Architecture of the French Enlightenment (1980) by Allan Braham. This is a well-illustrated, thorough survey of the period, which includes a study of pre- and post-Revolutionary architecture.

The Writing of the Walls: Architectural Theory in the Late Enlightenment (1986) by Anthony Vidler. Another, more particularized, investigation of architectural theory of the period.

Laugier and Eighteenth Century French Theory (1962) by Wolfgang and Anni Herrmann. This is a translation of *An Essay on Architecture* (1753) by Marc-Antoine Laugier. Whereas the source text may be hard to read, the introduction by the Herrmanns provides an excellent guide to the theorist who, using the idea of the 'primitive hut', proposed a 'natural' architecture.

Boullée and Visionary Architecture (1976) by Helen Rosenau. Covers the grandiose building projects of one of the most extraordinary architects of the period.

Claude-Nicolas Ledoux – Architecture and Social Reform at the End of the Ancien Régime (1990) by Anthony Vidler. This is one of the few thorough English-language studies of the visionary architect Ledoux.

Sources of Architectural Form: A Critical History of Western Design Theory (1995) by Mark Gelernter. Chapter 6 (The Enlightenment) and Chapter 7 (The 19th Century) are useful in presenting the background of ideas to the development of architecture.

History of Modern Architecture (1971) by Leonardo Benevolo. This work is in two volumes. Volume 1 covers the period from 1740 to the 20th century, and has important sections on the birth of industrial towns that are relevant to a study of 19th-century architecture.

The Modern City: Planning in the 19th Century (1970) by Françoise Choay. This book covers one of the most important themes in the development of 19th-century architecture.

Architecture: Nineteenth and Twentieth Centuries (1958) by Henry-Russell Hitchcock. Readable general study by a major architectural historian.

The Four Elements of Architecture and Other Writings (1851–69; translated 1989 by H F Mallgrave and W Herrmann) by Gottfried Semper. Semper was one of the most important 19th-century architectural theorists. The style of these texts may be harder to read, but they are of great importance in establishing his ideas about the origins of architecture, and how structure might relate to architecture and the expression of style.

Heavenly Mansions and Other Essays (1949) by John Summerson. John Summerson was one of Britain's foremost architectural historians in the 20th century. This is a series of readable essays including a fascinating text on Viollet-le-Duc.

The Rise of an American Architecture (1970) edited by Edgar Kaufmann Jr. Interesting account that includes the development of cities and parks, and the skyscraper.

The Gothic: Literary Sources and Interpretations through Eight Centuries (1959) by Paul Frankl. Important study of Gothic architecture that includes its incarnation in 19th-century architecture. See also *Gothic Architecture* (1960) by the same author.

Mechanization Takes Command (1948) by Sigfried Giedion. A look at construction in terms of concepts of comfort and its acquisition; for example, bathing and hygiene. Although there are many omissions, or issues covered too thinly, it at least addresses and introduces the cultural climate in which architecture was developing in the 20th century.

In Search of Modern Architecture – A Tribute to Henry-Russell Hitchcock (1982) by Helen Searing. This book was produced as a festschrift for the famous architectural historian. It includes an interesting range of essays including architectural and urban design topics from 1740 up to the 20th century.

20TH-CENTURY ARCHITECTURE
Rosamund Diamond

The history of modern architecture could be described as a history of ideas, in which the apparent divergence of approaches, and the number of movements, in contrast to previous centuries, resulted from the wide range of possibilities made available by new technologies. This not only made architects address different methods of construction, but also the social effects of their buildings, individually and collectively, in shaping and reflecting the way people live in the modern age. Architects such as Le Corbusier projected visions of whole conurbations and environments to support the new social structures that they envisioned.

It is hard to be precise in attempting to trace the start of modern architecture when one considers both its technological and its visionary characteristics. In one sense its origin may be found in the origins of the Industrial Revolution, but in another it lies as much in the development of ideas in the middle of the 18th century. The individual's place in an increasingly mechanized field of production is often questioned in the debates of 20th-century architecture, and this growing dilemma is expressed in the late century's divergence of stylistic approaches.

The machinery of society, profoundly out of gear, oscillates between an amelioration, of historial importance, and a catastrophe. The primordial instinct of every human being is to assure himself of shelter. The various classes of workers in society today no longer have dwellings adapted to their needs; neither the artisan nor the intellectual. It is a question of building which is at the root of the social unrest of today; architecture or revolution.

LE CORBUSIER

History of Modern Architecture (Volume 2, 1971) by Leonardo Benevolo. This is a very interesting history of modern architecture because, unlike many of the personality-dominated histories, it sets architecture and urbanism into its industrial, economic, and social contexts.

Space, Time and Architecture: The Growth of a New Tradition (1941) by Sigfried Giedion. This study of modern architecture and its development in the USA has been one of the most frequently read by students. It avoids some of the ideological influences that Benevolo and Tafuri (see below) present as central to their studies of modern architecture.

Modern Architecture: A Critical History (1980) by Kenneth Frampton. This is one of the most valuable recent brief introductory studies of modern architecture, by one of the leading critical writers on the subject, including contemporary work.

Theory and Design in the First Machine Age (1960), *Age of the Masters* (1962), *Architecture of the Well-Tempered Environment* (1969), all by Reyner Banham. Banham's work is always carefully researched, placed in a general cultural context, and very readable. On the one hand, he apparently has an easy style which concerns his sense of the power of things contemporary and immediate; on the other, it is this, together with his scholarship, that allows him to question the developments of modern architecture, their successes and failures, rather than freezing them as historical events. The last title is still important as a critical study of the impact of environmental engineering.

Programmes and Manifestos on 20th-Century Architecture (1970) edited by Ulrich Conrads, translated by Michael Bullock. This is a good source book of some of the most important statements of position made by architects between 1900 and the early 1960s.

Architecture Culture 1943–1968 (1993) by Joan Ockman with the collaboration of Edward Eigen. This is another version of the previous book with the inclusion of a later generation of architects.

Sources of Modern Architecture (1967) by Dennis Sharp. A very useful bibliography listing many significant architects of the Modern movement, with basic information on their lives and their work, and publications by or on them.

Modern Architecture (2 volumes; 1986) by Manfredo Tafuri and Francesco Dal Co. Like the work of Benevolo, this sets architecture into a political and cultural context, that is prepared to reassess history and with it the Modern movement.

Key Buildings of the Twentieth Century (1985, 1990) by David Dunster. Volume 1 covers houses 1900–44 and Volume 2 1945–89. Both consist of brief studies of individual buildings significant to the development of 20th-century architecture, providing a useful companion to the broader histories.

Oeuvre Complète (1910–65) by Le Corbusier, edited by W Boesiger. In seven volumes, an extraordinary record of one of the century's most important architects, including his own descriptions of his work.

Complexity and Contradiction in Architecture (1966) by Robert Venturi. One of the few architectural treatises of the late 20th century. It presages what is now described as Post-Modern architecture.

Learning from Las Vegas (1972) by Robert Venturi, Denise Scott Brown, and Steve Izenour. This is a study of the popular culture that the authors identify as confronting contemporary architecture.

The Language of Post-Modern Architecture (1984) by Heinrich Klote, translated by Radka Donnell. Thorough general review of the main Post-Modernists, although to understand this late 20th-century development, general cultural works that examine other arts should be studied.

CLASSICAL MUSIC

EARLY MUSIC – *David Fallows*

B roadly speaking, the notion of 'early music' has two quite separate meanings. The first is the history of Western music before Bach and Handel (both born in 1685), an enormous repertory that goes back to Gregorian chant (reputedly assembled by Pope Gregory the Great around 600 AD) and includes a large number of major composers, among them Perotinus (c. 1200), Guillaume de Machaut (c. 1300–1377), Guillaume Dufay (c. 1400–1474), Josquin des Prez (c. 1450–1521), Giovanni Pierluigi da Palestrina (1425–1594), William Byrd (1543–1623), Claudio Monteverdi (1567–1643), Arcangelo Corelli (1665–1713), and Henry Purcell (1659–1695). The second meaning is the application of historical performing techniques to any music before about World War II: there have been many changes in the construction of instruments, in the way performers react to music on the page, in the way they phrase the music, in aesthetic attitudes.

The 18th-century musician was taught to see the whole of musical history as a hill rising gently and undulatingly out of the darkness, with the music of his own time standing on the sunlit summit: the modern musician is encouraged to view it as a rather alarming slope, studded like Easter Island with titanic heads, far larger than life. And he may even have an uneasy suspicion that the slope is a downward one.

THURSTON DART

A Dictionary of Early Music (1981) by Jerome Roche and Elizabeth Roche. Thumbnail information on all the main composers, repertories, instruments and concepts in music down to the time of Monteverdi. This is an excellent and authoritative summary.

Western Plainchant: A Handbook (1993) by David Hiley. A comprehensive orientation to the state of research on the melodies of the Catholic church, a repertory that formed the basic musical training of all composers before the Reformation and continued to have a massive impact on composers until the 19th century.

Music in Medieval Europe (1989) by Jeremy Yudkin. Takes the story up to about 1400 with clear and engaging explanations and copious musical examples.

Studies in Medieval and Renaissance Music (1950) by Manfred F Bukofzer. This remains one of the most gripping books for the general reader who wants a glimpse at how a musical historian goes to work on early materials. Mainly concerned with the 15th century.

The Rise of European Music, 1380–1500 (1993) by Reinhard Strohm. An extended panoramic view of how these central years are seen today, bursting with original and controversial insights.

Music in the Renaissance (1976) by Howard Mayer Brown. An elegant bird's-eye summary of music from 1420 to 1600, with its focus on the main composers and their work.

Music in the Seventeenth Century (1987) by Lorenzo Bianconi. Perhaps the clearest and most incisive recent survey of music in the years from the beginnings of opera to the time of Corelli.

The Interpretation of Music (1954) by Thurston Dart .Though old and occasionally eccentric, this is a glitteringly brilliant introduction to the performer's problem in music down to the Baroque era.

Authenticity in Early Music (1988) edited by Nicholas Kenyon. Essays that explore the problems of historical performance as seen today. After its publication nobody dared use the word 'authenticity' again, and performers were much more cautious in their claims of historical correctness.

Early Recordings and Musical Style (1992) by Robert Philip. By exploring the earliest recorded performances, Philip draws attention to the many aesthetic changes within the last century, to musical styles that would not now be acceptable in any circumstances, and to how difficult it would be to reconstruct the sounds of the early 20th century if no recordings had survived. It is a solemn lesson to those attempting to recover the sounds of the 18th century and earlier.

BAROQUE MUSIC – *David Maw*

The word 'baroque' comes from the Portuguese *barroco* for a pearl of irregular or bulbous shape. It found its way into critical writing during the middle part of the 18th century, when it was used with a pejorative connotation; thus 'A baroque music is that in which the harmony is confused, charged with modulations and dissonances, the melody is harsh and little natural, the intonation difficult, and the movement constrained' (Jean Jacques Rousseau, *Dictionnaire de musique*). In modern times, the word has been used to refer to music of the period 1600–1750, irrespective of its ornateness or frowardness; what the general characteristics of the style are is still an open question. During the period, important developments were made in opera and instrumental music (the virtuosity attained in violin and keyboard repertories being noteworthy); and elaborate theories were formulated about the conveyance of the affections through music.

> *Music hath two ends, first to please the sense, and that is done by the pure dulcor of harmony ... and secondly to move the affections or excite passion. And that is done with measures of time joined with the former. And it must be granted that pure impulse artificially acted and continued hath great power to excite men to act but not to think ... The melody is only to add to the diversion.*
>
> ROGER NORTH

Music in the Baroque Era (1947) by Manfred Bukofzer. Though now old, this stately tome is still the best account of the developments in musical style during the period.

Source Readings in Music History: The Baroque Era (1950) selected and annotated by Oliver Strunk. A selection of passages from contemporary writers is here presented in excellent translations. The topics covered are: the *stile rappresentativo*, musical practice, operatic rivalries and criticism, and developments in musical theory.

Monteverdi (1962) by Denis Arnold. This is a vivaciously written account of the composer's life and work. Denis Arnold was the foremost scholar of 16th- and 17th-century Venetian music, and in this book he used his extensive knowledge to good effect in explaining Monteverdi's pivotal position between Renaissance and Baroque styles.

The Purcell Companion (1995) edited by Michael Burden. An excellent collection of essays concerning many different aspects of the composer and his music, published to coincide with the tercentenary of his death.

Couperin (1982) by David Tunley. A brief and intelligent study of the most eminent composer of the French Baroque.

Vivaldi (1978) by Michael Talbot. Vivaldi deserves to be better known for pieces other than the *Four Seasons*: Michael Talbot's book explains why.

Rameau (1968) by Cuthbert Girdlestone. This is the classic work on one of the most characteristic and controversial musicians working in 18th-century France. In addition to his major contributions to musical theory, Rameau was a composer of considerable accomplishment.

Scarlatti (1953) by Ralph Kirkpatrick. This elegantly written book covers every aspect of Scarlatti's life and work and also contains much interesting information about the performance of his 555 keyboard sonatas.

Handel (1994) by Donald Burrows. Handel's was a varied life, often very much at the heart of society. Donald Burrows presents a balanced picture of the man, his context and work, righting the lopsided impressions that have arisen.

Bach (1983) by Malcolm Boyd. This is a remarkable book, conveying a considerable breadth and depth of insight within relatively few pages. Of course, the subject matter warrants nothing less.

CLASSICAL MUSIC – *David Maw*

There is more general acceptance for the notion of a classical style in music – being that of Haydn, Mozart, and Beethoven, according to Rosen's contention – than for a classical period. In so far as the latter has any validity, then it is to designate the years 1750–1820; but really the phenomenon is more localized than a simple temporal segment would suggest. The style is characterized by the formal conventions of the 'sonata principle', which are the stock in trade of sonatas, symphonies, concertos, string quartets, and operatic set pieces; these being the genres principally cultivated. The term 'classical' is justified both by the universality of these formal characteristics, and on account of the balance that they effect between the various elements of music; it has nothing at all to do with a recrudescence of antique values.

Nevertheless, the passions, whether violent or not, should never be so expressed as to reach the point of causing disgust; and music, even in situations of the greatest horror, should never be painful to the ear but should flatter and charm it, and thereby always remain music.

WOLFGANG AMADEUS MOZART

The Classical Style (1976) by Charles Rosen. The definitive exposition of this subject.

Source Readings in Music History: The Classic Era (1950) selected and annotated by Oliver Strunk. An anthology of passages from contemporary writers concerning changes in musical practice, operatic rivalry and criticism, and the musical life of Europe.

The String Quartet (1983) by Paul Griffiths. The string quartet was one of the most significant developments of the 18th century. Paul Griffiths tells its story right up to the present day, cunningly structuring his book in the form of the music.

The Piano: A History (1976) by Cyril Ehrlich. The invention and development of the piano had a more significant impact upon the nature of musical thought than did any other technological innovations before the production of sound by electronic means. Cyril Ehrlich is one of the most eminent socioeconomic historians of music, and his book a classic.

C P E Bach Studies (1988) edited by Stephen L Clark. J S Bach's second son was one of the most unusual and influential of the composers who effected the transition between Baroque and classical modes of musical thought. This collection of essays (some rather technical) affords insights into many areas of a composer who merits greater attention.

Haydn, his Life and Music (1988) by H C Robbins Landon and David Wyn Jones. This is an excellent survey of a long and productive life with much relevant background material on the composer's artistic and cultural surroundings.

The Mozart Companion (1956) edited by H C Robbins Landon and Donald Mitchell. For a composer as multifaceted and oft written about as Mozart, the best introduction is a collection of essays by various authors. The full range of his output is covered here by writers as distinguished as Friedrich Blume, Arthur Hutchings, Hans Keller, and the editors themselves.

Beethoven (1985) by Denis Matthews. The author maintains an admirable distance on the life and the work, where these are elsewhere so often mythologized; but he conveys also the enthusiasm and awe that so monumental a subject requires.

Schubert (1987) by John Reed. This is a good introduction to a composer who was caught between Classicism and Romanticism but properly belonged to neither.

ROMANTIC MUSIC – *David Maw*

The word *Romantik* entered the common currency of the German language after its use by E T A Hoffman in an essay on Beethoven's instrumental music, written in 1813. This owes more to Hoffman than to Beethoven, and it would be wrong to confuse the novel forms of Beethoven's later music, impelled by a complete fidelity to his material, with the formal vagaries of subsequent music, where expressive caprice was the guiding light. Romanticism can be dated, then, from around 1820; many of its traits lingered on well into the 20th century. While music was generally regarded in the 19th century as the highest art form, it frequently looked to literature and the fine arts for inspiration: symphonic poems, songs without words, nocturnes, evocations, fantasies, rhapsodies, and countless other pieces of a fanciful inclination were among the most experimental and typical genres cultivated. Yet, even where the form was ostensibly abstract – in symphonies, concertos, and sonatas – there was a strong suggestion that it was being narrated by the material, rather than emerging inexorably from it.

It is the art of music which most completely realizes this artistic ideal, this perfect identification of matter and form. In its consummate moments, the end is not distinct from the means, the form from the matter, the subject from the expression; they inhere in and completely saturate each other; and to it, therefore, to the condition of its perfect moments, all the arts may be supposed constantly to tend and aspire.

WALTER PATER

Romantic Music (1984) by Leon Plantings. A highly readable introduction to the ideas and styles of music in the 19th century.

Source Readings in Music History, the Romantic Era (1950) selected and annotated by Oliver Strunk. This is an invaluable collection of excerptions presenting the literary background to romanticism and the writings of composer-critics of the period (Carl von Weber, Hector Berlioz, Robert Schumann, Franz Liszt, and Richard Wagner).

The Memoirs of Hector Berlioz (1969) translated and edited by David Cairns. Berlioz was no less significant as a literary figure than as a musical one. His memoirs are a compelling read, telling of his upbringing and education, literary and musical passions, amorous adventures, travels, life as a critic, and progress towards compositional success. David Cairn's translation is excellent.

Berlioz (1982) by Hugh Macdonald. A considered appraisal of the man and his music by the most eminent scholar of the subject.

The Cambridge Companion to Chopin (1992) edited by Jim Samson. It is a paradox that Chopin's music should be so classical in technique, given its highly romantic sound. This excellent collection of essays helps to explain why this is so, setting the music in the context of its influences, borrowed and bequeathed. One or two of the essays may be slightly too technical for the general reader; but most are quite approachable.

Schumann and his World (1994) edited by R Larry Todd. Many minds come together here to consider the enigmatic work, elusive personality, and turbid milieu of one of the 19th century's most characteristic composers.

Liszt (1990) by Derek Watson. Liszt's flamboyant personality and the legends that accrued around it have for a long time hindered evaluation of the compositional legacy. Derek Watson's excellent study rectifies this with a clear-sighted account of an oeuvre that is often masterly and frequently innovative.

The Wagner Compendium, a Guide to Wagner's Life and Music (1992) edited by Barry Millington. To encompass Wagner in a single volume is an impossibility; I suspect that Barry Millington's compendium comes as close to achieving this unfeasible task as can be reached.

Brahms (1990) by Malcolm Macdonald. Brahms rued his having been born 'too late'; the figure of Beethoven was a blessing and a bane to him. Malcolm Macdonald's is a careful study of a scrupulous and complicated artist.

Tchaikovsky (1973) by Edward Garden. No account of Tchaikovsky could satisfactorily separate the life and the work; so Edward Garden integrated the two in a very sensitive evaluation.

20TH-CENTURY MUSIC – *Paul Griffiths*

Two themes stand out in the history of Western music in the 20th century: change and accumulation. Instances of the first include, in the early part of the century, Schoenberg's break with tonal harmony and Stravinsky's renewal of rhythmic pulse; and the growing power of electronic technology, particularly since the World War II, has altered how music is composed, performed, and heard. What Western classical music has simultaneously accumulated has been a deeper awareness not only of its own past but of traditions outside itself, including especially the many musical cultures of Asia. Western composers in 1900 were working within a tradition that was essentially Germanic and that extended back no more than 150 years or so. Their colleagues now survey many centuries, and the world.

You cannot tell where music is going any more than you can tell where people are going. Each time creates its own needs.

IGOR STRAVINSKY

Modern Music: A Concise History (1994) by Paul Griffiths. A general introduction to the modern age in Western music, from Claude Debussy to the present. The next step would be to move to the following three volumes, which divide up the period, and which need some acquaintance with musical notation.

Music in Transition (1977) by Jim Samson. A study of the first two decades of the century, and in particular of the breakdown of tonal harmony, as it occurred in the music of Arnold Schoenberg, Alexander Skryabin, and others.

Music Since the First World War (1977) by Arnold Whittall. This is an excellent, companionable read; Whittall shows wide sympathies in considering how composers dealt with broadening musical possibilities.

Modern Music and After (1995) by Paul Griffiths. This book works from the detonation of radical change that came in the late 1940s (John Cage, Pierre Boulez, electronic music) to the exuberant confusion of music in the 1990s.

Stravinsky in Pictures and Documents (1978) by Vera Stravinsky and Robert Craft. From the time of *The Firebird* (1910) to his death (1971), Stravinsky was the dominant musical force by virtue of his influence and prestige, not to mention the variety and brilliance of his achievement. This compendium is full of tang, colour and insight, despite its other, quite un-Stravinskian, quality of disorder.

The Music of Stravinsky (1988) by Stephen Walsh. For a more consistent view of Stravinsky's output – and also a lively one – this is the best choice. The author has been working on a major biography of the composer.

Schoenberg (1975) by Charles Rosen. There should be more books like this: a concise introduction, steered, by the author's intelligence, between reverence and scepticism, and requiring from the reader nothing but curiosity.

Silence (1961) by John Cage. A classic collection of essays by the man who persuaded us that music is not an art, still less a means of communication, but an attitude of mind, a way of being attuned, even to silence.

JAZZ

Miles Kington

A year or two back I did a book for HarperCollins called *The Jazz Anthology* which, if I did again now, I'd call *A Jazz Anthology*, but I wouldn't change a lot else; it's still quite a good sampler. In the introduction I see I wrote that most writing on jazz is not very good (including almost all the novels and poetry ever written on the subject) and I stick to that now. The best of it tends to be anecdotal, like the best conversation of jazz musicians, which explains this selection. The best musical history of jazz is not yet finished – Gunther Schuller has written the first two volumes and has got up to about 1940.

---

*Most of the people who have any respect for jazz in this country
are those who can make a buck out of it.*

BILLIE HOLIDAY

We Called It Music (1992) by Eddie Condon. Condon embraced jazz, the guitar, and the bottle during the Prohibition years. He wasn't a great guitarist but he was a wonderful storyteller and this is the most funny, colourful, prejudiced account of jazz between the wars ever written. Sample phrase: 'I arrived at the club in a perfect state of equilibrium – half man, half whisky.'

Raise Up Off Me (1979) by Hampton Hawes. Miles Davis's autobiography is commonly thought to be the toughest, frankest book by a modern black musician about drugs, racism, Charlie Parker, and so on. It isn't, though it's good. This is.

The McJazz Manuscripts (1979) by Sandy Brown. Sandy Brown was a wonderful Scots clarinettist who learned to play at the sort of Edinburgh clubs where Sean Connery learned to be a teenage bouncer. He later became a genius of an acoustic architect and a damned good writer; this book contains all the writings he left behind, including an unfinished autobiography.

Close Enough for Jazz (1983) by Mike Zwerin. Zwerin played trombone with Miles Davis in 1949 and never played with anyone as good again, but he did become the resident jazz writer on the *International Herald Tribune* (in Paris), where he still is, and, in my opinion, is the best jazz writer alive today. This is his odd, freewheeling life story, which takes in everything from playing on tours in Russia to inheriting a steel company he didn't want. (He has also translated a book by the wonderful French writer Boris Vian and written a sombre history of jazz under the Nazis.)

Jazz Anecdotes (1993) edited by Bill Crow. The best collection of (genuine) jazz anecdotes ever printed. Bill Crow is a musician himself (very good bass player) and knows how to get, and tell, a story from other players.

Mama Said There'd Be Days Like This (1991) by Val Wilmer. Val Wilmer is the complete opposite of the jazz stereotype. Typically, a jazz person is American, black, male, and heterosexual. Wilmer is English, white, female, and lesbian. She is also one of the best photographers and writers ever to fall in love with jazz, and has got closer inside black culture than most white people ever get.

POP MUSIC

Charles Shaar Murray

Pop provides one of the broadest cultural umbrellas which the 20th century has to offer: sheltering beneath it can be found such wildly dissimilar flora and fauna as Bing Crosby and Howlin' Wolf, Gracie Fields and Madonna, Barry Manilow and Ice-T, the Bay City Rollers and the Butthole Surfers. By the same token, pop books come in a bewildering variety of flavours and weights, as well as shapes and sizes. They range from potboiling biographies to train spotter's guides; from addled memoirs to academic tracts; from dryly fact-packed laundry listings to airily free-flying theory; from solemn social and cultural history to scabrously bawdy anecdote; from the most impenetrably parochial of subcultures to the most all-encompassingly ubiquitous manifestations of the international mass market. Pop means an infinite number of things to an infinite number of people, and the sheer diversity of the field has been well served by its equally diverse chroniclers.

Rock and roll is the most brutal, ugly, vicious form of expression – sly, lewd, in plain fact, dirty ... rancid-smelling, aphrodisiac ... the martial music of every delinquent on the face of the earth.

FRANK SINATRA

The Faber Book of Pop (1995) by Hanif Kureishi and Jon Savage. With an 800-page celebration of precisely that diversity covering the full half-century and drawing on contributions from (among hundreds of others) Malcolm X, Angela Carter, Hunter S Thompson, Greil Marcus, Nik Cohn, Iggy Pop, Andy Warhol, Lester Bangs, Colin MacInnes, and Paul Johnson, Kureishi and Savage cater for every conceivable taste and interest, delivering as sumptuous a smorgasbord of pop-culch text bites as anyone has ever served up between a single pair of covers.

AwopBopALooBop ALopBamBoom: Pop from the Beginning (1969) by Nik Cohn. Inaccurate, opinionated, shamelessly unfair, and unashamedly biased, this is the best and most influential book about pop music ever written by an Englishman. Barbecuing every sacred cow he could find – he was the first pop critic to damn the Beatles' *Sgt Pepper's Lonely Hearts Club Band* as the emperor's psychedelic new clothes – Cohn wrote this book as a funeral oration for the corpse of pop at the end of the 1960s, a time when the Flash McTrash aesthetic he adored had been seemingly subsumed beneath a welter of solemnity and pretension. This eulogy for superpop is the most relentlessly quotable pop book ever written: Cohn's coining of the term 'boring old fart' is almost the least of his achievements.

Mystery Train (1975) by Greil Marcus. Modern rock criticism starts here. Marcus was unravelling the subtexts of pop before most of his peers even knew what a subtext was, and these essays – on Robert Johnson, Sly Stone, Randy Newman, Elvis Presley, and the Band – address the expression, in popular music, of the classic themes of American literature, providing both cross-disciplinary continuity and a signpost towards new ways of listening.

Hellfire: The Jerry Lee Lewis Story (1982) by Nick Tosches. The most audacious, imaginative, and unorthodox rock biography ever written: an intoxicating, magic-realist account of the life and times of a white 1950s rocker more radical and challenging than Presley could ever have dreamed of being, who straddled the implicit contradictions of who he was and what he did until they tore him apart.

Revolution in the Head: The Beatles' Music and the Sixties (1995) by Ian MacDonald. A virtuoso example of just how scholarly pop criticism can get, and also of how spectacularly this approach can pay off when it's done properly. MacDonald – the author, incidentally, of a rather good book about Shostakovich – analyses each and every Beatles song in order of recording and in doing so links the band's rise and fall with that of the Sixties Dream.

Psychotic Reactions and Carburettor Dung (1988) by Lester Bangs. The late Lester Bangs took the 1960s notion of 'new journalism' as far as anyone who ever wrote about popular music: he was pop's Tom Wolfe, Hunter Thompson, and Norman Mailer all stuffed into the same battered black leather jacket. This collection of a decade and a half's demented scribblings – on Kraftwerk, John Coltrane, the Clash, Elvis Presley, and his personal hero and *bête noir*, Lou Reed – is the most highly charged and deeply committed writing about pop available anywhere. For Bangs the music he wrote about was a matter of life and death, and it shows. Includes his famous essay *James Taylor – Marked for Death*.

The History of the Blues (1995) by Francis Davis. A huge story, intelligently told; Davis succeeds in his gargantuan task not least because he knows what to leave out. Witty, perceptive, compassionate, and incisive, this self-proclaimed 'pop critic's history of the blues' is the finest single-volume introduction to pop's primal root music that any general reader could desire.

The Death of Rhythm and Blues (1988) by Nelson George. Whites – specifically, white males – have traditionally enjoyed a near monopoly on the analysis of popular music, even though the bulk of the music worth writing about has been black. Here Nelson George, the doyen of African-American pop commentators, redresses the balance (partially, anyway) and tells you what the white boys can't: that the great black music upon which modern notions of pop is founded thrived under segregation and lost much of its impetus and identity in the wake of the civil-rights movement, and that white patronage of the music and its makers has proved a far from unmixed blessing.

The Ice Opinion (1994) by Ice-T and Heidi Siegmund. Rap is the most word-intensive form of pop since the mid-1960s heyday of Bob Dylan (whose 'Subterranean Homesick Blues' is itself one of rap's ancestor records), and therefore it's not surprising that rap's most prominent standard-bearer has a lot to say for himself, albeit with the aid of a ghostwriter. The chapters on race relations and the social origins of gang culture are fascinating and the chapters on sex rather less so, but the material on his famous conflict with Time Warner over his 'Cop Killer' song provides a unique account of a classic music-biz confrontation between a street hustler with a story to tell and a megacorporation with assets to protect.

The Sex Revolts (1995) by Simon Reynolds and Joy Press. The best and most ambitious of the current crop of books dealing with pop's gender agenda, this transcends the narrow confines of the women-in-rock debate to examine what pop's treatment of sexuality is actually telling us. Sometimes irritatingly rock-centric (black music scarcely gets a look in), it's nevertheless challenging, well argued, and innovative.

DANCE

Susanne Lahusen

Recent dance literature has expanded far beyond biography and technical manuals. Writers have looked at dance from all imaginable angles: dance as a form of communication, dance in its social, political, and cultural contexts, dance in education and therapy. The books here chosen range from general histories of both Western and non-Western traditions in stage and social drama, to biographical accounts and inspirational texts for the teacher and participant.

I would only believe in a God who knew how to dance.

FRIEDRICH NIETZSCHE

The History of Dance (1981) by Mary Clarke and Clement Crisp. A comprehensive history, covering more than 2,000 years and crossing many cultural boundaries, that illustrates how dance has always played an important role in every society.

Ballet and Modern Dance (1988) by Susan Au. A concise and lucid text, vividly describing the great performers and performances of the past, as well as exploring today's Western theatre dance.

Time and the Dancing Image (1988) by Deborah Jowitt. A fascinating account of how European and American theatrical dance has evolved in its social and cultural settings during the last two centuries.

Let's Dance: Social, Ballroom and Folk Dancing (1978) by Peter Buckman. Amusing anecdotes, lively descriptions, a useful glossary – a superbly illustrated compendium of social, ballroom and folk dancing.

Rhythm in Joy: Classical Indian Dance Traditions (1987) by Leela Samson. An introduction to the variety and richness of five of India's classical dance forms.

The Black Tradition in American Dance (1989) by Richard Long. A beautifully illustrated book which looks at the African-American contribution to social and theatre dance from the early minstrels to the Dance Theatre of Harlem.

The World of Diaghilev (1971) by John Percival. A book on the great impresario who had become the focal point for many leading artists of the early 20th century.

Martha, the Life and Work of Martha Graham (1991) by Agnes De Mille. Probably the most interesting of the numerous biographies of the famous modern dancer and choreographer, and an insider's view of the American modern-dance scene.

In Touch with Dance (1993) by Marion Gough. A stimulating book encouraging teachers to make the dance lesson a dynamic and highly creative experience for young people.

THEATRE

WORLD THEATRE – *Graham Ley*

Study and appreciation of the theatre have expanded in recent decades from close attention to scripts and plays to a consideration of performance. In this reading list I have concentrated on introductions with that emphasis, accepting that readers may wish to 'travel' in their interests outside Britain and Europe, and back from the present to the past. Illustrations are undoubtedly important in any appreciation of performance, and, with some specific exceptions, the books listed here are helpful in that respect.

By whatever means it is accomplished, the prime business of the play is to arouse the passions of the audience so that by the route of passions may be opened up new relationships between a man and men, and between men and Man.

ARTHUR MILLER

Theatre Through the Ages (1975) by Cesare Molinari. A clear and coherent presentation, with excellent illustrations, that concentrates on Europe.

Illustrated Encyclopedia of World Theatre (1977) edited by Martin Esslin. A broad introduction edited by one of the most impressive of modern critical thinkers on the theatre.

Illustrated History of British Theatre (1994) by Simon Trussler. An ambitious and informative new survey of British theatre from its beginnings to the present day.

Shakespeare's Theatre (1992) by Peter Thomson. The second edition of an excellent and thoroughly readable introduction to the Elizabethan and early Jacobean theatrical performance.

A Short Introduction to the Ancient Greek Theatre (1991) by Graham Ley. A companion for those particularly interested in the performance of Greek tragedy and comedy.

The New Comedy of Greece and Rome (1985) by Richard Hunter. An excellent introduction to the forms of Greek and Roman comedy which anticipate modern social comedy.

The Cambridge Guide to Asian Theatre (1993) by James Brandon. An excellent, short introduction to the immense range of theatrical performance in Asia by a leading expert.

Indian Theatre: Traditions of Performance (1990) edited by Farley Richmond and others. A thoughtful appreciation, in informative detail, of traditions which include a strong emphasis on dance as well as drama.

The Cambridge Guide to African and Caribbean Theatre (1994) by M Banham and others A new survey of drama and theatre practice which offers an unparalleled introduction.

A Dictionary of Theatre Anthropology (1990) by E Barba. This look at intercultural theatre practice and experiment has fascinating illustrations.

The Director and the Stage (1982) by E Braun. On the art of the director.

British Theatre Design: The Modern Age (1989) by J Goodwin. This has superb illustrations, and is a good starting point for an interest in this aspect of theatre.

SHAKESPEARE – *Derek Parker*

One of Dr Johnson's chief regrets at being mortal was the thought of leaving this world for one in which Shakespeare's works were no longer available. I am on his side. A good edition of the *Complete Works* is an essential: probably in the celebrated Arden edition, though there are plenty of handy individual paperbacks of the plays and poems. Shakespeare is quite simply inexhaustible: and if the time comes when you think you have exhausted him, there is a long line of critics and biographers to remind you that far from touching bottom, you are still splashing in the shallows. My favourite biography is Samuel Schoenbaum's wonderful *Shakespeare: A Documentary Life*, which came out in 1975 and reproduced every contemporary document remotely connected with the poet. This is sadly long out of print, but is well worth seeking out; and happily, Professor Schoenbaum has followed it up with a simpler edition, *William Shakespeare: A Compact Documentary Life* (1977). As for the rest, we shall never be able to put our hand on Shakespeare's shoulder, but through the plays, the criticism, the biographies, we can make an effort to clutch at his sleeve – and sometimes seem to feel it flutter in our grasp, across four centuries.

Shakespeare's writing was a magic circle in which he himself could only tread ... He invented a work which was peculiar to himself, and not to be compared with the productions of any writer of any nation – in which he had no follower nor second.

SAMUEL TAYLOR COLERIDGE

Shakespeare: A Documentary Life (1975) by Samuel Schoenbaum. Contrary to popular belief, we know a great deal about Shakespeare's life – perhaps more than about any other Elizabethan except the Queen herself. Schoenbaum gives it to us straight: no interpretation, no guesses – just the facts.

Going to Shakespeare (1978) by J C Trewin. Trewin saw every notable Shakespearean production between 1920 and 1980; his comments on the plays are based on *performance*, and in this book he shows us *how they work*, illuminating many a scene by remembering how Laurence Olivier declaimed a particular speech, or how Godfrey Tearle moved on a particular line. For sheer insight, this beats many a scholarly tome hollow.

Young Shakespeare (1988) and *Shakespeare: The Later Years* (1992) by Russell Fraser. There are more lives of Shakespeare in and out of print than the strongest man could shake the largest number of sticks at; these two are among the most accessible. There is a certain amount of conjecture, but it is sensible conjecture, and Fraser not only presents all the alternatives, but supports the most likely with good argument – and gives us at the same time some excellent background to the age.

Shakespeare: Court, Crowd and Playhouse (1993) by François Laroque. A charming little book which gives us a vivid picture of life in Shakespeare's time – with excellent and often unusual illustrations – and a selection of the most important contemporary documents.

The Elizabethan World Picture (1943) by E M W Tillyard. One of the difficulties about reading Shakespeare is his age is so remote to us: his anti-Semitism and vivid chauvinism ring strangely in our ears. Professor Tillyard helps us over all the stiles with an insight into the Elizabethan world which is dazzlingly interesting as well as illuminating.

The Characters of Shakespeare's Plays (1817; recent editions available) by William Hazlitt. Hazlitt was perhaps the most sympathetic of all 19th-century critics of Shakespeare. Wonderfully readable, his opinions have dated little – and he is man enough to know when he is beaten: he wishes he did not have to write about *Lear*, because 'all that we can say must fall far short of the subject'.

Shakespeare's Workmanship (1918) by Arthur Quiller-Couch. Here is a critic who, first beaten down by F R Leavis, has remained stubbornly out of fashion; but there are few writers about Shakespeare's plays in whose company I would rather be. Quite simply and above all, the king of enthusiasts, he makes you *want* to read the man.

Prefaces to Shakespeare (1923–47) by Harley Granville Barker. Barker, one of the great Shakespeare directors of all time, sadly failed to write prefaces to all the plays; but those he did prepare are among the great examples of practical Shakespeare criticism.

A Notebook on William Shakespeare (1948) by Edith Sitwell. Nobody would now put forward Edith Sitwell as a great critic, but her devotion to Shakespeare gave her quirky insights and a sense of excitement which raise the short hairs on the back of the neck.

ELIZABETHAN AND JACOBEAN DRAMA
Derek Parker

The best option is, of course, to read about the plays and then see them in performance. However, the best dramas can well bear reading as well as seeing, and there is beauty in Marlowe, fun in Ben Jonson, darkness and horror in John Webster and Thomas Middleton which delight and intrigue almost as much on the page as on the boards. If the Elizabethans had an unequalled way with language, the harsher, more astringent tragedies of the Jacobeans can be as exciting – and in the absence of novels, bring their period alive with quite extraordinary brilliance.

Great drama is the souvenir of the adventures of a master
among the pieces of his own soul.

GEORGE JEAN NATHAN

Five Pre-Shakespearean Comedies (1934) edited by F S Boas. Among these, Nicholas Udall's *Ralph Roister Doister* 1553 is the earliest known English comedy, about the courting of the Widow Custance, and Henry Medwall's *Fulgens and Lucrece* 1486 the earliest 'straight' secular play. They show a distinct debt to the ancient Greek and Roman dramatists, though thoroughly anglicised.

The Collected Plays (1590–1604; several modern editions) by Christopher Marlowe. The bloodshed, treachery and titanic ambition of *Tamburlaine the Great*, the isolated pathos of *Edward II*, and above all the tragic, ironical dignity and majesty of *Doctor Faustus*, make Marlowe's plays pioneering works for their time, and a considerable influence on Shakespeare.

The Collected Plays (1598–1631; several modern editions) by Ben Jonson. 'O rare Ben Jonson!' says the stone over his grave in Westminster, and if his plays now seem stronger in production than on the page, *The Alchemist* and *Bartholomew Fair* repay reading, bringing the London of the early 1600s vividly alive – swindlers and mountebanks, lawyers and pickpockets, idle women and busy gossips.

Early English Stages (1959) by Glynne Wickham. To understand fully just how the Elizabethan dramas appeared on the stages of the time, we need to know about the boy players, methods of staging, the theatrical politics of the time, the rivalries between the various companies – and how the productions slowly began to take a form we would recognize today.

English Plays and Players (1956) by G B Harrison. A fascinating survey of the 35 years or so which comprised the great period of Elizabethan drama – that is, from the writing of Marlowe's *Tamburlaine* in the 1580s to Shakespeare's *Hamlet* at the turn of the century, with just a few reputable dramas in the following 15 years. Stage and university, the boy players, the lives of Jonson, Marlowe, Robert Greene, Essex's rebellion ... all written with vigour and commitment.

The Rise of the Common Player (1962) by M C Bradbrook. It takes a real effort of imagination, now, to believe that a boy could have played Cleopatra or Lady Macbeth; but reading a good account of the actors of the Elizabethan theatre we begin to understand how it may have been – and how the often clumsy comedy must have been leavened by the jigs and knockabout farce of the period.

ENGLISH DRAMA 1700–1900 – *Derek Parker*

Really excellent dramatists were thin on the ground between the end of the Restoration period and the years of the solid, safe Victorian theatre – where nevertheless a number of anti-Victorian dramatists beavered away subversively – Wilde, Shaw, Arthur Pinero, T W Robertson, Henry Arthur Jones managing to entertain but also shock and educate audiences.

We do not go to the theatre like our ancestors to escape from the pressure of reality, so much as to confirm our experience of it.

CHARLES LAMB

Four English Comedies (1950) edited by J M Morrell. Just four plays give us a bird's-eye view of the English theatre between 1606 (when Ben Jonson's *Volpone* was first performed at Lincoln's Inn) and 1777, when Richard Brinsley Sheridan's *The School for Scandal* delighted audiences at Drury Lane. In between are William Congreve's *The Way of the World* 1700 and Oliver Goldsmith's *She Stoops to Conquer* 1773 – four of the best, wittiest, most delightful plays in the language.

Restoration Tragedy (1930) by Bonamy Dobrée. A first-rate survey of the subject, including the work of John Dryden, George Etherege, Thomas Shadwell, and John Vanbrugh – most of whose plays are brilliant comments on the period and its foibles.

The Plays of Oscar Wilde (1892–95) by Oscar Wilde. If there is any British comedy after *She Stoops to Conquer* which can compare with Wilde's *The Importance of Being Earnest* 1895, it is probably one of Wilde's other plays; his theatrical instincts were impeccable, his wit coruscating; here are four plays that are as enjoyable to read as to see.

Our Theatre in the Nineties (1932) by George Bernard Shaw. For a general survey of English drama towards the end of the 19th century, turn to Shaw, who remains the most entertaining (if not always the shrewdest) of all theatre critics, even including the great William Hazlitt. The articles he wrote for the *Saturday Review* between 1895 and 1898 are quite simply wonderful.

Around Theatres (1953) and *More Theatres* (1969) by Max Beerbohm. Beerbohm succeeded Shaw as drama critic for the *Saturday Review*, and his essays lead us gently into the 20th century with articles on all the major plays produced between 1898 and 1910.

BRITISH DRAMA 1900 TO THE PRESENT
Derek Parker

World War I changed the theatre just as it changed everything else; soon came Coward, ready to show the 1920s their own face in *The Vortex* 1924, putting drugs on stage for the first time. There was a brief flirtation with poetic drama, led by T S Eliot and Christopher Fry, with W H Auden and Christopher Isherwood in the wings; Terence Rattigan, with elegant, mannered comedies, bridged the period between the 1930s and the 1950s, when came the new generation – Samuel Beckett, Harold Pinter, Arnold Wesker, John Arden followed by Tom Stoppard, Edward Bond, David Storey, David Hare – and the most fruitful period of English drama for 400 years.

We do not think that a play can be worth acting and not worth reading.

W B YEATS

The Complete Plays of Bernard Shaw (1882–1948; several modern editions) by Bernard Shaw. Here is the Goliath of modern drama, who produced a body of work that cannot be ignored. Few of his plays failed to rouse audiences to argument, from *Widowers' Houses* (and in 1892 a play about a prostitutes' madam and her daughter made a sensation) to *The Apple Cart* 1929, which ends with America pleading to be allowed to rejoin the Commonwealth. It is difficult to conceive of anyone who would not find the majority of these plays amusing and stimulating.

The Voysey Inheritance (1905) and *The Madras House* (1907) by Harley Granville Barker. The former, about a scandal which destroys a family business, and the latter, a feminist social comedy, show what can be done in the way of skilful workmanship (Barker started life as an actor) combined with a strong sense of social values. Read, too, Barker's *Prefaces to Shakespeare* (1923–47), the best of Victorian Shakespearean criticism.

The Collected Plays of Noël Coward (several editions) by Noël Coward. Two of Coward's plays may be (a dangerous prophesy) as near immortal as any writer could hope: *Hay Fever* 1925 and *Private Lives* 1930. These are comedies such as the English stage had not seen since Congreve. But recent productions have shown other, less regarded plays – *Design for Living* (1933) and even *Peace in Our Time* (1949) to be well worth revival.

Rosencrantz and Guildenstern are Dead (1967), **Jumpers** (1972), and **Arcadia** (1994) by Tom Stoppard. All his plays are examples of high wit and dramatic ingenuity. These three at least should be read. Elegance is not a quality we immediately associate with most contemporary playwrights; here it energizes rather than weakens the plays.

The Birthday Party (1958), **The Caretaker** (1960), and **No Man's Land** (1965) by Harold Pinter. *The Caretaker* bears perhaps a stronger resemblance to traditional drama than any other of his pieces. These lead into the writer's private dream world; asked what any line of his play 'means', the author replies that it means what it says, and we must make what we can of that; but few people will read his work without at the very least a puzzled fascination, and at best a feeling of being in the presence of a very considerable dramatist.

Murder in the Cathedral (1935) by T S Eliot. Arguably the best verse drama of our time, though *The Family Reunion* (1939) has fine passages; Eliot wrote three other plays, none of which has found a place in the contemporary repertory.

The Lady's Not for Burning (1949) by Christopher Fry. Fry is the only other verse dramatist since 1900 whose work survives in occasional production; this remains his best play, and still delights through his pleasure in playing with language; but some of his others – notably *A Phoenix Too Frequent* (1946) – are better than some critics allow.

Look Back in Anger (1956) by John Osborne. A seminal play which altered the face of English drama by its rage, invective, emotional conviction, and determination to present on stage the passions of our time. It must be read for that reason, though recent revivals have proved it irredeemably second-rate as drama. *The Entertainer* (1957) is a somewhat better play.

Waiting for Godot (1955) by Samuel Beckett. Many a playgoer went to see *Waiting for Godot* convinced that it was nonsense, only to emerge – perhaps without 'understanding' the play – convinced that s/he had been in the presence of greatness. It now seems easier than it did 40 years ago; *Happy Days* 1962, *End Game* 1958 and others still present difficulties for the literal-minded, but cannot, should not, must not be ignored.

The Norman Conquests (1974) by Alan Ayckbourn. The astonishingly prolific Ayckbourn has probably brought more audiences to the edge of hysteria than any dramatist since Coward. His plays must be seen, but many of their qualities come through on the page – including his amazing ingenuities of construction, and his darkly effective talent for showing us tragedy through the lens of comedy.

AMERICAN DRAMA – *T J Lustig*

'There are no dramatic subjects in a country which has witnessed no great political catastrophes and in which love invariably leads by a straight and easy road to matrimony' – Alexis de Tocqueville, *Democracy in America* (1835). Right about so much else, de Tocqueville was signally wrong in this, for the political and emotional problems of 20th-century American democracy have produced a rich body of dramatic work. The tradition has been a predominantly realist one, though it has often strained that overstretched word well beyond its breaking point. But within its characteristic concentration on the relation between the (mainly middle-class) individual and society, American drama has told the story of the nation from the period of colonial expansion to that of imperial domination. It has dramatized the political in the personal in its treatment of the individual and the family. And it has staged the personal in the political in its analysis of the American dream and its spiritual evacuation. Often concerned with property, violence, truth, and the presence of the past, 20th-century American drama has seen itself both as weapon and as cure.

American drama stages a nation thinking (or not thinking) in front of itself.

MATTHEW ROUDANE

Trifles (1916) by Susan Glaspell. An early one-act play with a poignant and beautifully crafted feminist twist. Glaspell's treatment of women from their own point of view has not been equalled until the more recent works of Marsha Norman and Beth Henley.

Desire under the Elms (1924) and *Long Day's Journey into Night* (1956) by Eugene O'Neill. Precise notations of family conflict, underwritten by an eerie sense of the presence of the past and the hard American landscape. O'Neill's use of language and symbol can seem heavy-handed, but these are works of unparalleled dramatic intensity, crucial statements of the central dynamic forces in American drama.

Waiting for Lefty (1935) by Clifford Odets. With its triumphant final chorus of 'Hello America! ... We're stormbirds of the working class', this is the definitive American agitprop play.

A Streetcar Named Desire (1947) by Tennessee Williams. Unique in its raw intensity, but apparently committed to emotional sensationalism at the cost of any political or philosophical engagement.

Death of a Salesman (1949) and *Broken Glass* (1993) by Arthur Miller. The most powerful, coherent, and ethically engaged of American dramatists, Miller has made his work a long attempt to assert the value of connection, of the individual's profound relation and responsibility to wider communities.

True West (1980) by Sam Shepard. This highly focused treatment of sibling rivalry resonates with American myths.

Fences (1985) by August Wilson. Beginning with family life in the back yard of a black American family, this play goes on to expose inexorably the historical determinants of 20th-century African-American experience.

Oleanna (1992) by David Mamet. Misunderstood by some audiences of the first production as an attack on political correctness, Mamet's latest play is in fact a classic liberal study of the ineluctable corruptions of power.

CINEMA

Stanley Kauffmann

Film books in the English language were relatively scarce until around 1960 when the so-called Film Generation burst forth. To accommodate this phenomenon, publishers began pouring out books. That generation's energy has decreased somewhat as serious consideration of film became less of a novelty and assumed a place in our lives more or less like that accorded older arts. With that settling-down, publication of film books has also declined. The great wave of the 1960s and 1970s produced predictably many inferior books, some of them catchpenny even in their arty pretentiousness, but some valuable works appeared. Now that the very idea of a film literature is established, we can anticipate a steady flow of books – biographies, histories, and criticism, which will always include the theoretical vogue of the moment. Since the cultivated person no longer ignores the treasury of film that is part of our artistic legacy, such a person can increase his or her appreciation of that treasury by judicious reading. Here are some primary suggestions.

On the screen man is no longer the focus of the drama,
but will become eventually the centre of the universe.

ANDRÉ BAZIN

What is Cinema? (1967) by André Bazin and others. Exceptional perception and exceptional commitment to the artistic and spiritual possibilities of film.

Bergman on Bergman (1973) by Stig Björkman, Torsten Manns, and Jonas Sima. Three Swedish film critics interview Ingmar Bergman on his entire career to date. The result is more than a director's biography, it is the summation of a life in art.

Notes on Cinematography (1977) by Robert Bresson. A great director's wisdom, enlightening and, quite often, thrilling.

Film Form and ***Film Sense*** (1957) by Sergei Eisenstein. These two books, here in one volume, are cornerstone works in any serious study of the subject.

The Movies as Medium (1970) edited by Lewis Jacobs. A highly useful conspectus of practical and aesthetic problems.

The Film Encyclopedia (1994) by Ephraim Katz. By far the best one-volume job. Imperfect, like all one-volume encyclopedias on any subject, but still inexhaustibly useful.

American Film Criticism: From the Beginnings to Citizen Kane (1972) edited by Stanley Kauffmann and Bruce Henstell. Reviews of significant American and foreign films at the time of their first appearance in the USA. A chronicle and a commentary.

The Phantom Empire (1993) by Geoffrey O'Brien. A poetic exploration of our conscious and unconscious, our waking lives and our dreams, after the first 100 years of film's existence.

Film History: An Introduction (1994) by Kristin Thompson and David Bordwell. The best one-volume world history. See my comments on Katz.

Stage to Screen (1949) by A Nicholas Vardac. A vivid account of the growth of the cinematic impulse through the 19th-century popular theatre until the flowering of the film itself.

PHOTOGRAPHY

Susan Sontag

To write about photography, as I discovered when I was writing my own essays on the subject, is nothing less than to write about the world. There is no activity that is distinctively modern which so evidently touches on and obliges us to confront the principal issues of modernity – political, moral, and aesthetic. We all take photographs or think we could or should. More important, we all understand a great deal of the world – indeed, reality itself – through the medium of, and by the standards set by, photographed images. Resisting the temptation to use my allotment of recommendations to cite some contemporary favourite books of photographs, from *The Americans* (1958) by Robert Frank to *The Silence* (1995) by Gilles Peress, I've chosen instead to list a number of books which can give the curious reader a complex sense of the history of photography and the rich debate about the many issues raised by its imperious scope.

Earlier much futile thought had been devoted to the question of whether photography is an art. The primary question – whether the very invention of photography had not transformed the entire nature of art – was not raised.

WALTER BENJAMIN

Looking at Photographs (1973) by John Szarkowski. One hundred pictures from the collection of the Museum of Modern Art chosen and commented on by John Szarkowski, the director of the Department of Photography at MoMA for several decades and a leading influence in the formation of contemporary photographic taste.

Art and Photography (1968) by Aaron Scharf. A rapid, lucid historical overview of the relation between photography and other visual arts, particularly painting.

Photographers on Photography (1966) edited by Nathan Lyons. An anthology of statements by some of the great photographers, starting from the turn of the century. Among those included are Alfred Stieglitz, Berenice Abbott, Man Ray, Ansel Adams, Paul Strand, Henri Cartier-Bresson, and Robert Frank.

Photography in the Modern Era (1989) edited by Christopher Phillips. A more ample collection of statements by important photographers and critical writings and manifestoes about photography covering the period from 1913 to 1940. The critics (many of them visual artists in their own right) and photographers are all European. Among them are Jean Cocteau, Laszlo Moholy-Nagy, August Sander, Alexander Rodchenko, and F T Marinetti.

Photography in Print (1981) edited by Vicki Goldberg. Another anthology of statements by photographers and critics, this one covering the whole history of photography from Niépce and Fox Talbot forward. Perhaps not surprisingly (so rich is this literature), there is hardly any overlap between the documents selected for this anthology and the two listed above.

On Photography (1977) by Susan Sontag. A cycle of six essays written between 1973 and 1976 about some of the problems, aesthetic and moral, posed by the omnipresence of photographed images. The first book-length consideration in English on photography as such.

Camera Lucida (1980) by Roland Barthes. One of the last books by the great French critic, and a highly personal, partly autobiographical, meditation on the pathos and seductiveness of certain kinds of photographed images.

The Waking Dream (1993) by Maria Morris Hambourg and Pierre Apraxine (curators). The catalogue for the exhibition in 1993 at New York's Metropolitan Museum of Art of selections from the Gilman Paper Company holdings, which may be the world's most beautiful and original private photography collection. The span of the collection, which includes great photographs by unknown photographers as well as little-known masterpieces by most of the great names, is from 1839, the inception of photography, to the 1930s.

The Photographic Experience, 1839–1914: Images and Attitudes (1993) by Heinz K Henisch and Bridget A Henisch. A sophisticated, sociologically alert retelling of the complex development of photography in all genres: as art, as commerce, as an adjunct to science and to the exercise of political power.

Photography Against the Grain: Essays and Photo Works 1973–1983 (1984) by Allan Sekula. An incisive early example of the recent literature on the ideological implications, frequently conformist, of the taking of photographs in many conventional contexts.

FASHION

HISTORY OF FASHION – *Jacqueline Herald*

The first histories of dress were published in the 19th century. They focused on period costume and were used as a visual reference source for theatre designers and artists depicting historical themes. In the early 20th century, more radical texts on fashion considered the psychological dimension of dress and identity. More recently, books on historic and contemporary fashion have fallen into four main categories: manuals on cut and construction of historic garments; glossy descriptive books about *haute couturiers*, emphasizing style, texture of fabrics, and ingenious decorative details; educational books with line drawings, presenting a chronology of dress and how it reflects the lifestyle of a particular period; and socio-anthropological studies of dress as cultural system of signs, denoting distinctions of gender, class, and attitude, both individually and collectively.

> *Common sense and most historians of costume have assumed that the demands of either utility, status or sex must have been responsible for the invention of clothing. However ... scholars have recently informed us that the original purpose of clothing was magical.*
>
> ALISON LURIE

A History of Men's Fashion (1993) by Farid Chenoune. Generally fashion histories have focused on women; this is an interesting overview of the development of menswear since the French Revolution.

Adorned in Dreams: Fashion and Modernity (1985) by Elizabeth Wilson. An excellent introduction: a brief history followed by discussion of the industry, eroticism, gender and identity, fashion in the city, popular culture, and dress reform.

Chic Thrills: A Fashion Reader (1992) edited by Juliet Ash and Elizabeth Wilson. A compilation of essays on the language of clothes, the relationship between high fashion and popular culture, and on utopian and alternative dress.

Costume and Fashion: A Concise History (1985) by James Laver. Laver pioneered the study of dress history in the 1960s, setting fashion in the context of cultural and economic change.

Dress and Morality (1986) by Aileen Ribeiro. A historical inquiry into attitudes towards extravagance and modesty and how individuals, church, and state affected the clothed image.

Dress and Gender: Making and Meaning (1992) edited by Ruth Barnes and Joanne B Eicher. An intriguing range of anthropological case studies on the meaning of apparel and textiles in determining women's status within different cultures around the world.

Fashion, Culture and Identity (1992) by Fred David. A sociological analysis of what makes the fashion industry tick, partially based on interviews with fashion designers.

Fashions of a Decade: 1920s to 1990s (1991–93) by Patricia Baker, Vicky Carnegie, Yvonne Connikie, Maria Constantino, Elane Feldman, Jacqueline Herald. Aimed at teenagers, lively, with images of the period and newly commissioned illustrations. Succinct text, nevertheless introduces many aspects of fashion history. A good starting point for the younger reader.

Seeing Through Clothes (1975) by Anne Hollander. Discusses the history of different ways of depicting people, attitudes of the period, especially in historic painting and sculpture.

The Face of Fashion (1993) by Jennifer Craik. An up-to-date sociocultural approach; well argued and accessible text on how identities are communicated through clothes.

20TH-CENTURY FASHION AND STYLE
Jacqueline Herald

The study of dress style is currently in vogue. In the last decade or so more books dedicated to fashion designers and looks have been published than ever before. Some are glossy picture books on the creations of a particular couturier; others are fun visual references to the story of a particular garment or cult accessory (the Hawaiian shirt, the necktie, the handkerchief). Other books concentrate on the means of creating a particular image, through fashion photography or illustration. There are also the more flippant manuals or style, taken seriously by some dedicated followers of fashion, which guide the reader about what to wear, where to buy, either for a particular social occasion or an effect – Madonna look-alike, for example. Other, more serious studies include reference dictionaries on design and designers and more discursive texts on the meaning of style among different class, age, and cultural groups.

A style does not go out of style as long as it adapts itself to its period. When there is an incompatibility between the style and a certain state of mind, it is never the style that triumphs.

COCO CHANEL

The Fashion Conspiracy (1988) by Nicholas Coleridge. A lively, gossipy, and highly entertaining account of the top designers' fashion empires, from catwalk to sweatshop, written by the editor of *Harpers and Queen* magazine.

Jocks and Nerds (1989) by Richard Martin and Harold Koda. This is a witty visual history of men's fashion in the 20th century. It examines the leaders of style within social types and the particular looks associated with them, including the Cowboy, the Military Man, the Rebel, Joe College, the Businessman, and the Man about Town.

Fashion Sourcebook (1988) by Amy de la Haye. A general directory of the key people, ideas, and looks in 20th-century fashion.

Street Style (1994) by Ted Polhemus. The book of the Victoria and Albert Museum exhibition of that name, tracing the transition of subcultural dress from sidewalk to catwalk. It looks at punks, New Romantics, New Age travellers, and other groups which have hit the music stage and the news headlines and then influenced mainstream fashion in modified forms.

Women of Fashion (1991) by Valerie Steele. A look at some of the most influential women in the world of fashion in this century, including the great Coco Chanel and Elsa Schiaparelli.

Cult Objects (1985) by Deyan Sudjic. The 'yuppie' 1980s is the period in which, arguably, conspicuous consumption adopted an unprecedented degree of status for everyone. Cult looks and individual credibility did not just depend on clothes, but on the gadgets and accessories worn or displayed with them. Sudjic discusses with humour and irony the reasons behind the language of Rolex watches, Anglepoise lamps, four-wheel drive vehicles in town, and dress classics such as Levi 501s and the Burberry raincoat.

CRAFT AND DESIGN

HISTORY OF CRAFTS – *Jacqueline Herald*

There are numerous books on the crafts, which fall into distinct categories. Potted histories can be found in dictionaries of decorative arts, which are useful for general reference: more detailed and often generously illustrated books on craft are devoted either to a particular craft discipline or the types of objects most closely associated with it (such as textiles, ceramics, jewellery), or to a particular country or culture. In an industrial or postindustrial world, the crafts are often viewed with nostalgia, being perceived as traditional and handmade from natural materials, even though contemporary craft practice incorporates machines, computers, and synthetic media. A very large proportion of the books available are of the 'how to do it' type, extremely instructive but sometimes lacking in imagination.

The story of craft is not only the story of man's increasing skill with materials and increasing power over the natural environment; it provides in addition, evidence of the way in which society itself has developed. Men often define themselves through the skills they acquire, and the uses to which they put them.

EDWARD LUCIE-SMITH

World Crafts (1992) by Jacqueline Herald. Written in collaboration with Oxfam Trading, this explains the processes and meaning behind crafts from around the world, particularly in developing countries where women especially have turned to craft as a means of generating income. It explains the reasons for changes to traditional designs in adapting products to the Western tourist and export markets.

The Story of Craft (1981) by Edward Lucie-Smith. To the expert, this is an infuriatingly general history. However, it is a worthwhile introduction to the craftsperson's role in society from the ancient world to today's craft revival. The focus is Europe, but Islam and the Far East are discussed for their contribution to craft skills and organization, and in relation to modern craft movements.

International Crafts (1991) edited by Martina Margetts. This is a compendium of the best of contemporary craft from around the world, covering many different techniques and media. Although highly selective, it is a useful survey and includes a good introductory essay on the state of crafts in the late 20th century.

The Unknown Craftsman (1989) by Soetsu Yanagi. Subtitled 'A Japanese Insight into Beauty', this book by the poet and art critic Yanagi, who was close to the British potter Bernard Leach and to the Japanese potter Shoji Hamada, questions the value of handwork. He was instrumental in the 1920s in cultivating the appreciation of Japanese folk art as the country was rapidly industrializing. His collection of folk art became the nucleus of the Mingei-kan, the Japanese Folk Art Museum in Tokyo. The questions raised have a universal relevance in that they consider the artistic role of the studio-based maker within a mechanized world.

Women and Craft (1987) by Gillian Elinor and others. A feminist look at women's craft as personal creativity in domestic and professional settings.

DESIGN – *Guy Julier*

Since its inception as a professional activity in the late 19th century, design has been a haphazard activity. In bridging the gap between the conception and execution of objects, designers have invariably moved between the creative and the formulaic, the intellectual and the manual, the cultural and the commercial. Its lack of 'rules' or professional norms is mirrored in the breadth of design writing. In its early form, design publications sought professional legitimacy by drawing on traditional modes of architectural and art criticism and history. Design was explained as the result of the work of individual 'hero' designers. However, in recent years, with the development of design history and criticism as a separate academic discipline, design writing has taken in a broader range of perspectives. On the one hand writers have sought explanations for the look or existence of artefacts in terms of their production, taking into account such aspects as technology, materials, the organization of labour, and distribution systems. Consumption has also been taken into account: thus design has begun to be read from the point of view of the user's experience. This may range from the very scientific approach within ergonomics to the more theoretical readings of the role of desire and fantasy in consumerism, informed by a psychoanalytical approach. It remains clear, however, that with the growing professionalization of design practice and its ascendant academic status, the historical gap between its practice and criticism is narrowing.

Design has a twofold relation, having in the first place, a strict reference to utility in the thing designed; and secondarily, to the beautifying or ornamenting that utility. The word design, *however, with the many has become identified rather with its secondary than with its whole signification – with ornament, as apart from, and often even as opposed to, utility. From thus confounding that which is in itself but an addition, with that which is essential, has arisen many of those great errors in taste which are observable in the works of modern designers.*

HENRY COLE, 1849

Pioneers of the Modern Movement (1936) by Nikolaus Pevsner. Republished as *Pioneers of Modern Design* 1960. Invariably invoked as the first design-history book to be published, Pevsner's account tracks the development of design practice and ideas from the doctrines of William Morris in the late 19th century to the Modernist canons of Walter Gropius in the 1920s. Relying on an account of individual architect/designers, the book assesses each of them in terms of their contributions towards Modernism as the zenith of design.

Mechanization Takes Command: A Contribution to Anonymous History (1948) by Sigfried Giedion. Whereas Pevsner was clearly a Modernist, Giedion's history of design is that of a technological determinist. His study tracks the rise of the designer and designed objects as the result of developments in industrial production and materials technology.

Theory and Design in the First Machine Age (1960) by Reyner Banham. This lively text suggests that the history of design in the early 20th century was not so much a development to a purist aesthetic as Pevsner had argued. Rather, the pioneer European modernists were in fact responding to the exciting new challenges of technological development such as transportation and electrification.

Objects of Desire (1985) by Adrian Forty. Forty places the history of design within social history. He reads the development of office design as part of the changing patterns of labour, the development of bathrooms through attitudes to hygiene. Thus he retrieves the 'consumer' as a key force in the shaping of design practice and ideas.

An Introduction to Design and Culture in the Twentieth Century (1986) by Penny Sparke. Key developments in design are treated thematically in this inquiry: issues such as education, materials technology, mass consumption, and the rise of consultant design are covered in this global account. The book therefore reveals the eclectic nature of design history.

Twentieth-Century Ornament (1990) by Jonathon Woodham. Lavishly illustrated, this book eschews a discussion of heady design philosophy in favour of popular artefacts – ceramics, textiles, fashion, posters, public monuments, and entertainment architecture. The text analyses interactions between taste and consumerism, the decorative arts, the fine arts and architecture and design, to reveal tensions which invariably give rise to reaffirmations of nostalgia and nationalism in ornament.

A View from the Interior: Feminism, Women and Design (1989) edited by Judy Attfield and Pat Kirkham. Drawing on a range of feminist readings of design and the consumption of design, this discursive book largely centres on women and design in Britain since the mid-19th century. It analyses how views of femininity have been constructed within design as well as the lived experience of women designers and consumers.

Graphic Design: A Concise History (1994) by Richard Hollis. Covering most 20th-century graphic design forms – from the poster to digitization – this whirlwind tour links the major graphic designers to their commercial and theoretical contexts.

Quotations and Sources on Design and the Decorative Arts (1993) by Paul Greenhalgh. This compendium of quotations is arranged thematically and provides a useful short cut to source material as well as key reflections within the historiography of design.

The Meanings of Modern Design (1990) by Peter Dormer. This highly readable critique considers design as the product of economic forces. It then analyses the various, and sometimes contradictory, value systems which define and guide design practice. Thus he discusses such contemporary conceptions as 'craft', 'style', 'engineering', and 'high design'.

Design After Modernism (1986) edited by John Thackara. After two decades of design history and criticism that either confirmed the Pevsnerian approach or struggled free from it, this book brought together a series of texts reflecting the eclecticism of design writing. It also marked the convergence of practice and theory in design – some of its contributors, such as Nigel Coates, were also professional practitioners of design. New challenges to design, such as the development of digitized technologies, were thus brought into the debate for the first time.

Manufactured Pleasures: Psychological Responses to Design (1994) by Ray Crozier. A discursive text which examines the major psychoanalytic theories and subsequently considers how our perception of artefacts is governed by the subconscious.

SCIENCE AND TECHNOLOGY

SCIENCE

GENERAL REFERENCE BOOKS – *Derek Gjertsen*

In 1704 John Harris, a mathematician and cleric, published his *Lexicon Technicum, a Universal Dictionary of Arts and Sciences*, the first comprehensive technical dictionary to be published in Britain. Since then the need for such works has grown enormously. The literature of science has become so vast, and sometimes so technical and unfamiliar, that general readers and experts alike frequently need to consult a reference work of some kind. While each individual science will have its own corpus of detailed reference works, there is also a large class of works covering the whole of science, some of the more important of which are listed below.

The largest encyclopedia which has been at our constant disposition has been the Thu Shu Chi Chheng, *that magnificent collection produced by imperial order in 1726, consisting of 32 sections, 6,109 subsections, and 10,000 chapters ... in some 1,700 volumes.*

JOSEPH NEEDHAM

McGraw-Hill Encyclopedia of Science and Technology (1994) edited by Sybil P Parker. 20 volumes with 7,500 alphabetically sequenced entries and 50,000 cross-references, *McGraw-Hill* is the most comprehensive work available. Profusely illustrated, it contains both long technical articles and many shorter, more accessible entries.

Chambers Science and Technology Dictionary (1988) edited by Peter M B Walker. A widely available 1,300-page single volume. *Chambers* can be recommended for its comprehensiveness. It also contains a number of useful tables.

Penguin Dictionary of Science (1993) by E B Uvaroa and Alan Isaacs. Although less comprehensive than the Chambers dictionary, the Penguin text is easier for the nonscientist.

Dictionary of the History of Science (1983) by W F Bynum, E J Browne and Roy Porter. Contains more than 700 entries explaining the origins, meaning, and significance of many of the main ideas of science and medicine.

Companion to the History of Modern Science (1989) by R C Olby, G N Cantor, J R Christie and M J S Hodge. An extensive and authoritative survey consisting of 67 essays covering the period 1500–1900. Also discussed are a number of related themes including science and literature, marginal science, science and war, and science and imperialism.

Dictionary of Scientific Biography (1975) edited by Charles C McGraw-Gillispie. 13 volumes, published by Simon and Schuster. The most comprehensive and authoritative dictionary available, though it is only likely to be found in large libraries. Because it excludes living scientists, it is now in need of a major revision.

Biographical Encyclopedia of Scientists (1994) by J Daintith, S Mitchell, E Toothill and D Gjertsen. More accessible and up to date than the Simon and Schuster, this is also the most comprehensive of the currently available dictionaries of scientific biography. It contains accounts of the life and work of over 2,000 scientists from the earliest times to the winners of the 1993 Nobel prizes.

Breakthroughs: A Chronology of Great Achievements in Science and Mathematics (1985) by Claire L Parkinson. The work lists on a year-by-year basis many of the major breakthroughs in science from antiquity until recent times.

GENERAL TEXTS – *Derek Gjertsen*

Science has come to exercise such a profound influence over modern society that its presence can be felt in almost every area of life. One effect of this has been the production of an enormous number of popular works attempting to present science to the general reader. And few in this field have improved upon the mature work of Isaac Asimov. Today there is scarcely an aspect of science, however recondite and technical it might be, that cannot be approached through some popular introduction. At the same time, scholars from what were previously thought to be unrelated fields such as sociology and literature have realized that their own work is incomplete without some understanding of science and its history.

Some 80 or 90 per cent of all scientists that have ever been, are alive now.

DEREK DE SOLLA PRICE

Great Scientific Experiments (1981) by Rom Harré. Harré describes with great lucidity and with numerous illustrations '20 experiments that changed the world'. The experiments discussed include J J Thomson's discovery of the electron, Louis Pasteur's work on artificial vaccines, and Stephen Hales's demonstration that sap circulates in plants.

Science Good, Bad and Bogus (1983) by Martin Gardner. A superb and entertaining defence of science against the attacks and claims of pseudoscientists. The collection includes essays on Uri Geller, the psychic surgery of Arigo, the biorhythms of Fliess, and the claim that quantum theory can justify belief in ESP.

The Two Cultures and a Second Look (1993) by C P Snow. In 1959 C P Snow first argued that many highly educated people had as much familiarity with the Tibetan language as with some of the basic principles of science. His critique of modern education and society, and his argument that the 'two cultures' – the arts and the sciences– need to be brought together, are still relevant.

The Sociology of Science (1973) by Robert Merton. Recent times have seen the creation of the discipline of the sociology of science. The modern founding father of the discipline in Robert Merton, whose writings in this collection of his more important papers show a wit, style, imagination, and judgement rarely found in his followers.

Asimov's Guide to Science (1973) by Isaac Asimov. Dealing with both the physical and the biological sciences, and the basic principles of science as well as the results of the latest researches, Asimov writes with a lucidity and enthusiasm few have ever equalled.

Science and Change 1500–1700 (1972) by Hugh Kearney; **Science and Social Change 1700–1900** by Colin Russell. These two works, though written about different periods and in different styles, show how developments in science have produced changes not only in such obvious fields as warfare and navigation, but in the structures of society itself and in the ways in which we see the world around us and our place within it.

Darwin's Plots (1983) by Gillian Beer. Beer was one of the first scholars to show how much the imaginative literature of a period can be deeply influenced by the science of the day. The work of George Eliot and Thomas Hardy in particular, she argues, pursue explicitly Darwinian themes.

The Art of the Soluble (1967) by Peter Medawar. A collection of essays in which Medawar argues that if politics is the art of the possible, then science is the art of the soluble. The collection also contains Medawar's ruthless destruction of the theories of Teilhard de Chardin.

Popper (1973) by Brian Magee. A brief and clear introductory account of the work of Karl Popper, one of the most influential philosophers of science.

Little Science, Big Science (1963) by Derek de Solla Price. A pioneering and entertaining attempt to show how the growth, value, and productivity of science can be objectively measured.

HISTORY OF SCIENCE – *Derek Gjertsen*

In the past historians have tended to see in science an uninterrupted advance to ever more and deeper truths about ever more aspects of nature. In the process, it was thought, poverty, disease, and superstition would simply disappear from the face of the Earth. But it is only too apparent that superstition, disease, and poverty are as entrenched as ever, while many previously lauded scientific truths have turned out to be simple errors. Consequently, contemporary historians of science are more concerned with understanding how science changes – what factors, for example, have influenced the acceptance and rejection of particular theories. They are further concerned to understand the supposed uniqueness of the scientific revolution and why this crucial process seems to have occurred in the West alone.

New systems of nature were but new fashions, which would vary in every age; and even those who pretended to demonstrate them from mathematical principles would flourish but a short time, and be out of vogue when that was determined.

JONATHAN SWIFT

The Rise of Scientific Europe 1500–1800 (1991) by David Goodman and Colin A Russell. This richly illustrated text is probably the best single-volume general work for the period in question. It is of particular interest in dealing with science in such so-called 'fringe' areas as Sweden and the Iberian peninsula, countries usually ignored in most earlier histories of science.

The Cambridge Illustrated History of the World's Science (1983) by Colin Ronan. A more comprehensive work that the Goodman and Russell text, Ronan's history covers the period from the origin of science in antiquity to recent times. Most unusually, it also has separate chapters on Chinese science, Arabian science, and Indian science.

The Revolution in Science 1500–1750 (1983) by A Rupert Hall. Historians have long tried to understand the nature and origin of the apparently unique scientific revolution. Hall provides a classic survey of the problem and explores the extent to which the revolution can be derived from the structure of European society. He concludes that no particular reason can be singled out since 'every feature of European civilization was a contributing factor'.

The Classics of Science (1984) by Derek Gjertsen. The work deals with 12 classic scientific texts ranging in time from the *Elements* of Euclid to Darwin's *Origin of Species*. The contents of the 12 works are analysed and described, placed in their historical context and their subsequent publishing history recounted.

The Structure of Scientific Revolutions (1962) by T S Kuhn. One of the most important and influential work on the history and philosophy of science published this century. Kuhn's book argued that science alternated between periods of 'normal' science, when scientists work within the confines of a particular paradigm, and 'revolutionary' periods, when the old paradigm is overthrown and replaced by a new model.

Science and Religion (1991) by John Hedley Brooke. An authoritative discussion of the interaction between science and religion from Galileo to the 1980s. Brooke shows that the boundaries between religion and science have frequently shifted and that past attempts to see nothing but conflict in their relationship are merely partisan.

The Fontana History of Science. The following four volumes on this ongoing series had been published by 1995: ***Chemistry*** (1992) by William Brock; ***The Environmental Sciences*** (1992) by Peter Bowler; ***Technology*** (1994) by Donald Cardwell; ***Astronomy and Cosmology*** (1994) by John North. Further volumes on mathematics, physics, biology, and medicine will appear in due course. The volumes published so far, while incorporating the results of much recent scholarly research, have remained admirably readable.

Augustine to Galileo: Science in the Middle Ages (1952) by A C Crombie. Crombie's work is still the most easily available and accessible account of medieval science. It covers the period from the 5th to the 17th century and is most notable for displaying long-ignored continuities between medieval and 17th-century science.

The Shorter Science and Civilisation of China (1978–) by Colin Ronan. Four volumes, covering mathematics, astronomy, physics, and engineering have already appeared of this abridgement of Joseph Needham's *Science and Civilisation in China*. It provides in a readable form an account of the development of science in China and argues that science was not the exclusive invention of Western scholars.

MATHEMATICS

INTRODUCTION – *Ian Stewart*

The big problem with school mathematics, apart from the way it puts most people off the subject for life, is that it gives the impression that there are no problems left to solve. Real mathematics is far broader, and more vigorous, than most of us ever imagine. The difficulty is to make contact with genuine mathematics without getting submerged in technical details. All these books manage to achieve just that.

Only an elephant or a whale gives birth to a creature whose weight is 70 kilograms or more. The President's weight is 75 kilograms. Therefore the President's mother was either an elephant or a whale.

STEFAN THEMERSON

The Mathematical Experience (1981) by Philip J Davis and Reuben Hersh. Best-selling book about what it is like to be a mathematician, for people who aren't.

3.1416 and All That (1985) by Philip J Davis and William G Chinn. A witty collection of short, simple items on all aspects of mathematics.

Mathematics, the Science of Patterns (1994) by Keith Devlin. Highly illustrated, in the Scientific American Library series. Gives an overview that is strong on both ancient and recent history.

For All Practical Purposes (1994) edited by Solomon Garfunkel. The book of a US TV series that brought real mathematics to the people. Highly illustrated and very up to date.

Mathematics, a Human Endeavour (1994) by Harold R Jacobs. Subtitled 'A book for those who think they don't like the subject', it has sold over a million copies because it *is*.

Invitation to Mathematics (1992) by Konrad Jacobs. Based on a course called 'Mathematics for Philosophers' at Erlanger-Nuremberg University: it assumes no more than high-school mathematics.

e, The Story of a Number (1994) by Eli Maor. The only book I know whose hero is a number other than pi – and a fascinating historical tour through large chunks of the mathematical scenery.

Innumeracy (1988) by John Allen Paulos. The surprise *New York Times* best seller that sharpens your mathematical grip on the everyday world.

The Most Beautiful Mathematical Formulas (1992) by Lionel Salem, Frédéric Testard, and Coralie Salem. Tackles formula-aversion head on by making formulas the focus of the story: accessible, strewn with cartoons.

Concepts of Modern Mathematics (1975, 1995) by Ian Stewart. I wrote this 20 years ago when 'modern mathematics' was just coming into schools: it's just been reissued.

NUMBERS – *Ian Stewart*

The most fundamental concept in mathematics is number. Ignore logicians and philosophers who try to tell you otherwise and start waffling about sets and propositions – numbers are where it all started. And numbers lead on to higher things, among them combinatorics (sophisticated counting) and algebra (general properties of numbers and other numberlike entities). All are represented here, but good old-fashioned numbers are in the majority.

---

*I once had a conversation with a doctor who, within approximately
20 minutes, stated that a certain procedure he was contemplating
(a) had a one-chance-in-a million risk associated with it; (b) was
99 per cent safe; and (c) usually went quite well.*

JOHN ALLEN PAULOS

A History of Mathematics (1968) by Carl B Boyer. An extremely well-written
account of the history of mathematical thought, offering many insights into numbers.

Descartes' Dream (1986) by Philip J Davis and Reuben Hersh. How numbers behind
the scenes rule our world, and whether that is a Good Thing.

A First Course in Abstract Algebra (1989) by John B Fraleigh. Algebra from the
modern abstract viewpoint, for those who want to know what's involved.

Concrete Mathematics (1994) by Ronald L Graham, Donald E Knuth, and Oren
Patashnik. Combinatorics – the art of counting – from the viewpoint of computer science.
Worth reading for the students' marginal notes alone.

Number (1991) by John McLeish. An often idiosyncratic but highly readable account
of the origins and developments of the number concept.

Beyond Numeracy (1991) by John Allen Paulos. How numbers feed into more general
mathematical ideas, presented as a series of quick bites at a variety of simple topics.

Elementary Number Theory (1988) by Kenneth H Rosen. An undergraduate-level
text that can be read by anybody interested in the deeper properties of numbers.

Galois Theory (1989) by Ian Stewart. Galois was a colourful character who proved
that the equation of the fifth degree cannot be solved and was killed in a duel over a
woman. Read it for its history and the pictures.

Galois' Theory of Algebraic Equations (1988) by Jean-Pierre Tignol. An accessible discussion of what led up to Galois' epic work on equations of the fifth degree and higher.

The Penguin Dictionary of Curious and Interesting Numbers (1986) by David
Wells. Arranged in numerical order from –1 to Graham's Number; a collection of curious
facts about every interesting number in existence – and also the first uninteresting one.

GEOMETRY – *Ian Stewart*

Once upon a time geometry was easy, because there was only one of it – the one laid
down in great logical detail by Euclid. Then we began to discover alternatives –
spherical geometry, non-Euclidean geometry, finite geometries ... even topology, a modern arrival that focuses on concepts such as 'inside' or 'knotted' that remain unchanged
when a shape is stretched, bent, or twisted. What do all these disparate geometries have
in common? The visual element, humanity's most powerful mental tool.

---

*Mad Mathesis alone was unconfined / Too mad for mere material chains to bind, /
Now to pure space lifts her ecstatic stare, / Now running round the circle, finds it square.*

ALEXANDER POPE

Introduction to Geometry (1969) by H S M Coxeter. An elegant survey of virtually every area of geometry. Demanding, but worth it.

A Budget of Trisections (1987) by Underwood Dudley. Why angles cannot be trisected with ruler and compasses, and hundreds of attempts to do it despite that. After all, what do mathematicians know about it?

Ideas of Space (1989) by Jeremy Gray. Historical introduction to Euclidean, non- Euclidean, and relativistic models for the shape of the universe.

Euclidean and Non-Euclidean Geometries (1993) by Martin Jay Greenberg. There are more geometries than we usually imagine, and parallel lines need not behave the way we usually think.

Geometry in Nature (1993) by Vagn Lundsgaard Hansen. How geometry sheds light on form in the natural world.

Knot Theory (1993) by Charles Livingston. An excellent introduction to a major area of topology, the geometry of continuous transformations. How to prove that a knot can't be untied.

Poetry of the Universe (1995) by Robert Osserman. The contribution of mathematics to our understanding of the shape of the universe and the physics that goes with it, from Flat Earth to Big Bang.

Fearful Symmetry: Is God a Geometer? (1992) by Ian Stewart and Martin Golubitsky. How the geometrical concept of symmetry is deeply involved in the creation of nature's patterns.

Journey into Geometries (1991) by Marta Sved. Alice in Geometryland.

The Shape of Space (1985) by Jeffrey R Weeks. Exotic geometries stimulated by speculations about the nature of space and time.

FOUNDATIONS OF MATHEMATICS – *Ian Stewart*

Numbers are fundamental to the historical development of mathematics and to the way human beings learn it and think about it. But you can dig down underneath the number concept and turn up ideas upon which it logically rests. The ideas include the notion of a set, and the various disciplines of mathematical logic. These books cover a variety of topics in the philosophy and foundations of mathematics.

And new Philosophy calls all in doubt, / The Element of fire is quite put out, / The Sun is lost, and th'earth, and no mans wit / Can well direct him, where to looke for it.

JOHN DONNE

Founders of Modern Mathematics (1982) by F Gareth Ashurst. Historical account of where modern mathematics came from, and who did it.

Algorithmic Information Theory (1987) by Gregory J Chaitin. What do we really mean by 'random'? One of the great original minds of recent decades provides some surprising answers.

What Is Mathematical Logic (1990) by J N Crossley, C J Ash, C J Brickhill, J C Stillwell, and N H Williams. Technical, readable, and brief account of the basic ideas of mathematical logic and foundations.

Logic and Information (1991) by Keith Devlin. What mathematical logic can tell us about intelligence, knowledge, and the communication of information.

Abraham Robinson (1995) by Joseph Warren Dauben. Extensive biography of one of the founders of modern mathematical logic.

Berkeley's Philosophy of Mathematics (1993) by Douglas M Jesseph. History of one of the great controversialists in the foundations of mathematics, and why he was worried about them.

The Nature of Mathematical Knowledge (1984) by Philip Kitcher. Philosophical analysis of the meaning and significance of mathematics, and the development of its own internal view of what it's all about.

Mathematics and the Search for Knowledge (1985) by Morri Kline. What has mathematical thinking done for humanity, and how has it changed our view of what it means to 'know' something?

Introduction to Mathematical Logic (1964) by Elliott Mendelson. This one *is* technical; but it's a brilliant description of the nuts and bolts of logic and set theory which to my mind has never been bettered.

Sets, an Introduction (1990) by Michael D Potter. Undergraduate textbook providing an unusually accessible introduction to the foundational concepts of set theory. Don't be put off by the apparent level of difficulty.

APPLIED MATHEMATICS – *Ian Stewart*

Today's mathematics is general and abstract, littered with curious ideas invented for their own sakes. Yet it pays its way through applications that range across the whole spectrum of science, and into the humanities, business and medicine ... No corner of human culture is untouched by mathematics. These books mostly describe new and exciting applications of new and exciting mathematics, but a few of the more orthodox applications are represented too.

One factor that has remained constant throughout all the twists and turns of the history of physical science is the decisive importance of mathematical imagination.

FREEMAN DYSON

Fractals Everywhere (1993) by Michael F Barnsley. The intricacies of fractals, a new and beautiful type of geometrical object, and their uses in image compression.

Reality Rules (1992) by John L Casti. How to build mathematical models of the world, solve them, and gain insight into how the universe works.

Symmetry in Chaos (1992) by Michael Field and Martin Golubitsky. Glorious technicolour picturebook of some novel applications of exotic mathematics. Order and chaos combined in a nutshell.

Let Newton Be! (1988) edited by, John Fauvel, Raymond Flood, Michael Shortland, and Robin Wilson. Multi-author volume on the life, works, and influences of Isaac Newton.

Introduction to Physical Mathematics (1985) by P G Harper and D L Weaire. Basic mathematical concepts that prove useful in physics, with plenty of physical motivation.

Complexity (1992) by Roger Lewin. The recent creation of the mathematics of complex adaptive systems, and its implications for evolution, history, economics, and the kitchen sink ...

Fractals, Chaos, Power Laws (1991) by Manfred Schroeder. Some of nature's deepest symmetries are related to changes of scale. This simple insight leads to beautiful and powerful new mathematical theories.

Games of Life (1993) by Karl Sigmund. Applications of mathematics to the games that living creatures play in order to survive, reproduce, and evolve.

Nature's Numbers (1995) by Ian Stewart. The role of mathematics in understanding the world. In the widely praised Science Masters series.

The Geometry of Biological Time (1990) by A T Winfree. How a visual approach to dynamics sheds light on the biological world.

FRONTIERS OF MATHEMATICS – *Ian Stewart*

How can you do research on mathematics? Haven't all the numbers been discovered? Well, no, but that's not really the point. Research mathematics is no more about studying bigger numbers than biology is about making a bigger elephant. It's what you do with the numbers that matters. These books will open your eyes to the enormous breadth, variety, and vigour of mathematics on the front line.

Aelius Donatus (4th century) is quoted by his student St Jerome as saying Pereant qui ante nos nostra dixerum, *freely translated as 'Damn the guys who published our stuff first'.*

RALPH P BOAS JR

The Collapse of Chaos (1993) by Jack Cohen and Ian Stewart. What is the relation between simplicity and complexity in science? The new mathematics of complexity theory, intermingled with biology, physics, and evolution.

Mathematics: The New Golden Age (1988) by Keith Devlin. When was the Golden Age of mathematics? Now!

Mathematics and the Unexpected (1988) by Ivar Ekeland. An elegant little book about modern theories of change and their connections with chance and prediction.

Bridges to Infinity (1984) by Michael Guillen. A friendly, formula-free trip through the human side of mathematical research.

Fuzzy Thinking (1993) by Bart Kosko. How to think precisely about vagueness. If there were a Society of Fuzzy Logicians you would be able to be a 37% member, paying 37% fees and receiving 37% benefits.

Understanding the Infinite (1994) by Shaughan Lavine. The best discussion I know of the philosophy of mathematical theories of the infinite. Tough going in places, but worth the effort.

The Mathematical Tourist (1988) by Ivars Peterson. An extremely readable survey of a variety of areas of frontier research in the mathematical sciences.

Islands of Truth (1990) by Ivars Peterson. Sequel to *The Mathematical Tourist*. More of the same, as you'd expect.

Does God Play Dice? (1989) by Ian Stewart. Best-selling introduction to chaos theory which cuts out the hype and explains the mathematics.

The Problems of Mathematics (1992) by Ian Stewart. A sweeping survey of today's mathematical frontiers, originally aimed at undergraduates. Soon to be reincarnated as *From Here to Infinity*, aimed at everybody.

PHYSICS

INTRODUCTION – *Brian Pippard*

Until the last years of the 19th century, the principal aim of physics was to find the basic rules governing the movement of bodies, and to use them in solving a wide variety of problems, including the practical problems of engineering. Isaac Newton's laws of motion and his discovery of universal gravitation form the heart of this venture, and were followed after a century by the exact description of electric and magnetic processes which culminated in James Clerk Maxwell's linking of light to electromagnetic waves.

The resulting, very nearly consistent, picture of the general behaviour of matter (as distinct from chemistry and other studies of particular forms) is now known as classical physics. It was found to be seriously incomplete with the discovery, between 1895 and 1900, of X-rays, radioactivity, the electron, and the quantum; in 1905 Albert Einstein formulated the relativity principle. From those remarkable ten years has sprung the whole of modern physics, which in no way relegates classical physics to the scrapheap, but delineates its limits of applicability. To grasp the ideas of modern physics and its vast range, from the human scale downwards to atoms and their constituents, and upwards to the very bounds of the cosmos, one must first appreciate how classical physicists discovered what they knew and how they made sense of it.

Although mathematics is the most powerful and convenient language with which to develop the logical consequences of the fundamental laws, one does not need mathematical facility to obtain a good feeling for how success has been achieved.

It behoves us to remember that in physics it has taken great men to discover simple things. They are very great names indeed which we couple with the explanation of the path of a stone, the droop of a chain, the tints of a bubble, the shadows in a cup.

D'ARCY WENTWORTH THOMPSON

General principles of physics:

Physics for the Inquiring Mind (1960) by E M Rogers. An introduction to the general ideas of physics, with much historical detail, aimed at the nonspecialist reader by an outstanding and innovating teacher; copious line drawings by the author.

The Laws of Nature (1955) by R E Peierls. Similar to the above but on a smaller scale, and with more emphasis on relativity and particle physics.

The Character of Physical Law (1965) by R P Feynman. Based on a television series by a great physicist and brilliant expositor. Concentrates on basic concepts such as conservation, symmetry, the concept of time, and probability in quantum physics.

From Falling Bodies to Radio Waves (1984) by E Segrè. A historically based account of classical physics through the achievements of such as Galileo, Isacc Newton, Michael Faraday, Rudolf Clausius, James Clerk Maxwell, and Josiah Gibbs.

The transition from classical to modern physics:

The Evolution of Physics (1938) by Albert Einstein and L Infeld. The greatest of modern physicists describes the developments he pioneered – relativity and quantum physics – as the outcome of earlier achievements.

Order, Chaos, Order (1994) by P Stehle. A largely nontechnical account, with more detailed appendices, of the complex early years of the 20th century during which the perceived weaknesses of classical physics were resolved through the invention of quantum mechanics.

Thermal physics:

The Refrigerator and the Universe (1993) by M and I F Goldstein. Energy and entropy in physics, chemistry, and cosmology (including the greenhouse effect).

The Quest for Absolute Zero: Meaning of Low Temperature Physics (1977) by K Mendelssohn. A nonmathematical account of how very low temperatures are produced, and the phenomena, such as superconductivity and superfluidity, that occur at these extreme conditions.

Matter in all its forms:

The Cambridge Guide to the Material World (1985) by R Cotterill. An extraordinarily wide and copiously illustrated survey of the varieties of matter from fundamental particles to the constituents of plants and animals, taking in crystals, liquids, glasses, polymers, and many others.

Social and political aspects of physics:

The Making of the Atomic Bomb (1986) by R Rhodes. A very full account of the physics, technology, and organization involved in one of the greatest of all industrial ventures, and its appalling outcome.

Biographies of great physicists:

It is hard to make a choice, but the following deserve serious consideration for their breadth of coverage:

Energy and Empire (1989) by C Smith and M N Wise on William Thomson Kelvin;

Rutherford (1983) by D Wilson;

Subtle Is the Lord (1982) by A Pais on Einstein;

Niels Bohr's Times (1991) by A Pais;

Uncertainty (1992) by D C Cassidy on Werner Heisenberg;

The Life of Isaac Newton (1993) by R Westfall. A shorter version of his magisterial *Never at Rest* (1980).

PARTICLE PHYSICS – *Christine Sutton*

Particle physics is the study of the basic building blocks of matter and the forces that act upon them. Over the past 50 years research in this field has shown that the matter we observe is built from only a few elementary particles called quarks and leptons, and that only four fundamental forces operate on these particles to yield the great diversity of the universe. More recently, discovering how these particles and forces evolved in the very early universe has forged intimate links between particle physics, cosmology, and astrophysics, and yielded a remarkable synthesis of ideas.

We now know that in the maelstrom of high density and temperature that existed in the early moments of the universe, only the most primordial objects could exist; any transient combinations, such as protons, let alone molecules, would decompose more quickly than a butterfly in the core of a volcano. It is for this reason that the search for what is elementary underlies both particle physics and the cosmology of the early universe.

LEON LEDERMAN AND DAVID SCHRAMM

The Discovery of Subatomic Particles (1983) by Steven Weinberg. An intriguing discussion of the early history of particle physics. It covers in particular the discoveries of the electron and the atomic nucleus by introducing a number of basic physical principles and emphasizing how they underlie our ability to 'see' within the atom.

Quarks: The Stuff of Matter (1984) by Harald Fritsch. A straightforward account of the peculiar world of quarks and the strong force that binds them together, never to let them appear alone.

The Cosmic Onion: Quarks and the Nature of the Universe (1983) by Frank Close. A first guide to particle physics by a gifted and inspirational lecturer, who presented the Royal Institution's Christmas lectures 1993–94. The many illustrations include photographs, diagrams, and the author's own cartoon quarks.

The Particle Explosion (1987) by Frank Close, Michael Marten, and Christine Sutton. A highly illustrated, loosely historical account describing the different particles and how they were discovered. At the same time it reveals how the field has developed with advances in experimental techniques for making particles and tracking them down.

The Forces of Nature (1986) by Paul Davies. A valuable companion to any of the books that are mainly about quarks, 'building blocks' of matter, this concentrates on the 'mortar'. It provides an introduction to how modern deals with forces at a quantum level.

Particles and Forces: At the Heart of the Matter (1990) edited by Richard Carrigan and Peter Trower. A collection of articles from *Scientific American*, mainly from the 1980s, which brings particle physics into the 1990s. All are good, some are classics.

From Quarks to the Cosmos: Tools of Discovery (1989) by Leon Lederman and David Schramm. An experimental particle physicist and a theoretical astrophysicist team up to show how the physics of the very small has become inextricably linked with our understanding of the universe on cosmic scales. Well illustrated. The emphasis is on what we know through experiment.

Dreams of a Final Theory (1993) by Steven Weinberg. The most eloquent of particle physicists, and a Nobel prizewinner, presents the case for research in particle physics, and in particular the ill-fated Superconducting Supercollider. That this was later cancelled does nothing to detract from the unfolding arguments, but adds poignancy to a tale well told.

The Particle Garden (1994) by Gordon Kane. A fascinating, up-to-date introduction to particle physics, which also presents a personal view of the field as it heads towards the 21st century. It places the present state of understanding in better context than many other books and articles.

QUANTUM THEORY AND RELATIVITY
Stephen Webster

Quantum physics give an atom's-eye view of the world; relativity theory makes the link between space and time, gravity and motion. Both theories are 20th-century developments and both have revolutionized physics. The books listed here reveal some of the peculiarities that these days dominate the working life of a physicist.

When I first came across quantum mechanics I rang my mum and told her: This is it – I'm going to be a physicist.

FROM THE HANDBOOK *CAREERS IN PHYSICS*

No Ordinary Genius (1994) edited by Christopher Sykes. An amply illustrated tribute to Richard Feynman, Nobel prizewinner and pioneer in the understanding of quantum mechanics, who died in 1988.

Genius: Richard Feynman and Modern Physics (1992) by James Gleick. Full-scale biography of the attractive and brilliant Richard Feynman.

The Quantum Self (1990) by Danah Zohar. An encouraging book which attempts to make the links between our understanding of atomic behaviour and our understanding of ourselves.

The Quantum Society (1994) by Danah Zohar and Ian Marshall. This sequel to *The Quantum Self* carries the argument further, making links between the quantum idea and a new and better society.

Schrödinger's Kittens (1995) by John Gribbin. The well-known science writer takes a look at the behaviour of light, and searches for quantum and relativistic interpretations.

Einstein for Beginners (1993) by Joseph Schwartz and Michael McGuinness. A cartoon treatment of the great physicist and his ideas which no one can fully understand. This book will at least get you started, and relatively painlessly.

Relativity for the Layman (1969) by James A Coleman. One of the great classics of popular science, in spite of the sexist title. Written with a sure economy of words, this is a book of great clarity and elegance.

Einstein's Universe (1979) by Nigel Calder. A full account of the history of relativity theory and its implications for the way we understand the universe. Included is enough material about Einstein for the reader to get an idea of what the man was like.

CHEMISTRY

GENERAL – *Julian Rowe*

Getting familiar with what chemistry is all about is more important now, at the end of a century, than at the beginning, when this science was comparatively primitive. Now we need to know why the ozone layer is under chemical attack, why book and magazine printers now choose to use water-based inks, and what the analysis on every packet of food means. Increasingly, the boundaries between different scientific disciplines are blurred: the subtle mixture of chemistry and physics that underlies the manufacture of the microchip means that we are dealing with physics, chemistry, and electronics simultaneously. These books provide a firm basis for pursuing such questions further.

The more we know, the more we feel our ignorance; the more we feel how much remains unknown; and in philosophy, the sentiment of the Macedonian hero can never apply – there are always new worlds to conquer.

HUMPHRY DAVY

A Short History of Chemistry (1937) by J R Partington. A prolific author of textbooks on chemistry and author of a multivolume history. This is a clear and authoritative account of the history of chemistry. It draws on many original sources and although it starts with alchemy and ends with radioactivity and the transmutation of the elements, this excellent and concise book concentrates on the foundation of modern chemistry and the great scientists who lead the way.

Asimov on Chemistry (1975) by Isaac Asimov. In 17 wide-ranging essays this experienced science popularizer effectively covers the entire field of chemistry in an accessible manner. Everything from the chemistry of the planet Earth, inorganic, organic, and nuclear chemistry are entertainingly treated, and there is an essay on the Nobel prizewinners at the end.

The Nature of the Chemical Bond (1940) by Linus Pauling. A double Nobel prizewinner. A classic, perhaps ambitiously included in a general reading list, but showing how real advances in understanding are made as a result of modern chemical research.

The Chemical History of the Candle (1861) by Michael Faraday. Often acknowledged as one of the greatest scientists of all time, during the Christmas holiday (1860–61) Michael Faraday gave a series of talks on physics and chemistry to an audience of young people in London. He engaged their imagination and made them feel the challenges and delights of science. *The Chemical History of a Candle* is clearly one of the best and covers the chemistry of combustion in an original and astonishingly comprehensive way. These talks became an institution and have been given ever since by distinguished scientists over the Christmas period at the Royal Institution, London.

Success in Chemistry (1982) by Jean Macqueen, series editor. One of the brilliant Success Studybooks – really aimed at pre A-level students, but giving an excellent basic, nontrivial coverage of the subject.

The Penguin Dictionary of Chemistry (1990) by D W A Sharp. Useful, updated compendium of definitions of chemical terms. Not just examination fodder.

The Alchemists (1976) by F Sherwood Taylor. The author is a former director of the Science Museum, London. No reading list on chemistry would be complete without a look at the alchemists. Widely misunderstood, much of their pioneering work under-lay the astonishing expansion of chemistry from the 17th century onwards.

The Dorling Kindersley Science Encyclopedia (1994) by Heather Couper and Nigel Henbest (consultants). Covers many topics in chemistry and applied chemistry in a highly illustrated and informative way.

ORGANIC AND INORGANIC CHEMISTRY
Julian Rowe

Inorganic chemistry is probably what most people regard as chemistry – memories of school laboratories, smells, flashes, and bangs. The laboratory scenes beloved by movie directors that show an antiquated distillation apparatus, smoke and bubbling, coloured solutions belong rightly to popular mythology. This reading list should redress the balance.

So it happens, therefore, that every element says something to someone (something different to each) like the mountain valleys or beaches visited in youth.

PRIMO LEVI

The Consumer's Good Chemical Guide (1994) by John Emsley. A good guide, thoroughly dippable – just what its title implies.

Structure and Change – An Introduction to Chemical Reactions (1981) by R A Richardson, A C Blizzard, and D Humphreys. A high-school text that successfully blends a factual and theoretical approach to chemistry. It succeeds in giving an appreciation of the vital role of chemistry in the world.

Usborne Introduction to Chemistry (1983) by Jane Chisolm and Mary Johnson. A highly illustrated and simple introduction to chemistry that covers an amazing amount of ground.

Chemistry in the Service of Man (1925) by Alexander Findlay. A wonderful text from what now seems like a bygone era. Nonetheless it is a substantial introduction to chemistry, very readable, and the chapter on radioactivity and atomic structure, written in the prenuclear age, is particularly absorbing.

Men and Molecules (1960) by Carl R Theiler. What chemistry is and what it does. The author takes the reader through the transformation of first ideas into reality – the building up of mighty industries and the production of astonishing new materials. The reader grows familiar with chemical formulae and their strange names in this well-illustrated book which has a very good glossary.

BIOCHEMISTRY – *Julian Rowe*

To understand what the life sciences are about, some biochemistry is a necessary requirement. Modern biology has travelled a great distance from the observational stance of the naturalist, without, it is necessary to say, in any way invalidating it. The route was certainly via biochemistry. To understand genetics, to understand the molecular sciences or molecular basis of life, start with biochemistry. This list is in part informative, in part a march of progress.

When you cannot measure it, when you cannot express it in numbers,
your knowledge is of a meagre and unsatisfactory kind.

WILLIAM THOMSON KELVIN

A Guide-Book to Biochemistry (1959) by Kenneth Harrison. Many standard books on biochemistry are very thick, 500–1,000 pages. This excellent book is a deliberate exception and provides a good guide that is brief and to the point.

The Physical Basis of Life (1951) by J D Bernal. Based on a prescient lecture delivered to the Physical Society, this speculative survey discussed the conditions under which life may have emerged from an inorganic world – biochemistry in action.

Readings in Molecular Biology by W B Gratzer. Selected from *Nature* by W B Gratzer, these short essays in journalism were aimed at the working scientist and chart the progress of the then emergent branch of science – molecular biology.

Principles of Biochemistry (1993) by A L Lehninger. A comprehensive American undergraduate text, written with masterly clarity. The author properly declares that biochemistry is now the lingua franca of the life sciences, and no one consulting this introductory text should be the poorer for having done so.

Dynamic Aspects of Biochemistry (1967) by E Baldwin. A book that first highlighted the fact that biochemistry is an interesting and a quite different discipline from chemistry. Many thousands of undergraduates must have cut their novice teeth on this particular book and were probably grateful.

APPLIED CHEMISTRY – *Julian Rowe*

There are few products around us at home or at work that do not owe their existence to the ever more sophisticated application of chemistry. From prescribed drugs to paints, better petrol or food analysis, crime detection or perfume – all have at base an understanding of chemistry. These books are selective, but they cover the ground. The general reference works noted in this section are also, of course, equally useful for any inquiry into a subdivision of chemistry.

They leave such things alone and busy themselves with their fires and learning the steps of alchemy, which are distillation, solution, putrefaction, extraction, calcination, reverberation, sublimation, fixation, separation, reduction, coagulation, tinction, and the like.

PARACELSUS

The Life Savers (1961) by Richie Calder. The cover blurb says: 'the enthralling story of today's revolution in medicine – the discovery and development of the life-saving drugs'.

Butter Side Up or The Delights of Science (1978) by Magnus Pyke. Reviewed by the *Evening Standard*: 'An opencast mine of unexpected information that can be understood even by someone who cannot tell a Bunsen burner from a laser beam.'

Chemistry: The Conquest of Materials (1957) by Kenneth Hutton. A good account, by a teacher and author, of the scope of modern chemistry, telling a clear story from the elements to modern drugs. On the way fuels, modern materials such as plastics, pesticides, and explosives are dealt with at a usefully informed level.

Metals in the Service of Man (1972) by W Alexander and A Street. How metals are obtained and worked and the part they play in modern life. An ideal introduction for the general reader.

Plastics in the Service of Man (1956) by E A Cousins and V E Yarsley. A description of the structure, manufacture, properties and the contemporary use of plastics.

Science and Technology (1993) by Open University Press. A good work of reference which covers just what its title implies and includes applied chemistry. Well illustrated and up to date, it is a good volume for browsing.

The following encyclopedias provide sound, accessible articles on a wide range of chemistry topics:

Junior Britannica Surprisingly readable articles on any aspect of science – chemistry and applications thereof covered adequately.

The World Book Covers the ground more than adequately.

ASTRONOMY

COSMOLOGY – *John Gribbin*

Where do we come from? Cosmology deals with the big questions, the origin and evolution of the entire universe, and its ultimate fate. This means that it also deals with our own origins, giving the subject the same fascination for many people as religion or philosophy. And yet, cosmology is one of the youngest sciences. Until the 1920s, no astronomer seriously doubted that the universe was eternal and unchanging. That cosy assumption was overturned by the discovery of universal expansion, leading to the idea of a definite origin in the Big Bang, some 15 billion years ago. Today, cosmologists are even prepared to tackle the question of what happened before the Big

Bang. The books mentioned below will give you the opportunity to peer over their shoulders at this work in progress, and to see how these ultimate questions are being tackled, even if the ultimate answers are not yet in.

Credit must be given to observation rather than theories, and to theories only in so far as they are confirmed by the observed facts.

Aristotle

The Anthropic Cosmological Principle (1986) by John Barrow and Frank Tipler. An exhaustive overview of the cosmos and humankind's place in it, daunting in parts but quite readable if you skip the technical stuff.

Afterglow of Creation (1993) by Marcus Chown. The best book about the 'cosmic background radiation' that fills all of space and is a remnant of the Big Bang itself.

The Creation of the Universe (1952) by George Gamow. Fascinating (if slightly dated) 'horse's mouth' account from one of the pioneers of the Big Bang theory.

In Search of the Big Bang (1986) by John Gribbin. Historical account of the development of cosmology in the 20th century, from the expanding universe to the theory of inflation.

The Stuff of the Universe (1990) by John Gribbin and Martin Rees. The Astronomer Royal, Martin Rees, joins forces with science writer John Gribbin to describe the 'dark matter' that makes up 99% of the universe.

Lonely Hearts of the Cosmos (1991) by Dennis Overbye. The story of the quest for the secret of the origin of the universe, told in terms of the personalities involved. Gives a real flavour of how cosmologists work and think.

Time Machines (1993) by Paul Nahin. Goes beyond the black hole, mixing science fiction and science fact to discuss the extraordinary implication of Albert Einstein's general theory of relativity, that time travel may not be impossible.

Was Einstein Right? (1986) by Clifford Will. The answer, of course, is yes. The most accessible guide to Einstein's theories for the nonscientist.

History of astronomy – *Derek Gjertsen*

More than most exact sciences, astronomy lends itself to historical treatment. For one thing, along with mathematics, it was the first science to establish itself in antiquity and therefore has a longer and more fully documented history than most other sciences. Furthermore, the records of ancient astronomers contain data still valuable to the astronomers of today. But also, as much of modern astronomy changes so rapidly with books becoming out of date within a decade, the only way to estimate the value of any theory or observation is to see it within some kind of historical context. Consequently it is no accident that almost every work on modern cosmology, popular or scholarly, will begin with the structure of the universe proposed by Copernicus in the 16th century and lead via Galileo, Johannes Kepler, and Isaac Newton to the Big Bang.

People give ear to an upstart astrologer who strove to show that the Earth revolves, not the heavens. This fool wishes us to reverse the entire science of astronomy; but sacred scripture commanded the Sun to stand still, and not the Earth.

MARTIN LUTHER ON COPERNICUS

Astronomy and Cosmology (1994) by John North. A new, authoritative, and readable history (part of the excellent Fontana History of Science series), this book covers astronomy from prehistory to Stephen Hawking.

The Sleepwalkers (1960) by Arthur Koestler. Mainly an account of how Copernicus, Kepler and Galileo battled to show that it was the Sun and not the Earth that lay at the centre of the universe. Despite bias against Galileo and some inept theorizing, Koestler's work remains – at the narrative and biographical level – an extraordinarily exciting book.

In Search of Ancient Astronomies (1979) edited by E C Krupp. An account of the astronomical knowledge, techniques, and monuments of neolithic Europe, North and Meso-America, and Egypt.

Megaliths, Myths and Men: An Introduction to Astro-Archaeology (1976) by Peter Lancaster Brown. A critical and expert survey of the supposed astronomical background of Stonehenge, the Pyramids, and several other ancient remains. Lancaster Brown manages to dispose of some of the more outlandish claims commonly made about ancient astronomy.

The Expanding Universe 1900–31 (1982) by Robert Smith. A scholarly but readable account of the theoretical arguments and observational evidence that enabled such astronomers as Edwin Hubble to conclude that the universe is expanding. The same period and argument is covered in the more popular and lavishly illustrated *Man Discovers the Galaxies* (1976) by R Berendzen, R Hart, and Daniel Seeley.

The Great Copernicus Chase and Other Adventures in Astronomical History (1992) by Owen Gingerich. An engrossing collection of 36 short essays ranging from 'Egyptian Sky Magic' to 'The Great Comet of 1965'.

The Astronomical Scrapbook (1984) by John Ashbrook. A fascinating collection of 91 short articles, mainly gleaned from the more curious byways of the history of astronomy, which originally appeared in the popular magazine *Sky and Telescope*.

History of the Telescope (1955) by Henry King. The standard history of the telescope from the earliest times to the 1950s.

The Story of Jodrell Bank (1968) by Bernard Lovell. The story of Lovell's attempts to design, finance, and build a huge steerable parabolic radio telescope. Against all the odds, it was opened in 1957. More detail about the various telescopes built by Lovell can be found in *The Jodrell Bank Telescopes* (1985).

Halley and the Comet (1985) by Peter Lancaster Brown. Probably the best of the many popular works written to commemorate the return of Halley's comet in 1986. It contains historical, biographical, and astronomical material.

A History of Japanese Astronomy (1969) by Shigeru Nakayama. There are, of course, non-Western astronomical traditions. Nakayama provides a sound account of the development of astronomy in Japan. A comparable account for China can be found in *The Shorter Science and Civilisation in China* (1978–94) by Colin Ronan.

PLANETS AND THE SOLAR SYSTEM
Derek Gjertsen

Until the 1960s, books on the Solar System could do little more than describe such grosser features of the planets as their size, mass, and distance from Earth. But with the launch of the Orbiter, Apollo, Mariner, Voyager, and other planetary probes, astronomers could at last speak significantly about the geology, meteorology and history of the planets. They also had access to many stunning colour photographs of planetary surfaces and such remarkable phenomena as the rings of Saturn. As a result, current books on the Solar System are much more plentiful, detailed, and colourful than those produced only a few years before.

It is most beautiful and pleasing to look upon the lunar body distant from us by about 60 terrestrial diameters as if it were distant by only two of these measures. Anyone will then understand that the Moon is by no means endowed with a smooth and polished surface but is rough and uneven ... crowded everywhere with deep chasms and convolutions.

GALILEO GALILEI IN 1610 ON FIRST SEEING
THE MOON THROUGH A TELESCOPE.

Orbiting the Sun: Planets and Satellites of the Solar System (1981) by Fred Whipple. A comprehensive account of the solar system incorporating satellite data and photos from the various Viking missions. Patrick Moore's *New Guide to the Planets* (1993) covers much the same ground at a less technical level.

Guide to the Sun (1992) by Kenneth Phillips. Though somewhat technical in parts, this book provides a readable account of the chromosphere, photosphere, corona, and interior of the Sun, and how best it can be observed.

Times Atlas of the Moon (1969) by H A Lewis. A detailed 110-page map of the Moon. Less detailed and with more general information about the Moon – its origin, orbit etc – is Patrick Moore's *The Moon* (1985).

Comets: Readings from Scientific American (1981) edited by John C Brandt. A collection of authoritative articles covering such topics as the tails, spin, and nature of comets. A simpler account can be found in *Guide to Comets* (1977) by Patrick Moore.

Solar System: Readings from Scientific American (1975) by W H Freeman. A useful and readable collection of articles on the Solar System including individual papers on the planets, their origin, and interplanetary fields.

The Discovery of Neptune (1979) by Morton Grosser. A fascinating account of the discovery in 1846 of the existence of a previously unknown planet.

Nemesis (1988) by Richard Muller. The exciting story of the search by astrophysicists in the 1980s for the 'killer star' Nemesis. Nemesis is thought to be orbiting the Sun and – as it approaches the Earth every 26 million years – causing such catastrophes as the extinction of the dinosaurs.

We Are Not Alone (1970) by Walter Sullivan. A sensible but interesting discussion of whether or not life exists on worlds outside our Solar System.

STARS AND GALAXIES – *Derek Gjertsen*

Until relatively recent times the only books on stars were concerned with the mythic origin of their names. Nothing more was known about stars than that they were numerous, twinkled, and were very far away. In the 19th century things changed radically when it was shown that detailed knowledge of a star's composition, temperature, density, and much more besides could be derived by analysing the light it emitted. The Milky Way was still, however, assumed to represent the whole of creation, and it was not until the 1920s that it became apparent that a profusion of other galaxies could be found beyond the Milky Way. They have been studied intensively ever since.

I was contemplating the stars in a clear sky when I noticed a new and unusual star shining almost directly above my head where there had never been any star in that place in the sky. Unable to accept the evidence of my eyes I called upon my servants and a passing peasant to verify my observations.

TYCHO BRAHE ON THE SUPERNOVA OBSERVED IN 1572

The Milky Way (1973) by S L Jaki. A historical account of the growth of our knowledge of the Milky Way from the speculations of Aristotle to the observations in the 1920s of Edwin Hubble.

The Guide to the Galaxy (1994) by Nigel Henbest and Heather Couper. A lavishly illustrated, popular but detailed work on the Milky Way. It has chapters on the discovery of the Milky Way, its geography, its centre, and the Perseus, Orion, and Sagittarius arms.

Supernovae (1985) by Paul Murdin and Lesley Murdin. The Murdins begin their popular work with descriptions of the supernovae of 1066, 1572, and 1604 and go on to show how supernovae are related to pulsars, black holes, neutron stars, and the creation of the elements. *End in Fire* (1990) by Paul Murdin describes the discovery in 1990 of SN1987A, the first supernova to be visible to the unaided eye since 1604. Murdin traces the development of the supernova and shows its connection to theory.

Frontiers in Astronomy: Readings from Scientific American (1970) edited by Owen Gingerich; **The Universe of Galaxies: Readings from** Scientific American (1984) edited by Paul W Hodge. The two works are valuable collections of articles on such topics as quasars, dark matter, the Milky Way, the red shift, and exploding galaxies.

The X-Ray Universe (1985) by Wallace Tucker and Riccardo Giacconi. X-ray stars were first observed in 1962. The authors describe the discovery and the resulting research which led to the launch of the two X-ray telescopes UHURU in 1970 and EINSTEIN in 1978 and the results gathered.

Observing the Universe (1984) by Nigel Henbest. A collection of short articles from *New Scientist* dealing with research into X-ray astronomy, ultraviolet astronomy, the gamma ray sky, cosmic rays, the infrared sky, and optical and radio astronomy.

The Cosmic Perspective (1990) by M Zeilik and J Gauttard. A major 800-page-plus single-volume textbook dealing with the evolution of the stars and the galaxies. Although technical in parts, much of the text remains within the competence of the general reader.

Star Names: Their Lore and Meaning (1899; republished 1995) by Richard Allen. A standard and comprehensive survey of the meaning of star names in English, Greek, Arabic, and other languages.

AMATEUR ASTRONOMY – *Patrick Moore*

Many books on astronomy have been published in recent years. Many of them are specialized; in my list I have included only books which give a general picture – and which do not include complex mathematical formulas. You may note that some of my choices appeared in 1990 or 1991, but I have selected them because of their excellence and because the material in them has not become outdated.

Astronomy is perhaps the science whose discoveries owe least to chance,
in which human understanding appears in its whole magnitude, and
through which man can best learn how small he is.

G C LICHTENBERG

Heavenly Bodies: Beginner's Guide to Astronomy (1995) by Iain Nicolson. A simple outline, based on the recent BBC television series of the same name.

The Natural History of the Universe (1994) by C A Ronan. A well- written, beautifully illustrated general survey of modern astronomy; it has been widely acclaimed.

Concise Dictionary of Astronomy (1991) by Jacqueline Mitton. A very clear, well organized 'A to Z', which includes a tremendous amount of information and is very easy to digest.

Images of the Universe (1991) edited by Carol Stott. Mainly an observer's book; each chapter is written by an expert in his particular field. Most of the authors are closely linked with the British Astronomical Association.

The Hidden Universe (1991) by Roger Tayler. A very clear account of some of the problems of modern cosmology – problems which are no nearer solution in 1995 than they were in 1991!

PRACTICAL ASTRONOMY – *Derek Gjertsen*

Astronomy is probably the only exact science in which amateurs can play a significant role and operate, just like their professional colleagues, in their own scaled-down observatories with their own, much smaller telescopes. To this end they need a large number of practical aids, ranging from catalogues and dictionaries to books on how to make and use a telescope. The first published star catalogue, compiled by Ptolemy in about 150 AD, listed 1,022 stars in 48 constellations. In contrast, the *Bonn Catalogue* compiled by Friedrich Argelander in 1863 listed 324,198 stars from the northern hemisphere alone.

In order to the finding out of the longitude of places and perfecting
navigation and astronomy, we have resolved to build a small observatory
within our park at Greenwich.

WARRANT OF CHARLES II, 1675

Exploring the Night Sky with Binoculars (1986) by Patrick Moore. A book for beginners. After offering advice on choosing binoculars, Moore writes about the planets, comets, and the Moon. Half the book is devoted to charts of the constellations.

Astronomy with a Small Telescope (1985) by James Muirden. Introductory chapters describe the various telescopes and their mounting and are followed by advice on how to observe the Sun, Moon, planets, meterorites, comets, constellations, and galaxies. There is also a chapter on photography.

Telescope Making for Beginners (1974) by Roy Worrill. For those prepared to make their own telescope Worrill offers a simple guide. More detailed advice and information can be found in *Handbook for Telescope Making* (1962) by M E Howard.

Norton's 2000 (1989) by Arthur Philip Norton. *Norton's Atlas* first appeared in 1910; the latest edition (18th) is calculated for the year 2000. A similar approach can be found in the *Cambridge Star Atlas 2000* (1991) by Will Trion.

Sundials (1969) by Frank Cooper. A standard work giving instruction on how to construct horizontal, vertical, polar, and equatorial sundials.

Both the ***Penguin Dictionary of Astronomy*** (1993) by Jacqueline Mitton and the ***Macmillan Dictionary of Astronomy*** (1988) by Valerie Illingworth are excellent concise guides for the amateur.

Dictionary of Space (1986) by Malcolm Plant. An essential aid for those who cannot remember whether *Apollo 7* went to Mars or the Moon or which rocket first landed on Venus.

The Guinness Book of Astronomy (1992) by Patrick Moore. A familiar and informative guide to the Solar System and the stars with a 90-page star catalogue, and brief sections on the history of astronomy.

NAVIGATION, CALENDARS, AND HOROSCOPES
Derek Gjertsen

Astronomy has always been an abstract and speculative science as well as a practical and precise discipline. The first signs of specialized astronomical skills become apparent in the lengths of the year and the month. This was no simple matter and it was not until the 16th century, for example, that a reasonably reliable calendar was introduced into Europe. The data compiled in this way could be and from early times was used by astrologers to forecast horoscopes. Practical and technical skills were needed to navigate successfully over the oceans and, eventually, to guide missiles and planes through the skies. For this reason astronomy was one of the first sciences to receive substantial government support and under the broad umbrella of the 'space race' has continued to receive huge financial assistance.

The Calendar was so out of joint that Caesar placed between the months of November and December two intercalary months of 67 days, having already intercalated 23 days in February, which gave 445 days to that year.

CENSORINUS ON 46 BC, THE SO-CALLED YEAR OF CONFUSION

The Haven Finding Art. A History of Navigation from Odysseus to Captain Cook (1971) by E G R Taylor. An account of how sailors have navigated first by wind rose and stars, then by compass and chart, next by instruments and tables, and finally, with the introduction of the chronometer in the 18th century, with the full accuracy provided by being able to find a precise longitude.

From Sails to Satellites (1992) by J E D Williams. Covering with less historical detail but with more illustrations much of Taylor's ground, Williams also extends the story to recent times to include the use of radio and radar in navigation.

Greenwich Time and the Discovery of Longitude (1980) by Derek Howse. The first part of the book deals with the discovery of longitude and the role of Greenwich Observatory in the solution. Howse also relates how Greenwich came to be accepted as the prime meridian and the role of Greenwich time in the world.

The Voyaging Stars (1978) by David Lewis. An account of how throughout Oceania islanders in traditional canoes navigate from one small island to an equally small but distant island.

Time and the Calendars (1975) by W M O'Neil. Details are provided of the Egyptian, Roman, Babylonian, Indian, Chinese, and Meso-American calendars and the extent to which they rely upon astronomical investigation.

Gregorian Reform of the Calendar (1983) edited by M Hoskins and O Pedersen. A full and fascinating account of the historical and astronomical problems of introducing the Gregorian calendar into Europe.

A History of Western Astrology (1987) by Jim Tester. A detailed and scholarly history of Western astrology from the 5th century BC to the 17th century.

Astrology: Science or Superstition (1984) by H J Eysenck and K B Nais; *The Truth about Astrology* (1984) by Michel Gauquelin. Two works in which the traditional claims of astrology are tested against a variety of empirical evidence.

EARTH SCIENCE

GEOLOGY – *Dougal Dixon*

Geology is a very wide subject. It contains so many subdisciplines – such as mineralogy, petrology, geophysics, geochemistry, palaeontology, sedimentology – that it is almost impossible to produce a list that covers them all. The following, however, should give the interested reader a good start.

These rocks, these bones, these fossil ferns and shells, / Shall yet be touched with beauty, and reveal / The secrets of the book of earth to man.

ALFRED NOYES

Rocks, Minerals and Fossils of the World (1990) by Chris Pellant. It is normally not a good idea to base mineral identification on photographs – the diagnostic properties do not show. However, the photographs in this book are particularly good.

The Practical Geologist (1992) by Dougal Dixon. A useful coverage of the various aspects of geology and the techniques used to study them.

The Cambridge Encyclopedia of Earth Sciences (1982) edited by David G Smith. Rather academic treatment of all the physical earth sciences (of which geology is a part), but well illustrated.

The Principles of Physical Geology (1965) by Arthur Holmes. The standard university textbook that deals principally with landscape formation.

Earth and Life Through Time (1986) by Steven M Stanley. The whole panoply of Earth's history, with the different types of rocks formed at different times, and the different animals and plants found preserved in them.

Understanding the Earth (1992) by G A Brown and others. The updated version of the Open University's textbook on earth science, bringing the original 1972 classic completely up to date.

Natural History Museum, Earth Galleries booklets:

The Age of the Earth (1980) by John Thackray. An excellent rundown on the techniques used to work out geological time.

Britain Before Man (1978) by F W Dunning and others. Covers the development of the British Isles and so includes sedimentary rock formation, plate tectonics, fossils, and the concept of geological time.

PALAEONTOLOGY – *Brian Rosen*

Palaeontology, the study of fossil remains of former life, lurks benignly in its quiet backwater – surely, little to do with the real world. Children reel off the tongue-twisting names of dinosaurs as though they were playground friends, though no one has ever seen a live one. Anybody can go out at weekends fossil-hunting, and they don't have to be professional palaeontologists to make discoveries. Appearances, however, are misleading. Every so often, the subject rears up and bares its intellectual teeth. It had a critical role in giving us the very concept of geological time, and hence the great age of the Earth, ideas that were shocking in their time and later became vital in dating the past and discovering natural resources. Palaeontology is dragged from its lair and into the witness box for the perennial battle between creationists and evolutionists, and has startled the world with the awe-inspiring notion that large slices of life on our planet are wiped out almost instantly in mass extinction events, some say on a regular basis every 26 million years in response to Earth collisions by extraterrestrial bodies. Palaeontology gave us 'deep time', 'macroevolution', and *Jurassic Park*, and is, quite simply, the only direct evidence we have for over 3,000 million years of life on our planet before we humans arrived here ourselves. And if you want to know what global change has in store for us, and for the rest of life, ask the palaeontologists, for much of the future has already been written in the past. What is this science that contemplates strange and beautiful organic objects found in the rocks, and yet can shake the Earth by studying them?

We [palaeontologists] try to discover as many facts as possible that might be connected, the more the better. We let the problem become complicated. We want to know all the factors that must be taken into account, so we let the difficulties accumulate. We get a great kick out of this...

L B HALSTEAD

Before the Deluge (1968; translated 1970) by Herbert Wendt. The history of palaeontology, its issues and its personalities, rich in narrative and with a balanced international perspective.

The Meaning of Fossils (1972) by Martin Rudwick. Widely regarded as the standard scholarly reference to the historical scientific issues and intellectual questions posed by palaeontology.

The Message of Fossils (1991; translated 1993) by Pascal Tassy. An easy-going essay focused on the interface between palaeontology and evolution, which includes its more recent controversies.

Fossils (1960) by H H Swinnerton. A notable contribution to the classic New Naturalist series, this inevitably has a very homely British bias. No matter – the range of fossil-bearing rocks in Britain is a good enough sample of the fossil record, which Swinnerton sets out with charm, enjoyment, and enthusiasm.

Earth and Life Through Time (1986) by S M Stanley. Earth and life and the meaning of nearly everything. This is the American college solution to everything you wanted to know about fossils, evolution, and geology. Don't worry about the self-assessment questions unless you are a student – this book is here on its encyclopedic merit.

History of Life (radically expanded edition 1990) by Richard Cowen. A delightfully individual and good-humoured account, complete with arcane limericks and other incidental entertainment, which highlight the science without distracting from it. Good on invertebrates.

The Book of Life (1993) edited by Stephen Jay Gould. The thinking person's palaeontological coffee-table book (and why not? See Gould's panegyric on the significance of coffee tables and their books). First-class illustrations and chapters by an impressive cast list of other distinguished specialists with emphasis on vertebrates, including humans.

The Natural History Museum Book of Dinosaurs (1995) by Angela Milner. No book list in this subject can be without something on dinosaurs. This is an up-to-date look at their biology – what we can deduce about their lifestyles from modern research and new finds – together with the history and practice of dinosaur studies, from bones in the rock to a restoration of the whole animal.

The Nemesis Affair. A Story of the Death of Dinosaurs and Ways of Science (1986) by David Raup. Treats extinction generally, and discusses controversial collisions between extraterrestrial bodies and Earth, between organisms and their physical world, and between scientists and mass culture.

Wonderful Life (1989) by Stephen Jay Gould. Gould is palaeontology's most virtuoso narrator and interpreter. Here he brings to life in epic style the famously mysterious, and miraculously preserved, animals of the Burgess Shale, and the personalities who have studied them, using them as the raw material for expounding his ideas about the significance of chance.

Fossils: The Key to the Past (1991) by Richard Fortey. Bringing fossils to life and applying this knowledge to geology and biology. An effortless browse through all the branches of the subject, introducing all the main fossil organisms at the same time.

EARTHQUAKES, VOLCANOES, AND TECTONICS
Dougal Dixon

When it comes to volcanoes the reading public is not well served by books at a popular level. Beware, particularly, of the block diagram showing a cone of a volcano cut in half, fed by a red thread of liquid cutting through the rocks below, exiting through side vents as well as the main crater. There never was a volcano like that, and the oversimplification is misleading. That said, however, the following are probably the best books available.

It is useful to be assured that the heavings of the earth are not the work of angry deities. These phenomena have causes of their own.

LUCIUS ANNAEUS SENECA

The Natural History Museum's Earth Galleries (formerly the Geological Museum) produce a series of booklets covering a range of earth sciences. All are published by Her Majesty's Stationery Office.

Earthquakes (1983) by Susanna van Rose. Describes the various phenomena associated with an earthquake, covers the known causes, and gives some case histories.

The Story of the Earth (1981) by F W Dunning and others. Gives an overview of the concept of plate tectonics and shows how volcanoes and earthquakes fit into the grand scheme.

Dorling Kindersley Eyewitness Guides: Volcano (1992) by Susanna van Rose. An elegantly illustrated book with photographs and artwork showing all sorts of phenomena associated with volcanic activity.

The Dorling Kindersley Science Encyclopaedia (1993) edited by Heather Couper and Nigel Henbest. Has good sections on earthquakes and volcanoes.

Mountains of Fire: The Nature of Volcanoes (1991) by R W and B B Decker. A well-illustrated introduction to volcanoes, their rock types, and their effects.

Natural Disasters: Volcanoes (1991) by Jacqueline Dineen. A good, simple book, but beware the block diagrams!

METEOROLOGY – *Chris Pellant*

The swirling, circulating atmospheric systems that control the Earth's daily weather and seasonal climate are driven by the principles of physics, especially those relating to how fluids heat up, cool down, and move. Meteorology is concerned with understanding these processes and the events they cause, and because of man's dependence on his atmospheric surroundings, the prediction of changes in weather and climate is a very important part of the science. Today, possibly as much as at any time in the past, the atmosphere is changing and being changed. Temperatures are rising, new gases are appearing and established ones are changing in quantity; circulation is being altered. The effects of these, often man-induced, changes is a new area to tax the skills of meteorologists.

Yesterday it thundered, last night it lightened. I have a leech in a bottle, my dear, that foretells all these prodigies and convulsions of nature.

WILLIAM COWPER

The Restless Atmosphere (1953–67; various reprints) by F Kenneth Hare. A very readable account this, covering physics and related science in easily understood language. The section on the depressions of middle latitudes even hints at the effects these cyclonic air masses have on the humans who continually suffer from them, by reference to 'cyclonic man'.

Climate and the British Scene (1975) by Gordon Manley. Originally one of the now collectable Collins New Naturalist series, this classic account opens with a fascinating history of meteorological recording and, after detailed coverage of the climate of Britain, finishes with the impact of weather and climate on man.

Atmosphere, Weather and Climate (1992) by Roger G Barry and Richard J Chorley. A heavyweight volume for the dedicated reader. Everything is here from the gas content of the sky to the causes of climatic change.

The Weather Book (1982) by Ralph Hardy, Peter Wright, John Gribbin, and John Kington. A book to fascinate anyone with an interest in meteorology. Packed with colour pictures and amazing facts.

The Weather Machine (1974) by Nigel Calder. A very readable account of meteorological phenomena and events, by an expert in putting science into everyday language.

Ice Age Earth (1992) by Alastair Dawson. A detailed account of the meteorological and geological evidence for the changes in the climate during the ice age. What we know about the current changes in the world's climate is in great measure reliant on what we know about past climatic change. The Ice Age changes in climate were not man-made. Today, in addition to man's interference with the climate, there are still many natural causes of global warming and cooling.

GEOGRAPHY – *Simon Ross*

G eography is all around us, whether it be the built world of cities, motorways, and industry or the natural world of deserts, beaches, and tropical forests. With the recent growth of the environmental movement and concerns about global poverty and famine, natural disasters and climate change, geography has become much more issue-based than it used to be, although it still retains the important qualities of inquisitiveness, sensitivity, and sheer wonder and excitement which are at the heart of geographical study. The Earth is a fascinating, diverse, yet very vulnerable and fragile place and only through the careful understanding and management of its peoples and resources will it retain its character and support the generations to come. This is the very essence of geography and it therefore comes as no surprise that the subject has witnessed a tremendous boom in popularity and status in both school and university.

My journey around the world gave me a sense of global scale, of the size and variety of this great planet, and of the relation of one country and one culture to another which few people experience and many ought to.

MICHAEL PALIN

The Gaia Atlas of Planet Management (1985; new edition 1994) by Norman Myers. There are many atlases and reference books on the market today but there are few that are as informative and lavishly illustrated as this. It is intelligent and thought-provoking and there are many excellent thematic maps and colour photographs. It is divided into several sections including the land, the oceans, the elements, evolution, and civilization. I strongly recommend this book for all those with an interest and concern for the issues affecting the future of our planet.

Around the World in 80 Days (1989) by Michael Palin. An extremely readable, amusing, and, in places, poignant account of the author's attempt to follow in the foot-steps of Phileas Fogg. Superbly illustrated and divided into bite-size pieces, it makes an excellent escapist's bedtime read for dark winter nights.

Quest for Adventure (1981) by Chris Bonington. This wonderful book, dedicated to some of the world's greatest adventurers, is superbly written and well illustrated. It trans-ports the reader into territories that the ordinary person can only dream about and sets the imagination racing. Among the adventures described are the *Kon-Tiki* voyage, the flight of *Apollo 11*, the scaling of Mount Everest, and the crossing of Antarctica.

Maps and Map-Makers (1987) by R V Tooley. Maps have always been at the heart of geography and they are also extremely collectable antiques, being attractive to look at and holding their value well. This book forms an excellent introduction to maps and the cartographers that painstakingly produced them and it will probably whet the appetite for seeking out some originals in second-hand bookshops.

How to Shit in the Woods (1989) by Kathleen Meyer. This is an extremely amusing paperback which will bring a wry smile to all those who have been camping or back-packing in the bush. There is, however, a serious side to this American book: 'No longer can we drink even a drop [of mountain water] before purifying it without running the risk of getting sick.'

Restless Earth (1972) by Nigel Calder. This book represented something of a land-mark in being one of the first general readers (it accompanied a television series) to examine the role of the newly forming concept of plate tectonics in accounting for the major physical features of the Earth's surface. It is superbly illustrated and is still highly regarded today.

Human Geography: Evolution or Revolution? (1975) by Michael Chisholm. In the 1960s and 1970s there were a number of important developments and innovations in the nature of geography and Professor Michael Chisholm attempted to make some sense of the changes. 'The primary purpose in writing is to convey an account of the direction and purpose of recent changes in human geography as conceived by some-one fairly close to the scene.' Chisholm's book is a fascinating read for it traces the his-tory of the subject to the mid-1970s and attempts to look ahead into what was then regarded as a very uncertain future.

Discovering Landscape (1985) by Andrew Goudie and Rita Gardner. This book aims to 'discover and try to explain some of the most appealing features of the natural landscape'. It is a splendid book for all those with an inquisitive mind who want to know a bit more about the history and geology of well-known British sites such as Helvellyn, Lulworth Cove, and Cheddar Gorge.

Disasters (1980) by John Whittow. This fascinating book looks at the causes and effects of the major natural hazards such as earthquakes, landslides, and floods, writ-ten by a very well-respected author. It contains some amazing and often chilling eye-witness accounts.

Geology and Scenery in England and Wales (1971) by A E Trueman. For those with an interest in the geological development of particular landscapes in England and Wales such as the West Country moors, the Cotswolds, or the Lake District, this is a must for it is both informative and highly readable.

Inside the Third World (1979) by Paul Harrison. This powerful and thought-provoking book is highly recommended for all those who have an interest in the Third World. As a freelance journalist Paul Harrison travelled extensively, particularly in Africa, and this book describes his many experiences in the general field of development. It contains some marvellous and often highly moving descriptive passages of landscapes and people.

BIOLOGY

INTRODUCTION – *Stephen Webster*

The job of biology is to look at life: where it came from, how it works, and what it is made of. Yet, surprisingly, even biologists find it hard to define what is meant by 'life'. An elephant, of course, is a living thing, but what about a virus, or a length of DNA? Or a glucose molecule? The books below show how broad a subject biology has become in its attempt to make scientific sense of the living world.

Tyger! Tyger! burning bright / In the forests of the night, / What immortal hand or eye / Could frame thy fearful symmetry?

WILLIAM BLAKE

Pedigree: Words from Nature (1973) by Stephen Potter and Laurens Sargent. A wonderful collection of revelations about the origins of the names we give to plants and animals. From where, for example, does the porcupine get its name? And did you know that the collective noun for the starling is a murmuration?

The Double Helix (1968) by James D Watson. A terrific read about arguably the greatest scientific breakthrough of our age – the discovery of the structure of DNA by the two young Cambridge scholars James Watson and Francis Crick. If you think that scientists are remote and cold, this book will quickly change your mind.

Life on Earth (1979) by David Attenborough. One of the best-written introductions to the variety of life on Earth – and beautifully illustrated too. Based on his award-winning TV series of the same name. Attenborough takes you through the whole 'story of evolution', beginning with the primeval soup and ending up with us.

The Panda's Thumb (1980) by Stephen Jay Gould. A collection of essays by a master science writer able to breathe life into facts both general and particular. Here, Gould reflects on the evolution of the panda, investigates Charles Darwin, and wonders whether 'dinosaurs were dumb'. Fine bedtime reading.

What Is Life? (1944) by Erwin Schrödinger. This is one of the great science classics of the 20th century, elegantly written by an eminent physicist. His theoretical approach to the question of life involved an analysis of how genes must work, an analysis that set the agenda for the new study of molecular biology.

Why Big Fierce Animals Are Rare (1980) by Paul Colinvaux. A good introduction to the science of ecology. Each chapter looks at a feature of the complex and fascinating set of relations that exist between plant animals and environment. If you want to read about how animals and plants get on with their normal day-to-day life, undisturbed by people and pollution, this book would be a good start.

CELLULAR BIOLOGY – *Stephen Webster*

All living things are made of cells – you could almost call cells the atoms of life. Yet these tiny things are themselves immeasurably complicated and the subject of constant research. Inside the cell lie the genes and an intricate series of mechanisms for making proteins and other substances. The books below show that cells are fundamental to biology – yet are still only partially understood.

> *Let's begin this way, then: there is a cell, and this cell is a unicellular organism, and this unicellular organism is me, and I know it, and I'm pleased about it. Nothing special so far.*
>
> ITALO CALVINO

The Chemistry of Life (1991) by Steven Rose. This is an up-to-date and authoritative survey of the chemical goings-on inside a cell. Rose is a professor at the Open University and here makes a technical subject pretty approachable.

Immunology (1991) edited by Paul William. Authoritative papers from the *Scientific American*, covering the fascinating science of immunology. Difficult in parts but a wonderful book for conveying how clever cells can be.

The Science of Aids: Readings from Scientific American (1989) by various authors. More papers from *Scientific American*, this time on how the HIV virus mounts an attack on the cellular immune system.

The Doctrine of DNA (1991) by Richard Lewontin. Lectures originally given on Canadian radio. A sustained attack on the idea that DNA controls people – or even cells.

The Red Queen Hypothesis (1993) by Matt Ridley. Highly readable account of the way the genes inside our cells have organized life in favour of sex.

Cell Biology (1986) edited by Barry King. Different contributors give their account of some of the most interesting aspects of cell biology, including evolution, motility, and protein synthesis.

Time and the Hunter (1967) by Italo Calvino. Short stories inspired by science. Several of the stories spring from the wonders of cell division, and have their own kind of truth.

The Growth of Biological Thought (1982) by Ernst Mayr. Included in this great book is a fascinating account of the 19th-century delvings by biologists interested in the mysterious world of the cell.

DNA – *Stephen Webster*

It is easy to think that with so much talk about genes, the question of how DNA works must be resolved by now. Not true. We may know the genetic code and the positions of some genes, but precisely how they work remains a riddle. Furthermore, as the books below show, there is no agreement about the extent of the power genes have in the daily life of an organism.

I, —————, being a natural born human being, do hereby forever copyright my unique genetic code, however it may be scientifically determined, described or otherwise empirically expressed ...

PART OF A 'CERTIFICATE' OFFERED BY THE US
CONCEPTUAL ARTIST LARRY MILLER

Perilous Knowledge (1993) by Tom Wilkie. Useful account of the Human Genome Project – the mapping and decoding of each and every one of our genes. Wilkie is a science journalist and so well placed to understand and express public concerns over the moral consequences of molecular biology.

Blueprints (1989) by Maitland A Edey and Donald C Johanson. A brilliantly written and exciting account that shows just how much has been achieved by the geneticists. The history of science made vivid.

Not in Our Genes (1984) by Steven Rose, Leon Kamin, and Richard Lewontin. Political as well as biological, these essays are an argument against the so-called reductionist ideas that suggest genes are in charge.

The Language of the Genes (1993) by Steve Jones. Entertaining yet restrained, the celebrated geneticist gives a reliable account of what we do and don't know about our genes.

The DNA Mystique (1995) by Dorothy Nelkin and M Susan Lindee. Two American authors give fascinating insights into the way the gene has invaded popular culture, turning up in comics, pop songs, and soap commercials.

The Science and Politics of IQ (1974) by Leon Kamin. More than 20 years old, this is a passionate and compelling study of the dubious idea that intelligence is determined by genetics.

The Mismeasure of Man (1981) by Stephen Jay Gould. The Harvard scientist and science writer turns his skills to examining the history of attempts to link intelligence to genetics.

EVOLUTION – *Richard Dawkins*

All living creatures, though superficially diverse, are cousins of each other and all give the illusion of being superbly designed for the purpose of continuing the genetic instructions that built them. Darwin's theory of evolution by natural selection is the unifying theory of life and it explains everything that we know about living things, their diversity, and their appearance of design. With the addition of Mendelian genetics, Darwinism became neo-Darwinism. Neo-Darwinism today goes from strength to strength, and it is itself still in a rapidly evolving phase, as many of the following books show.

Let me lay my cards on the table. If I were to give an award for the single best idea anyone has ever had, I'd give it to Darwin, ahead of Newton and Einstein and everyone else. In a single stroke, the idea of evolution by natural selection unifies the realm of life, meaning and purpose with the realm of space and time, cause and effect, mechanism and physical law. But it is not just a wonderful scientific idea. It is a dangerous idea.

DANIEL DENNETT

The Origin of Species (1859) by Charles Darwin. Easier to read than many people imagine. In addition to the brilliant theory itself, Darwin has astonishingly wise and far-sighted things to say about a great variety of related topics, from ecology to biogeography. The only thing he got badly wrong (along with all his contemporaries except Mendel) was genetics.

The Theory of Evolution (1958) by John Maynard Smith. Clear, authoritative, and readable account of the modern neo-Darwinian theory.

Adaptation and Natural Selection (1966) by George C Williams. A seminal work which succeeds in combining inspiration with tough-minded correction of error. The book has exerted an increasing influence in the decades since it was written, and Williams is now respected as perhaps the dominant figure among American Darwinians.

Darwinism Defended (1982) by Michael Ruse. Darwinism hardly needs defending, but this worthwhile book includes a rip-roaring attack on creationism.

The Blind Watchmaker (1986) by Richard Dawkins. Argues that Darwinian natural selection is the only known theory that could, in principle, explain adaptive complexity.

The Problems of Evolution (1986) by Mark Ridley. Witty and cultivated essays on particular topics of controversy, or of lively discussion, in the field of evolution.

The Ant and the Peacock (1991) by Helena Cronin. A beautifully written account of two important evolutionary topics, altruism and sexual selection, tracing them from their origins in the writings of Darwin and Alfred Russel Wallace to the sophisticated theories of modern times.

The Cambridge Encyclopedia of Human Evolution (1992) edited by Steve Jones. Edited by a team led by Steve Jones, the well-known geneticist. A comprehensive and up-to-date survey of all aspects of human evolution, with some fascinating information.

The Origin of Humankind (1994) by Richard Leakey. A brief and readable personal view of human fossils by today's leading authority on them.

Darwin's Dangerous Idea (1995) by Daniel Dennett. The penetrating view of a philosopher with a deep understanding of modern Darwinism, showing the importance of Darwinism for all aspects of human thought. Filled with fascinating and original insights.

HUMAN EVOLUTION – *Chris Stringer*

Interest in our origins was a human characteristic long before the biblical version in the Book of Genesis was written. New evidence from fossils and archaeology show that the

5-million-year history of human evolution was not a simple ladder of inevitable progress, but a complex bush of radiating lineages, with ours as the sole survivor.

We are all Africans under the skin.

CHRIS STRINGER

Links (1988) by John Reader. A very readable introduction to the history of fossil discoveries and the personalities involved.

Lucy: The Beginnings of Humankind (1981) by Don Johanson and Matt Edey. A very popularly written insider's view of palaeoanthropology.

Human Evolution: An Illustrated Guide (1993) by Roger Lewin. An excellent general review of the topic.

The Cambridge Encyclopaedia of Human Evolution (1992) edited by Steve Jones, Robert Martin, and David Pilbeam. Good general coverage of primates, fossils, archaeology, and recent human variation.

Encyclopaedia of Human Evolution and Prehistory (1988) edited by Ian Tattersall and others. An alphabetically arranged in-depth coverage of palaeo-anthropology, although not so strong on the behavioural side.

The Origin of Modern Humans (1993) by Roger Lewin. An up-to-date review of this controversial topic.

In Search of the Neanderthals (1993) by Chris Stringer and Clive Gamble. All aspects of these fascinating extinct people are covered here by Chris Stringer and an archaeologist coauthor.

REPRODUCTION – *Peter Tallack*

All living things can generate new individuals of the same species. But sex is not absolutely necessary. With asexual reproduction, individuals are derived from one parent – by division or budding, for instance – and no special reproductive structures are involved. But although simple and direct, this method produces offspring that are genetically identical to the parent. Sexual reproduction, on the other hand, involves specialized reproductive cells of two parents – typically male and female – that fuse to produce a new individual with a different genetic make-up. This mode of reproduction apparently has great advantages, as most complex plants and animals have adopted it. Even many bacteria and other organisms that normally reproduce asexually engage in occasional bouts of sexual reproduction. But just why sex evolved and what benefits it brings are two of the biggest unsolved problems in biology. And with the advent of new medical technologies, we are now faced with the difficult question of deciding when it is right to interfere with our own reproductive futures. Reproductive biology is a fast-moving field, and most books on the subject rapidly become out of date. Those listed below look set to stand the test of time.

If you want to know, life is the principle of self-renewal, it is constantly renewing and remaking and changing and transfiguring itself.

BORIS PASTERNAK

Reproduction (1977) by Jack Cohen. A standard, well-illustrated introduction that collects together information on all aspects of biological reproduction.

Reproduction in Mammals (1982) edited by C R Austin and R V Short. A scholarly, comprehensive, and authoritative reference series justly famous for its clear and interesting presentation of up-to-date data and theory. Early volumes cover germ cells and fertilization, hormones in reproduction, embryonic and fetal development, reproductive patterns, and the manipulation of reproduction.

Peacemaking Among Primates (1989) by Frans de Waal. The author draws on detailed observations by himself and other leading experts to describe primate reproductive behaviour in captivity and in the wild. A stimulating tale of relationships, rivalries, and reconciliations.

Sperm Wars (1996) by Robin Baker. Since the 1970s, biologists have been fascinated by the biological and evolutionary implications of sperm from different males competing for fertilization of the egg in the female reproductive tract. This is the first popular book on the phenomenon in humans. It summarizes an immense amount of information, all carefully documented. Iconoclastic and provocative.

The Triumph of the Embryo (1991) by Lewis Wolpert. A limpid and engaging account of embryology and development – the coordinated process leading from a fertilized egg to an adult that is itself capable of becoming a parent.

The Red Queen Hypothesis (1993) by Matt Ridley. A wide-ranging and erudite examination of the scientific debates over the hows and whys of sex and the unending evolutionary battle between males and females that results once it gets going. Up to date, provocative, and stylish.

Life Cycles (1993) by John Tyler Bonner. An evolutionary biologist who has devoted his life to the study of slime moulds. Writing with clarity and humour, he sets reproduction in the context of the life cycle – a linkage of evolution, development, and the complex activities of adult organisms. Filled with wonderful insights and interesting examples.

The Pill (1995) by Bernard Asbell. The development of the oral contraceptive pill and its liberating impact on the lives of millions of women is a remarkable tale of scientific discovery, fortuitous discovery, dogged persistence, and moral dilemmas over reproductive choices. The story is told in this riveting book, a skilful combination of history, biography, science, and public policy.

The Human Body Shop (1993) by Andrew Kimbrell. The author reviews the technological and commercial controls of human reproduction, arguing that our current legal and technical framework is inadequate to deal with advances in biotechnology.

A Question of Life (1984) by Mary Warnock. The author is a British philosopher who has had enormous influence on the issue of what it is permissible to do with embryos. Intended for a broad general readership, this is a clear and balanced report of a committee she chaired that looked into human fertilization, embryology, and the ethics of assisted reproduction.

EMBRYOLOGY AND DEVELOPMENT
Stephen Webster

All living things grow and change, yet usually in quite predictable ways. For example, as children get older we expect them to get bigger. And a lettuce seed, planted in the ground, will quite soon become a leafy vegetable. How? What controls development? The books below will start you on one of the greatest puzzles of biology.

But other [seed] fell into good ground, and brought forth fruit,
some an hundredfold, some sixtyfold, some thirtyfold.

THE BIBLE, MATTHEW 13:8

Ontogeny and Phylogeny (1977) by Stephen Jay Gould. This account of the 19th-century idea of recapitulation – that individual development mirrors evolutionary development – is a fascinating piece of research into the history of biology.

When Did I Begin? (1988) by Norman D Ford. In-depth analysis of an important ethical problem: when, exactly, does a human embryo become an individual?

The Triumph of the Embryo (1991) by Lewis Wolpert. A straightforward and informative account of the development of the vertebrate embryo. This is Wolpert's own research field, and he writes with verve.

How the Leopard Changed Its Spots (1994) by Brian Goodwin. As an outspoken critic of those biological models that see the gene as all-powerful, Goodwin here presents his own ideas about the nature of development.

Richard Owen: Victorian Naturalist (1994) by Nicholaas Rupke. A contemporary of Charles Darwin and an opponent of the theory of natural selection, Owen is more or less forgotten today. This biography gives sympathetic treatment to Owen's 'romantic' views of biological change.

On Growth and Form (1917) by D'Arcy Thompson. This scientific classic lays out in fabulous detail the different forms we see in living things – and attempts a theory of unification.

The Engineer in the Garden (1993) by Colin Tudge. Sometimes disturbing account of how animals and plants may grow up to be different – thanks to genetic engineering.

MEDICINE

HISTORY OF MEDICINE – *Roy Porter*

Aside from medicine proper, interest is growing today in the historical, cultural, and social dimensions of medicine. These are the aspects dealt with in the books I have chosen, which set out to explain why we have the medicine we have. They look at such central issues as the way medicine relates to other features of a culture, such as science and technology, religion and mythology, and the question of whether modern medicine really serves the interests of patients or the medical profession.

Formerly, when religion was strong and science weak, men mistook magic for medicine; now, when science is strong and religion weak, men mistake medicine for magic.

THOMAS SZASZ

A Short History of Medicine (1968) by Erwin H Ackerknecht. Probably the best short history, it provides an ideal introduction to the subject.

Limits to Medicine: The Expropriation of Health (1977) by Ivan Illich. A stimulating book that argues that modern medicine serves the profession and not the patient.

The Role of Medicine: Dream, Mirage or Nemesis? (1979) by T McKeown. A thoughtful book, it questions how far medicine is really responsible for today's revolution in health.

The Body in Question (1978) by Jonathan Miller. A fascinating exploration of the functioning of our bodies and our experience of them. The book is based on a popular television series.

The Illustrated History of Medicine (1992) by Jean-Charles Sournia. Superbly illustrated, this book is particularly strong on its coverage of contemporary medicine.

The Western Medical Tradition: 800 BC to AD 1800 (1995) by Lawrence Conrad, Michael Neve, Vivian Nutton, and Roy Porter. An up-to-date scholarly survey.

Companion Encyclopedia of the History of Medicine (1993) by W F Bynum and Roy Porter. The most up-to-date work of reference dealing with the history of all the world's medical cultures.

MEDICAL BIOGRAPHY AND PRACTICE
James Le Fanu

Medicine may be a science but, though it may be a truism to say so, it is primarily about people – the personalities of the doctors who practice it and the patients who seek their attention. This humanistic side of medicine is a source of endless fascination. More than any other profession, medicine provides opportunities for a vast range of talents from those content with the humdrum life of everyday general practice to the white-coated scientist in his laboratory, from the missionary doctor to the sophisticated teaching-hospital specialist. Few leave a permanent record of their lives, so medical biographies and autobiographies are a particularly useful means of understanding the real nature of medical life. They are complemented by two collections of medical anecdotes from the *British Medical Journal* and the *Lancet* which focus on the particularity of medicine, its idiosyncrasy and humour.

It was wonderful to see the Vietcong flag raised on Berkeley campus, but it felt even better when the staff and workers at Bethnal Green Hospital voted to occupy against its threatened closure.

DAVID WIDGERY

Talking Sense (1972) by Richard Asher. This series of essays by the late Dr Asher exemplifies better than anything else I know the humane common sense that is the hallmark of good medical practice. It contains such gems as the Seven Sins of Medicine (obscurity, cruelty, bad manners, overspecialization, love of the rare, common stupidity, and sloth), the Dangers of Going to Bed and the first description of Münchhausen's syndrome.

Soundings (1992) edited by Ruth Holland. The best of contemporary medical writing are the contributions by a series of eight doctors and journalists to be found at the back of the *British Medical Journal* each week. This is a collection of their mini-essays, 800 words each, covering every aspect of modern medical practice.

The Lancet: In England Now (1989) For many years, but regrettably no longer, the *Lancet* ran a column, In England Now, consisting of anonymous anecdotes sent in by readers describing the idiosyncratic, perverse, and unusual events of everyday medical practice.

Weary, the Life of Sir Edward Dunlop (1994) by Sue Ebury. The most sustained instance of the dedication and ingenuity of doctors was exhibited by those working on the Burma–Thailand railway during World War II. Of these the most remarkable was Edward 'Weary' Dunlop. By his example, 'he held this body of men from moral decay in bitter circumstances which they could only meet with emotion rather than reason'.

A Doctor's Life (1989) by David Selbourn. These are the diaries covering the years 1960–63 of Hugh Selbourn, consultant physician, edited by his son. They provide a fascinating insight into the everyday life of a busy provincial doctor with three grid references to the political and cultural events of the time.

Churchill's Doctor: A Biography of Lord Moran (1992) by Richard Lovell. Moran is most famous for being Churchill's doctor who was much criticized for the inclusion in his autobiography of the details of the great man's illnesses. This biography places Moran's achievements in a wider context as well as illustrating the sort of wide-ranging intelligence with which leaders of the profession guided and shaped the emergence of the National Health Service.

The Fibre Man, the Life Story of Dr Denis Burkitt (1985) by Brian Kellock. Burkitt is best known for his espousal of the role of dietary fibre in preventing disease but his most remarkable achievement was the discovery of the cause of Burkitt's lymphoma while working as a physician in Uganda and the introduction of effective treatment. This biography illustrates the great scope offered by medicine for the enterprising doctor in the years after World War II.

Pain: The Gift Nobody Wants (1993) by Paul Brand and Philip Yancey. Paul Brand is an inspirational orthopaedic surgeon who was the first person to understand the cause of leprosy's characteristic disfigurement and developed both methods for its prevention and surgical repair. His subsequent research into the mechanisms of pain transformed medical approach to this serious problem.

Some Lives! A GP's East End (1991) by David Widgery. David Widgery was a general practitioner in London's East End for 20 years and this is a highly personal account of one man's fight against the medical and social consequences of prolonged unemployment, homelessness, and poverty.

MEDICAL RESEARCH – *James Le Fanu*

Research is central to the intellectual life of medicine and the application of the scientific method has repaid enormous rewards. There are regrettably few good descriptions of the practice of medical research but the examples noted here give a flavour of what is involved. The story of the world's first test-tube baby emphasizes the reality of the frustrations and false avenues that can so frequently hinder the resolution of an apparently quite straightforward problem. The saga of self-experimentation catches the fanaticism and urgency which lies behind the onward march of medical progress.

*So the substance and the ways of the living are broken down,
and from the bits and pieces tomes are gathered in encyclopaedic
summary; what is known of a cell, or part of a cell, may fill a volume.*

EDRED CORNER

The Youngest Science: Notes of a Medicine Watcher (1984) by Lewis Thomas. Lewis Thomas's medical career saw the beginning of the transformation of medicine into a science-based discipline throughout the 1950s and 1960s. This book captures the enormous excitement of these thrilling decades.

A Matter of Life: The Sensational Story of the World's First Test Tube Baby (1981) by Robert Edwards and Patrick Steptoe. This is much more than the description of a heartening medical success story as it describes in fascinating detail the enormous frustrations encountered when developing pioneering techniques and the tenacious force of character which is necessary to see them through.

Who Goes First: The Story of Self-Experimentation in Medicine (1988) by Lawrence K Altman. This is the remarkable story of many medical self-experimenters who deliberately acted as human guinea pigs in the furtherance of their research. Its main theme might be characterized as obsessionalism – the determination of those involved in medical research to get at the truth no matter what the cost.

The Encyclopaedia of Medical Ignorance (1984) by R Duncan and M Weston-Smith. As its title suggests, this fascinating volume describes not what is known but rather what is not known. This is interesting not only in itself but as a useful antidote to the claims of omniscience of the medical profession, particularly the belief that medicine has all the answers. Rather, medicine's great achievement has been the application of technological solutions to diseases whose causes for the most part remain unknown.

CRITIQUE OF MODERN MEDICINE AND MEDICAL ETHICS – *James Le Fanu*

The two great projects of modern medicine have been the prevention and treatment of disease. The achievements of prevention stretch from the great sanitary reforms of the 19th century to the elimination by vaccination of life-threatening infectious diseases. By contrast, a completely different intellectual approach, mostly empirical and technical, has produced a cornucopia of new drugs and operations for the chronic degenerative diseases which are not amenable to prevention but rather a necessary consequence of the marked general increase in life expectancy. Though apparently complementary, in fact the philosophies of prevention and treatment have been in constant conflict over the last 50 years. Many diseases, it is argued, are caused by an unhealthy lifestyle and so resources should be directed towards preventing rather than curing them. Contrariwise the claims of the preventability of such diseases, it is alleged, are based on faulty science and a desire to medicalize all aspects of society. This conflict of perception lies at the heart of understanding the role of medicine in contemporary society and the diversity of the arguments are well presented in the following books.

It is silliness to live when to live is torment; / And then have we a prescription to die / When death is our physician.

WILLIAM SHAKESPEARE

Limits to Medicine, Medical Nemesis – the Expropriation of Health (1976) by Ivan Illich. This was much the most influential book in encouraging the steady disillusionment with technologically based medicine that occurred from the 1970s onwards. Illich focused on the adverse features of medicalization – the robbing of personal autonomy, medicine's inhumanity, and the high price patients paid in terms of medical complications. (There is an interesting reply to Illich by David Horrobin called *Medical Hubris – A Reply to Ivan Illich* 1977).

The Role of Medicine (1979) by Thomas McKeown. McKeown was very influential in the 1960s by challenging the belief that medicine could take the credit for improvements in life expectancy and disease control which he claimed were almost entirely attributable to social factors such as improvements in the standard of living, better housing and nutrition. It formed the basis for the rise of what has been called the 'new public health', an idea, particularly favoured by the government, that prevention is better than cure and that resources are better spent on such things as health education and health promotion than on curative medicine.

The Death of Human Medicine (1994) by Peter Skrabanek. Skrabanek's position is almost directly opposed to that of McKeown. He contrasts the traditional human medicine with doctors caring for individual patients who seek their aid, with the false pretensions of prevention – what he calls 'healthism' – the propagation of health promotion, screening to encourage ordinary people into adopting a 'healthy' lifestyle.

Preventionitis: the Exaggerated Claims of Health Promotion (1994) edited by James Le Fanu. This collection of essays has a similar position to that of Skrabanek and focuses in particular on the weaknesses in the scientific evidence concerning the preventability of disease.

Philosophical Medical Ethics (1986) by Raanan Gillon. This is the best general introduction to medical ethics from a British perspective and covers all the main issues concerning autonomy, paternalism, and justice in the practice of medicine.

Life's Dominion: An Argument about Abortion and Euthanasia (1993) by Ronald Dworkins. This is a masterful elucidation of the arguments around the two most important ethical issues of abortion and euthanasia. Dworkins writes so well and seductively that even those totally opposed to these practices might almost be convinced.

PSYCHIATRY – *Anthony Clare*

Psychiatry is the branch of medicine that applies knowledge from the biological and social sciences, including genetics, pharmacology, physiology, psychology, and epidemiology, to the care and treatment of patients suffering from disorders of mental activity and behaviour. Psychiatry's emergence in the 18th century as a separate speciality coincided with the splitting of medicine into an increasingly triumphalist biological science and a geographically isolated, stigmatized, and neglected psychological domain. Over the past two decades, the growing interest in and understanding of brain function has resulted in an explosion of interest in the biological basis of many psychiatric disorders and a growing reintegration of psychological and physical approaches to health and disease.

Canst thou not minister to a mind diseas'd, / Pluck from the memory a rooted sorrow, / Raze out the written troubles of the brain, / And with some sweet oblivious antidote / Cleanse the stuff'd bosom of that perilous stuff / Which weighs upon the heart?

WILLIAM SHAKESPEARE

The Discovery of the Unconscious (1970) by Henri Ellenberger. A brilliant account of the historical development of the study of mind and the birth, evolution, and vicissitudes of dynamic psychiatry and psychotherapy. It includes a detailed assessment of the dynamic systems associated with the names of Pierre Janet, Alfred Adler, Sigmund Freud, and C G Jung, and traces the origins of modern dynamic psychotherapy back to the healing practices of primitive peoples, to the role of the shaman and the practices of exorcism, magnetism, and hypnotism.

General Psychopathology (1946) by Karl Jaspers. This book, the first edition of which appeared in 1913, the seventh and last in 1959, is a monumental examination of psychopathology which comprises the study of causal connections and general laws underpinning mental events and so-called empathetic understanding involving empirical experiment and free existential achievement.

The Foundations of Psychoanalysis (1984) by Adolf Grunbaum. This constitutes the most intellectually formidable and devastating critique of the claims and achievements of psychoanalysis. The need to provide adequate supportive evidence for psychoanalytical principles before their application to other fields is underscored but the book itself reveals just how far psychoanalytical theories outstrip the scientific evidence available to support them.

Darkness Visible (1991) by William Styron. An intimate personal account by a gifted writer of his tortured descent to the edge of self-destruction into what he terms the 'inexplicable agony' of severe depression.

Psychiatry in Dissent (1980) by Anthony W Clare. A nontechnical account of the major controversial issues in modern psychiatry – including the nature of mental illness, the concept of schizophrenia, compulsory treatment, and ECT – placed within the context of psychiatry as it is currently practised.

Manic-Depressive Illness (1990) by Frederick K Goodwin and Kay Redfield Jamison. A substantial analysis of the nature and extent of manic depression, its cyclical course, and contemporary treatment. Vividly portrays the complexity of this particular form of psychiatric disorder and the intermingling roles of biology, personality, and environment in its genesis, impact, and outcome.

Schizophrenia and Related Syndromes (1994) by P J McKenna. A lucid account of the most baffling psychiatric disorder comprehensible to lay and professional reader alike.

The Faber Book of Madness (1991) edited by Roy Porter. A diverting and informative anthology on the subject of madness, including a rich selection of the writings of those who have themselves suffered serious mental instability.

The Oxford Textbook of Psychiatry (1989) edited by Michael Gelder, Dennis Gath, and Richard Mayou. The most comprehensive yet manageable textbook of psychiatry currently available.

PSYCHOANALYSIS – *Anthony Storr*

Freud ranks with Charles Darwin and Karl Marx as one of the three pioneers who most altered man's vision of himself in the 20th century. Darwin demonstrated man's kinship with other animals, Marx postulated that history was governed by economic forces over which the majority of human beings have no direct influence. Freud laid siege to Victorian notions of rationality, and claimed that men were much more governed by unconscious forces and emotional drives than they were by reason. Although Freud's psychoanalytic theories have been sharply criticized in recent years, psychoanalysis has had such a powerful influence on our thinking about ourselves that it cannot simply be dismissed because it does not fulfil the criteria of science. Even if every idea that Freud put forward could be proved wrong, we should still be greatly in his debt.

Analysis does not set out to make pathological reactions impossible,
but to give the patient's ego the freedom *to decide one way or the other.*

SIGMUND FREUD

The Discovery of the Unconscious (1970) by Henri F Ellenberger. Subtitled 'The History and Evolution of Dynamic Psychiatry', this is an invaluable source book which has won worldwide acclaim.

Freud: A Life for Our Time (1988) by Peter Gay. The best and most recent biography of Freud by an American historian who is also trained in psychoanalysis.

The Unconscious before Freud (1962) by Lancelot Law Whyte. An irreplaceable account of how the idea of unconscious mental function and events gradually developed over several centuries to culminate in Freudian theory.

The Psychoanalytic Movement (1985) by Ernest Gellner. A witty, irreverent account of how psychoanalysis developed from being a theory of neurosis in a widespread movement which conquered the Western world.

Anxiety and Neurosis (1968) by Charles Rycroft. A penetrating account of how the psychoanalytic method can be used to treat neurotic symptoms, which relates psychoanalytic theory to biological principles.

Freud and His Followers (1975) by Paul Roazen. Based on interviews with some 70 people who had known Freud personally, this is a readable, scholarly, sometimes scandalous account of the history of psychoanalysis.

Freud (1989) by Anthony Storr. A brief account of Freud's life and thought which may be found useful as an introductory text.

Freud: Biologist of the Mind (1979) by Frank J Sulloway. An outstanding contribution to Freudian studies which is still indispensable reading for anyone interested in psychoanalysis and its founder.

PSYCHOLOGY – *Hans Eysenck*

Psychology is the scientific study of human (and animal) behaviour. It has its classics, of course, but for nonprofessional readers general overviews of recent research are probably to be preferred – science constantly advances, and the latest research, and the most recent theories, build on what was done before and advance it further. For most readers interest will probably centre, not so much on purely technical issues, but on topics relevant to the human condition. Psychology has made important contributions to our understanding of crime, neurosis, personality, intelligence, and many other important topics; it has also pioneered methods of curing neuroses, rehabilitating criminals, and generally improving the quality of life. There has in recent years been a recognition that human beings are bisocial animals, and hence the old-fashioned disregard of genetics and biology in general has given way to a more inclusive theory taking into account both social and biological factors.

Everything that exists exists in some quantity, and can therefore be measured.

E L THORNDIKE

Conditional Reflexes (1927) by I P Pavlov. Pavlov's book is a classic, and worth reading in spite of its age. Many people have built on this secure foundation, and anyone wanting to see how a science of behaviour is possible can do no better than read this monumental contribution. The experiments are mainly done on dogs, but the general principles have been found to apply equally to humans.

Personality and Individual Differences: A Natural Science Approach (1985) by H J Eysenck and M Eysenck. Personality is of central importance in modern psychology, and many important advances have been made in the experimental study of personality and in the social importance of these advances. This book gives a brief overview of where we are now.

Handbook of Effective Psychotherapy (1993) by T R Giles. In the last 12 years or so behaviour therapy, based on the principles of conditioning and learning, has been shown to be much more effective in curing neurotic disorders than the psychotherapies based on Freudian speculations. This book discusses methods and evidence in detail.

Biological Approaches to the Study of Human Intelligence (1993) by P A Vernon. The study of intelligence has been transformed in recent years by successful attempts to look at the brain processes underlying cognitive functioning, and the psychophysiological differences between high- and low-IQ people. This book gives a good summary of what has been achieved.

The Psychopathology of Crime (1993) by A Raine. Raine has summarized a great deal of recent work demonstrating that high criminality (and antisocial behaviour generally) has a strong genetic basis, so that we can identify the hormonal influences and the neural transmitters mediating these effects. These findings have important consequences for our thinking about crime.

Biological Psychology (1994) by F J McGuigan. McGuigan explains the biological basis underlying our emotions, memory, learning, social behaviour, and so on. It is a successful attempt to show the close links between psychology and biology, and to get beyond the simplistic, purely social approach hitherto prevalent.

Perspectives on Bias in Mental Testing (1984) by C R Reynolds and R Brown. Reynolds and Brown deal in detail with the problems raised by bias in mental testing, and in particular the arguments about the influence (if any) of race in this connection. They give an unprejudiced account of the problem, and tell the reader what factual knowledge is available.

Nature and Nurture in Psychology (1993) by R Plomin and G McClearn. Plomin and McClearn give a detailed account of the present status of the age-old nature–nurture controversy, covering the personality and intelligence, attitudes and other topics. This is an easy-to- read but very up-to-date account written by leading experts.

ANIMALS

THE LIVES OF ANIMALS – *Stephen Webster*

Life for an animal has its simple priorities, feeding and reproduction being just two. However, actually finding out how an animal lives, and where, is an often uncomfortable experience requiring patience and diligence. Any of the books below might inspire you to go out into the wild and take a look for yourself.

Sing a song of sixpence / A pocket full of rye, / Four and twenty blackbirds, / Baked in a pie; / When the pie was opened, / The birds began to sing; / Was not that a dainty dish / To set before the king?

TRADITIONAL NURSERY RHYME

Life of the Bee (1901) by Maurice Maeterlink. A beautiful account of one man's study of the bees in his care. The author is almost poetic in his descriptions of the efforts of the bees, working to look after hive and queen. Still an apicultural classic.

The Goshawk (1951) by T S White. A gripping account, suitable for younger readers too, of the author's attempt to train a hawk. The story shows how profound can be the relationship between animal and owner. One of the best books on the art of falconry ever written.

Life at the Edge (1989) edited by James Gould and Carol Grant Gould. This book is a series of articles from *Scientific American* and is a detailed scientific account of how animals live in even the strangest and fiercest places – in the Antarctic or inside volcanoes, for example. Quite technical and challenging but with a little effort this book makes an excellent read.

The Formation of Vegetable Mould, through the Action of Worms, with Observation on Their Habits (1881; new edition 1985) by Charles Darwin. As an old man Darwin chose the common earthworm as the final object of his curiosity, and wrote this splendid book on its habits and its intelligence.

Last Animals at the Zoo (1991) by Colin Tudge. An inquiry into the places most of us must visit if we want to see elephants and rhinos, lions and tigers. An interesting and thought-provoking description of how, through captive-breeding programmes, zoos can assist endangered species.

Primate Visions (1992) by Donna Haraway. A detailed survey of the nature of primate research, looking especially at how issues of gender and race have influenced the scientists' work.

LIFE IN THE SEA – *Gordon L J Paterson*

Sea covers much of our planet. Hidden beneath the waves lives a rich diversity of plants and animals, appearing to us as bizarre, fantastic, and intriguing. The oceans and their inhabitants represent the last great frontier on the planet. It is significant that we know more about processes on other planets than our marine ecosystems. Even now startling discoveries are made. New habitats, such as the hot vents, and huge animals like megamouth sharks have been found in the last 20 years, reminding us how little we really know about our planet. Marine biology and oceanography are the branches of science that study life in the sea.

Every living thing is descended from marine life. Indeed, we carry the ancient sea inside us, for the isotonic composition of the blood of vertebrates on land bears an unmistakable resemblance to seawater ...

ELLIOTT A NORSE

The Open Sea – Its Natural History, Part 1. The World of the Plankton (1972) by Alister Hardy. This is a classic text, wonderfully written, which will serve as a good introduction to the open sea and the intriguing creatures that live in it. Slightly dated now but nevertheless a fascinating account.

Deep-Sea Biology – A Natural History of Organisms at the Deep-Sea Floor (1992) by J D Gage and P A Tyler. The deep sea is one of the largest ecosystems, covering some 50% of the planet. This scholarly work introduces the reader to how oceanographers study the animals and their ecology in this alien world, where the temperature is only just above freezing and the pressure reaches several tonnes per square centimetre.

Global Marine Biological Diversity (1993) edited by Elliott A Norse. It is often forgotten that the sea represents one of the most diverse systems on the planet. This book explains the problems facing, conserving, and sustaining biodiversity in the marine environment. It provides a readable account of the current debate about biodiversity and how and why we should try to sustain it.

Reader's Digest Book of the Great Barrier Reef (1984). The Great Barrier Reef is without doubt one of the great natural phenomena of the world. But even more amazing are the plants and animals that live on, in, and around this coral wonderland. The book beautifully illustrates the vast diversity of life to be found.

The Greenpeace Book of Coral Reefs (1992) by Sue Wells and Nick Hanna. The main thrust of this book is explaining the coral ecosystem and the complex cycles of life that are increasingly under threat by human activities.

Oceans – A Mitchell Beazley World Conservation Atlas (1991) edited by Danny Elder and John Pernatta. This atlas gives useful background to conservation problems in the marine environment.

Water Baby (1992) by Victoria A Kaharl. This is a fascinating account of the building and development of the research submersible *Alvin*. It is one of a handful of vehicles that take scientists down into the depths to glimpse this alien realm. *Alvin* has been the platform from which researchers have made many startling discoveries. It is the oceanographic equivalent of the space shuttle.

Sharks in Question – The Smithsonian Institution Answer Book (1989) by Victor G Springer and Joy P Gold. No book list on marine life would be complete without something on sharks. Our fascination with this group of top marine predators is mirrored by the format of the book, which is based on the most frequently asked questions. The book is a mine of useful information.

Guardians of the Whales – The Quest to Study Whales in the Wild (1992) by Bruce Obee and Graeme Ellis. Much of what we know about the behaviour and ecology of whales comes from dedicated bands of scientists studying whales from boats – a kind of professional whale-watching. This beautifully photographed book recounts the people and the methods they use to study whales in the NE Pacific.

There are numerous field guides to help those interested in marine life identify the plants and animals they encounter on shores and while diving. Collins, Hamlyn ,and the Marine Conservation Society produce general guides to marine life and fish for Europe and further afield. The Audubon Society and Peterson guides cover the North American coasts.

The Hutchinson University Library series provided a range of books about various groups of marine animal and although these are aimed at students they contain a wealth of biological detail. Examples of volumes in the series are: *Marine Mammals, Annelids, Molluscs, Sponges*.

FISHES – *Darrell J Siebert*

Ichthyology is the study of fishes, in all their aspects. This includes trying to figure out the evolutionary relationships among them (their history) and attempting to understand their ecology (how they live). The history of fishes provides insight into panevolutionary theories of how life and Earth have evolved together. Fish ecology will be the key to the sustainable development of an important food source worldwide. Fishes also give great pleasure to many people as pets. A well thought-out and maintained aquarium is a beautiful sight. The diversity of modern fishes is bewildering. If there is among vertebrates a biodiversity crisis of species it is the fishes: perhaps only half of all living fishes are known. They deserve better.

Fishes are a necessary part of our environment. During the past couple of decades millions of people have come to realize that our planet is in danger and have dedicated their energies to protecting and improving the world we live in. I am reminded of a dialogue in an old Pogo comic strip which starts when one of the

characters says that 'everyone is talking about it'. 'I'm not talking about it.'
'You're not everyone.' 'No, but without me, no one is everyone.' This is the way it
is with our environment: nothing in it is really expendable.

C LAVETT SMITH

Fish of the World: A Collection of 19th-Century Paintings (1990) by Hiroshi Aramata. A beautifully compiled work of the amazing artwork of illustrators from the 19th century.

Dr Axelrod's Atlas of Freshwater Aquarium Fishes (1985) by Herbert R Axelrod, Warren E Burgess, Neal Pronek, and Jerry G Walls. A huge work of colour photographs for which there is as yet no substitute. Arranged by region of the world with information on husbandry.

Fishes: Expedition Field Techniques (1993; 2nd edition 1995) by Brian W Coad. An excellent introduction to ichtyhological fieldwork, for the amateur and professional alike.

The Fishes of Tennessee (1993) by David A Etnier and Wayne C Starness. As good an example of an American 'state' book as there is, lavishly illustrated with colour photographs, some of which show the amazing world of fish colours.

The Rise of Fishes: 500 Million Years of Evolution (1995) by John A Long. A surprising introduction to fossil vertebrates (fishes). An academic work but so well illustrated it will be of interest in the popular literature.

Fishes of the World (1976; 3rd edition 1994) by Joseph S Nelson. The only real introduction into the realm of fish classification. Now in its 3rd edition, it has improved with time.

Encyclopedia of Fishes (1994) edited by John R Paxton and William N Eschmeyer. Arranged systematically, this is the best of the compendia written for the layman.

Fish Watching: An Outdoor Guide to Freshwater Fishes (1994) by C Lavett Smith. A delightful introduction to fish watching in nature, by a dedicated fish watcher. You can learn to do it yourself from this book.

Sharks in Question (1989) by Victor G Springer and Joy P Gold. Simply the best, most informative shark book on the market.

The Aquarist's Encyclopaedia (1983) by Günther Sterba. One of the hobbyist volumes, but filled with biological information.

Trout (1991) edited by Judith Stoltz and Judith Snell. A wonderful, well-illustrated compilation of information on the world's most important freshwater game fishes.

Fishes of the World: An Illustrated Dictionary (1975) by Alwyne Wheeler. A dictionary of fishes and fish terms. Most of what you want to know can be found here.

INSECTS – *Paul Eggleton*

The study of insects is known as entomology, and covers a very broad range of disciplines from behaviour to molecular biology. Insect biology is one of the most important areas of biology, and one of the least well-known, given that of the 5 million probable insect species perhaps only 1 million have been formally described. Of those 1 million, perhaps 100,000 have their biologies known in any detail, and at the present rate of habitat destruction, many species will go extinct before anything at all is discovered about them. The enormous number of insect species has recently led ento-mologists to become concerned with insect biodiversity as an area of research in itself, and especially with insect conservation and the effect of human disturbance on insect diversity.

I feel like an old warhorse at the sound of the trumpet when I read about the capturing of rare beetles ... It really makes me long to begin collecting again.

CHARLES DARWIN

Bugs in the System: Insects and Their Impact on Human Affairs (1995) by May R Berenbaum. A simple and readable introduction to insects, their classification, biology, and effects on people. It gives a good overview of the extraordinary diversity of the insect world.

Life on a Little-Known Planet (1993) by Howard Ensign Evans. Covers similar ground to the first book, but might be considered either more poetic or more pretentious, accord-ing to taste. Throughout, however, the author's love of his subject shines through.

A Field Guide to the Insects of Britain and Northern Europe (1982) by Michael Chinery. An excellent introduction to the natural history of British insects, with identifica-tion keys and good illustrations.

Insects of Australia (1991) edited by the Commonwealth Scientific and Industrial Research Organization. In contrast to the Chinery book, this deals in detail with a tropical fauna which is much richer and more varied than the European one. It also has useful chapters on insect systematics, morphology, and biogeography.

Insect Conservation Biology (1994) by M J Samways. A good introductory book deal-ing with the problems and principles of insect conservation, a topic that has been neglected compared with the conservation biology of larger vertebrate animals.

The Ants (1990) by B Hölldobler and E O Wilson. A Pulitzer prizewinning book dealing with a group of animals with one of the most complex and interesting social systems of any organism. A unique contribution to biology. The same authors' *Journey to the Ants* (1994) is shorter and more accessible, intended for the general reader.

Insect Phylogeny (1981) by W Hennig. Although out of date and in places difficult to read, this still remains a seminal work by the great German entomologist Willi Hennig. It was one of the first works to apply the principles of cladistics to estimating evolutionary relationships between organisms, and many of its conclusions are still accepted today.

Imm's General Textbook of Entomology (1957; 10th edition 1977) volume 2 by O W Richards and R G Davies. An excellent textbook introduction to insect diversity, dealing with each group in detail. A good primer for those interested in the whole range of insect forms.

The Insects: Structure and Function (1982) by R F Chapman. A textbook that emphasizes a functional approach to the study of insects. Readable and highly informative.

BIRDS – *Robert Prys-Jones*

Birds fascinate people. Colourful, vocal, and accessible, they provide an avenue through which we can begin to obtain understanding of the selective forces moulding the living world to which we belong. Partly as a result, the breadth of knowledge available on birds is unrivalled for other animal groups. This knowledge, combined with the affection with which most are held, has placed birds at the forefront of efforts by conservation organizations worldwide to maintain natural environments in the face of overwhelming and ever accelerating human-induced change. Birds thus demand our attention, not only for the amazing creatures they are, but also for the role they can play as a shield for the great unknown world that is vanishing around us.

The pleasure of studying birds and the pleasure of finding out new things can be combined at small cost in money, though more in time, by anyone so inclined.

DAVID LACK

The Life of the Robin (1943) by David Lack. A classic, highly readable account of the life of a bird species, written by one of the century's pre-eminent ornithologists.

Finches (1972) by Ian Newton. Written with enthusiasm from great personal experience, this is a model of how to write a comparative account of the behaviour and ecology of a bird family.

The Web of Adaptation (1976) by David Snow. A strangely little-known but compellingly readable account of the behaviour of fruit-eating birds in the American tropics.

The Age of Birds (1980) by Alan Feduccia. The evolutionary history of birds is a topic of great current research, but this remains the best introduction to the subject.

Bird Migration (1983) by Chris Mead. A wide-ranging, well-illustrated overview of a subject that holds a particular fascination for many bird-watchers.

Save the Birds (1987) by Anthony Diamond. Produced in a number of languages and national editions, this book provides authoritative and beautifully illustrated insight into the problems that endanger a depressingly large number of bird species worldwide.

The Cambridge Encyclopedia of Ornithology (1991) edited by Michael Brooke and Tim Birkhead. Undoubtedly the place to begin pursuing an interest in almost any aspect of ornithology. Well arranged and illustrated, and clearly written by an impressive team of contributors.

Dunnock Behaviour and Social Evolution (1992) by Nicholas Davies. Fifty years on from Lack's *Life of the Robin*, this is a brilliantly written account of the insights that arise from combining detailed fieldwork on a species with modern evolutionary theory.

Handbook of the Birds of the World (1992, continuing) edited by Josep del Hoyo, Andrew Elliott, and Jordi Sargatal. With two of a proposed 12 volumes now published, it is impossible to praise this work too highly. Immensely ambitious and astonishingly illustrated, it combines exceptionally readable family-level reviews with brief but comprehensive species accounts and distribution maps for every bird species.

The Beak of the Finch (1994) by Jonathan Weiner. Written by a journalist, this books succeeds well in conveying the fascination inherent in the profoundly important, long-term studies by Peter Grant and his co-workers into the action of natural selection on Galapagos finch populations.

ANIMAL BEHAVIOUR – *Peter Tallack*

In order to survive and reproduce successfully, animals have evolved clever ways of finding food, shelter, and mates, avoiding predators, caring for their young, and so on. Ethology – the study of animal behaviour – views animals as machines with fascinating mechanics, as organisms with complex life histories, and as the end products of natural selection that have evolved from ancestors who themselves lived and behaved and were successful in producing offspring. The subject ranges from microscopic investigations of genetic mechanisms and nervous systems, through experimental work of the behaviour of whole organisms, to long-term studies on groups of animals in forests, fields, and oceans. There are four underlying questions of animal behaviour – what are the mechanisms that control it? why or how are they useful? how did they develop? what is their evolutionary history? – and a vast array of splendid books that attempt to provide answers.

We are survival machines – robot vehicles blindly programmed to preserve the selfish molecules known as genes. This is a truth that still fills me with astonishment.

RICHARD DAWKINS

The Oxford Companion to Animal Behaviour (1981) edited by David McFarland. A standard handbook that anyone interested in animals can enjoy. Contains more than 200 articles, each written by a specialist, on a wide range of topics.

King Solomon's Ring (1952) by Konrad Lorenz. A gripping introduction to modern animal behaviour by one of its founders, an advocate of the view that most animal behaviour is genetically fixed or innate. Full of original insights and a pleasure to read.

The Study of Instinct (1951) by Niko Tinbergen. A systematic discussion of the beginning of ethology written with brilliant clarity by the pioneer of the biological study of animal behaviour under natural or near-natural conditions. Important and influential.

The Dance Language and Orientation of Bees (1967) by Karl von Frisch. A definitive account of von Frisch's marvellous observations and experiments on the waggle dance and other forms of honeybee communication behaviour. The culmination of more than 50 years of research, this is a genuine classic.

In the Shadow of Man (1983) by Jane Goodall. Goodall's work with the chimpanzees of Gombe is one of the great scientific achievements of the 20th century. Her detailed revelations of their behaviour first appeared in this lyrical book, written with sympathy and understanding.

Sociobiology (1975) by Edward O Wilson. This groundbreaking study of the biological basis of all social behaviour on social animals was the subject of much controversy when it first appeared, principally because of the final chapter focusing on humans. Authoritative, encyclopedic, and readable.

The Selfish Gene (1976) by Richard Dawkins. The author's first book and still his most famous. An engrossing look at evolution and behaviour from a gene's-eye perspective, expounded with clarity, wit, and verve. Forceful and persuasive.

How Monkeys See the World (1990) by Dorothy L Cheney and Robert M Seyfarth. The authors describe their superb study of signalling in vervet monkeys. The enthralling ideas and lucid presentation combine to make this the best exploration so far of what goes on inside the mind of another species.

The Red Queen (1993) by Matt Ridley. A brilliant look at the evolution of sex and its implications for behaviour, providing a rich collection of insights into the private lives of a whole host of creatures.

The Tangled Wing (1982) by Melvin Konner. A poetic and masterly survey of the biological constraints on human nature, including what animal behaviour can and cannot tell us about ourselves.

ANIMAL RIGHTS – *Andrew Linzey*

The moral status of animals has emerged as a new field of study in its own right. In the area of philosophy alone, within the last 20 years contemporary moral philosophers have written more on the topic of human responsibility to other animals than their predecessors had written during the previous 2,000 years. In fact, ethical concern for animals is not new. Although Western culture has generally accorded animals a low status, almost every thinker from Pythagoras to Schweitzer has at least considered the question of duties to animals. What is new is a major shift in ethical sensitivity. The old idea that animals are simply resources, machines, tools, things here for our use, is slowly but surely giving way to another perception that sentient beings have value in themselves, inherent dignity, and rights. This revolution of sensibility has been facilitated by a number of pioneering works in the field of ethics, philosophy, and religion. Listed here are some of the major works that have been significant during the modern period.

The time is coming, however, when people will be astonished that mankind needed so long a time to learn to regard thoughtless injury to life as incompatible with ethics.

ALBERT SCHWEITZER

Civilization and Ethics (1923) by Albert Schweitzer. Although Schweitzer was not the first to embrace the humane treatment of animals, his doctrine of 'reverence for life' has been widely influential. *Civilization and Ethics* is the second volume of his wide-ranging critique of Western philosophy. According to Schweitzer, reverence for life is the 'basic principle of the moral'. 'It is good to maintain and encourage life; it is bad to destroy life or to obstruct it.' Although Schweitzerian doctrine – in its original form at least – has few followers today, it is difficult not to be impressed by the sheer profundity of this thought. Readable and very challenging.

Animal Rights (1976) by Andrew Linzey. This slim volume effectively heralded the modern animal rights movement. It argues that sentiency (the ability to experience pain and suffering) rather than 'personhood', 'soulfulness', or 'rationality' should be the criterion for rights; and examines our current use of animals as food, for science, and for sport. Criticizes the Judaeo-Christian tradition for its theological insensitivity to animals. Linzey's later works, *Christianity and the Rights of Animals* 1987 and *Animal Theology* 1994, develop his theological critique of Western religious attitudes.

Animal Liberation (1976) by Peter Singer. Following on the heels of *Animal Rights*, Singer's work is a philosophical defence of the sentiency criterion for moral considerability. If a being suffers, there can be no good reason why that suffering should not be taken into consideration. Argues that many contemporary practices are 'speciesist'; that is, the result of an arbitrary and unjustifiable prejudice against animals. Hugely popular and readable book, still in print.

The Moral Status of Animals (1977) by Stephen R L Clark. Another heavyweight philosophical defence of animals. It argues that the humanitarian tradition against cruelty within Western culture should compel us to rethink our attitudes to animals and become vegetarians. Not an easy read but full of challenging insights.

Man and the Natural World: Changing Attitudes in England 1500–1800 (1983) by Keith Thomas. Consummately impressive history of the origins of modern sensibility to animals. Charts with great skill the movement of ideas from medieval views of human supremacy to the emergence of Victorian philanthropy. Especially good on the religious aspects and the role of theology for and against animal welfare. Thomas is a celebrated historian and a very fine writer.

The Case for Animal Rights (1983) by Tom Regan. Yet another heavyweight philosophical book. Argues that all animals are 'subjects of a life' and have intrinsic value, and therefore rights. Maintains that only a theory of rights can do justice to our moral obligations to animals. A significant philosophical contribution, nicely textured writing, but no easy read.

The Unheeded Cry: Animal Consciousness, Animal Pain and Science (1989) by Bernard E Rollin. Rollin is one of the few animal-rights theorists equally versed in physiology, philosophy, and bioethics. This is a powerful critique of the view that animals do not have a mental life and cannot suffer, especially critical of experimental scientists who work with animals. Rollin developed the world's first course in veterinary ethics and animal rights at Colorado State University.

Political Theory and Animal Rights (1990) edited by P A B Clarke and Andrew Linzey. A major anthology comprising 60 extracts from political theorists, philosophers, and theologians including Plato, Aristotle, Augustine, Thomas Aquinas, René Descartes, David Hume, John Locke, George Berkeley, Thomas Hobbes, Jean-Jacques Rousseau, Gottfried Leibniz, Montaigne, Richard Hooker, Karl Marx, Albert Schweitzer, and Bertrand Russell. The anthology shows how various concerns about animals form part of a long historical tradition and details the major shifts of thinking about the status of animals. Indispensable to understanding the emergence of the modern animal-rights movement.

Created from the Animals: The Moral Implications of Darwinism (1991) by James Rachels. A powerful defence of Darwin, arguing that, correctly understood, Darwinism provides a strong theoretical basis for animal rights. Maintains that Darwin, in holding that humans are 'created from the animals', laid the foundations for a new inclusivist ethic. Chapter 5 on 'Morality without the idea that humans are special' is provocative and challenging. Written in an accessible style with wit and elegance.

The Heretic's Feast: A History of Vegetarianism (1993) by Colin Spencer. The first major history of vegetarianism from early humanoids to the ethical vegetarianism of the 1990s. Spencer's conclusion echoes the words of Henry Beston: 'We need another and wiser and perhaps a more mystical concept of animals ... They are not brethren; they are not underlings; they are other nations caught with ourselves in the net of life and time, fellow prisoners of the splendour and travail of the earth.' A fascinating volume, remarkable for its breadth and lucidity.

PLANTS

INTRODUCTION – *Sandra Knapp and Bob Press*

Plants are the basis for all life on Earth. Their ability to convert the Sun's energy into a usable form places them at the base of the pyramid of life. Plants range from simple to highly complex organisms and occupy a bewildering variety of niches in the natural world. They can be parasites, carnivores, mimics, and are often equal partners with animals in intricate associations. The science of botany comprises the study of plants, their diversity of form and function, their distribution, and their uses.

I indulged the fancy once upon a time that a botanist was one who distinguished plants by sight: but I observe that, unless scent, taste and touch come in and that very obviously, a botanist is of no account.

CARL VON LINNÉ

The Compleat Naturalist (1971) by Wilfred Blunt is a lively and beautifully illustrated biography of the world's most influential botanist, Carl von Linné (otherwise known as Carolus Linnaeus). In the 18th century he devised not only the first adequate system for classifying plants – the then notorious sexual system – but also the binomial system of Latin plant names which remains the universal currency among botanists.

The Life of Plants (1964; revised 1981) by E J H Corner is a successful solution to the problem of writing a 'small book about plants *in toto*' and an enthusiastic counter to previous 'thoroughly dull and dully thorough' works on the subject.

The Plant Book (1990) by David Mabberly follows in the footsteps of classic works by J C Willis, A Cronquist, and others. It is as complete a reference to the vascular plants as it is possible to have, with entries for evey currently accepted family and genus. Brief text gives information on interrelationships, morphological characteristics, distributions, numbers of species, and uses.

Plant Taxonomy (1990) by Tod Stuessy is a heavyweight text by one of the most authoritative taxonomists around. Slightly daunting but comprehensive and thought-provoking.

Biology of Plants (5th edition 1992) by Peter Raven, Ray Evert, and Susan Eichorn. As well as explaining form and function, the authors address the themes of heredity, evolutionary relationships, and ecology, providing a rounded picture of plant biology.

The New Royal Horticultural Society Dictionary of Gardening (1992) edited by A Huxley is a comprehensive work covering most plants ever cultivated. It is liberally sprinkled with explanations of gardening terms and techniques as well as describing numerous cultivars, hybrids, and cultivated plants of both wild and purely garden origin.

The Plant Finder (1994–95 edition) published by the Hardy Plant Society is the ultimate plant catalogue, listing 55,000 different plants and where to obtain them in the

UK. This is where to find those little-known species you have always wanted to cultivate.

The Private Life of Plants (1995) by David Attenborough is an eminently readable and lavishly illustrated account of different aspects of the lives of plants, from dispersal, growth, and nutrition to plant–animal interactions and survival strategies. Based on his television series for the BBC.

PLANT VARIETIES – *Sandra Knapp and Bob Press*

There are in excess of 250,000 species of vascular plants alone in the world and species new to science are discovered and described almost daily, especially from tropical regions where the biodiversity is still nowhere near being adequately quantified. Gardeners and horticulturalists have added enormously to this natural variety by producing cultivars of purely garden origin. The limits and defining characteristics of taxa are constantly under review, changing with the increase in our understanding of the plants involved. Two common methods of getting to grips with this wealth of life are taxonomy and floristics. Taxonomy is the describing, naming, and classifying of organisms – in this case plants. Floristics focuses on the whole flora of a geographical region.

Locality often makes plants a little different, but it has never changed one species into another, not even in the brain of any sane botanist.

CARL VON LINNÉ

Carnivorous Plants (1979) by Adrian Slack is still probably the best book describing a fascinatingly macabre and diverse group of plants which are linked by their unique method of supplementary nutrition.

Palms (1982) by Alec Blombery and Tony Rodd. A good example of a study of a single group of plants, this book deals with the cultivation, care, and economic importance of palms as well as describing the world's species.

A World of Ferns (1991) by Josephine Camus, Clive Jermy, and Barry Thomas is a general introduction to the subject of ferns, organized by habitat. The beautiful photographs show the diversity of the group.

Crucifers of Great Britain and Ireland (1991) by Tim Rich. Number six in a series of seven BSBI Handbooks by various authors, pitched at the more committed botanist. The series covers difficult and taxonomically challenging groups of plants in the British Isles flora, including sedges, umbellifers, docks, willows, and roses. All are written and illustrated to the highest standards.

Field Guide to the Trees of Britain and Europe (1992) by Bob Press is typical of the New Holland Field Guides. The books in this series, by various authors, epitomize the most common style of photographic guides to identifying plants, and reflect the increasing tendency to include all species in Europe rather than a limited selection of them.

Guide to Flowering Plant Families (1994) by Wendy Zomlefer is a synoptic treatment of the flowering-plant families that occur in the USA. Despite this apparent geographical limitation, it is useful almost anywhere and has the added bonus of lucid, easily assimilated sections on modern taxonomic methods, cladistics in taxonomy, and botanical terminology.

STRUCTURE AND FUNCTION
Sandra Knapp and Bob Press

Living things are complex and a first step in their study is to know how and why they are constructed as they are. Structure and function are indivisible; to study one without the other is to understand only half the story. The basic principles of different functions are similar throughout the plant kingdom but the means by which they may be achieved and, therefore, the range and type of structures required, are much more varied. Habitat, too, is highly influential on plant structure. Plants occur in a wide range of habitats, from boiling springs to ice-bound tundra and from sea beds to mountaintops; their structural diversity is equally broad. Within this diversity of form there are also examples of superficial similarity between unrelated groups of plants; for example, the cactuses of North and Central America and succulent *Euphorbia*s from the deserts of the Old World. Different organs may be modified to meet the same environmental demands, and homology, the principle of comparing like with like, is especially important when dealing with morphological features of plants where a 'leaf' may be a true leaf, a leaf stalk, a stipule, or a stem, and a 'bulb' may derive from a root, a stem, a leaf base, or a bud.

A biologist, regardless of his specialty, cannot afford to lose sight of the whole organism if his goal is the understanding of the organic world.

KATHERINE ESAU

Anatomy of Flowering Plants: An Introduction to Structure and Development (1987) by Paula Rudall is a concise but comprehensive description of plant anatomy and its pre-eminent role in plant taxonomy. Stunningly illustrated.

Plant Form. An Illustrated Gude to Flowering Plant Morphology (1991) by Adrian Bell is a rapid-reference guide to the architecture and construction of plants, giving concise explanations of the derivation and interpretation of morphological features. Suitable for users of varying abilities.

Bark: The Formation, Characteristics and Uses of Bark Around the World (1993) by Ghillean and Anne Prance. Bark is one of the defining tissues of woody plants. This work uses photographs to explain its variety of form, function, and use worldwide.

THE LIVES OF PLANTS – *Stephen Webster*

Plants are the producers of our planet. They are the organisms that absorb the Sun's light and manufacture the food on which animals depend. The waste product of that process we also need rather a lot: oxygen. As these books show, plants are every bit as fascinating and important as animals.

> *The thirsty earth sucks up the rain, / And drinks, and gapes for drink again. / The plants suck in the earth, and are / With constant drinking fresh and fair.*
>
> ABRAHAM COWLEY

The Fate of the Forest (1989) by Susanna Hecht and Alexander Cockburn. A measured account of the destruction of the Amazonian tropical rainforest. Filled with interesting details on the flora of Amazonia.

The Pollination of Plants (1973) by Michael Proctor and Peter Yeo. A rich source of information on the many and varied ways plants have found of getting pollen from one to another.

The Private Life of Plants (1994) by David Attenborough. Beautifully illustrated account of the lifestyles of plants, combined with detailed text and the traditional Attenborough enthusiasm.

The Day of the Triffids (1951) by John Wyndham. Fiction, but still a compelling story of the worst nightmare – the day the plants turned against mankind. Quite a lot of interesting botanical detail too.

A Passion for Plants (1995) by Clive Langmead. The subject of the book is as much Ghillean Prance as it is plants. For Prance is director of Kew Gardens and is a man in love – with things botanical. Essential reading for someone who thinks plants are dull.

Mushrooms (1990) by Roger Phillips. Strictly speaking, mushrooms are fungi, not plants, but we eat them and tread on them as though they were plants. This book will open up a completely new world for you – and help you distinguish between the safe and the dangerous.

Vegetables (1995) by Roger Phillips and Martin Rix. A survey of the edibles we normally see in the greengrocery or down at the allotment, plus some oddities. Fascinating, scientific, and well illustrated.

AGRICULTURE AND MEDICINAL PLANTS
Sandra Knapp and Bob Press

Agriculture played no part in the earliest human societies but once the first plant domestications took place, crops became a major factor in shaping our civilization. In its broadest sense, modern agriculture encompasses such aspects as gene manipulation and conservation of wild progenitors as well as the more prosaic planting, growing, and harvesting of crops. Medicinal usage of plants almost certainly dates from man's earliest history. Initially there was probably little or no difference between plants as healthful foods and plants as curatives in the crudest sense. When these roles diverged, medicinal use gradually became entwined with folklore, mysticism, and other philosophical accoutrements, often to the point of entirely obscuring the original purpose of the plant. Synthetic drugs and chemicals have largely replaced herbal remedies in the industrialized world, but extracts derived from plants maintain an important role in modern medicine and for many peoples traditional drugs remain their only available source of treatment. The renewed interest in natural plant extracts is a reminder that, once upon a time, we were all similarly reliant on herbs and herbal lore.

> *I have oft-times declared, how by the outward shapes and qualities
> of things we may know their inward virtues.*
>
> PARACELSUS

Nightshades, the Paradoxical Plants (1969) by Charles Heiser successfully uses a 'let's tell' style to convey the importance of an intriguing group of medicinal plants.

Medical Botany – Plants Affecting Man's Health (1977) by Walter Lewis and Memory Elvin-Lewis. A reference work with the information organized both by plant and by the conditions treated. The coverage is worldwide and the data easily accessible.

Seed to Civilization (1981) by Charles Heiser covers the origins and evolution of agriculture in a readable style by focusing on the major food species.

The New Age Herbalist (1988) by Richard Mabey is an up-to-date herbal in the European tradition. Mabey uses modern interpretation and relevant medical research to explain and justify the use of traditional remedies.

Field Guide to the Crops of Britain and Europe (1989) by G de Rougemont is a useful tool for identifying the numerous crop plants grown in the region.

Plants and People (1990) by Anna Lewington is a book of the uses of plants by people for agriculture and medicine. Beautiful coffee-table style disguises a highly authoritative work.

Earthly Goods (1994) by Christopher Joyce tackles the complex relationships between medicinal plant hunters, local peoples, conservationists, and pharmaceutical companies, as well as emotive issues including 'ownership' of biodiversity. The book is leavened with descriptions of eccentric scientists, the author's travels, and examples of useful plants.

A Dictionary of Folklore (1995) by Roy Vickery is a source of information on plants in folklore and ethnobotany in the British Isles, including superstitions and customs, legends, folk medicine, and other uses. Unusually for the subject matter, Vickery emphasizes present-day practices and beliefs (those current during 1975–94) as well as dealing with older traditions.

ENVIRONMENT

BIODIVERSITY – *Nigel Dudley*

Biodiversity, or biological diversity, refers to the richness and variety of life, measured by the number of species of plants and animals, their genetic variety, and the ways they interact in ecosystems. Ten years ago 'biodiversity' did not even appear in dictionaries, yet in 1992 it received international attention through agreement of the Convention on Biological Diversity at the Earth Summit in Rio de Janeiro. The concept marks an increasing sophistication in our understanding of ecology. Plants and animals need a working ecosystem. Variety within a species may be as important, from an evolutionary standpoint, as several different species. Preservation of nothing but a relic population may not be much better than complete extinction. Yet at the moment, biodiversity is disappearing faster than at any time in the Earth's history, due to habitat destruction, overexploitation and pollution. Biodiversity already commands an impressive library of books. The titles listed below help show how the idea is developing, give a range of viewpoints about the importance of biodiversity, and outline some options for management of biodiversity in the future.

Ecosystems are not only more complex than we think, but more complex than we can think.

FRANK EGLER

The Sinking Ark (1979) by Norman Myers. Argues that we face a massive loss of species, particularly through tropical deforestation, and that conservation efforts are manifestly failing to counter this trend. In this book he also puts the practical case for preserving species, in terms of their use as genetic resources for foodstuffs, medicines, and so on; a theme which he has continued to developed in a number of further titles, including *The Primary Source*.

Gaia: A New Look at Life on Earth (1979) by James Lovelock. Proposes the still heretical theory that the planet itself is, biologically speaking, a self-regulating mechanism. Whether you agree with Lovelock or not, he presents a sober and well-argued case, and his book helped focus attention on the role that different components play in the ecology of the planet, thus paving the way for discussion on biodiversity.

Biodiversity (1988) edited by Edward O Wilson. The first book to crystallize the debate about biodiversity, which also brought the word itself to public attention. A fascinating array of articles, papers, and even poems about biological diversity around the world. Still the best single introduction to the subject. See also *The Diversity of Life* by Wilson himself for a readable introduction to the subject.

Conserving the World's Biological Diversity (1990) by Jeffrey A McNeely, Kenton R Miller, Walter V Reid, Russell A Mittermeir, and Timothy B Werner. The most comprehensive attempt so far to set an agenda for international conservation of biodiversity. Much of the thinking was later incorporated into proposals for the Convention on Biological Diversity.

The Threatened Gene: Food, Politics and the Loss of Genetic Diversity (1990) by Cary Fowler and Pat Mooney. Biodiversity loss does not only affect natural systems; during the 20th century we have lost hundreds of traditional crop strains and livestock breeds. This meticulously researched and readable book looks at what has happened, how genetic diversity has been lost in food production, and why it matters.

Biodiversity: Social and Ecological Consequences (1992) by Vandana Shiva. Proposes that biodiversity conservation has to be tackled by first addressing problems of intensive farming and North–South relations. It is one of a series of books by a noted Indian scientist and feminist; her *Staying Alive* looks at women's issues in more detail.

Global Biodiversity: The Status of the Earth's Living Resources (1992) edited by Brian Groombridge. A massive review of biodiversity around the world, looking at the status of key ecosystems, the human uses of plants and animals, rates of change in natural systems, and so on.

Saving Nature's Legacy (1994) by Reed F Noss and Allen Y Cooperrider. Guidelines on practical biodiversity conservation at a landscape level.

ECOLOGY – *Nigel Dudley*

E cology has become one of the fastest-growing scientific disciplines of the latter 20th century, and the serious student can refer to a seemingly endless stream of textbooks, monographs, journals, and conference proceedings. The following list has a more modest aim: to introduce some basic and accessible books for the general reader that will outline some of the key ideas for the nonspecialist. As such, it includes two historical titles from people who started to focus attention on issues of ecology, and looks at some accessible modern interpretations.

I wish to speak a word for Nature, for absolute freedom and wildness, as contrasted with a freedom and culture merely civil – to regard man as an inhabitant, or a part and parcel of Nature, rather than a member of society.

HENRY THOREAU

The Natural History of Selborne (1789; several recent editions) by Gilbert White. Why should a series of letters about natural history, written by an obscure parson living near the English South Downs, become a perennial bestseller? Perhaps because White was one of the first to seek the interrelationships in nature, and to look beyond simple classification of biology. Still fascinating, even if White did make a few mistakes, perhaps most famously that swallows and martins overwintered by hibernating in burrows rather than by migrating.

The Portable Thoreau (1980) edited by Carl Bode. An excellent introduction to one of the best nature writers of all time, including the complete text of *Walden* (1854), Thoreau's account of living in a remote house in the Maine woods and of the surrounding nature, along with selections from his journals, *The Maine Woods*, *A Week on the Concord and Merrimack Rivers*, and other works.

History of the Countryside (1990) by Oliver Rackham. For much of the world, ecology is now intimately tied up with human history, and with the changes that farming, forestry, industry, and migration patterns have made on the landscape. Rackham's book, which concentrates particularly on England, shows how ecology and history can be matched to explain the current landscape and ecology. Fascinating and provocative.

Ecology (1990) by M Begon, J L Harper, and C R Townsend. One of the more readable of a series of textbooks on ecology, looking at relationships within populations and communities.

Ecological Imperialism (1993) by Alfred W Crosby. Looks at the biological expansion of Europe over 1,000 years, with particular emphasis on the colonial period, and argues that displacement of native peoples by Europeans in most temperate regions was driven as much by ecology as by military conquest. Interesting for its perspectives linking ecology with historical movements.

Global Marine Biological Diversity (1993) edited by Elliott A Norse. Looks at the ecology of marine systems and at steps to address current problems facing the world's seas and oceans.

The Private Life of Plants (1995) by David Attenborough. A stimulating introduction to plants and the way that they function, by one of the world's best-known natural-history filmmakers and writers. Important because plant ecology is so often ignored by anyone but the professional academics. Attenborough has written many fascinating books; watch out also for *Life on Earth*, which starts from a more general ecological perspective.

ENVIRONMENTAL PROBLEMS – *Nigel Dudley*

Environmental awareness did not suddenly emerge, fully fledged, some time during the 1980s. A concern about environmental impact of human society can be traced back for hundreds of years and, for example, the first pamphlet on air pollution, *Fumifugion: or the smoake of London dissipated*, was published by John Evelyn in London in 1666. Since then, ideas have developed gradually, and have been refined and sometimes revised as our understanding of the environment has become more sophisticated. The list below gives some of the milestone publications of the 'modern' environmental movement. A few of the earlier titles may now sometimes seem a little simplistic, or their ideas have been so incorporated into mainstream thinking that they hardly seem radical any more. All of them have played important roles in shaping, and often changing, people's thinking about our relationship to the planet.

> *Pollution has a long history. The creation of wastes has been one of the distinguishing characteristics of every human society.*
>
> CLIVE PONTING

Silent Spring (1962) by Rachel Carson. Probably the one book that, more than any other, kick-started today's environmental movement. Rachel Carson was a marine biologist, who drafted this passionate exposé about the impact of pesticides on the environment when she was already seriously ill. The book caused a furore and Carson spent her last months being bitterly attacked by industry representatives. She helped change the outlook of a generation. Beautifully written and cogently argued, still fresh after 35 years.

Small Is Beautiful (1973) by E F Schumacher. The title of the book, which delighted or infuriated readers during a period when technology and transnational business practices were increasingly being challenged, was actually suggested by the publisher. The essays give a theoretical background to such developments as intermediate technology. The best, such as 'Buddhist economics', remain pertinent and readable today.

The Limits to Growth (1975) by Donella L and Dennis L Meadows, Jorgen Randers, and William W Behrens III. An early and influential attempt to map the likely impacts of resource depletion using computer modelling. Coming immediately after the 1973 oil crisis, the book helped create new attitudes towards nonrenewable resources. The predictions have proved to be overly pessimistic in terms of time scale, although the central argument remains valid, and the team produced a new analysis, *Beyond the Limits*, almost 20 years later.

How the Other Half Dies – The Real Reasons for World Hunger (1976) by Susan George. It is commonly argued that 'overpopulation' is the greatest threat facing the human race, and the major cause of hunger and famine. Susan George elegantly and comprehensively demolishes these claims, showing that access to food has more to do with the priorities of international agribusiness and the ways that development aid is used and abused.

Soft Energy Paths: Towards a Durable Peace (1977) by Amory Lovins. At a time when solar and wind power were regarded as little more than utopian dreams, Lovins turned the argument around and boldly claimed that, using established technologies, renewable sources will supply all our energy in the future. Part research paper and part polemic, it provided much of the inspiration for current developments of wind farms, solar villages and small-scale hydropower projects. 'Soft energy' became synonymous with post-oil energy sources.

The Nuclear Barons (1981) by Peter Pringle and James Spiegelman. The other half of the energy debate: a detailed and readable analysis of the rise of nuclear power, from early weapons-testing through to then current debates about energy. Written in advance of the major US nuclear accident at Harrisburg and the disaster at Chernobyl in the Ukraine, the book sounds prophetic warnings about the dangers of nuclear energy and remains the best one-volume history of the first 40 years of nuclear development.

In the Rainforest (1984) by Catherine Caufield. Repeated opinion surveys show that tropical deforestation is the single environmental issue that causes the most concern around the world. This book, written by an American journalist, is the account of a personal investigation into causes and effects of tropical forest loss that covered Africa, Asia, and Latin America.

Brundtland Report: Our Common Future (1987) by World Commission on Environment and Development, chaired by Gro Harlem Brundtland. The most comprehensive official international attempt to define 'sustainable development' and to harmonize the needs of people and environment, coordinated by the then prime minister of Norway. Like most such efforts at consensus, it contains contradictions and compromises. Important because of its influence on many governmental and United Nations initiatives.

The Green History of the World (1991) by Clive Ponting. A history of the world from an environmental standpoint, packed with information but also presenting a sustained argument about the links between ecology and human activities, and linking in the influence of religious thought and political philosophy. An excellent one-volume introduction.

How Much is Enough? (1992) by Alan Thein Durning. Addressing the issue that will increasingly dominate the debate about the environment in the next few years; how the rapidly increasing levels of consumption – of raw materials, energy and other resources – by the rich fifth of the population can be reconciled with the needs of the environment and of the poorer human majority.

CONSERVATION – *Peter Tallack*

Around the globe, biological communities that took millions of years to develop are being devastated by human action. What is bad for biological diversity will almost certainly be bad for the human population, because we too are dependent on the natural environment. Conservation biology is the scientific discipline born of this crisis. Its aim is to study and prevent the loss of biological diversity: specifically, the extinction of species, the loss of genetic variation, and the destruction of biological communities. It brings together people and knowledge from many different fields.

When the last individual of a race of living things breathes no more, another heaven and another earth must pass before such a one can be again.

WILLIAM BEEBE

The Diversity of Life (1992) by Edward O Wilson. An outstanding overview of the biodiversity crisis, as well as basic concepts such as evolutionary change, extinction, and speciation, written for the general public. The all-encompassing range, the compelling case for conservation, and the delightful natural history are virtues enough to recommend this book.

Why Big Fierce Animals Are Rare (1980) by Paul Colinvaux. An excellent readable guide to how the living world works.

The Theory of Island Biogeography (1967) by Robert MacArthur and Edward O Wilson. This seminal text presents and explores the relationship between the number of species on an island and its size, distance from the mainland, and biogeographical history. The book has stimulated more research in conservation than any other work and remains controversial.

Nature's Keepers (1995) by Stephen Budiansky. An environmental journalist explains in simple terms the new science of mathematical ecology, which is providing tools for effective environmental management by revealing how ecosystems really work and interact.

Reflections of Eden (1995) by Biruté M F Galdikas. A pioneering primatologist and world leader in conservation tells the enthralling story of her 25-year study of the orangutans of the Borneo rainforests. A powerful advertisement for the preservation of these great apes and their habitat.

The Last Panda (1992) by George D Schaller. A fascinating account of the author's efforts to study and save the giant panda. He successfully mixes natural history with the politics of conservation: the exposé of the countless cover-ups and fatal mistakes of zoos, governments, and international wildlife groups makes for gripping and often depressing reading.

Last Chance to See (1990) by Douglas Adams and Mark Carwardine. Adams, author of *The Hitchhiker's Guide to the Galaxy*, teams up with a zoologist in this lively but poignant tour of the imminent threat of extinction facing many well-known species.

Gerald Durrell's Army (1992) by Edward Whitley. Gerald Durrell – the world's most intrepid animal collector, who died in 1995 – was also the 'commander' of an army of local people trained to save their own wildlife. This is a first hand globetrotting account of their trials and tribulations.

Noah's Choice (1995) by Charles C Mann and Mark L Plummer. Explores the politics of endangered species with some good reporting on what goes on inside the US Fish and Wildlife Service.

Last Animals at the Zoo (1991) by Colin Tudge. A look behind the scenes at the difficulties and successes of captive breeding. The author convincingly argues that zoos are now an essential part of modern conservation strategy.

ANTHROPOLOGY

BIOLOGICAL ANTHROPOLOGY – *Helen M MacBeth*

Biological anthropology arose out of physical anthropology, which involved measuring and comparing, on the one hand, living peoples worldwide and, on the other hand, the fossilized bones of early humans or their even earlier ancestors. The study of this prehistory is also called palaeoanthropology. The aspects to study about living humans mushroomed with the increase in biochemical and molecular science, to include genetics, protein analysis, nutrition, parasites, diseases, and all aspects of human physiology and biochemistry. Anthropology means the science of humans, but the subject matter is usually concentrated on humans in groups.

Interest in the evolution, past and ongoing, of human biology is central to the subject. So a closely related discipline is the study of our closest relatives, the monkeys and apes. Although humans are clearly biological organisms like other animals, they are distinctive because of the extent of their thought processes and social organization. Whereas some biological anthropologists are specialists in genetics, biochemistry, nutrition, and so on, the contribution of others is much more generalist as they integrate social processes into their perception of biological outcomes. Biological anthropology is a subject for everyone with or without background education in biology, for it is only human to be interested in ourselves.

The extent of human variability is enormous, so large that no two individuals who have ever lived or will ever live can ever be exactly the same. The fundamental causes for this variability lie in ... the genes inherited from our parents, and the infinity of environments which act upon and within individuals from conception to death.

G AINSWORTH HARRISON

Introduction to Physical Anthropology (6th edition 1994) by R Jurmain and H Nelson. An excellent first reader for the layman or new student.

Human Biology: an introduction to human evolution, variation, growth and ecology (3rd edition 1988) by G A Harrison, J M Tanner, D R Pilbeam, and P T Baker. More difficult, but probably the central textbook for the discipline.

Human Variation, Races, Types and Ethnic Groups (3rd edition 1992) by Stephen Molnar. Intermediate between the above two books; gives useful insight into that politically sensitive topic commonly known as 'race'.

Human Populations: Diversity and Adaptation (1995) edited by A J Boyce and V Reynolds. A very recent collection of research papers on a wide spectrum of biological anthropological topics, collated in honour of the retirement of Professor G A Harrison, who for over a generation has been a central figure in the discipline.

Humankind Emerging (1976) by B G Campbell. Now rather dated but a well-illustrated book for those who like a Time-Life approach to understanding human evolution.

The Book of Man, the Quest to Discover Our Genetic Heritage (1994) by W F Bodmer and R McKie. A clear and simple book with an emphasis on the understanding of genetics for understanding ourselves.

The Language of the Genes, Biology, History and the Evolutionary Future (1993) by Steve Jones. A fascinating and painless way into understanding genetics by the Reith lecturer.

Human Biology and Ecology (1977) by A Damon was written for the layman or first-year student and despite its date gives useful insight.

SOCIAL ANTHROPOLOGY – *Chris Holdsworth*

Who are we? The answer to this question, more than any other, inspires anthropology. We are all fundamentally alike, yet we live in an amazing diversity of cultures. By participating in and observing everyday life in other cultures, anthropologists hope to obtain an understanding of how others experience life. At the heart of anthropology is ethnography: a written description of the culture of another society and an account of the anthropologist's experience within that culture. It is through the comparative study of other cultures that anthropologists hope to understand who we are. But anthropology is a discipline in turmoil. It consists of a multiplicity of theoretical approaches and areas of concern, is a uniquely Western development, and the ethnography is now recognized as essentially autobiographical. In recent years this has led many anthropologists to question the validity of their methods, epistemology, and some of their most basic concepts such as culture, society, the self, rationality, and human nature.

In anthropology we study ourselves, precisely because it requires us to change our conception of who 'we' are, from an exclusive, Western 'we' to an inclusive, global one. To adopt an anthropological attitude is to drop the pretence of our belonging to a select association of Westerners, uniquely privileged to look in upon the inhabitants of 'other cultures', and to recognize that along with the others whose company we share (albeit temporarily), we are all fellow travellers in the same world. By comparing experience – 'sharing notes' – we can reach a better understanding of what such journeying entails, where we have come from, and where we are going.

TIM INGOLD

Argonauts of the Western Pacific (1922) by Bronislaw Malinowski. A classic account of the interrelationship between magic and the ceremonial exchange of valuables in the South Seas by one of the founders of modern anthropology. Malinowski's methodological introduction established the standard for future anthropological fieldwork.

Return to Laughter (1954) by Elenore Smith Bowen (pseudonym of Laura Bohannan). A vivid and moving description of life and death in a Nigerian village as it copes with a smallpox epidemic. The book was one of the first to provide an introspective account of the fieldwork experience.

Witchcraft, Magic and Oracles among the Azande (1937; abridged edition 1976) by Edward Evans-Pritchard. A description of Azande beliefs about witchcraft, magic, and sorcery. Evans-Pritchard's theoretical insights about the nature of human rationality have been very influential, the book being quoted as much by philosophers as anthropologists.

Yanomamö: The Fierce People (1968) by Napoleon Chagnon. A compelling study of the well-known Amazonian tribe, whose traditional violent way of life is now under threat from deforestation and the activities of gold miners. Chagnon argues that their social organization is a dynamic process controlling their chronic warfare.

The Interpretation of Culture (1973) by Clifford Geertz. A collection of essays by America's leading anthropologist examining the concept of culture, its role in society, and how it should be studied.

Anthropology and Anthropologists: The Modern British School (1973) by Adam Kuper. Anthropology is perhaps best understood through its history. Kuper's well-written account of the theories and characters involved in the development of British social anthropology is the best there is.

Orientalism (1978) by Edward Said. A controversial critique of the West's interpretation of 'the Orient' that questions some of our most basic assumptions about ourselves as Westerners.

Time and the Other: How Anthropology Makes its Object (1983) by Johannes Fabian. A fascinating discussion of how anthropology uses time to define the relationship between the self and the other.

The Gender of the Gift (1988) by Marilyn Strathern. A spirited critique of cross-cultural comparisons that examines initiation rites and ceremonial exchange in a Melanesian society where male–female relations are based on gift exchange.

Companion Encyclopedia of Anthropology: Humanity, Culture and Society (1994) edited by Tim Ingold. Consisting of 38 essays on a diversity of topics, it is a comprehensive and readable overview of current thinking in the subject.

ARCHAEOLOGY

INTRODUCTION – *Paul Bahn*

Archaeology is the study of the human past – from the earliest tools to yesterday's garbage – through its material remains. It developed over the course of centuries from a natural curiosity about the past into antiquarianism and eventually the unique blend of science and art that characterizes archaeology today. It covers a vast array of topics, from the Stone Age to recent times, and encompasses many specialities, such as Egyptology and underwater archaeology. Although it is associated in most people's minds with excavation, this is in fact only one of the many ways that information can be obtained about the past; and archaeology now calls on specialists from many other subjects, and especially from the sciences, to extract an ever increasing range of evidence in order to learn more about, to understand, and to explain the form and behaviour of past societies.

The archaeological excavator is not digging up things, he is digging up people ... the life of the past and the present are diverse but indivisible ... Archaeology, in so far as it is a science, is a science which must be extended into the living and must indeed itself be lived if it is to partake of a proper vitality.

MORTIMER WHEELER

Archaeology from the Earth (1954) by Mortimer Wheeler. A classic text by one of modern archaeology's greatest pioneers and practitioners.

The Archaeologist's Handbook (1986) by Jane McIntosh. A useful and readable survey of how we know what we know about the past.

Past Worlds: The Times Atlas of Archaeology (1988) edited by Chris Scarre. A major encyclopedic survey of past cultures by a battery of specialists.

Archaeology: Theories, Methods and Practice (1991) by Colin Renfrew and Paul Bahn. A leading textbook that explains, with examples from all over the world, how archaeologists obtain the evidence to answer the wide range of questions that interest them.

The Collins Dictionary of Archaeology (1992) edited by Paul Bahn. The most up-to-date reference book offering definitions of sites, cultures, artefacts, technical and theoretical terms.

Understanding Archaeological Excavation (1993) by Philip Barker. The best available introduction to archaeology's traditional methods of extracting information from the ground.

Time Detectives (1995) by Brian Fagan. A collection of essays comprising a wide variety of case studies that show how archaeology uses modern science to obtain information about the past.

The Cambridge Illustrated History of Archaeology (1995) edited by Paul Bahn. A fully illustrated survey of archaeology's history, from its beginnings to the present, in all parts of the world.

The Story of Archaeology (1995) by Paul Bahn. A beautifully illustrated collection of 100 spreads – 'archaeology's greatest discoveries' – that display the subject's tremendous range.

INDUSTRIAL ARCHAEOLOGY – *Anthony Burton*

This is a new subject: the term 'industrial archaeology' appeared in print for the first time in 1955. It can be loosely defined as the recordings and investigation of the remains of industrial buildings and structures. At first, the work was largely limited to the period of the Industrial Revolution and that was generally taken as being centred on the vast range of developments that took place in Great Britain in the 18th and early 19th centuries. A feature of the early years was that much of the investigation was left to amateurs doing work on local cities. Over the years the subject (and its literature) has developed, so that it has become worldwide and extended to cover the recording and, where appropriate, conservation of industrial sites from any period. There has also been a movement to place the sites in their human and social as well as a technological context.

It is difficult to carry our minds back to a time when buildings of such overwhelming presence were not familiar objects, and to understand the impact their first appearance must have made. They belonged to a whole new range of man-made objects of superhuman scale, by means of which the transformation of England from an agricultural to an industrial country, and later from a largely rural to an urban one, was given physical form.

J M RICHARDS

The Functional Tradition (1958) by J M Richards. A seminal work that showed industrial buildings were worthy of study, and through Eric de Maré's superb photographs disclosed they could even be beautiful.

Industrial Archaeology (1972) by Arthur Raistrick. One of the first, and one of the best, attempts to show how the subject could be treated in a logical and scholarly fashion.

Remains of a Revolution (1974) by Anthony Burton. A study of the classic period of the British Industrial Revolution, which combines a study of the physical remains with their human history.

Industrial Archaeology (1975) by Neil Cossons. A standard work which deals systematically with the different branches of the subject, and an ideal starting point for beginners.

Industrial Archaeology (1976) by Theodore Anton Sanck. This is an introduction to American industrial history, based on a detailed look at a number of key sites.

Monuments of Industry (1986) by Geoffrey D Hay and Geoffrey P Stell. Although it is limited to Scotland, it is a model of how sites should be recorded in words, photographs, and drawings.

Civil Engineering 1839–1889 (1991) by Mike Chrimes. One of the few books to look at engineering structures on a worldwide basis.

TECHNOLOGY

INTRODUCTION – *Trevor I Williams*

Today, technology is generally regarded as the application of science for practical purposes, but it must be remembered that many technologies – such as the smelting and working of metals and the processing and weaving of fibres – were well developed before science as it is now understood existed at all. Others, such as plastics, have emerged almost within living memory. The term 'technology' (as the German *technologie*) was coined in 1777 by Johann Beckmann of Göttingen.

The most important and urgent problems of the technology of today are no longer the satisfaction of the primary needs or archetypal wishes, but the reparation of the evils and damages wrought by the technology of yesteryear.

DENNIS GABOR

A History of Technology: The Twentieth Century c. 1900 – 1950 volumes 6 and 7 (1978) edited by Charles Singer, E J Holmyard, A R Hall, and Trevor I Williams. This is the recognized comprehensive work on the history of technology, from the dawn of civilization to the mid-20th century. It deals primarily with the Middle East, Egypt, Europe, and North America.

Science and Civilisation in China (1954) edited by Joseph Needham. This multivolume work, internationally acclaimed – commenced in 1954 and still appearing –

complements the above with its penetrating and largely original study of the history of technology in China, relating this to the Middle East and Europe. This is available in an abridged form: *The Shorter Science and Civilisation in China* (1978–97; continuing) by Colin A Ronan.

An Encyclopaedia of the History of Technology (1990) edited by Ian McNeil. A team of 20 acknowledged experts cover the history of technology from the Stone Age to the Space Age.

Oxford Illustrated Encyclopedia of Invention and Technology (1992) edited by Monty Finniston. One of eight volumes of the comprehensive *Oxford Illustrated Encyclopedia*.

Chambers Science and Technology Dictionary (1988) edited by P Walker. The latest version of *Chambers Technical Dictionary*, which first appeared some 50 years ago. A comprehensive and reliable guide to many thousands of technical terms.

The Power of the Machine (1992) by R A Buchanan. Reviews the social implications of technological revolution, worldwide, and finds it to be very uneven.

The Materials Revolution (1988) edited by T Forester. A collection of reprinted articles from a variety of sources, intended for the general reader.

The Uses of Life: A History of Biotechnology (1993) by R Bud. Although biotechnology has been practised for millennia – as in brewing – it has become an important industrial force only in comparatively recent years. This book is the first authoritative review of its history.

MATERIALS – *Trevor I Williams*

The term 'material' covers a range of substances from which things can be made. While some fall into broad categories – such as metals and plastics – others have little in common except their utility. Such, for example, are ceramics and glass, wood and leather, all used from the dawn of civilization but now appearing in increasingly sophisticated forms.

Today, plastics generally denote some kind of synthetic material – such as polythene or nylon – but it must be remembered that similar materials abound in nature and have long been in common use. Such, for example, are rubber and shellac. The first important artificial product to be developed commercially was celluloid (originally Parkesine), a form of cellulose nitrite plasticized with camphor, invented by Alexander Parkes in 1865.

Metals have played so important a role in the history of civilization that they have been used to designate whole epochs. The Stone Age was followed by the Bronze Age, the Iron Age, and – since roughly the mid-19th century – the Steel Age. For the greater part of human history no more than eight metals were in common use – gold, silver, copper, iron, lead, zinc, tin, and mercury. Platinum was introduced in the early 19th century and only more recently have aluminium, magnesium, and titanium been used in substantial quantities. Others, such as tungsten, vanadium, chromium, molybdenum, and nickel are used in relatively small quantities for special purposes such as making alloys or electroplating.

The whole of our present material civilization depends on the efficient harnessing of power, but the control of this power is made possible only by the use of many varieties of metals and alloys. Without metals no railway, aeroplane, motorcar, electric motor, or turbine could operate.

W A ALEXANDER AND A STREET

Artifice and Artifacts: 100 Essays in Materials Science (1992) by Robert W Cahn. A compilation of articles written over a span of 25 years by an acknowledged expert in the field.

Engineering Materials: An Introduction to their Properties and Application (1980) by M F Ashby and D R H Jones. A guide to the choice of materials for particular purposes.

Advancing Materials Research (1987) by Peter A Psaras and A Dale Langford. A review of recent progress in materials-science research.

Physical Metallurgy (1974; 3rd revised edition 1993) edited by Robert W Cahn and Peter Haasen. Generally rated the most authoritative and up-to-date book in this field.

Metals in the Service of Man (1972) by William Alexander and Arthur Street. A short, reliable guide for the general reader.

A Hundred Years of Metallurgy (1963) by W H Dennis. A good general account of developments in metallurgy from roughly the middle of the 19th century.

Metals, Ceramics, and Polymers (1974) by O Wyatt and D Dew-Hughes. A comprehensive review of three major fields, effectively linking engineering and science.

Pioneers in Polymer Science (1989) edited by Raymond B Seymour. Basically a biographical study, but contains much background information.

The First Century of Plastics (1963) by M Kaufman. A comprehensive review, published under the imprint of the Plastics Institute.

NONRENEWABLE ENERGY – *Alan Williams*

The majority of the country's energy, with one or two exceptions, is produced by fossil fuels or a combination of fossil and biofuels. This is reflected in a considerable number of publications directed towards combustion but, because of the importance of the subject, these are generally specialized books in science and engineering. Most general energy books are preoccupied with the fact that fossil fuels are finite and consequently look very much to the future and to alternative energy sources such as renewable energy suppliers or, indeed, nuclear energy.

The meek shall inherit the earth, but not the mineral rights.

PAUL GETTY

The Energy Question (1992) by Gerald Foley. This is a well-known book which deals with systems and resources – including coal, petroleum, natural gas, and the tar sands and oil shales. It also deals with energy flows and storage, which is a necessary part of combustion in a world where climate warming and pollution are pre-eminent in one source. The last part deals with the future, including energy forecasting and conservation.

Energy Around the World: An Introduction to Energy Studies. Global Resources, Needs, Utilization (1984) by J C McVeigh. This book covers such sources as petroleum, natural gas, hydro power, and biomass, and then moves into future energy sources. Again, this is a very general book. The major energy sources, such as coal and petroleum, are treated at approximately the same level as solar energy, geothermal energy, and so on.

Energy (1984) by Joseph Priest. A good general coverage of energy and just enough on combustion.

Energy and the Atmosphere: A Physical-Chemical Approach (1986) by Ian M Campbell. An interesting analysis of atmospheric pollution, including a useful introduction to combustion.

An Introduction to Combustion (1993) by Warren C Strahle. A detailed scientific analysis of all aspects of combustion. Not for the beginner.

Combustion and Pollution Control in Heating Systems (1994) by V I Hanby. An interesting book detailing the principle of combustion and pollution control in the context of heating systems.

Combustion of Liquid Fuel Sprays (1990) by Alan Williams. A good coverage of liquid-fuel sprays and, more importantly, the key aspects of combustion pollution control applicable to almost any fuel.

Coal: Resources, Properties, Utilization, Pollution (1995) edited by Orhan Kural. A useful contemporary survey of all aspects of coal.

Fire: Technology, Symbolism, Ecology, Science, Hazard (1993) by Hazel Rossotti. Combustion can have adverse consequences and fire is a classic case. Well illustrated.

Dictionary of Energy Technology (1979) by Alan Gilpin and Alan Williams. A last resort if the words are unfamiliar.

RENEWABLE ENERGY – *Mary Cobbett*

The natural world has many complex processes for maintaining its own survival. If we want to survive into the future – and have a relatively smooth ride – our best bet lies with understanding and working with those natural processes, rather than trying to 'conquer' nature. Technologies that support rather than harm the environment exist in the form of obtaining power from wind, the sun, and rain. Utilizing methods of environment-conscious building and sewage systems and generally being aware of the conservation of energy that we use every day are all positive ways of assisting the Earth in coping with the pressures we lay upon it. Through a combination of cost-effective energy-efficient improvements and low-impact renewable energy; technologies it may be possible to cut the use of fossil fuels by half. In many parts of the world fossil fuels have never been a viable option, whereas the abundance of sun and wind in some areas are infinite resources waiting to be tapped.

It's only when we put our energies into what we're for, rather than what we're against, that we can really change things.

PAUL ALLEN

Energy Without End (1991) by Michael Flood. Shows how the UK can start to meet the challenge of switching to less polluting, renewable energy resources. Positive and comprehensive, recommended reading for anyone concerned about the future of energy use and the environment.

The Future of Energy Use (1994) by Robert Hill and others. Introduction to the uses of different kinds of energy and their social and environmental impacts throughout the world.

Power Surge (1994) by Christopher Flavin, and Nicholas Lenssen. The world is being pushed towards more efficient, decentralized, and cleaner energy systems, and this clearly outlines the massive changes ahead in transport, the home, and society.

The Solar Electric House (1993) by Steven Strong. This will tell you everything you need to know to decide whether photovoltaics are for you, including system options and economics; how to determine your electricity requirements; stand-alone and interactive systems; designing a solar house; and descriptions of all key components.

Real Goods Solar Living Resource Book (8th edition 1994) by John Schaeffer. A guide to all aspects of solar, wind, water, and other sustainable resources: solar panels, water pumps, batteries, and so on. Chapters on home safety, ecology, food growing, and how to make a living that doesn't compromise your values. It has become the bible of the US alternative-energy world. Despite being aimed at the US market, it is also a treasure trove for UK readers.

Windfarm Location and Environmental Impact (1988) by Alexi Clarke. Increasingly becoming a very topical subject, this is an important assessment of a hitherto relatively unexplored field. Also looks at other siting constraints such as conflicting land uses, public attitudes, and planning permission.

Wind Power for Home and Business (1993) by Paul Gipe. A comprehensive reference book covering all aspects of modern wind-energy machines – the new wind machines are efficient, powerful, and inexpensive in the long run. Contains lists of manufacturers, test centres, and so on in many countries, including the UK, the USA, and continental Europe.

Micro Hydro Design Manual (1993) by Adam Harvey and Andy Brown. Examines every stage of planning and installation of a small-scale system. Worked examples with illustrations and notes to help with all the practical aspects of the project, with detailed sections on turbines, governing, drive systems, electrical power, and maintenance.

Micro-Hydro Electric Power (1986) by Ray Holland. Concise, reliable introduction to the technology of small-scale water power.

Micro-Hydro Power (1991) by Peter Fraenkel and others. Essential for those involved in designing, implementing, or operating microhydropower schemes in developed and developing countries. Covers civil works, economics, turbines, electrical power, and more.

APPROPRIATE TECHNOLOGY – *Colin Garden*

Technology usually implies engineering and machinery but these are only part of what has become known as appropriate technology or AT. Advocates of appropriate technology aim to provide solutions to the problems resulting from poverty and mass unemployment in developing countries and they are concerned as much with the social appropriateness of the technologies they use as they are with techniques. They aim to benefit all members of a community, not just the well-educated and the wealthy, and to support, rather than replace, local strategies. As the books listed will show, AT is about a self-help, community-based approach to development and making the most economical use of available resources and skills.

If that which has been shaped by technology, and continues to be so shaped, looks sick, it might be wise to have a look at technology itself. If technology is felt to be becoming more and more inhuman, we might do well to consider whether it is possible to have something better – a technology with a human face.

E F SCHUMACHER

Small Is Beautiful: A Study of Economics as if People Mattered (1973) by E F Schumacher. Introduces the concepts of 'intermediate' and 'appropriate' technology. Schumacher argues that the pursuit of profit and unlimited economic growth will not provide solutions to the problems of the modern world.

The AT Reader: Theory and Practice in Appropriate Technology (1985) by Marilyn Carr. The standard introduction to AT. Explains the origins of the idea and demonstrates its application in a wide range of contexts.

Appropriate Technology: Technology with a Human Face (1978) by P Dunn. Written by an engineer; covers the actual practice of appropriate technology in a clear, simple style.

The Third World Tomorrow (1980) by Paul Harrison. First-hand reports on projects in Africa, Asia, and Latin America. Shows how the concepts of appropriate technology, people's participation, self-help, and small-scale enterprise are put into practice.

The Economies of Small: Appropriate Technology in a Changing World (1990) by Raphael Kaplinsky. A study of the economics of AT. Gives a good overview of the development of the AT movement and its concern with environmental, social, and economic issues. Moves from case studies of AT in developing countries to considering the relevance of an AT approach in industrially advanced countries.

Tinker, Tiller, Technical Change: Technologies from the People (1990) edited by Matthew Gamser, Helen Appleton, and Nicola Carter. Emphasizes the need for 'experts' to recognize local innovation when offering technical assistance to poor communities. Seventeen case studies of locally developed technologies.

The Critical Villager (1993) by Eric Dudley. A look at the cultural aspect of appropriate technology. The author argues that, if technical aid is to be effective, development workers must give due consideration to local culture and conditions.

HISTORY OF COMPUTING – *Doron Swade*

The electronic digital computer has emerged as one of the most significant features of late-20th-century technology. The word 'computer' is now universally associated with electronic digital devices of which the desktop personal computer is perhaps the most common example. But as recently as the 1950s computers were not machines but people who performed calculations. Some of the finest minds of past centuries have attempted to build calculating devices to relieve humans from the tedium and difficulty of calculation. An account of these attempts and the development of machines for arithmetic calculation into the versatile modern electronic computer is a rich and fascinating tale. The following selection captures the major features of the history and prehistory of computing from the different standpoints of a variety of authors.

Who can foresee the consequences of such an invention?

LUIGI MENABREA, 1842

Computing before Computers (1990) edited by William. Aspray An authoritative compilation of book chapters covering the prehistory of computing by five leading computer historians. An accessible account of calculating devices from mechanical contrivances starting with the abacus and ending with the early electronic calculating machines of the 1950s.

Passages from the Life of a Philosopher (1864) by Charles Babbage. Less about computing than about the views and recollections of the so-called first pioneer of computing. A highly readable and delightfully mischievous book, autobiographical in nature, by the beleaguered, controversial designer of vast mechanical calculating engines in the 19th century.

Irascible Genius: A Life of Charles Babbage, Inventor (1964) by Maboth Moseley. Energetic biography of Charles Babbage. Provides a vivid portrait of Babbage's life and his ultimately doomed efforts to construct mechanical calculating machines.

Charles Babbage and his Calculating Machines (1991) by Doron Swade. Short, nontechnical, and well-illustrated book written to accompany the Babbage bicentennial exhibition at the Science Museum, London.

Bit by Bit: An Illustrated History of Computers (1985) by Stan Augarten. Arguably the best single-volume history of computing, starting with the earliest mechanical devices and ending with the early days of the personal-computer revolution.

The Dream Machine: Exploring the Computer Age (1991) by Jon Palfreman and Doron Swade. Popular account of computing written to accompany a BBC TV series. History and prehistory is used as a context for the modern computer, especially the personal computer and its emerging multifunctional role.

A Computer Perspective: Background to the Computer Age (1990) by Charles Eames and Ray Eames. Superbly illustrated time-line history of computing. Essentially a captioned visual history starting with the electromechanical census devices of the 1890s and ending with the electronic devices of the 1940s.

Early British Computers: The Story of Vintage Computers and the People That Built Them (1980) by Simon Lavington. A short, invaluable account of British pioneering developments in electronic computing during the crucial three decades from the 1930s to the 1950s.

The Origins of Digital Computing (1982) by Brian Randell. Seminal collection of original historic papers in the history of computing from the mechanical devices of the 19th century to the electronic machines of the 1940s. Some material is inevitably technical. An essential reference source.

COMPUTING – *Jack Schofield*

In one sense, computing is just part of the electronics industry. The boom in computers has been produced by the availability of low-cost integrated circuits – silicon chips – which powered earlier booms in pocket calculators, video-games consoles, and other consumer products. (That's why it's called Silicon Valley, not Computer Valley.) In another sense, computing is special because a computer is a tool for processing information. No one finds it threatening that binoculars and telescopes allow us to see further, or that wheeled and winged vehicles enable us to travel faster. However, the idea that computer 'brains' can store more data and process it faster and more accurately produces all sorts of phobias. But computers are not mysterious. They are machines, designed by men and manufactured for profit. Understanding the process and its context will help remove any such fears. That's important, because computing is one of today's biggest industries, and the one on which many of our futures depend.

The best way to predict the future is to invent it.

ALAN KAY

Microchip: The Story of a Revolution and the Men who Made It (1985) by T R Reid. The power of the chip industry is based on one big idea, the Monolithic Idea that you could combine different kinds of components on an integrated circuit. In the late 1950s, this idea came separately to two men, Robert Noyce and Jack Kilby. Its application launched the Information Revolution.

The Soul of a New Machine (1982) by Tracy Kidder. A novelistic account of how a new type of computer came together out of the efforts of hardware designers and software writers. If Kidder had been lucky, the machine would have been a huge success. As it wasn't, the story now has little historical interest, though it's still the only computer book to have won its author a Pulitzer Prize.

Father, Son & Co: My Life at IBM and Beyond (1990) by Thomas J Watson Jr and Peter Petre. IBM is by far the world's largest computer company, and dominated the business for 25 years from 1964. Tom Watson Jr, son of the company's founder, was the man most responsible.

Innovating for Failure: Government Policy and the Early British Computer Industry (1989) by John Hendry. In the 1940s and 1950s, the British computer industry was at least level with the Americans and miles ahead of the Japanese. What went wrong?

Computer Lib (1987) by Ted Nelson. Nelson understood the microcomputer industry and self-published a book about it in 1974 – which is impressive when you remember the microcomputer wasn't even invented until 1975. At the time it was a mixture of handbook and religious tract for the freaks and hackers who got the industry rolling. It's still a cult classic.

West of Eden: The End of Innocence at Apple Computer (1989) by Frank Rose. One of the ideas that drives the computer industry is that a couple of young hackers can start a company in their garage and develop it into a multibillion dollar international corporation. The two Steves, Jobs and Wosniak, did that at Apple, before losing control of their company ...

Gates (1993) by Stephen Manes and Paul Andrews. In 20 years, Bill Gates went from college dropout to the world's richest individual: according to *Fortune* magazine, his personal net worth is about $12.9 billion. The success of Microsoft, Gates's company, was bound up with the huge success of the personal computer, particularly the IBM PC-compatible, for which Microsoft supplies most software.

The Cuckoo's Egg (1990) by Clifford Stoll. What starts as an attempt to account for a few cents turns into a hunt for a mystery hacker and then into international espionage. It sounds like a techno-thriller but it's nothing more than the truth. The book thus provides more insight into the world of hacking than the many more sensationalized accounts.

Virtual Reality (1988) by Howard Rheingold. A pioneering account of the origins of cyberspace, and where it might take us.

Mind Children: The Future of Robot and Human Intelligence (1988) by Hans Moravec. Moravec, a leading roboticist, thinks that we may be moving from the biological to the postbiological world, and that our true children may not be flesh and blood but self-replicating machines.

CYBERSPACE – *Wendy M Grossman*

Cyberspace is one of the hot topics these days. Most of the books on the market that talk about it are geared towards telling people how to get on-line and what to do when they get there. Those books are useful, but they're not much fun to read, and they're not much use as an introduction for people who don't want to go on-line themselves but just want to know what's happening out there. The books on this list are geared towards the latter type of reader.

It is a region without physical shape or form. It exists, like a standing wave, in the vast web of our electronic communication systems. It consists of electron states, microwaves, magnetic fields, light pulses and thought itself.

MITCH KAPOR AND JOHN PERRY BARLOW

Surfing on the Internet (1995) by J C Herz. The ultimate travel guide to cyberspace, whether you want to go there or not. Herz samples all sorts of different Internet offerings and reports back with a lot of humour.

The Media Lab (1987) by Stewart Brand. The Media Lab at the Massachusetts Institute of Technology was set up in 1985 to bring together artists and computer scientists to invent the future of technology. Brand's reporting on the many projects and thinkers at the lab introduces many of the concepts behind today's new developments.

Cyberia: Life in the Trenches of Hyperspace (1994) by Douglas Rushkoff. The youth culture of today: acid-house rock, virtual reality, on-line communities, and cyberpunks.

Virtual Reality: Through the New Looking Glass (1993) by Ken Pimentel and Kevin Teixeira. An introduction to the technology behind virtual reality and what can be done with it.

Great Mambo Chicken and the Transhuman Condition: Science Slightly Over the Edge (1990) by Ed Regis. Not specifically about cyberspace, but in its entertaining Tom Wolfe style recounting of the further reaches of science it wanders into the related areas of artificial intelligence and artificial life.

The Hacker Crackdown (1992) by Bruce Sterling. Sterling is best known as a science-fiction writer, but a series of raids in the US inspired him to write this non-fiction book to explore the extension of law and civil liberties to what he and many others like to call the Electronic Frontier.

The Cuckoo's Egg (1989) by Clifford Stoll. The more we depend on computer networks, the more vital it is that they have adequate security. This is the story of an astronomer turned computer-security specialist who set out to solve the small accounting problem of a $0.75 discrepancy and wound up helping to trap an international hacker.

Neuromancer (1984) by William Gibson. This science-fiction novel, Gibson's first, is the book that invented the word 'cyberspace'. The story of a data thief and the development of artificial intelligence inside a computer matrix, this book is somewhat difficult to read; it launched a new type of science fiction, known as 'cyberpunk'.

PARANORMAL

Wendy M Grossman

Every year a great tidal wave of books is published that defies everything we know about science on subjects like UFOs, psychics, faith healing, ghosts, alternative medical treatments, spontaneous human combustion, creationism, astrology, and even angels. If that weren't bad enough, more books promote pseudoscientific myths that have little basis in fact. The books below attempt to redress the balance and go a long way to show that truth, in many cases, really is stranger than fiction.

No more things should be presumed to exist than are absolutely necessary.

WILLIAM OCCAM

Innumeracy: Mathematical Illiteracy and Its Consequences (1988) by John Allen Paulos. One reason pseudoscience and paranormal claims seem so convincing is that most people are so innumerate they can't evaluate their likelihood. Paulos shows you how.

Psychic Investigator (1991) by James Randi. Randi turns his experience of 35 years' worth of paranormal investigation to explaining psychic phenomena like dowsing, psychometry, and spiritualism. Based on a 1990 television series.

Science: Good, Bad, and Bogus (1981) by Martin Gardner. Martin Gardner was for many years the mathematical-games columnist for *Scientific American*; his second passion is debunking improbable claims and bad science.

Sorry, You've Been Duped! (1986) by Melvin Harris. A historian ferrets out the truth behind well-known mysteries such as the Amityville horror and the Bloxham tapes.

The Mask of Nostradamus (1990) by James Randi. This sceptical biography of the world's most famous prophet unearths some of the background to his most often quoted prophecies.

The Prevalence of Nonsense (1967) by Ashley Montagu and Edward Darling. An enjoyable and authoritative debunking of myths and common fallacies.

Pseudoscience and the Paranormal: A Critical Examination of the Evidence (1988) by Terence Hines. A lively and thoroughly researched introduction to all areas of pseudoscience, in which category Hines includes psychoanalysis.

The Mismeasure of Woman (1992) by Carol Tavris. A brilliant re-analysis of many of the most prevalent myths about women, many of them due to bad science. Subtitled 'Why women are not the other sex, the inferior sex, or the opposite sex'.

The Mismeasure of Man (1981) by Stephen Jay Gould. Intelligence testing pervades our education systems and thinking. Gould investigates the shameful history of intelligence research and its abuse.

High Weirdness by Mail (1988) by Ivan Stang. A book that proves there's nothing so weird that you can't find people who believe it. A directory of the world's most bizarre mailing lists, with samples of their output.

HISTORY

INTRODUCTION

John Stewart

The study of the past is something that has fascinated human societies from at least the time of the ancient Greeks and Romans, and before this in certain eastern cultures. This does not mean, however, that those who study the human past in a scholarly way, that is professional historians, can necessarily agree on the usefulness or otherwise of such a pursuit. For some, history can provide a guide, albeit an imprecise one, to an understanding of the present and, more problematically, the future. Others see this as an unrealistic or pretentious claim for history, arguing instead that its virtues lie in such matters as evaluating evidence and in beginning to understand the complexities of human existence. The latter group tend to be 'conservative' in their historical practice, and are unhappy about any alliances between history and other disciplines such as sociology. Such debates go to the heart of what we mean by 'history', and the books listed below provide an introduction to these debates from a number of different standpoints.

Not to know what took place before you were born is to remain for ever a child.

MARCUS TULLIUS CICERO

History and Social Theory (1992) by Peter Burke. This work argues for a closer relationship between history and the social sciences, and for the use of appropriate 'theory' in historical study. A number of case studies are also provided suggesting how such a relationship might work in practice. Burke is a distinguished historian in this field, and his arguments therefore come right from the heart of the debate.

What is History? (1961) by E H Carr. A controversial figure, Carr claimed a 'scientific' basis to historical study, while acknowledging, in a famous phrase, that history was an 'unending dialogue between past and present'. Of particular concern to his critics, however, was his definition of historical 'facts'. Although difficult to defend nowadays as a whole, this work was significant not least in provoking other historians to try and describe and analyse exactly what it was they did when undertaking research and writing.

The Practice of History (1967) by Geoffrey Elton. The late Geoffrey Elton was one of the most articulate exponents of the more 'traditional' approach to history. In this work he reveals, clearly and lucidly, the kind of painstaking procedures a historian has to go through in order to produce a useful piece of historical research. Elton also makes clear his scepticism about any predictive or 'scientific' qualities which might, mistakenly, be attributed to history. In part, this work is a response to Carr.

Return to Essentials (1991) by Geoffrey Elton. In a sense, the title says it all. Elton attacks those who would distort history by seeking to force historical evidence into predetermined theoretical patterns. Instead, Elton seeks to emphasize the traditional historical practices of which he himself was such an admirable exponent. This book is worth reading alongside Marwick, Tosh, and, especially, Burke.

What Is History Today? (1988) edited by Juliet Gardiner. This is a collection of essays on the different branches of history – political history, economic history, and so on – by experts in the various fields. Clearly written and with a useful introduction, this work brings out both the diversity of historical study and the range of opinions about its value.

The Nature of History (1989) Arthur Marwick. Writing in a witty and provocative style, Marwick seeks to show the 'necessity of history', by which he means the need for societies to study and attempt to understand the past in order to be able to make sense of present-day society. The book also deals with such topics as the development of historical studies and the problematic nature of primary sources.

Introduction to History (1986) by the Open University. Designed for an Open University distance-learning course, and written by Arthur Marwick, this is one of the best places for any newcomer interested in the nature of historical study to start. Marwick carefully takes readers through various meanings of the word 'history', and again argues the case for the necessity of society's understanding its historical origins. There are a number of video recordings also associated with this course which, if access can be gained to them, further illustrate the points being made.

The Pursuit of History (1991) by John Tosh. Like Marwick, Tosh sees a necessity for historical study. His work is particularly useful in alerting readers to some of the main types of historical study, and to recent developments such as the use of quantitative methods.

ANCIENT HISTORY

ANCIENT EGYPTIAN HISTORY – *Geraldine Pinch*

The birth of Egyptology is usually dated to Jean François Champollion's decipherment of the Egyptian hieroglyphic script in 1822. Egyptologists are concerned with every aspect of the civilization of ancient Egypt; not just with those topics, such as pyramids and mummies, that have caught the popular imagination. Egypt is important in the history of humanity as the first large state to be ruled by a central government. The 'pharaonic' culture created in the late 4th millennium BC lasted for over 3,000 years and produced some of the world's most impressive art and architecture. In spite of the huge quantity of surviving remains, and frequent new discoveries, many aspects of life in ancient Egypt remain mysterious.

I now proceed to give a more particular account of Egypt; it possesses more wonders than any other country, and exhibits works greater than can be described, in comparison with all other regions; therefore more must be said about it. The Egyptians, besides having a climate peculiar to themselves, and a river differing in its nature from all other rivers, have adopted customs and usages in almost every respect different from the rest of mankind.

HERODOTUS

Ancient Egypt: A Cultural Atlas (1980) by John Baines and Jaromír Málek. A reliable introduction to ancient Egyptian history and culture. It includes a guide to all the main ancient sites with many excellent maps and plans.

Ancient Egypt: The Land and Its Legacy (1988) by T G H James. A journey through Egypt describing the surviving towns, temples, and tombs. A beautifully illustrated book that combines impeccable scholarship with sensitivity to the atmosphere of ancient sites.

Ancient Egypt: Anatomy of a Civilization (1989) by Barry J Kemp. A thought-provoking study of the political, social, and economic life of the ancient Egyptians written by a leading archaeologist.

Conceptions of God in Ancient Egypt (1982) by Erik Hornung (translated by John Baines). A challenging book for anyone seriously interested in understanding the complex world of ancient Egyptian religion.

Building in Egypt: Pharaonic Stone Masonry (1991) by Dieter Arnold. A detailed, technical book that answers every conceivable question about how the pyramids, and all the other great monuments, were built.

Egyptian Painting and Relief (1986) by Gay Robins. An essential, brief guide to understanding and enjoying Egyptian paintings and sculptured reliefs. It explains the materials, methods, and unique conventions of ancient Egyptian art.

Egyptian Hieroglyphs (1987) by W V Davies. The best short introduction to the languages and scripts of ancient Egypt.

Ancient Egyptian Literature volumes 1–3 (1973, 1976, 1980) by Miriam Lichtheim. These books allow the ancient Egyptians to speak for themselves. They include translations of stories, love poems, royal inscriptions, and passages from the famous *Book of the Dead*

Akhenaten, King of Egypt (1988) by Cyril Aldred. A comprehensive study of a ruler who has been called 'the first individual in history'. It explores the religious reforms of the 'heretic pharaoh' and his wife Nefertiti, and the troubled history of the controversial Amarna period.

The Complete Tutankhamun (1990) by Nicholas Reeves. A full, and magnificently illustrated, account of the reign of the boy pharaoh Tutankhamun, and of the astounding contents of his tomb.

GREEK AND ROMAN HISTORY – *Graham Ley*

There is an abundance of general histories of both Greece and Rome, which vary from the lavishly illustrated to detailed studies of the available archaeological and literary evidence about events and personalities. I have included in this list primarily books that provide a reliable overview of extensive periods, and that incorporate in an accessible form the results of continuing scholarship. The Greek and Roman historians, of whom the most important for general study are Herodotus and Thucydides (for classical Greece) and Livy and Tacitus (for republican Rome and the early Roman Empire), have been translated in the Penguin Classics series. Also fascinating, for their suggestive portraits of individuals, are the biographies written by Plutarch (of Greek and Roman military and political leaders) and by Suetonius (of the early Roman emperors).

It will be enough for me if these words of mine are judged useful by those who want to understand clearly the events which happened in the past and which (human nature being what it is) will, at some time or other and in much the same ways, be repeated in the future.

THUCYDIDES

The Routledge Atlas of Classical History (1971; revised edition 1994) by Michael Grant. A graphic presentation of the major historical events and eras.

The Historians of Greece and Rome (1969) by S Usher. An informative and accessible introduction to the major ancient writers themselves.

The Fontana History of the Ancient World (1976 onwards) by various authors. A comprehensive and accessible multivolume account by specialists, which pays attention to social and cultural history as well as to economics, military affairs, and politics. The volumes are: *Early Greece* by O Murray, *Democracy and Classical Greece* by J Davies, *The Hellenistic World* by F Wallbank, *Early Rome and the Etruscans* by R Ogilvie, *The Roman Republic* by M Crawford, *The Roman Empire* by C Wells, *The Later Roman Empire* by A Cameron.

The Early Greeks (1976) by R J Hopper. A clear and interesting survey of Greek history from the Minoan period to the emergence of the classical Greek city-state.

The Greek World 479–323 BC (1983) by Simon Hornblower. Probably the best short survey of a crucial period in Greek history, which saw the rise and decline of classical Athens.

The Miracle That Was Macedonia (1991) by N Hammond. A recent account of the growth and apogee of Macedonian power under Philip and his son Alexander the Great by a leading historian.

Alexander to Actium: The Historical Evolution of the Hellenistic Age (1990) by Peter Green. A detailed picture of the changing historical and cultural relations in the Mediterranean in the period of the gradual decline of Greek power, and of the growth of Rome.

A History of the Roman World 753–144 BC (1980) by H Scullard. A continually revised, authoritative history of the first six centuries of the Roman republic.

The Roman Revolution (1939) by Ronald Syme. The classic study of the transformation of the Roman republic into a principate under Augustus.

For up-to-date studies of the Roman Empire, in its earlier and later periods, I should recommend the books by Wells and Cameron in the Fontana series.

Three other books deal with areas that may be of particular interest to readers:

The Roman Invasion of Britain (1980) by Graham Webster;

Greeks, Romans and Barbarians (1988) by Barry Cunliffe;

The Ancient Economy (1984) by M Finley.

ANCIENT MIDDLE EASTERN HISTORY
Stephanie Dalley

The civilizations that once flourished in the Middle East have been uncovered grad-ually during the past 150 years. Their numerous and varied writings on stone and clay are still being excavated and are mostly deciphered, so that we can reconstruct very ancient life and literature in astonishing detail. Sumerians, Babylonians, Assyrians, Hittites, Canaanites, Elamites, and Persians are all linked together by their use of cuneiform (wedge-shaped) writing, by trade and empire, and by splendid cities. They made extraordinary progress in art, architecture, astronomy, and technology, and we are only just beginning to appreciate the true extent of their achievements.

It is indeed one of the most remarkable facts in history, that the records of an empire, so renowned for its power and civilisation, should have been entirely lost; and that the site of a city (Nineveh) as eminent for its extent as its splendour, should for ages have been a matter of doubt; it is not perhaps less curious that an accidental discovery should suddenly lead us to hope that these records may be recovered, and this site satisfactorily identified.

AUSTEN HENRY LAYARD

Ancient Iraq (1980) by George Roux. A beautifully constructed account which introduces Mesopotamian history and culture to the nonspecialist.

The Greatness That Was Babylon: A Survey of the Ancient Civilization of the Tigris-Euphrates Valley (1988) by Harry W F Saggs. An excellent overview showing clearly why this civilization ranks among the foremost in world history.

Mesopotamia (1991) by Julian Reade. A brief, elegant account containing brilliant illustrations taken mainly from the superb collections in the British Museum.

Cultural Atlas of Mesopotamia and the Ancient Near East (1990) by Michael Roaf. This fine book gives an overview of the whole subject, beginning with the remark-able prehistoric cultures. It is lavishly illustrated throughout the text.

Ancient Near Eastern Art (1995) by Dominique Collon. If you ever got the impres-sion that the Egyptians and Greeks invented fine architecture or freestanding statues, carving in very hard stone or narrative sculpture with lifelike scenes to take your breath away, read this and think again.

Myths from Mesopotamia (1991) by Stephanie Dalley. Even earlier than the Iliad, the Odyssey and the Mahabharata, the ancient Mesopotamians were writing epics and myths that still have power to compel modern man. These translations are eminently readable, and show how scholars have pieced together the oldest stories in the world.

Early Mesopotamia: Society and Economy at the Dawn of History (1992) by J Nicholas Postgate. An original and fascinating book which combines archaeology and texts to give new insights into the development of ancient civilization. Beautifully illus-trated too.

From the Omens of Babylon: Astrology and Ancient Mesopotamia (1994) by Michael Baigent. This remarkable book, by a nonspecialist who has taken great care with the scholarly material to write an account that is highly readable, is the envy of specialists. It shows that Chaldaean astrologers did not become famous worldwide without good cause, and how their learning contributed to humanism in the Renaissance.

The Hittites (1990) by Oliver R Gurney. This remains one of the best books to describe the ancient Indo-European people of Anatolia who took over much of the learning of Mesopotamia and helped to transmit it to Hebrews and Greeks.

The Bible and Recent Archaeology (1987) by P Roger and S Moorey. An extensive revision of Kathleen Kenyon's book of 1978. It relates with great clarity and fine photographs how the tricky linkage between archaeology and the Bible continues to excite furious debate.

EUROPE

MEDIEVAL EUROPEAN HISTORY – *Simon Hall*

Since World War II, medieval historians have pioneered alternatives to the traditional, event-based study of history. Today, most medievalists attempt either to present a snapshot recreation of medieval culture as a whole – intellectual, economic, and material – from as wide as possible a selection of its surviving records, or to trace long-term changes in the ideas, economic trends, technology, demography, and even environment of the medieval world. The following selection offers an introduction to both traditional and new medieval history.

These may seem small things ... but taken together they build up a complicated sense of the past, which must always be made up of small things vividly perceived.

R W SOUTHERN

The Oxford Illustrated History of Medieval Europe (1992) edited by George Holmes. A superbly illustrated, modern, thematic introduction which combines both traditional and new approaches.

Cambridge Medieval History 8 volumes (1923–36) by various authors. A multivolume series offering the most authoritative traditional account of the Middle Ages.

Feudal Society (1965) by Marc Bloch. A ground-breaking analysis by an extraordinary historian and Resistance hero that helped to create the new approach to history.

The Making of the Middle Ages (1953) by R W Southern. The best short introduction to the medieval world, transcending the division between traditional and new history, by possibly the greatest British medievalist of all.

The World of Late Antiquity (1971) by Peter Brown. An outstanding short, illustrated introduction to the early medieval period, from AD 200 to about 800, packed with thematic insights.

The Three Orders: Feudal Society Imagined (1978) by Georges Duby. The most influential book by the most celebrated modern French medievalist, tracing the emergence, importance, and disappearance of a concept fundamental to medieval social thought.

Reason and Society in the Middle Ages (1978) by Alexander Murray. An exploration of all aspects of the interaction between the mental and real worlds of medieval Europe.

Medieval Monasticism (1984) by C H Lawrence. A straightforward factual introduction to one of the most complex and important features of medieval culture, and one of the most alien to modern readers.

Medieval Civilization (1988) by Jacques Le Goff. A unique combination of narrative history with an analysis of time and space, material culture, Christian society, and mentalities, sensibilities, and attitudes in medieval Europe.

THE RENAISSANCE – *Martyn Rady*

The Renaissance is commonly considered to extend from the 14th to the 16th century. The Renaissance was a cultural movement which sought to restore the forms of classical Roman and Greek civilization which had been lost during the period of the Middle Ages. This restoration involved not only art, architecture, and sculpture, but also a renewal of interest in Latin and Greek texts, poetry, and drama. The Renaissance had its place of birth in Italy, in particular in the courts of the north Italian princes who acted as patrons of the arts. Italy was also the home of the earliest humanists, so called because of their interest in 'human letters' (*literae humaniores*): poetry, literature, and history. The humanists edited classical works, the original texts of which had been corrupted during the Middle Ages, and sought to perfect the Latin and Greek languages used in their own day. The Renaissance spread out from its Italian birthplace during the 15th century and affected art, architecture, and literature across most of Europe.

> *The 16th century ... runs from Columbus to Copernicus, from Copernicus to Galileo, from the discovery of the earth to the discovery of the heavens. That is when man found himself.*
>
> JULES MICHELET

Cultural Atlas of the Renaissance (1993) by C F Black and others. A very well-illustrated volume which covers the principal trends of the period.

The Art of the Renaissance (1963) by Peter Murray and Linda Murray. Another well-illustrated book which concentrates primarily on developments in art and architecture in Italy.

The Italian Renaissance in its Historical Background (1961) by Denys Hay. The author investigates not only the values and meaning of the Renaissance in Italy but also its political background and subsequent dissemination north of the Alps.

The Renaissance in National Context (1992) edited by Roy Porter and Mikulas Teich. Although the volume includes several chapters on the Renaissance in Italy, the bulk of the work is devoted to the Renaissance in northern Europe. It thus provides a valuable counterweight to the 'Italianocentric' approach of most books on the Renaissance.

The Impact of Humanism on Western Europe (1990) by Anthony Goodman and Angus MacKay. Provides a thorough survey of the humanist 'programme' and includes discussion of the relations between humanism and the Reformation, court patronage, and magic.

Renaissance Europe 1480–1520 (1971) by J R Hale. Provides valuable and entertaining social, religious, economic, and cultural background.

Lives of the Painters, Sculptors and Architects (1550; several translations) by Giorgio Vasari. Vasari records the biographies of the leading Italian artists from Cimabue and Giotto in the late 13th century to Leonardo and Michelangelo in his own day.

The Prince (1513) by Niccolò Machiavelli. By separating politics and government from theology and ethics, *The Prince* may be considered one of the first works of political science.

PROTESTANT REFORMATION – *Martyn Rady*

The Protestant Reformation began as a reaction to the theology and practices of the Catholic church. It is frequently considered to have commenced in 1517 when the German monk Martin Luther launched a public attack on the Catholic practice of selling indulgences, which were documents absolving the purchaser from sin. Luther's protest and his desire to 'purify' and reform the church won him immediate and widespread support in Germany. The success of Protestantism in Germany owed much, however, to the backing of the princes who protected Luther and established churches of their own independent of the pope. The movement of religious protest and renewal begun by Luther was given clarity and coherence by the Swiss reformer John Calvin, who composed his seminal theological text *The Institutes of the Christian Religion* in Geneva during the 1530s. By the middle years of the 16th century, Germany, Scandinavia, England, Scotland, the Low Countries, and large parts of France and central and eastern Europe had been won over to the Protestant Reformation. The reaction of the Catholic church (known as the Counter-Reformation) was to define its theology more closely, to eliminate abuses, and to urge the persecution of Protestants.

> *All the strength, all the weakness of the German character was reflected and magnified in his [Luther's] passionate temperament, its tenderness and violence, its coarseness in vituperation and old-fashioned Biblical piety ... its conviviality and asceticism, its homely common sense and morbid self-scrutiny, its paroxysms of contrition and heady self confidence.*
>
> H A L FISHER

Reformation Europe 1517–1559 (1963) by G R Elton. Provides a thorough historical account of the origins and early development of the Reformation in Europe.

Reformation and Society (1966) by A G Dickens. A well-illustrated text which covers the principal themes of the period. The author explains the popular appeal of the Reformation with reference to the social conditions of the period and the role of the printing press in the dissemination of ideas.

Luther: His Life and Work (1963) by Gerhard Ritter. A leading German scholar explains not only the life and theology but also the popular appeal of Martin Luther.

Martin Luther: Selections from his Writings (1961) edited by John Dillenberger. Luther's writings still retain, even in translation, a strong and emotive power.

John Calvin (1975) by T H L Parker. An introduction to Calvin's life and work which explains his theology in simple and straightforward terms.

Popular Culture and Popular Movements in Reformation Germany (1987) by R W Scribner. A collection of essays which analyse the progress and impact of the Reformation from the point of view of popular belief, hierarchy, and social anthropology.

The Catholic Reformation (1971) by Pierre Janelle. A Catholic scholar traces the history of the Catholic or Counter-Reformation and discerns its origins in a movement for reform within the Catholic church which actually predates Protestantism.

The Dutch Revolt (1977) by Geoffrey Parker. From the middle of the 16th century onwards, the conflict between Protestantism and the revived Catholicism of the Counter-Reformation led to military contests in Germany, France, and the Low Countries. This book traces the history of the most violent of these confrontations.

MODERN EUROPEAN HISTORY – *Glyn Redworth*

The transformation of Europe between the Reformation and the 20th century is impossible to contain in one list. The period is characterized by the growth of powerful nation-states, whose antagonism had bloody consequences. It is also the age when capitalism came of age, and was too often unrestrained by notions of the common good. The democratic liberties championed during the French Revolution were not to be matched by economic and social liberties until this century.

> *And which is the first of these rights? That of existence. The first social law is, therefore, that which assures every member of society of the means of existence; all other laws are subordinate to it.*
>
> MAXIMILIEN ROBESPIERRE

The Perspective of the World (1979) by F Braudel. The third volume of this monumental work deals with the 15th to 18th centuries, and is no means confined to Europe. A masterpiece, it sets the scene for the economic and global setting of the rise of modern Europe.

The Thirty Years' War (1987) by Geoffrey Parker. Well illustrated, especially with maps, this gives an account of a conflict which still can claim to herald the beginning of a new phase in European politics. After 1648, wars are fought for secular rather than religious reasons.

The Embarrassment of Riches: An Interpretation of Dutch Culture in the Golden Age (1987) by Simon Schama. A breathtaking essay on art and representation in the first affluent culture of modern Europe.

Origins of the French Revolution (1980) by William Doyle. Recognized as the best introduction to the epoch of liberty, fraternity, and equality.

Spain: 1808–1975 (1982) by Raymond Carr. More wide-ranging than it appears. Liberalism was invented in early-19th-century Spain, and this account is an excellent introduction to efforts, in vain in Spain's case, to face the challenge of modernization.

The Russian Empire 1801–1917 (1967) by H Seton-Watson. A classic account of Russia's expansion of influence both in the Balkans and, territorially, into Asia. Its readability and authority make it a classic.

The Habsburg Empire, 1790–1918 (1969) by C A Macartney This period is examined in detail, though the poignancy of the Dual Monarchy is nowhere more vividly brought alive than in the novels of Joseph Roth.

Selected Writings of Karl Marx (1977) edited by David McLellan. This makes the works of the father of communism accessible. After all, Harold Wilson claimed he could never get beyond the first page of *Das Kapital*. A close study of Marx's own works reveals a more humane and sympathetic figure than the pronouncements of latter followers might suggest.

20TH-CENTURY EUROPE – *M R D Foot*

By the beginning of this century, Europe was the world's dominating continent; by the end of it, it had been displaced by North America, of which the predominance in turn was under threat from east Asia. Two European civil wars each spread into a world war, in 1914–18 and 1939–45, with catastrophic effects within Europe and outside it. From World War II, the part-European colossus of the USSR emerged strengthened, till its own internal contradictions destroyed it later in the century. At the western end of the continent, the French and the Germans, long opposed as enemies, formed the core of a European common market of which the principal aim was to prevent any more major European civil wars. Minor national differences can still make fierce trouble, as the current crisis in Bosnia shows: the catastrophe of 1914 began at Sarajevo, and it is unclear whether more such catastrophes can ever be stopped. At least European powers no longer own many colonies.

Other regions' claims to displace Europe in the centre of our world-picture are impressive. Africa, despised and disordered, boasts antiquity of human settlement; Asia encloses mature civilizations; North America is commercial by its economic might, South America by its rapid development; the Pacific rim by economic promise and achievement alike. All this competition has shrunk Europe's share of the map but has also forced Europeans into an increased dependence on each other and an enhanced European solidarity. They can no longer afford the internecine squabbles of the era of European world hegemony.

FELIPE FERNANDEZ-ARMESTO

Millenium (1995) by Felipe Fernandez-Armesto. Explains how Europe secured its temporary predominance over the other continents; it ranges far back in history – so much the better.

The Rise and Fall of Great Powers (1988) by Paul Kennedy. Also goes back, though only half as far as Fernandez-Armesto, before the 20th century; more diplomatic and less cultural in its coverage.

Europe 1880–1945 (1967) by John Roberts. An unusually lucid account of the diplomatic and political wrangles that attended the turn of the century and the two world wars.

The Myriad Faces of War (1986) by Trevor Wilson. Outstanding among the shelves-full of books that cover the Great War of 1914–18, which brought down four European empires and precipitated two revolutions in Russia.

A History of the Modern World (1983) by Paul Johnson. Begins with Lenin's revolution in Russia, and runs on into the early 1980s: Europe in these years cannot be considered in isolation from the rest of the world.

Lenin: Life and Legacy (1994) by Dmitri Volkogonov. Turns three generations of belief and misbelief upside down: a masterpiece of revisionist history.

The Oxford Companion to the Second World War (1995) edited by I C B Dear. Presents current scholarship on its formative subject.

The Age of Terrorism (1987) by Walter Laqueur. May well make its readers' hair stand on end: perils remain around us.

The Century of Warfare (1995) by Charles Messenger. Not confined to Europe, this is nevertheless Eurocentric.

THE HOLOCAUST – *David Cesarani*

The Holocaust was the first and only time that a state set out to annihilate every man, woman, and child of a designated group, wherever they lived, and however long it took. No other genocide has approached the intensity of the genocide against the Jews. Yet Nazi racial thinking had terrible consequences for other groups, too. There are varying explanations of why it happened, and why the Jews and the free world responded as they did. These are issues that haunt us today since genocide is clearly not a thing of the past. The Holocaust also lives on in the experiences of the survivors and has become a subject for artists, filmmakers, and novelists.

> *I could understand the desire to dissect history, the strong urge to close in on the past and the forces shaping it; nothing is more natural. No question is more important for our generation which is the generation of Auschwitz, or of Hiroshima, tomorrow's Hiroshima. The future frightens us, the past fills us with shame: and these two feelings, like those two events, are closely linked, like cause to effect. It is Auschwitz that will produce Hiroshima, and if the human race should perish by the nuclear bomb, this will be the punishment for Auschwitz, where, in the ashes, the hope of man was extinguished.*
>
> ELIE WIESEL

The Racial State – Germany, 1939–1945 (1991) by Michael Burleigh and Wolfgang Wipperman. A superb dissection of Nazi racial policy and practice, revealing how Jews, black people, Gypsies, gays, as well as other German men, women, and youth, were all adversely affected by Nazi race-thinking.

The Holocaust. The Fate of European Jewry (1990) by Leni Yahil. The most comprehensive one-volume account. Rich in detail, yet easy to read.

The Holocaust in History (1989) by Michael Marrus. A concise work that effort-lessly blends an outline of the Holocaust with a discussion of how the study of the sub-ject has evolved, including accounts of the main controversies.

Atlas of the Holocaust (1988) by Martin Gilbert. A valuable work of reference which, like his epic chronicle *The Holocaust* (1987), draws on survivor testimony to give a shocking blow-by-blow record of the catastrophe.

The Terrible Secret (1982) by Walter Laqueur. A precise and damning examination of how much the free world knew about the 'final solution' and how politicians, the press, and public opinion responded to the news.

The War Against the Jews (1975) by Lucy Dawidowicz. Although the account of Nazi policy is dated, this classic short history sympathetically explained Jewish responses for the first time and has hardly been bettered.

Anatomy of the Auschwitz Death Camp (1994) edited by Yisrael Gutman and Michael Berenbaum. The latest scholarship gathered together to unravel the complex history of the largest concentration camp and killing centre which has come to symbolize the Holocaust.

Out of the Whirlwind – A Reader of Holocaust Literature (1976) edited by Albert Friedlander. A fine collection of stories, extracts from novels, memoirs, and poetry by survivors that takes us as close as possible to the 'heart of darkness'. It includes extracts from the writing of Primo Levi and Elie Wiesel.

One by One by One. Facing the Holocaust (1990) by Judith Miller. For the sur-vivors the Holocaust did not end in 1945: it echoed on in their lives, touching their children, too. Every country involved in World War II had to confront its role in the 'final solution', a much delayed and painful process that is explored in perceptive essays on six different countries.

FRANCE – *M R D Foot*

France emerged gradually from the wreck of Charlemagne's empire. It was threat-ened by the Viking dukes of Normandy, who became kings of England, and at one stage of the Hundred Years' War owned about half of France's present territory, but were expelled by force of arms. Another threat came from the dukes of Burgundy, with whom the French crown eventually secured a marriage alliance. Religious wars in the 16th century were succeeded by a strong monarchy, run in turn by Cardinal Richelieu, Jules Mazarin, and Jean-Baptiste Colbert; which, late in the 18th century, ran out of cash. Revolution followed; so did terror; resolved by Napoleon Bonaparte's empire, which died of military overextension in 1814–15. The 19th century saw seven differ-ent regimes in France; for the last quarter of it, the Third Republic was relatively sta-ble, as industrial development began. An immense historical literature, most of it in French.

The Princess [Mathilde] was a portly little lady, with a startling
resemblance to her uncle Napoleon. 'If it weren't for him, I'd rather be
selling oranges in the streets of Ajaccio,' she would say, in the gruff,
plebeian voice of the Bonapartes. She sat, wearing a string of black pearls,
in a humble armchair to which her presence somehow gave the air of a
throne. She liked to feel that she was no stickler for etiquette, and would

*allow the ladies only to begin the movements of a curtsey before pulling
them up by main force for an embrace; while the gentlemen, once they had
shown their intention of kissing her hand, would receive an informal handshake.*

GEORGE D PAINTER

The Earliest Times (1927) by F Funck-Brentano (translated by E F Buckley).
Provides an old-fashioned medievalist's guide.

The Middle Ages (1922) by F Funck-Brentano (translated by E O'Neill). Does the
same.

France, Mediaeval and Modern (1918) by Arthur Hassell. Also has an old-
fashioned ring today.

The Ancien Regime and the Revolution (1856, several recent translations) by Alexis
de Tocqueville. Though much older, has a much more modern ring – the author fore-
saw the growth and the perils of democracy – and is still well worth reading.

France (1898) by J E C Bodley. Long the standard work. Begins at the revolution of
1789.

France (1969) by Douglas Johnson. A much more modern treatment, but also deals
mainly with events since 1789.

Marcel Proust (1959) by George D Painter. Though it runs over from the 19th century to the next, this is one of the best of biographies, and gives a splendidly complete
picture of the society of its day.

The Development of Modern France 1870–1959 (1940; revised edition 1967) by
D W Brogan. Remains much the best account of its subject; affectionate, sometimes
wayward, always interesting.

Grandeur and Misery of Victory (1930) by Georges Clemenceau. Covers the virtual dictatorship that saved France from Germany in 1917–18.

De Gaulle (1992) by Jean Lacouture. In two volumes, a life of France's saviour in the
following world war.

GERMANY – *Bob Moore*

The study of 19th-century German history really began to flourish in the 1970s and
1980s when historians began to look for the origins of the country's turbulence in
the 20th century. The amount of literature is enormous and the choices inevitably
highly selective, but the following do represent a cross-section of the best standard
works in the period and its leading personalities.

---

*Germany is a queer country: one can't regard it dispassionately. I alternate
between hating it thoroughly, stick stock and stone, and yearning for it fit to break
my heart. I can't help feeling it a young and adorable country – adolescent – with
the faults of adolescence.*

D H LAWRENCE

German History 1770–1866 (1989) by James Sheehan. On the history of Germany before unification, one cannot do better than this book which surveys the development of the Germanic states through the final years of the Holy Roman Empire and through the Napoleonic period into the 19th century, charting both the successes and the failures. Essential if one is to understand the federal nature of the post-1871 German Empire and the role of Prussia within it.

A History of Germany 1815–1985 (1987) by William Carr; *Germany 1866–1945* (1981) by Gordon Craig. Overlapping or adjoining the previous book are two other survey histories. Both have long timespans and have their own particular strengths. Again, one of these two should be considered essential reading.

Origins of the Wars of German Unification (1991) by William Carr. Provides a comprehensive account of the political and military circumstances which brought the German Empire into being. It includes all the debates, including the role of Otto von Bismarck and the fiendishly complex Schleswig-Holstein question which so bedevilled statesmen of the period.

Imperial Germany 1871–1914: Economy, Society, Culture and Politics (1994) by Volker Berghahn. This is exactly what the title suggests, namely an all-embracing survey of the 'Second Empire'.

Bismarck: The White Revolutionary (1990) by Lothar Gall. No reading list on 19th-century Germany would be complete without a biography of its leading statesman, Otto von Bismarck. There are many available, but the outstanding one of the present era is undoubtedly Gall's.

Similarly one cannot ignore the Emperor Wilhelm II. As one of the key figures in late-19th-century Germany, both his life and times demand attention. The following two titles are recommended: *The Kaiser and His Times* (1964) by Michael Balfour, and *The Kaiser and his Court* (1994) by John Röhl.

The Peculiarities of German History (1984) by David Blackbourn and Geoff Eley. This gives a more detailed insight into the debates on late-19th-century German history and beyond.

ITALY – *Glyn Redworth*

The geographical or cultural idea of Italy has existed since classical times, but it was only at the end of the 19th century that Italy became a political reality as well. Italian history is a series of invasions and betrayals, and it is perhaps little wonder that Italy gave birth to Machiavellianism.

There is, in fact, no law or government at all,
and it is wonderful how well things go on without them.

LORD BYRON

Italy and her Invaders ten volumes (1880s) by T Hodgkin. This work has not been superseded as an enthralling account of the various barbarian invasions which followed the decline of Rome.

History of the Popes (1886–89; translated 1891) by Ludwig Pastor. Another 19th-century masterpiece. Not easy to find, but a good library will be able to help. This work cannot fail to be readable owing to the colourful lives of many of the Roman pontiffs.

Kingdom of the Sun (1970) by John Julius Norwich. A lovingly penned account of some of Italy's less well-known invaders, the Normans, whose empire based on Sicily was one of the most fascinating of medieval societies.

The Prince (1513; translation by G Bull 1970) by Niccolò Machiavelli. Available in Penguin, as well as many other editions. His *Discourses* (1531) on Roman history are possibly even more shocking to the 20th-century moralist, but it is worth remembering that Machiavelli himself was a remarkably unconventional civil servant who was chastised by his superiors for being long-winded.

The Bourbons of Naples (1956) by Harold Acton. A fascinating account of one of Europe's most hedonistic dynasties.

Italy in the Age of the Risorgimento 1790–1870 (1983) by Harry Hearder. Deals with the period in which Italian nationalism led to the creation of a united and independent state.

Mussolini (1981) by Denis Mack Smith. A well-written life of *Il Duce* by Britain's leading historian of modern Italy.

A Political History of Italy: The Post-War Years (1983) by N Kogan. Bravely tackles the almost impossible.

RUSSIA TO THE END OF THE 19TH CENTURY
Martyn Rady

A Russian principality, with its capital in Kiev, reached during the early Middle Ages from the Baltic Sea almost to the Black Sea. Kievan Russia was destroyed, however, by the Mongol-Tatars in the 13th century. In the 15th century, petty princelings from Moscow (Muscovy) began to extend their power across northern and central Russia, defeating other Russian princes and eventually overcoming the Mongol-Tatars themselves. Ivan III (1462–1505) is commonly considered the first ruler of Muscovy to have assumed the title of tsar, or emperor. During the 16th and 17th centuries, the tsardom of Muscovy extended its territory across Siberia and into the Ukraine. It was not until Peter the Great (1682–1725), however, that Muscovite Russia became a European power. Peter not only engaged in substantial military and diplomatic activity across Europe but sought to reform the Russian state to make it akin to the states of western Europe. Although Peter built a new, Western looking capital in St Petersburg and obliged the nobles to shave their beards and dress in European fashions, he did not abolish the institution of serfdom. Nor did he establish any representative organs which might limit the autocratic powers of the tsar. Despite its major role in the defeat of Napoleon, Russia remained until the end of the 19th century economically backward and with a despotic system of government.

I have begun to sense what Russian writers have long revealed: that this is a place where the human spirit is made to struggle, thereby becoming fuller as well as more repressed.

GEORGE FEIFER

A History of Russia (1993) by Nicholas V Riasanovsky. A comprehensive account of Russian history which includes chapters on Russian culture, economy, and society.

Russia under the Old Regime (1974) by Richard Pipes. A thematic treatment of Russian history which seeks to explain the origins of Russian autocracy, serfdom, and economic backwardness.

The Russian Chronicles: A Thousand Years that Changed the World (1990) edited by Tessa Clark; more than 30 contributors. A survey of Russian history from the earliest times which is supported by extracts from contemporary documents and by illustrations.

Medieval Russia: A Source Book, 850–1700 (1991) by Basil Dmytryshyn. Provides useful extracts from Russian law codes and chronicles as well as descriptions given by contemporary visitors.

Prince A M Kurbsky's History of Ivan IV (1965) edited by J L I Fennell. A contemporary account of the life of Ivan IV (1533–84), reputedly the most brutal and ruthless of the tsars of Muscovy.

Peter the Great: His Life and World (1981) by Robert K Massie. A vivid and comprehensive biography by a leading popular historian.

The Cossacks (1969) by Philip Longworth. A history of the Cossacks of the steppeland and of the Ukraine, whose freebooting way of life fell victim to Russian expansion in the 17th and 18th centuries.

Journey for Our Time: The Journals of the Marquis de Custine (1953) by P P Kohler A French account of a journey to Russia in 1839 with some very telling observations on the nature of the Russian state and society.

SPAIN AND PORTUGAL – *Simon Baskett*

The two countries that now make up the Iberian peninsula have experienced a turbulent history, at time overlapping and intertwining, at others completely separate. The physical diversity of the peninsula has contributed to a many-stranded history, and its geographical location in Europe has led to an almost unique intermingling of cultures from Europe itself, Africa, and the Mediterranean. From the time of the first settlers arriving from N France in the early Stone Age, the peninsula has been exposed to the influence of a whole host of different peoples, from the Greeks and Romans to the Visigoths and the Moors, each leaving behind a distinct legacy.

In particular the Moorish conquest and subsequent *Reconquista* left an indelible imprint upon the whole peninsula. Both countries have experienced imperial grandeur followed by rapid decline, both have laboured under long-lasting dictatorships in the 20th century, and both have had to undergo the traumatic transition to democracy. The imperial past of the two countries has meant that they have been a shaping force in the histories of five continents: Africa, North and South America, Asia, and, of course, Europe. There is little doubt that the subject of Portuguese history has been relatively neglected in terms of English-language books and this is reflected in the book list.

A dry, barren, impoverished land. A peninsula separated from the continent of Europe by the mountain barrier of the Pyrenees – isolated and remote. A country divided within itself, broken by a high central table-land that stretches from the Pyrenees to the southern coast. No natural centre, no easy routes. Fragmented, disparate, a complex of different races, languages, and civilizations – this was, and is, Spain.

J H ELLIOTT

For a century and a half, from the mid-15th to the late 16th century, Portugal was the supreme power across the oceans of the earth. Its wealth, from its dominions and monopolies across the globe, was dazzling, the grandiose effect of the grandest of causes: discovery.

MARION KAPLAN

The Quest for El Cid (1989) by Richard Fletcher. An illuminating study of the 11th-century nobleman and soldier-genius. It provides an essential background to Moorish Spain and paints a vivid picture of Spain at this time.

Islamic Spain 1250–1500 (1992) by L P Harvey. A richly detailed account of this pivotal period in Spain's history from the fall of Seville to the Reconquista. It covers matters political, social, diplomatic, and cultural. Scholarly and comprehensive.

Spain 1469–1714: A Society of Conflict (1991) by Henry Kamen. An extremely thorough and up-to-date survey of Spanish history between these dates. It deals with the rise and fall of the imperial greatness of Spain. Kamen highlights the problems and tensions within Spanish society, and manages to create a fully integrated picture of all aspects of Spain at this time.

Imperial Spain: 1469–1714 (1990) by J H Elliott. The standard work on the Spanish Golden Age. It is elegantly written, highly readable, and is characterized by thorough research throughout.

Philip II (1995 3rd revised edition) by Geoffrey Parker. Entertaining, accurate, and revealing portrait of the most powerful man of his age, based upon Philip's personal papers and memoranda. Philip is brought to life in this compelling biography.

The Golden Age of Spain (1971) by Antonio Dominguez Ortiz. Interesting background on the literature, the arts, religion, economy, and society as well as the politics of Golden Age Spain.

The Spanish Armada (1988) by Colin Martin and Geoffrey Parker. A fascinating and impressive book vividly recreating the story behind the Armada. It makes use of the latest research and lays some of the old myths to rest. Well illustrated and a thoroughly good read.

The Portuguese Seaborne Empire (1991) by C R Boxer. An entertaining account of the deeds of the pioneers of maritime expansion, and the missionaries, soldiers, colonists, and merchants involved in the whole enterprise. Alternatively, *A World on the Move: The Portuguese in Africa, Asia and America 1415–1808* by A J R Russell-Wood provides an equally fascinating study of the first and one of the greatest colonial empires.

A Concise History of Portugal (1993) by David Birmingham. Highly accessible and true to its title – concise; running through Portuguese history up to the 1990s. Includes sections on Brazilian wealth, the wine trade, ties with England, and membership of the European Community, as well as the more obvious political history of topics such as the era of the liberal monarchy and the Antonio Salazar dictatorship.

They Went to Portugal Too (1990) by Rose Macaulay. An enduring account of Portugal as it once was; it deals with British travellers to Portugal, combining some excellent stories and entertaining anecdotes interwoven with the history of the country.

THE LOW COUNTRIES (NETHERLANDS AND BELGIUM) – *Bob Moore*

The history of the Low Countries has not generally been well served by books in the English language. For many years, there was no great publishing tradition among Dutch academics and even when books did start to appear, publishers seldom saw the need to produce English editions. As a result, many of the key texts listed here have been written by 'foreigners', with English and North American authors leading the way. Another distortion has been the immense interest in the Golden Age of the 17th century and the relative neglect of more recent periods. Obtaining a balance does mean that some of the cited works have been available for a long time, but this does not detract from their importance or readability.

I know some Persons of good sense and even of Quality that have no
clearer notion of 'em tho' they are next door to us, than they have
of the Mandarins in China; and what is worse, think themselves no
more obliged to know the one than the other ...

BERNARD MANDEVILLE

The Dutch Republic: Its Rise, Greatness and Fall 1477–1806 (1995) by Jonathan Israel. A volume from the **Oxford History of Early Modern Europe**. A comprehensive history which incorporates the latest scholarship but with a lightness of touch. An ideal, if not essential, starting point.

Rise of the Dutch Republic (1856) by John Lothrop Motley. A great book, not so much for the analysis which has been undermined by subsequent scholarship, but for its descriptions. His account of the siege of Leiden is a real classic. No recent edition but its early popularity means that copies can still be found in libraries and second-hand bookshops.

The Dutch Revolt (1979) by Geoffrey Parker. Just to set the record straight. The best recent scholarship on this colourful and turbulent period.

The Embarrassment of Riches: An Interpretation of Dutch Culture in the Golden Age (1988) by Simon Schama. How does one begin to provide reading on the Golden Age? Schama has his own inimitable style and a particular way of examining his subject which is always entertaining and often thought-provoking.

Culture and Society in the Dutch Republic During the 17th Century (1974) by J L Price. A more straightforward analysis of the period but a work which has stood the test of time.

Daily Life in Rembrandt's Holland (1962) by Paul Zumthor. Delivers some solid detail on everyday Dutch society in the Golden Age.

Plain Lives in a Golden Age (1990) by Adriaan van Duersen. A more recent work covering some of the same ground, and widely recommended by specialist historians and art historians of the period.

The Dutch Seaborne Empire (1965) by C R Boxer. A series of essays on maritime expansion, which was an essential element in the history of the Dutch republic.

The Low Countries 1780–1940 (1978) by E H Kossman. By far the best example of a common approach used by many Dutch and Flemish historians of the 19th and 20th centuries to combine the history of both the Netherlands and Belgium.

The Politics of Accommodation: Pluralism and Democracy in the Netherlands (1968) by Paul R Waibel. A work of political science, but one which provides an understanding of how contemporary Dutch politics and society are organized.

Literature of the Low Countries: A Short History of Dutch Literature in the Netherlands and Belgium (1971) by Reinder P Meijer. Perhaps the only general survey on Dutch and Flemish literature.

EAST-CENTRAL EUROPE (TO THE END OF THE 19TH CENTURY) – *Martyn Rady*

East-Central Europe is the term frequently used nowadays to refer to the lands lying between Germany and the historic Russian (later Soviet) frontier. It thus includes modern Poland, the Czech Republic, Slovakia, Hungary, Romania, and the Balkans. East-Central Europe is mainly Slavonic-speaking, but it also has large pockets of German, Hungarian, Romanian, and Albanian speakers, as well as Jews and Gypsies (Roma). Although during the Middle Ages, the territory of East-Central Europe included a number of independent kingdoms, it was dominated from the 14th century onwards by the empires. The Ottoman Turkish empire occupied the Balkans, while modern-day Hungary, the Czech Republic, Slovakia, Croatia, and parts of Romania and Serbia were ruled by the Austrian Habsburgs. At the end of the 18th century, the independent Polish state was partitioned between Prussia, Russia, and Habsburg Austria. During the 19th century, the peoples of East-Central Europe were strongly affected by the ideology of nationalism and sought to establish their own independent nation-states. Nationalism led to several abortive uprisings in the region, most notably in 1848. Several independent states were established in the Balkans during the late 19th century, but the rule of empires persisted in most of East-Central Europe until the end of World War I.

Historical Atlas of East Central Europe (1993) by Paul Robert Magocsi. Contains not only maps and tables but brief explanations of the principal historical developments in the region.

East Central Europe in the Middle Ages (1994) by Jean Sedlar. A thorough, thematically arranged survey of the region during the medieval period.

A History of the Habsburg Empire 1273–1700 (1994) by Jean Berenger. Traces the origins and growth of the Austrian Habsburg monarchy in East-Central Europe.

Eastern Europe, 1740–1985: Feudalism to Communism (1986) by Robin Okey. A valuable and comprehensive introduction to the more recent history of the region.

The Fall of the House of Habsburg (1963) by Edward Crankshaw. Traces the history of the Habsburg monarchy in the 19th century with particular reference to the fortune and fate of the ruling dynasty.

Hungary: A Short History (1962) by C A Macartney. A thorough account of Hungarian history from the earliest times.

Czechoslovakia at the Crossroads of European History (1990) by Jaroslav Krejci. Written before the split-up of Czechoslovakia, this remains the first substantial English-language history of the country to be written since World War II.

God's Playground: A History of Poland (1981) by Norman Davies. A masterful and entertaining account of Polish history. Arranged chronologically, the volumes are divided by the late-18th-century partition.

History of the Balkans: Eighteenth and Nineteenth Centuries (1983) by Barbara Jelavich. Despite its title, this work provides substantial historical material on the medieval and early modern periods. The bulk of the text is devoted to the wars of national liberation fought against the Ottoman Turks in the 19th century.

Danube (1989) by Claudio Magris. A travelogue which by its historical and cultural references yields a mine of observations and insights into the region.

A History of the Gypsies of Eastern Europe and Russia (1995) by David Crowe. Provides the first detailed history of one of East-Central Europe's largest and most neglected minorities.

The Everyman Companion to East European Literature (1993) by R B Pynsent and S I Kanikova. Gives biographies of East-Central European authors, and guides to the major literary trends in the region.

The Bridge on the Drina (1959) by Ivo Andric. A historical novel about a bridge in Bosnia, set between the 15th and the 20th centuries.

BRITAIN

CELTIC HISTORY – *Martin Henig*

The three lists on early British history (Celtic, Roman, and Anglo-Saxon to Norman) cover a period approximately from the 7th century BC until the 12th century AD. Nevertheless they cannot be entirely chronological. Celtic languages and art survived the Iron Age and Celtic culture reached its apogee in Ireland, Scotland, and Wales in the early Middle Ages. Although the traditional date for the end of Roman Britain is around AD 410, the provincial population can still be recognized, especially in western England, long afterwards, and besides traces of political continuity the Christian church seems to have had some Romano-British roots. The Normans – Vikings who had been settled in northern France for little more than a century – failed to extirpate the distinctive language and art of the Anglo-Saxons. The books selected here are ones I have found exciting to read and consult or, in two cases, to write. If there is a bias it is towards the cultural aspects (art, language, and literature) which define the 'souls' of these heterogeneous peoples.

Although people speaking Celtic languages had probably been present in Britain at least from the beginning of the 1st millennium BC, it is only with the arrival of the La

Tène art style in the 5th century with its characteristic and familiar S-scrolls, and with brief notices by Romans and Greeks from the 1st century BC onwards, especially Julius Caesar, Tacitus, and Dio Cassius, that they can be said to enter the light of history. Caesar shows us that Britain was fragmented into tribes often at war with one another and the position had not changed a century later. Nevertheless, despite their bloodthirsty ways and a religion which included human sacrifice, the abstract art of British smiths had reached a high level of virtuosity and beginnings had been made in introducing a monetary economy and in founding *oppida*, the precursors of Roman cities, at such places as Camulodunum (Colchester), Verulamium (by modern St Albans), and Calleva (Silchester).

All the Britons dye their bodies with woad, which produces a blue colour, and this gives them a more terrifying appearance in battle. They wear their hair long, and shave the whole of their bodies except the head and the upper lip.

JULIUS CAESAR

Iron Age Communities in Britain (1974) by Barry Cunliffe. This is the standard work on the subject, especially good on settlement and the economy.

Iron Age Britain (1995) by Barry Cunliffe. A more concise and accessible version of Professor Cunliffe's views, even better illustrated.

The Celtic World (1995) edited by Miranda J Green. This is a massive compendium by numerous authors discussing all aspects of the Celts, but very properly with an insular bias. It is, perhaps, an encyclopedia for library use rather than for the general book buyer but it will be consulted with profit for years ahead.

Exploring the World of the Celts (1993) by Simon James. Although the production is sometimes irritatingly trendy, this is the best general book on the Celts in all their aspects in Britain and beyond.

The Pagan Celts (1986) by Anne Ross. Dr Ross is a passionate enthusiast for all things Celtic, with a wide knowledge of later insular literature. Her wide learning is very apparent in this book, originally published in 1970 with the more accurate title of *Everyday Life of the Pagan Celts*.

Pagan Celtic Ireland. The Enigma of the Irish Iron Age (1994) by Barry Raftery. Although 'Irish' and 'Celtic' sometimes seem to be the same thing today, La Tène culture was evidently an imported phenomenon, confined to the northern half of the island. Whatever the language of Ireland previously, culture and for the most part the population shows strong continuity from the Bronze Age past. This is a very important book showing that invasion is not necessary for cultural change.

The Druids (1968) by Stuart Piggott. Here is the classic study of the well-known priestly caste and its place in Iron Age society, together with the story of the reinvention of the Druids by romantics and mystics in much more recent times.

Celtic Art from Its Beginnings to the Book of Kells (1989) by Ruth Megaw and Vincent Megaw. This is the best book on Celtic art in general, including insular art. It is superbly illustrated.

'The Work of Angels': Masterpieces of Celtic Metalwork 6th–9th Centuries AD (1989) edited by Susan Youngs. This is the catalogue of one of a series of exhibitions which really brought the past alive. No better proof is needed than this one that the greatest achievements of the Celts lay in post-Roman times. Included are works of art produced by the Picts of Scotland, Britons in western England and Wales, and of course Irish artists.

The Roman Conquest of Britain (1993) by Graham Webster. This is a classic trilogy to compare, for example, with that by Steven Runciman on the Crusades. Dr Webster explores through archaeology and historical sources the epic clash between Celts and Romans. It comprises revised editions of *The Roman Invasion of Britain* 1980, *Rome against Caratacus* 1981, and *Boudica* 1978.

ROMAN BRITAIN – *Martin Henig*

The Roman period begins with the invasion of four legions of the Roman army at the behest of the emperor Claudius, but quite quickly the leaders of native society were led to see the benefits of being incorporated into an empire which was generous in granting citizenship and political rights and encouraged the amenities of civilized life, including baths and banquets. With the exception of a serious outbreak of revolt among the Iceni tribe led by their ferocious queen Boudicca, aimed as much against other Britons as the Romans themselves, there was little trouble except in the frontier regions. Archaeology has revealed the prosperity of town and country, the flourishing of the arts, and a vibrant intermixture of Roman and native religion. In the 2nd century and beyond, virtually everyone thought of him- or herself as a Roman. When, from a combination of external circumstances, the Roman Empire disintegrated in the early 5th century, the Britons were one of the fragments that considered themselves heirs to the empire.

They create a desolation and call it peace.

PUBLIUS CORNELIUS TACITUS

The Oxford Illustrated History of Roman Britain (1993) by Peter Salway. This is the revised and illustrated edition of a book first published in 1981. This is the fullest and most readable overview of the subject, with many photographs in black and white and colour, although regrettably these lack scales.

Roman Britain (1995) by Martin Millett. Dr Millett is less concerned with the traditional version of Roman Britain centred on the doings of the army and more interested in the more subtle processes of cultural change. The book is both thoughtful and accessible.

Agricola (AD 97) by Cornelius Tacitus (translated 1970 as *The Agricola and the Germania*). One of the great classics of Latin literature. Tacitus' encomium on his father-in-law offers a near-contemporary account of one of Roman Britain's most influential governors.

Hadrian's Wall (1987) by David J Breeze and Brian Dobson. This is a lively account of Britain's most famous Roman monument. It deals with life on the Wall as well as military topics and should be in the luggage of any visitor.

The Towns of Roman Britain (1974) by John Wacher. Towns were the most characteristic institutions of the Roman Empire. This book has proved its worth over the years by bringing together all the evidence from place names, topography, inscriptions, and archaeology.

The People of Roman Britain (1988) by Anthony Birley. By means of a skilled use of inscriptions and other written sources, Professor Birley introduces us haltingly and fleetingly to the actual inhabitants of the province. This book gives a surprising insight into social history.

Religion in Roman Britain (1995) by Martin Henig. In this book I have tried to show that Roman tolerance towards and encouragement of religion was a profound agent of cultural change. Religion reflects both popular beliefs and profound faiths, some of which struck root in Britain.

Christianity in Roman Britain to AD 500 (1981) by Charles Thomas. In this very important work Charles Thomas assembles the evidence for Christianity in the province and makes an unassailable case for continuity into the so-called Dark Ages.

The Art of Roman Britain (1995) by Martin Henig. Until recently most scholars were content to disparage or at least ignore the art of Roman Britain. I have attempted to show that it has the same dynamism and originality as Celtic and Anglo-Saxon art and that it is one of the best indicators of the pagan, literary culture of the 4th-century British gentry.

The Age of Arthur (1973) by John Morris. Ever since it was published this book has been controversial. The story he tells is of the resistance of the Britons to the barbarians which crystallized around 'Arthur', and kept alive something of the spirit of Rome.

ANGLO-SAXON TO NORMAN HISTORY
Martin Henig

The coming of the English was not a single organized act. Groups of settlers from NW Europe (Netherlands to south Scandinavia) arrived in the 5th century, generally settling in deserted lands but sometimes involved in conflict with Britons or other Saxon groups. While large parts of western Britain, including Cumbria, Wales, and Cornwall, remained British-speaking, culturally England became Anglo-Saxon; however, the church may have kept Latin alive and it was certainly augmented (if not reintroduced) with the Augustinian mission of AD 597. Thereafter the Anglo-Saxons became highly cultivated, themselves sending missionaries to convert the heathen. In the late Saxon period there were constant problems of Viking raiding, conquest, and settlement.

In some respects the Norman Conquest of 1066 may be regarded as the final act of this drama. However, despite the ruthless suppression of English political freedom, which was made possible through the Norman military and fiscal regimes, Englishness continued to be apparent in art and ultimately the English language would supplant Norman French.

When we compare the present life of man with that of which we have no knowledge, it seems to me like the swift flight of a lone sparrow through the hall ... This sparrow flies swiftly in through one door, and out through another.

BEDE

Civitas to Kingdom: British Political Continuity 300–800 (1994) by K R Dark. Like John Morris's book, this deals with the Roman inheritance of western Britain and shows the extent to which the Britons of the early Middle Ages were legatees of Rome.

The Origins of Anglo-Saxon Kingdoms (1989) edited by Steven Bassett. Diverse essays by different authors showing that not all kingdoms had the same origin, and showing the part played by indigenous elements as well as the Germanic newcomers.

A History of the English Church and People (731; 1955) by Bede (revised 1990 as *The Ecclesiastical History of the English People*). Bede, born about AD 673, less than a century after the mission of St Augustine, demonstrates how quickly the Anglo-Saxons became civilized. This is a warm and moving account of politics and religious conversion by a great and highly readable historian.

The Making of England. Anglo-Saxon Art and Culture AD 600–900 (1991) edited by Leslie Webster and Janet Backhouse. Here, in a catalogue to a British Museum exhibition, is all the visual evidence for Bede's world and beyond, down to the reign of Alfred. There are excellent introductory essays.

The Golden Age of Anglo-Saxon Art 966–1066 (1984) by Janet Backhouse, D H Turner, and Leslie Webster. Although the late Saxon period was troubled, its cultural achievements, partly the legacy of King Alfred, were stupendous. This is another very important offering from the British Museum.

Anglo-Saxon Art: A New Perspective (1982) by C R Dodwell. This book looks at what the Anglo-Saxons achieved in its European context. It is one of those books that make one marvel at how those barbarian settlers in 5th-century Britain became (like the Irish) standard-bearers of culture, expressed in the most refined art.

The Anglo-Saxons (1982) by James Campbell, Eric John, and Patrick Wormald. This is a fine, illustrated general study of the Anglo-Saxons written by three of the leading authorities on the subject.

Alfred the Great. Asser's Life and Other Contemporary Sources (1983) by Simon Keynes and Michael Lapidge. This is a collection of texts, the most important of which is Asser's *Life of Alfred*. Here is the story of a king who is unique in being called 'Great' because his subjects loved him, because he fought off military catastrophe rather than because he undertook vast conquests, and because he educated his countrymen. Very Anglo-Saxon.

Viking Age England (1991) by Julian D Richards. A concise and well-written account of the Northmen who harried and invaded but also settled and traded in England. Recent excavation notably at York has very much brought them to life.

William the Conqueror (1964) by David C Douglas. This is the classic account of the Conqueror, a great warrior and administrator who changed the face of England.

English Romanesque Art 1066–1200 (1984) by George Zarnecki, Janet Holt, and Tristram Holland. This is the catalogue of an exhibition held at the Hayward Gallery, London, and still the most succinct account of the Norman artistic achievement. Introductory essays include one on architecture by Richard Gem, a worthy summary of one of the most obvious Norman contributions to the face of England.

MEDIEVAL BRITISH HISTORY – *Simon Hall*

The major questions in conventional British medieval history remain similar today to those which exercised 19th-century medievalists: whether the Saxon invasion of Britain was peaceful or violent, whether the Norman conquest introduced a new social order, whether the loss of the Angevin territories in France was a blessing or a disaster, how far the Hundred Years' War isolated England from the culture of late medieval Europe, how far the Scots, Irish, and Welsh managed to preserve their distinct identities. Progress, however, has been great, both from the cross-fertilization of history and archaeology and from the impact of new historical methods.

Here I am destitute of all help; I feel the palpable darkness of ignorance, and I have no lantern of an earlier history to guide my footsteps.

WILLIAM OF MALMESBURY

The Oxford History of England: The English Settlement (1985) by J N L Myers;

The Oxford History of England: Anglo-Saxon England (1971) by Frank Stenton;

The Oxford History of England: From Domesday Book to Magna Carta (1955) by A L Poole;

The Oxford History of England: The Thirteenth Century (1962) by Maurice Powicke;

The Oxford History of England: The Fourteenth Century (1959) by May McKisack;

The Oxford History of England: The Fifteenth Century (1961) by E F Jacob. The standard, large-scale, conventional guide to the whole field of English medieval history.

English Historical Documents volumes 1–5 (1953–75) edited by David C Douglas et al. A monumental, accessible and always fascinating collection of the major (and some minor) primary sources.

The Anglo-Saxons (1982) by James Campbell. A sumptuously illustrated introduction to all aspects of Anglo-Saxon England, filled with new ideas and insights.

The Norman Empire (1976) by John Le Patourel. The magisterial culmination of the career of the greatest modern authority on the world of the Normans.

From Memory to Written Record (1979) by M T Clanchy. An analysis of the development of literacy and a literate mentality which demonstrates that the most exciting new approaches to medieval history are not necessarily French.

Henry II (1973) by W L Warren. An outstanding biography of one of the most important medieval kings of England.

An Age of Ambition (1970) by F R H DuBoulay. An excellent thematic approach to later medieval England.

Domination and Conquest: The Experience of Ireland, Scotland and Wales 1100–1300 (1990) by Rees Davies. A good starting point for the history of the non-English kingdoms of medieval Britain.

TUDOR AND EARLY STUART ENGLAND
Glyn Redworth

England from the accession of the Tudors in 1485 to the early 17th century witnessed remarkable changes. Not only was unity in religion broken with the Reformation, but with the doubling of population in the space of 100 years, the stresses and strains of early modern society grew increasingly evident. Political disharmony went hand in hand with ideological diversity. The turbulence of the age is reflected in the writing of history. Older books stress the power of the state, especially over the spread of Protestantism, but more recent 'revisionist' work has stressed the importance of grass-roots movements.

This Realm of England is an Empire, and so hath been accepted in the world, governed by one supreme head and king, having the dignity and royal estate of the Imperial crown of the same.

ACT OF APPEALS 1533

England Under the Tudors (1974) by Geoffrey Elton. This classic textbook first appeared in the 1950s and portrays a Tudor state which is effectively ruled by, in the main, exceptionally strong monarchs.

Tudor England (1990) by John Guy. Incorporates the latest research and gives a greater insight into the mechanics of Tudor government.

Peace, Print, and Protestantism (1977) by C S L Davies. A wonderfully succinct account of English history from the Wars of the Roses to the mid-16th century, which reveals how early Tudor history is best studied with an understanding of the Middle Ages.

The Crisis of Parliaments (1971) by Conrad Russell. Also takes a less than usual overview of the period, and tackles developments in English life from the Reformation to the Civil War.

Bosworth Field and the Wars of the Roses (1966) by A L Rowse. A thoroughly well-written account of how, by fair means and foul, the Tudors seized the English throne.

The English Reformations (1993) by C A Haigh. A so-called revisionist account of the Reformation not as an event but as a series of processes. This work encapsulates the new consensus.

The Court of Henry VIII (1985) by David Starkey. A well-illustrated and vividly written account of the behind-the-scenes history of the king's reign. By emphasizing faction and not policy, Starkey brings alive the cut and thrust of the age.

Thomas More (1985) by Richard Marius. A highly controversial account of the martyr's life. Seeing him as much as sinner as saint, this is one of the more engaging of psychobiographies.

The Causes of the English Civil War (1990) by Conrad Russell. A forensic account of early Stuart history, where this son of the philosopher Bertrand Russell dissects what we mean by causes.

THE ENGLISH CIVIL WAR – *Glyn Redworth*

England's great civil war of the mid-17th century continues to divide modern historians just as much as it did contemporary observers. Did it have long-term causes, or was it really the result of Charles's political incompetence? Even the Marxist interpretations of the 1960s were foreshadowed by 17th-century writers, some of whom felt that the transference of land and power to the gentry after the Dissolution of the Monasteries left the crown at the mercy of its enemies. In the past 20 years, revisionists have eschewed deep-seated reasons for the conflict, but in recent years a return to old-fashioned 'telling the story' has reasserted the notion of constitutional conflict between the crown and Parliament.

Having by our late labours and hazards made it appear to the world at how high a cost we value our just freedom, and God having so far owned our caused as to deliver the enemies thereof into our hands, we do hold ourselves bound in mutual duty to each other to take the best care we can for the future, to avoid both the danger of returning into a slavish condition and the disagreeable remedy of war.

THE AGREEMENT OF THE PEOPLE, 1647

History of England from the Accession of James I to the Outbreak of the Civil War (1880s) by S R Gardiner. These ten volumes remain the best (and best-written) account of the lead-up to the Civil War. Gardiner's stock rises and falls, but successive generations of historians can never quite escape from his shadow. Not easy to find, but a good library will be able to help.

The Fall of the British Monarchies 1637–1642 (1991) by Conrad Russell. A bold attempt to use narrative detail to explain the Civil War partly as a short-term failure but also to show how difficult it was for Charles I to rule together an Anglican England, a Presbyterian Scotland, and a largely Catholic Ireland.

The Reign of King Pym (1941) by J A Hexter. Remains a powerful account of one of Charles I's most brilliant opponents. Despite its age, it reveals the complexities of the age.

Charles I and the Popish Plot (1983) by Caroline Hibbard. Details not only the fears of antipopery in England, but also Charles's somewhat naive attempts to have a diplomatic rapprochement with Rome.

Oliver Cromwell (1991) by B Coward. The most fair-minded and unsensational account of a character who still arouses much controversy.

The Rise of the New Model Army (1979) by Mark Kishlansky. This is the new military history at its best, explaining how military studies cannot be divorced from a wider understanding of politics and society.

The English Bible and the Seventeenth Century Revolution (1994) by Christopher Hill. A subtle study of the role of ideology by the greatest Marxist historian of the 1960s.

The Mental World of Stuart Women (1987) by Sara Heller Mendelson. Though not strictly speaking on the Civil War, this does help us understand how, in any time of historical crisis, women come to the fore in society.

Charles I on Horseback (1972) by Roy Strong. A fascinating account of the image of a king.

Divine Right and Democracy (1986) edited by D Wooton. A comprehensive selection of writings, ranging from James I's views on kingship to the radical thoughts of the interregnum.

RESTORATION TO HANOVERIAN HISTORY
Glyn Redworth

The period after the return of Charles II to the accession of Queen Victoria in 1837 saw England finally transformed from a rural monarchy to an industrialized democracy. The foundations were laid for the Industrial Revolution as well as for a worldwide empire overseas. A new national identity was painstakingly, and not wholly successfully, created as the notion of 'Britishness' evolved.

In every party there are two sorts of men, the Rigid and the Supple. The Rigid are an intractable race of mortals, who act upon principle. These are persons of a stubborn, unpliant morality. The Supple, who pay their homage to places, are as ready to change their conduct as their fashion.

ABRIDGED FROM *THE TATLER*, 1710

Court and Country 1658–1714 (1978) by J R Jones. An excellent introduction to the politics and culture of the age.

The Restoration (1987) by Ron Hutton. A highly intelligent account of the return of the House of Stuart.

Queen Anne (1984) by Edward Gregg. Deals with a much neglected monarch, in whose reign the relative decline of the monarchy is particularly apparent.

George I. Elector and King (1978) by Ragnhild Hatton. Probes how a Hanoverian monarch came to occupy the British throne and how his distance from the minutiae of English politics was a fillip to the growth of parliamentary government.

Jacobitism and the English People (1989) by P K Monod. Analyses the role of those who never quite came to terms with the Glorious Revolution and also casts much light on Scotland's absorption into the British kingdom.

English Politics and the American Revolution (1976) by John Derry. Deals with the loss of the American colonies and the divisions in England which precipitated it.

The Transformation of England (1979) by Peter Mathias. Remains the best introduction into the problems behind the notion of an industrial revolution.

A Polite and Commercial Society (1989) by P Langford. This has become almost an instant classic, as he deals with the social transformation of England.

Selections from the Tatler and the Spectator (1982) edited by A Ross. The liveliness of journalistic commentary in its first, golden, age is apparent on every page of these short extracts from the two leading journals of the 18th century.

19TH-CENTURY BRITISH HISTORY
Peter Martland

Nineteenth-century British history has something of a 'bad' reputation, partly because too much of the work achieved by historians has concentrated on the political aspects of the period. As a result they have succeeded in producing rather dry and complex accounts. That the 19th century holds considerable interest is clear in the continued popularity of its great writers – Charles Dickens, Anthony Trollope, Thomas Hardy – and good history can only further this. The books that follow are intended to represent this, providing readable coverage of all facets of a remarkable century of innovation and change.

The history of the Victorian Age will never be written: we know too much about it. For ignorance is the first requisite of the historian – ignorance, which simplifies and clarifies, which selects and omits, with a placed perfection unattainable by the highest art.

LYTTON STRACHEY

British History 1815–1906 (1991) by N McCord. Another superb work from the exemplary *Short Oxford History of the Modern World* series. The frequent use of headings and subheadings makes the narrative very easy to follow and absorb; couple this with a comprehensive bibliography and useful appendices and one gets the ideal introduction to 19th-century British history.

The Age of Improvement 1783–1867 (1959) by Asa Briggs. Standing the test of time, this seminal work is still 'total history' at its most accessible. Starting from the premise that the Industrial Revolution initiated an age of progress, Professor Briggs writes in what can only be described as an optimistic style, touching on fields as diverse as science and literature to produce a comprehensive overview of the period.

The Crisis of Imperialism 1865–1915 (1974) by Richard T Shannon. A lucid rendering of a period full of imperial confrontations and complicated diplomacy, helped by a very useful chronology and biographical notes on the major figures in foreign affairs. In spanning the centuries Shannon is able to show the failure of those involved to adapt their strategies to the changing situation, thus turning the great game of imperialism into one with consequences as catastrophic as World War I.

Aristocracy and People 1815–65 (1979) by Norman Gash. A very readable account of British political history, going beyond the major characters to produce a fascinating insight into the working of a political system. Particularly strong on the author's specialities in this period, notably popular unrest and Robert Peel.

Portrait of an Age: Victorian England (1953) by G M Young. When a historical work begins with 'A boy born in 1810 ...' one knows that one is in for a treat and Young does not disappoint. Written from an insider's point of view, it charts the rapid developments in all spheres of life during the Victorian era, creating in the reader's mind a mental picture which only the greatest of writers can produce.

The Origins of Modern British Society 1780–1880 (1969) by Harold Perkin. Thoroughly researched and convincingly argued, this is an engaging approach to social history and its bearings on political events. Stating that an industrial revolution initiated a concomitant social one, Perkin expounds the theory that just as technology is one step ahead of industry, so was society ahead of political action in the 19th century.

Gladstone 1809–74 (1986) by H C G Matthew .Towering like a leviathan over the second half of the century, Gladstone provided in his copious diaries rich pickings for the biographer. The merit of Matthew's account is his ability to make a complex man understandable without ever divorcing him from his age.

The Making of Victorian England (1962) by G Kitson Clark. Distilled from a course of lectures, this series of essays retains the rhetorical flair that made Kitson Clark such a sought-after speaker. At times overscholarly, this is still a stimulating book, although not one to be tackled without some knowledge of the period.

20TH-CENTURY BRITISH HISTORY
Peter Martland

Historians faced with assessing Britain in the 20th century are liable to be overcome by the wealth of evidence they have to work with and the plethora of approaches open to them. It is undoubtedly a challenge but one well worth confronting, offering insight into the current state of Britain and even welcoming prediction. Working so close to one's own time does carry the pitfall of partiality, but in the recommended reading that follows, the emphasis is very much on history and not on current affairs. It is too early to draw up a definitive list of topics that have shaped Britain in this all too unstable century, but attention should be directed away from the 'high' areas of parliamentary politics towards the growing power of society.

Great Britain has lost an empire and has not yet found a role.

DEAN ACHESON

Empire, Welfare, Europe: English History 1906–1992 (1993) by T O Lloyd. A well-structured book covering the predominant historical themes in chronological order. Ideal as an introduction, with a comprehensive bibliography and a very useful set of factual appendices.

English History 1914–1945 (1976) by A J P Taylor. Taylor's outstanding answer to his critics' accusations of 'popularism', a book to be savoured rather than dismissed. The erudition shines through without ever obscuring a fascinating story of rapid political change, told in Taylor's always readable style.

The People's Peace: British History 1945–1990 (1992) by K O Morgan. A rare example of recent events being treated as historical occurrences rather than current affairs. Morgan's objectivity never wavers, producing a lucid and entertaining account of Britain after World War II.

The Development of the British Economy 1914–1980 (1993) by Sidney Pollard. A book which makes economics understandable without recourse to complicated theories. Very strong on economic data, at times distractingly so, it charts the relative decline of Britain's economy in all too vivid detail.

Churchill: A Life (1991) by Martin Gilbert. To produce a multivolume biography of Churchill was a labour of love; to turn it into a comprehensive single edition must rank as a magisterial work of revision. This elegant account throws light both on Britain's most eminent politician of the century and on the overseas affairs in which he made his reputation.

British Society since 1945 (1982) by Arthur Marwick. A stimulating analysis of Britain's fluctuating social structure, charting the erosion of social class in the face of economic segregation.

The Eclipse of a Great Power: Modern Britain 1870–1975 (1983) by Keith Robbins. An excellent account of the demise of the British Empire and the various positions Britain adopted in an attempt to keep its place on the world stage. Major involvements are described in clear terminology, making the interests of Britain clear at all times.

State and Society: British Political and Social History 1870–1992 (1994) by Martin Pugh. An interesting work which places the main streams of political and social thought into a chronological framework. A sense of Britain's inexorable decline pervades the book, leading to assertions which can best be described as debatable.

USA

FROM THE 17TH CENTURY TO THE CIVIL WAR
Peter Martland

Understanding American history before the dawn of the modern era is fraught with difficulties. The colonial period (between 1607 and 1776) can be seen as a chronicle of settlement, expansion, and exploitation of the eastern hinterland of what became the USA. Against a background of social and economic development, the great cities of colonial America – Williamsburg, Philadelphia, and New York – were created, as were the institutions, like the slave trade, that dominated and eventually consumed the southern USA. Cutting across these developments were political moves – based on an ideology of reason and enlightenment – that led eventually to independence in 1776. The enduring interest in the Revolution, the founding fathers, and the first formative decades of the Union continues to inspire historians to research and produce books of both scholarly and general appeal. Those listed below reflect a tiny proportion of the most interesting, readable, and enjoyable.

We hold these truths to be self-evident, that all men are created equal, that they are endowed by their Creator with certain unalienable rights, that among these are life, liberty, and the pursuit of happiness.

THOMAS JEFFERSON (DECLARATION OF INDEPENDENCE 1776)

Colonial British America (1984) edited by J Greene and J Pole. A comprehensive set of essays covering both the issues and the contrasting approaches to them. The editors' introduction and conclusion gives the work a structure often lacking in collections of essays, while a useful index provides summaries of the major texts cited.

Red, White and Black: The Peoples of Early America (1974) by Gary B Nash. An outstanding work in the field of indigenous culture which has so dominated

American history in the last few decades. As the title suggests, this book deals with issues concerning Native Americans, settlers, and blacks and their all too antagonistic relations without ever resorting to generalizations or dogma.

The Economy of Colonial America (1980) by Edwin J Perkins. By comparing the English and American economies, Perkins is able to provide arresting angles on economic development which would be lacking from a more orthodox history of the economy.

America at 1750 (1971) by Richard Hofstadter. Limiting oneself to a fixed date can often be disastrous in historical analysis but Hofstadter carries it off with aplomb, catching the American *Zeitgeist* through a heady mix of primary sources and anecdotal evidence.

Entertaining Satan: Witchcraft and the Culture of Early New England (1982) by J Demos. Combining biographical, psychological, sociological, and historical approaches, this work weaves an inescapable spell, the lure of speculation having been avoided through concentrated original research.

The Urban Crucible (1979) by Gary B Nash. Good history is often achieved through novel approaches. This is certainly true in this book. For Nash, by eschewing the agricultural base of early America and concentrating on the significant growth in the mercantile sector, brilliantly succeeds in presenting detailed argument without losing the reader's attention. At times overtly Marxist in interpretation, it is nevertheless a work which demands at the very least recognition and partial acceptance from all quarters.

The Glorious Cause (1982) by Robert Middlekauff. A superb narrative of the complicated events which together form one of the most fascinating areas of American historical research: the Revolution. The extraordinary detail within this book never impinges on the story being told, this asset most apparent in Middlekauff's descriptions of the military encounters.

An Economic Interpretation of the Constitution of the United States (1913) by Charles Beard. This timeless seminal work emphasizes the weight given by the founding fathers to economic interests as forces in politics and in the formation of laws and constitutions.

The Era of Good Feelings (1963) by George Dangerfield. Covering the period from Thomas Jefferson to Andrew Jackson, this is a very well-written account, highlighting the change in both policies and personalities that occurred between their presidencies.

Liberty and Slavery: Southern Politics to 1860 (1983) by W J Cooper. Concentrating on the area of 'high' politics in the Southern states, Cooper's account conveys the sense of an enclosed world, a feeling that is instrumental to understanding the Civil War.

Journey to America (1833; 1959) by Alexis de Tocqueville. This celebrated early 19th century account of American political and social institutions has successfully weathered the passage of time. It is as relevant to our understanding the America of today as it is to understanding the times in which it was set.

FROM THE CIVIL WAR TO 1945 – *Peter Martland*

In the 80 years between the outbreak of the US Civil War in 1861 and the attack on Pearl Harbor in 1941 (which brought the USA into World War II), the nature of the country underwent a fundamental transformation, changing it from a predominantly rural society with an economy based largely on agriculture, into a mainly urban society underpinned by what had by 1941 become the world's most powerful manufacturing and financial base. These dramatic changes were set against the background of the Civil War and its aftermath, the opening up of the West and the influx of more than 25 million European immigrants seeking a better life. In an attempt to understand this extraordinary period of dynamic change, historians have over the years produced a wide array of books aimed at both the academic and general reader. The list below provides merely a small sample of recent and classic texts of this time.

Speak softly and carry a big stick.

THEODORE ROOSEVELT, ON THE ART OF DIPLOMACY.

The Origins of America's Civil War (1981) by Bruce Collins. Although designed primarily as a guide for students, this is an instructive work, covering both events and issues in a concise style which never strays into patronizing the general reader. As well as very helpful biographical notes and chronologies, it also sports a comprehensive reading list.

Battle Cry of Freedom: The Era of the Civil War (1988) by J M McPherson. This is an example of that rare kind of history which transports one back to the age it is describing, so vivid is the picture which McPherson paints. It is 'total' history at its best, covering numerous fields and achieving an almost seamless mix of popular and scholarly style.

Why The South Lost the Civil War (1986) by Richard E Beringer, Herman Hathaway, Archer Jones, and William N Still. This work demonstrates the relationship between military success, morale, and will and the weakness of Confederate nationalism when undermined by battlefield defeat.

The Age of Reform (1955) by Richard Hofstadter. This Pulitzer-prizewinning account covers the period from 1880 to 1940 and it makes compulsive reading. Hofstadter's premise is that the prominent political ideology during this half-century of dramatic change remained a constant one of conservative individualism, a bold statement but one that puts a new perspective on much of American policy.

Invisible Immigrants (1972) by Charlotte Erickson. The act of emigration led many ordinary working people to record their actions and attitudes. Charlotte Erickson's meticulous – though highly accessible – scholarship reveals a host of insights into the greatest movement of people the world has ever seen.

The United States Since 1865 (1960) by John A Krout. This standard college text has inspired two generations of students to know and understand their country. Structured as a survey of the period between the end of the Civil War and the end of World War II, this work is highly readable by either students or the general reader.

Theodore Roosevelt: Culture, Diplomacy and Expansion (1985) by Richard H Collins. In this book Collins attempts to re-evaluate the presidency of America's first larger-than-life imperial president: Theodore Roosevelt. Specifically, the creation of an American empire to reposition the USA internationally. Collins also chronicles Roosevelt's domestic legacy, from the creation of the National Park Service to trust-busting.

The Origins of the Second World War: American Foreign Policy and World Politics 1917–41 (1975) by Arnold A Offner. A brave book which confronts the widely held view that American foreign policy was isolationist and self-interested. Through a close analysis of America's relationship with the other world powers, it shows that even the prewar world was a close-knit one in which America was unable to stand as alone as perhaps it would have liked or tried to make it seem.

The Great Depression: America, 1929–41 (1985) by R S McElvaine. The strength of this work is its appreciation of the effects that abstract economic concepts have on the lives of all those who work for a living. It manages to transfer figures into feelings and provides a sobering read without ever straying into wild accusation.

FROM WORLD WAR II TO THE PRESENT
Peter Martland

It seems almost as if the USA, during the past 60 years, has been on a fast-moving roller coaster. It began with the triumph of World War II, continued through an age of boundless self-confidence which collapsed in the agonies of the fight for civil rights, political assassinations, the searing trauma of the war in Vietnam, the political scandal of Watergate and the politics of Ronald Reagan and beyond. To encapsulate this period of dramatic events and other equally rapid changes in American society is enough to tax the skills of even the greatest of historians. Below are some of the best and most readable works of this period. As a bibliography it is designed primarily to stimulate the reader into looking anew at the nation which more than any other defines the society we live in today.

Ask not what your country can do for you – ask what you can do for your country.

JOHN F KENNEDY

In the Shadow of FDR: From Harry Truman to Ronald Reagan (1983) by William E Leuchtenburg. Although he died in 1945, the legacy Franklin Delano Roosevelt left behind has dominated the American political landscape. In this highly readable book, William Leuchtenburg assesses and analyses that legacy in terms of Roosevelt's successors.

Since 1900: A History of the United States in Our Times (1959) by Oscar Theodore Barch Jr and Nelson Manfred Blake. By describing America's political, economic, social, diplomatic, and military history, this narrative succeeds in explaining the American experience of the first six decades of the 20th century.

The Rise and Fall of the New Deal Order America 1930–1980 (1991) edited by Steve Fraser and Gary Gersthe. In the wake of Ronald Reagan's watershed triumph in 1980, Fraser and Gersthe intended this work as an historical autopsy. In fact they attempt to identify and account for two generations of political thought and activity in the USA. However, in the end, the focus of the work has to be the decline and fall of the New Deal order.

A History of Our Time: Readings in Post War America (1983) edited by William H Chafe and Harvard Sitkoff. Arguing that contemporary America arose as a result of changes that have taken place since the beginning of World War II, the contributors of this scholarly work chronicle and interpret various aspects of modern American history. The themes evaluated include the sources of the Cold War, McCarthyism, the civil-rights movement, and the politics of the 1960s and 1970s.

The Unfinished Journey: America since World War II (1986) by William H Chafe. Set against the background of the USA's emergence as the world superpower at the end of World War II, Chafe's book charts in a highly distinctive manner the radical changes in American society after 1945, the Cold War, the movement towards civil rights, and the agony of Vietnam.

American High: The Year of Confidence: 1945–1960 (1986) by William L O'Neill. By using the novel – though controversial – device of juxtapositioning US national policy with social developments between 1945 and 1960, O'Neill succeeds in reinterpreting American history and placing it in a fresh perspective.

The Struggle for Black Equality: 1954–1980 (1980) by Harvard Sitkoff. This book is concerned with one of the most significant developments in American history: the struggle for racial equality and justice waged between 1954 and 1980. A highly readable narrative, placing as it does the civil-rights movement into a clear perspective. An excellent bibliographical essay at the end of the book provides a helpful jumping-off point for further reading.

AUSTRALIA AND NEW ZEALAND

David Lowe and Ruth Brown

Histories of Australia and New Zealand after the white settlement have in common the themes of British peoples exploring, landing, carrying out ever-expanding economic activity, and developing political systems, and all this with consequences for the respective indigenous populations. For a short time late in the 19th century, when New Zealanders took part in discussions leading to the federation of Australia's separate states, it seemed that their destinies would be more closely entwined, but New Zealand did not, in the end, join. In the 20th century the two countries have had very different experiences of immigration, of indigene–white relations, and relations with other states within the Asica-Pacific region.

AUSTRALIA AND NEW ZEALAND
IN THE 19TH CENTURY

How funny it'll seem to come out among the people that walk with their heads downwards! The Antipathies, I think ... Please, Ma'am, is this New Zealand or Australia?

LEWIS CARROLL

Pastiche I: Reflections on Nineteenth-Century Australia (1994) edited by Penny Russell and Richard White. An excellent collection of essays on early Aboriginal-colonial, social, cultural, political, and economic history of Australia, which also delves deep into the whole exercise of constructing histories of this period.

A Land Half Won (1980) by Geoffrey Blainey. A classic and influential account of the expansion and limitations of Australain capitalist endeavour, especially in the 19th century.

The Australian Colonists: An Exploration of Social History 1788–1870 (1974) by K S Inglis. A very good, readable survey of Australian social history in the 19th century, charting the development of the colonies and the changes to white Australian society after its convict origins.

The Australian Legend (1958) by Russel Ward. The classic and much debated account of the bush-worker inspired egalitarianism and mateship in Australian society, the legacy of which remains today.

The Oxford History of Australia volume 2 *1770–1860: Possessions* (1992) by Jan Kocumbas. The first volume in the Oxford series after white settlement is a good introduction to a thematic but integrated account of Australia's convicts' and colonizers' founding years and directions of expansion.

The Oxford History of Australia volume 3 *1860–1900: Glad, Confident Morning* (1992) by Beverly Kingston. Kingston sees the second half of the century as one of the most creative periods for the building of Australian institutions and beliefs. Her chapters on beliefs and the nature of politics are especially good.

Frontier: Aborigines, Settlers and Land (1981) by Henry Reynolds. A pioneering attempt to reconstruct the Aboriginal perspective of Aboriginal-European contact. Reynolds has also written on other dimensions of this contact, and is the most influential historian in this field.

Old New Zealand (1863) by F E Manning. A personal account by a timber trader who lived among the Maoris in the early days of white settlement, who wrote with an affection for the time and the people with whom he lived.

The Long White Cloud (1898) by W P Reeves. A highly readable account by a prominent politician and historian who wrote with classical 19th-century Whiggish optimism. New Zealand is proclaimed to be God's Own Country and a working man's paradise.

The New Zealand Wars and the Victorian Interpretation of Racial Conflict (1986) by James Belich. In lively style, Belich dismantles the Victorian conviction that Britain always won its battles against 'savages' in the Maori wars. He shows that only overwhelming numbers enabled the British to defeat the tactically superior Maoris.

AUSTRALIA AND NEW ZEALAND IN THE 20TH CENTURY

Australia is not very exclusive ... On the visa application they still ask if you've been convicted of a felony – although they are willing to give you a visa even if you haven't been.

P J O'ROURKE

When I was there, it seemed to be shut.

CLEMENT FREUD ON NEW ZEALAND

A Nation at Last? The Changing Character of Australian Nationalism 1888–1988 (1988) by S Alomes. A readable romp through the meanings and experiments of Australian nationalists who, for most of this century, had to contend with the formidable norm of the 'independent Australian Briton'. Alomes finds, perhaps harshly, that much so-called nationalism left a lot to be desired, or was stifled by Australian imperial cronies.

Australia in Peace and War (1991) by T B Millar. A very digestible history of Australia's overseas relations, including involvement in both world wars, Korea, and Vietnam. The balance is even, if mildly conservative, and this book serves as an excellent introduction for those wishing to explore further in this field.

A Nation for a Continent (1977) by Russel Ward. Three-quarters of 20th-century Australia through the eyes of a nationalist historian, concerned especially with politics and economics.

Immigration (1991) by James Jupp. The best introduction to one of the greatest themes in 20th-century Australia's history. This is a well-rounded account, not avoiding the 'white Australia' policy nor other hard questions that immigration has posed, but convincingly optimistic about the consequences of immigration for Australia.

After Mabo: Interpreting Indigenous Traditions (1993) by Tim Rowse. A very important interpretation of the consequences of the Australian High Court's recent ruling on the validity of Aboriginal legal title to areas of land. Aboriginality, politics, land, and even sovereignty are discussed.

The Oxford History of Australia volume 4 *1901–1942: The Succeeding Age* (1986) by S Macintyre. One of the best volumes in the Oxford history series. Macintyre is especially strong on social and economic themes between federation and the early years of World War II.

The Oxford History of Australia volume 5 *1942–1988: The Middle Way* (1990) by G Bolton. The final instalment in the Oxford series is very good on expansion and prosperity after World War II, and on the periodization of modern Australian history.

The End of Certainty: The Story of the 1980s (1992) by Paul Kelly. An account of how Australia's certainties, such as a huge social welfare net, a 'white' immigration policy, protection for local industry, and high fixed wages, were dismantled during the political-economic revolution of the 1980s. Kelly's 'certainty' that the new deregulated direction is the only path for the future is also challenging.

The Bone People (1984) by Keri Hulme. Winner of the Booker Prize in 1986, and probably the most famous New Zealand novel. It is a rich mixture of colloquial and mandarin styles, of unreal magic and harrowing violence, but most of all it is imbued with Maori spirituality.

To the Is-Land (1982) by Janet Frame. The first of a three-part autobiography, this is an evocative and often very funny account of growing up in New Zealand between the world wars, capturing especially the school fare of Romantic poetry and empire worship in that period.

AFRICA

History of Africa – *David M Anderson*

Since its birth as an academic subject in the early 1960s, the field of African history has blazed pioneering trails in historical method and inquiry. New sources are constantly being found, unearthed in archaeological excavations, collected as oral literature and histories, and recovered from libraries and archives, which deepen our knowledge of the African past and raise yet new questions to be answered. The scope and variety of research and writing is simply breathtaking, as many of the following titles indicate.

The heroism of African history is to be found not in the deeds of kings but in the struggles of ordinary people against the forces of nature and the cruelty of men.

John Iliffe

History of Africa (1989) by Kevin Shillington. A very readable general introduction to the African past. A good starting point.

African Civilisations: Precolonial Cities and States in Tropical Africa (1987) by Graham Connah. A lucid synthesis of the many complex societies of precolonial Africa, with plenty of illustrations and good maps.

Paths in the Rainforest (1993) by Jan Vansina. A classic work from one of the founding fathers of the academic study of African history, which reconstructs the history of political traditions across the vastness of equatorial Africa.

The African Poor: A History (1987) by John Iliffe. This wonderfully engaging book spans medieval to modern Africa to argue that the nature of poverty has been gradually changing as demographic patterns adjust the balance between land and labour.

Way of Death (1989) by Joseph C Miller. The best account of the Atlantic slave trade, richly textured and beautifully written. It deals with the history of the trade from Angola.

How Europe Underdeveloped Africa (1972) by Walter Rodney. This polemical account of European economic pillage remains essential to any discussion of the impact of colonialism.

The Making of Contemporary Africa (1984) by Bill Freund. A succinct history of Africa since 1800, thematically organized to emphasize the social changes brought about by colonialism.

Magomero: Portrait of an African Village (1987) by Landeg White. A microhistory of the village where David Livingstone set up the ill-fated mission to central Africa, this beautifully crafted book brings the experience of Africans to life.

The Scramble for Africa (1991) by Thomas Pakenham. This big, stylishly written book provides a colourful account of the European conquest of Africa at the end of the 19th century.

Studies in the Economic and Social History of the Witwatersrand 1886–1914 (1982) by Charles van Onselen. Essays on the astonishingly rapid transformations that shook the Witwatersrand after the discovery of gold. The author is South Africa's leading historian.

20TH-CENTURY AFRICA – *David M Anderson*

There is hardly a country in Africa that has not been beset by immense civil traumas of one kind or another in the final quarter of the 20th century. Among Africans themselves, and in the writings of those in the Western world, it is not surprising that the search for the causes and the cures of these crises should dominate all else. But alongside the image of modern Africa as a continent of famine, war, and suffering are other images too: images of rich cultural diversity, of artistic creativity, of innovation, of astonishing endurance, and of personal and collective dignity.

The question is not whether there is a crisis in rural Africa, but what its nature really is.

MICHAEL MORTIMORE

Africa (1995) edited by Phyllis Martin and Dan O'Meara. These essays offer an excellent introduction to the history and contemporary society of the African continent.

The Invention of Africa (1989) by V Y Mudimbe. Africa's best-known philosopher here discusses the multiple layers that form the foundation of contemporary African society. A thoughtful, erudite, and at times very surprising book.

In My Father's House: Africa in the Philosophy of Culture (1992) by K Antony Appiah. Another study which ranges widely through Africa's historical experience and sociological heritage to present an interpretation of the distinctiveness of African culture.

Siaya (1989) by Atieno Odhiambo and David W Cohen. This highly original book takes cameos of life in a rural district of western Kenya to reflect upon the wider sociology, politics, and culture of modern Africa.

The State in Africa: The Politics of the Belly (translated 1993) by Jean-François Bayart. Originally published in French, this brilliant and challenging work analyses the dynamics of political culture in modern Africa.

Africa in Crisis: The Causes and Cures of Environmental Bankruptcy (1985) by Lloyd Timberlake. Hard-hitting populist polemic, published by the pressure group Earthscan, advocating a wholesale reappraisal of economic and environmental policies in Africa.

More People, Less Erosion: Environmental Recovery in Kenya (1994) by Mary Tiffen, Michael Mortimore, and Francis Gichuki. An important book which presents significant evidence of innovation in African agriculture to counter the pervasive view of decay and productive decline.

Conservation in Africa: People, Policies, Practice (1987) edited by David Anderson and Richard Grove. These essays, mostly written by social scientists, deal with aspects of the conflicts between the conservation of wildlife and habitat and economic development.

The Anti-Politics Machine (1990) by James Ferguson. This influential and very readable critique of the development process takes projects in Lesotho as its focus.

Twentieth-Century South Africa (1995) by William Beinart. The best available account of modern South Africa, telling the story of segregation, apartheid, and liberation struggle up to the elections of 1994.

MIDDLE EAST

HISTORY OF THE MIDDLE EAST – *Edward Fox*

When we speak of the history of the Middle East, we are almost certainly speaking of the history of Islam, which emerged in Arabia in the 7th century AD and rapidly expanded through military-political conquest and conversion for the next two centuries. It is easy to see Islamic history in the form of a tree, which grew from a single stem and then branched out into the separate histories of the states that emerged as central authority in the Islamic empire weakened, particularly in Turkey and Iran. Although it is a common error nowadays to speak of Islam as a single thing, like 'Christendom', because of its huge cultural variety, the Islamic tradition and its history give a unity to the Middle East, north and Saharan Africa, Central Asia, and parts of the Indian subcontinent. To understand the Islamic religion, it is important to have a familiarity with its early history, and its early political and doctrinal splits.

History is a discipline cultivated widely among nations and races. It is eagerly sought after. The men in the street, the ordinary people, aspire to know it. Kings and leaders vie for it. Both the learned and the ignorant are able to understand it. For on the surface history is no more than information about political events, dynasties, and occurrences of the remote past, elegantly presented and spiced with proverbs ... The inner meaning of history, on the other hand, involves speculation and an attempt to get at the truth.

IBN KHALDOUN

Muhammad (1971) by Maxime Rodinson. Stimulating work by a French Marxist on the Prophet's life and the founding of the original Islamic state.

The Venture of Islam: Conscience and History in a World Civilization three volumes (*The Classical Age of Islam, The Expansion of Islam in the Middle Period, The Gunpowder Empire and Modern Times*) by Marshall G S Hodgson. A penetrating and detailed interpretive history of Islamic civilization, from the time of Muhammad to the Ottoman era.

A History of Medieval Islam (1965) by J J Saunders. Gives a good sweep of the development of Islamic civilization covering the time of the Prophet, the 'rightly guided Caliphs' who succeeded him, the empires of the Umayyad and Abbasid caliphs, the Fatimid anticaliphate, the Seljuk Turks, the Crusades, and the Mongol invasions, which culminated in the Muslim defeat in the sack of Baghdad in 1258.

The Crusades through Arab Eyes (1984) by Amin Maalouf. One of Lebanon's best living writers compiled this account from contemporary Arabic sources.

The Assassins: A Radical Sect in Islam (1967) by Bernard Lewis. The best available book on Hassan Sabah, the 'Old Man of the Mountain', and his faction of the Ismaili sect.

The Ottoman Centuries (1977) by Lord Kinross. A good one-volume history of the Ottoman Empire.

Mystical Dimensions of Islam (1975) by Annemarie Schimmel. The best single-volume account of Sufism, the mystical tradition of Islam.

A History of Islamic Philosophy (1983) by Majid Fakhry. A detailed historical survey which discusses the legalism, rationalism, and mysticism of Islamic thought.

An Anthology of Islamic Literature: From the Rise of Islam to Modern Times (1964) edited by James Kritzeck. An anthology representing a wide range of literary traditions.

THE MIDDLE EAST IN THE TWENTIETH CENTURY

Edward Barratt

Following the collapse and carving up of the Ottoman Empire after World War I, and the abolition of the caliphate – the symbol of Muslim unity – by Mustafa Kemal Atatürk, the Arab world was left destabilized. British and French suzerainty between the World Wars was replaced by Cold War rivalry, with the USA supporting Israel and the USSR the Arab nations. Ethnic conflict flared between Arabs and Israelis in 1948–49 after Israel's foundation as a state in Palestine, and erupted again in 1967 (the Six Days War) and 1973 (the Yom Kippur War). The economic power of Arab states was demonstrated in the world-wide oil crisis precipitated after the 1973 war, and Pan-Arabism and Islamic fundamentalism were touted as genuine Arab alternatives to the Western-style national structures created after World War I. However, the Iran-Iraq War in the 1980's and the contribution of most Arab nations to the defeat of Saddam Hussein in the Gulf War of 1990–91 demonstrated these ideas' limited practical usefulness. Whether the 1993 PLO-Israeli peace agreement demonstrated a new realism remains to be seen.

---

*The tormenting dilemma of the Middle East is this: either
we have one people too many, or one state too few.*

AFIF SAFIEH (PLO REPRESENTATIVE)

The Near East Since the First World War (1991) by M E Yapp. Clear narrative account focussing on individual national histories and their relation to the international and economic dimensions.

The Longman Companion to the Middle East Since 1914 (1987) by Ritchie Overdale. Short introduction to the major topics and a comprehensive reference section dealing with economic and social statistics, religion, and politics. In-depth guide to further reading.

Politics in the Middle East (1992) by Elie Kedourie. Analysis of the different ideological bases of Middle Eastern attitudes.

A Peace to End All Peace: Creating the Modern Middle East, 1914–22 (1989) by David Fromkin. Account of the creation of the modern states system after World War I.

Into the Labyrinth: The US and the Middle East 1945–1992 (1995) by H W Brands. Examines the role played by US interest in oil, antipathy towards the USSR, and support for Zionism in influencing events in the Middle East.

The Gulf Conflict 1990–91 (1993) by Lawrence Freedman and Efraim Karsh. Definitive account of the Gulf War, covering its origins, course, aftermath, and implications.

Visions and Marriages: The Middle East in a New Era (1995) by John Roberts. Discusses the prospects for peace following the 1993 Israeli-PLO peace agreement; also looks at individual nations with assessments of the wider ideological and economic situation.

The Israel-Arab Reader: A Documentary History of the Middle East Conflict (1985) edited by Walter Laquer and Barry Rubin. Gathers together all the principal documents of the Israeli-Arab conflict, in the framework of a clear and concise narrative.

INDIA

INDIAN HISTORY – *Burjor Avari*

The earliest records of Indian history date back to the Indus Valley culture, about 5000 BC to 1500 BC. India's oldest religion, Hinduism, originated during that period; but the finest of the Hindu religious literature dates after 1500 BC. A glorious and enriching Hindu-Buddhist-Jain civilization flourished in India between about 500 BC and AD 1000, and it exercised a major cultural and intellectual influence upon its immediate and distant neighbours. Islamic influences became more marked after AD 1000, and Islamic political power reached its apogee under the great Moguls between 1526 and 1707. The British followed the Moguls and, through the instrument of their Raj, Western civilization impacted upon India. The modern republics of India, Pakistan, Bangladesh, Sri Lanka, and Nepal are therefore heirs to a long and brilliant Asian civilization.

Not by wars and conquest has India influenced the outside world, but in the subtler and deeper realms of imagination and thought.

PERCIVAL SPEAR

The Penguin History of India (1990) by Romila Thapar and Percival Spear. These two short volumes are a useful introduction for the beginner. Elegantly written by two of the greatest historians of India in the 20th century, they provide a concise narrative of the entire span of Indian history.

The Wonder That Was India (1954; 1985) by A L Basham. A book that should be compulsory reading for all who are obsessed with the superiority of European culture. With the help of a rich array of sources, the author explores the social, cultural, and intellectual history of pre-Islamic India and provides evidence of the depth and width of Indian cultural influence in the world at that time.

The Arts of India (1981) edited by Basil Gray. A comprehensive survey of the art styles of India, covering sculptures, temples, and paintings from the earliest period of the Indus Valley culture to the late 20th century. The book examines the richness of the native tradition and the skill with which foreign influences are blended in that tradition.

Al-Hind: The making of the Indo-Islamic World volume 1 (1990) by Andre Wink. Examines the first encounter of Islam with India. This fascinating first volume looks at the four centuries between the 7th and the 11th centuries, the period before the rise of Islamic military and political power in India but during which the commercial and cultural connections were already beginning to draw India into the Islamic sphere of influence.

The Great Moghuls (1971) by Bamber Gascoigne. A sensitive study of the first six rulers of India's premier Muslim dynasty, their pride and vanity, wealth and pomp, wisdom and justice, but, above all, their sophisticated culture and horrendous cruelties. Anyone planning a tour of Mogul Indian sites will be well advised to read this book. There is also a TV series in six parts.

The Raj: India and the British 1600–1947 (1990) edited by C A Bayly. Contains valuable essays on a variety of social, cultural, and intellectual themes that highlight the British presence in India. More than 500 illustrations of paintings, photographs, furnishings, textiles, and artefacts further help to deepen our understanding of the British connection over nearly 350 years.

The Splendours of the Raj: British Architecture in India 1660 to 1947 (1985) by Philip Davies. The remarkable architectural achievement of British India, in the shape of monuments and buildings, bridges and railway stations, military headquarters and hill stations, gateways and gravestones, is brought to life in this book. The vision and motivation, style and design, functions and usage, which guided the architects and builders are explained, with the help of numerous original photographs.

Hobson-Jobson: a glossary of colloquial Anglo-Indian words and phrases and of kindred terms, etymological, historical, geographical and discursive (1886) by Henry Yule and A C Burnell. Republished 1994 with a brilliant historical perspective by Nirad Chaudhuri, the highly iconoclastic Indian writer of modern times. This volume of 1,000 pages is a mine of information on how words of Indian and Oriental origin crept into English and how English words acquired new meanings in the Indian context.

Divide and Quit (1964) by Penderel Moon. A first-hand description, by a member of the imperial Indian civil service, of the tragic catastrophe that engulfed millions of people when British India was partitioned in 1947. A book to be read if we are to understand the background of hostility between India and Pakistan.

Gandhi: The Traditional Roots of Charisma (1983) by Susanne Rudolph and Lloyd Rudolph. There is a vast literature on the life and works of Mahatma Gandhi, the most influential Indian leader of this century. This slim but thought-provoking volume argues that through the force of his ideas on courage, self-control, sacrifice, and morality Gandhi not only bequeathed to his people a sense of worth about themselves but also helped to modernize them.

20TH-CENTURY INDIA – *Mark Tully*

India is the home of one of world's oldest civilizations, a civilization which still survives. It is the cradle of an ancient family of religions. It has produced some of the greatest religious thinkers of all times, from the Buddha to Mahatma Gandhi. Its thought is regarded by many scholars as deeper than European religion and philosophy. India has always been an important trading centre. It has never been isolated, and has shown a remarkable ability to absorb the thought of other parts of the world without surrendering its own originality. It has been conquered but its civilization has never been overcome. It is one of the few countries to emerge from colonization a stable democracy. With their education to freedom of speech and of thought, their achievements in science and technology, their skills as traders, and their new- found freedom from bureaucratic socialism, Indians are set to make their nation one of the great economic powers of the 21st century.

India has, more fully than any civilization on earth, past or present, explored, embodied the highest, the most all-embracing realization of our human scope.

KATHLEEN RAINE

The Wonder That Was India (1954; many editions) by A L Basham. Still the best introduction to the foundations of Indian civilization.

The Hindu View of Life (1927; many editions) by Radhakrishnan. A concise and readable summary of the religion which is so difficult to understand for those brought up in the tradition of Semitic religions.

The Ramayana (1982) and **The Mahabharata** (1978) by R K Narayan. Easily accessible retellings of the two great Hindu epics.

Indian Muslims (1985) by M Mujeeb. A scholarly book on one of the world's largest Muslim communities and its interaction with Indian thought.

The Men Who Ruled India (1985) by Philip Mason. A sympathetic history of British rule in India by a Briton who served in the Indian civil service.

The Penguin History of India (1990) by Romila Thapar and Percival Spear. A concise history.

Jawaharlal Nehru (1975 onwards) by Sarvepalli Gopal. A biography in three volumes. Essential for understanding the conflict that dominated the independence movement between the Indian thought of Mahatma Gandhi and Nehru's Western ideologies. Essential also for understanding why Nehru's dream of an India modernized by European thought, political structures, and technology failed.

Raag Darbari (1992) by Shrilal Shukla. A satirical novel written originally in Hindi, about the rural Hindi heartland and the flaws in the political and administrative systems of independent India as they work in practice. Cynical but with the ring of truth.

Stories about the Partition of India three volumes (1994) edited by Bhalla Alok. This anthology of writing by Indian and Pakistani authors looks at the event which still affects the politics of S Asia and the lives of millions of citizens nearly 50 years after it took place.

Gandhi, Prisoner of Hope (1989) by Judith M Brown. A scholarly biography of one of the outstanding figures of the 20th century. A useful compendium of Gandhi's thoughts on many subjects is *The Mind of Mahatma Gandhi* (1967), compiled and edited by R K Prabhu and U R Rao.

FAR EAST

CHINA – *L B Lewis*

European fascination with China began in the 13th century, when the Venetian Marco Polo visited the Far East. Interest is even more intense today as we watch the developments of the world's most populous country – what will happen as China's octogenarian leadership dies off, and when Hong Kong is returned to Chinese control in 1997? As a huge land with one of the oldest continuous cultures in the world, China has much to see and much to understand. Reading Chinese history can become a numbing procession of dates and dynastic changes, and the political and social chronology of the last 100 years is as complex as that of any preceding period. Fortunately, it is much better documented. Recent events such as the Cultural Revolution (1966–76) and the massacre of Chinese students in Tiananmen Square, Beijing, in 1989 provoke heated opinions which colour most of the contemporary writing about China. Less controversial, Chinese art and literature (chiefly poetry), both dating back more than 2,000 years, have attracted many Western admirers. Because of the differences between Chinese and European languages, translation is particularly difficult. The words may be rendered more or less faithfully, but the distinctive style of an author or a genre is often lost, and the economy of expression built into the Chinese language tends to make prose sound simplified, like children's literature. Poetry may be more rewarding for the reader in translation.

Mao, the emperor, fitted one of the patterns of Chinese history: the leader of a nationwide peasant uprising who swept away a rotten dynasty and became a wise new emperor exercising absolute authority. ... He enabled the Chinese to feel great and superior again, by blinding them to the world outside.

JUNG CHANG

Riding the Iron Rooster: By Train Through China (1988) by Paul Theroux. There are two types of writing about travel in China: the first cannot praise enough, and the second cannot damn enough. If one travels alone by train in the midst of ordinary Chinese – as did the author – one is less insulated from sources of complaint than the pampered package tourist. Theroux complains a great deal without giving the impression of hating every minute. He travelled for a whole year, over tens of thousands of kilometres, when China was in a period of particularly rapid and baffling transition – when mobile phones, discos, and other trappings of Western commercial culture were just beginning to flood the country. He had the advantage of having made a previous trip, in 1980, against which to measure change. This comparison blends with his superb general knowledge of Chinese culture and history in a dryly funny, unsentimental, unsparing narrative, letting readers share the experience of seeing China with an exceptionally observant and amusing guide.

Ancestors (1988) by Frank Ching. For the Chinese, there is nothing more important than family – not merely the relatives alive in the present, but also the history of those who lived long in the past. Chinese-American journalist Frank Ching, whose family fled China when he was five, experienced profound isolation growing up away from his native land and unacquainted with a large family he had only heard about. In August 1973, as an adult, he entered China in search of his roots. Aided by priceless family documents, he soon found the grave of his clan's founder, the famous Song dynasty poet Qin Guan, who had lived 34 generations earlier. The story follows the Qin family through 1,000 years of Chinese history and tells the life stories of more than a dozen of its major figures of different generations.

Chinese Encounters (1979) by Arthur Miller, photographs by Inge Morath. The Pulitzer prizewinning American playwright and his wife visited China in 1978, when the country was just beginning to open up to the West. In addition to taking official guided tours, they were able to meet and talk quite freely with Chinese writers, actors, and artists. Thus they were among the first to publish the bitter feelings of educated Chinese about the years of repression under Mao Zedong's communist regime (culminating in the Cultural Revolution of 1966–76 and its wide-scale persecutions), and their hopes for the future. The text is a stately and sympathetic accompaniment to the photographs, many of them protraits in black and white, which are intimate and moving.

Dragon Lady (1992) by Sterling Seagraves. The Dowager Empress Ci Xi was long believed in the West to have been the real power behind the Chinese throne at the end of the last century. She died in 1908, leaving her two-year-old nephew P'u-i, the last Chinese emperor, in the hands of his weak regent father and a powerful clique of advisers. Within three years the empire was overthrown and a republic established. Ci Xi has commonly been portrayed as lewd, corrupt, and ruthless, to the extent of murdering P'u-i's predecessor, her adopted son; she was said to have bankrupted the Chinese navy to build herself a marble pleasure boat, at a time when the navy desperately needed funds to fight the encroaching Western powers and internal rebels. Sterling Seagraves presents a very credible and entertaining case in Ci Xi's defence – including the motives of various parties for slandering her – while giving a clear account of the power struggles in the disintegrating 2,000-year-old empire that led to civil war.

Red Star over China (1937; revised edition 1968) by Edgar Snow. The classic contemporary account of the progress of the Chinese revolution by an 'old China hand' who personally knew many of its leading figures: Mao Zedong, Zhou Enlai, General Zhu De. In the aftermath of the Tiananmen Square massacre of 1989, it is easy to dismiss the Chinese communist regime as merely bloodthirsty and totalitarian. To understand the faith placed by the Chinese people in the Party – and the extent of the betrayal at Tiananmen – it is necessary to know something about how the communists came to be in power, and the hope they offered in the early part of this century, when starvation, extortion by landlords, and terror at the hands of bandits were the daily lot of China's ordinary people.

Wild Swans (1991) by Jung Chang. The best-selling story of three generations of Chinese women, encompassing all the upheavals of the 20th century, from the chaotic early days of the new Chinese republic, through civil war and the long years of Mao Zedong's rule, to economic reform and the Tiananmen Square tragedy. The author was the first mainland Chinese to be awarded a doctorate at a British university.

Plum Blossom: Poems of Li Qingzhao (1980) translated by James Cryer. Li Qingzhao (1084–c. 1150) was China's greatest woman poet and belonged to one of the oldest literary traditions in the world. Her speciality was a form based on old songs, retaining the rhyme, tone, and line length but adding new words. Most classical Chinese poetry was inspired by nature; Li Qingzhao's poems are also filled with images from the natural world, but she was one of the few poets who wrote what is clearly love poetry. The delicacy and vividness of her work is captured in this translation. A glossary explains some of the literary allusions that occur throughout the poems and are unfamiliar to Western readers.

The Private Life of Chairman Mao (1994) by Li Zhisui. As personal physician to the chairman of China's Communist Party for several decades, Dr Li Zhisui was closer to Mao Zedong than almost anyone else. He knew not only the Great Leader at the centre of a volatile personality cult, whose portrait decorated millions of Chinese homes from 1950 to 1976; he was also intimately acquainted with Mao's physical and emotional make-up, his strengths and weaknesses – and the illnesses that these factors exposed him to. It is to be expected that Li's position – the modern equivalent of court physician to an absolute monarch – was an uncomfortable one, and that this book could not be written until the cult of Mao worship was truly disbanded.

JAPAN – *Toshio Watanabe*

Japan is a fascinating but not an enigmatic country. The easiest way to get to know modern Japan is to find a Japanese and build up a friendly relationship involving the family. In order to get more general or specific information on Japan there are excellent encyclopedias on Japan, such as the *Cambridge Encyclopedia of Japan* (1993) edited by R Bowring and P Kornicki, which also has an annotated list of further reading. The following list is a personal one which aims to stimulate the reader.

---

*It is hard to avoid the clichés about Japan, because both Japanese
and foreigners seem to feel most comfortable with them.*

IAN BURUMA

The Japanese Achievement (1990) by Hugh Cortazzi. A wide-ranging and lucid account of the history of Japan from Bronze Age to the present day. The author looks at all aspects of Japanese life, in particular the arts, literature, and religion. A good starting point.

Zen in the Art of Archery (1953) by Eugen Herrigel. The best introduction to what satori, 'the enlightenment', in Zen means. It has been criticized as hopelessly romantic, but he tries to be concise and avoids the usual abundance of florid adjectives employed by Western writers. For further exploration of Zen, Daisetsu Suzuki and Alan Watts are the best guides.

Unbeaten Tracks in Japan (1880; 1984) by Isabella Bird. This book tells the story of an incredible journey to northern Japan by an Englishwoman. It also shows Japan on the verge of modernization and gives a vivid insight into the lack of material comfort in the Japanese hinterland which was eventually overcome in the 20th century.

Barefoot Gen (1987) and *Barefoot Gen: The Day After* (1988) by Keiji Nakazawa. Anybody concerned with nuclear weapons should read this graphic novel depicting how the life of a very lively boy, Gen, is affected by the Hiroshima atom bomb. The scenes depicted are appalling and not for the squeamish, but it is also an intensely humane story. Anybody still in doubt should read the novel *Black Rain* by Masuji Ibuse.

A Japanese Mirror: Heroes and Villains of Japanese Culture (1984) by Ian Buruma. There are (too) many Western books trying to explain contemporary Japanese culture, but this one is stimulating, brilliant, and most readable. This is a must for anybody going to Japan.

Japan, Inc.: An Introduction to Japanese Economy (1988) by Shōarō Ishinomori. A graphic novel full of intrigues and even love stories, but it gently gives information relating to complex economic jargon and explains specific economic situations. Business people should find this book interesting. It represents an establishment view of Japan.

Underground in Japan (1992) by Ray Ventura. This is a real-life story of a Filipino illegal immigrant worker in Yokohama. It shows the darker side of Japan, but is not a negative book. I particularly recommend this book to Japanese readers.

Kitchen (1993) by Banana Yoshimoto. Among the most accessible of the contemporary writers in Japan. As in the film *Tampopo*, food and sexuality are intimately related in this novella. Those interested in the 'modern classics' should read any available works by Yasunari Kawabata, Yukio Mishima, Jun'ichirō Tanizaki, Kōbō Abe, Shūsaku Endō, or Kenzaburō Ōe.

Points and Lines (1970) by Seichō Matsumoto. Japan has a flourishing crime and detective-story industry, though unfortunately only a very few are translated into English. Perhaps the most senior figure is Seicho Matsumoto, who combines a meticulous plot with social critique.

SOUTH AND CENTRAL AMERICA

PRE-COLUMBIAN CIVILIZATIONS – *Colin McEwan*

The last 30 years have witnessed remarkable breaktroughs in our understanding of the origins and accomplishments of pre-Columbian civilizations in the Americas. The great riverine networks of the tropical forest lowlands are now known to have fostered the beginnings of agriculture, settled village life, and ceramic art as early as the 4th millennium BC. Archaeologists, art historians, epigraphists, and ethnohistorians have combined to make inroads into the interpretation of Classic Maya and other Central American writing systems, documenting fierce dynastic rivalries and the rise and fall of city-states. In South America, independent cultures evolved successful adaptations to the harsh Andean environment, culminating in the Inca empire with its distinctive calendar, cosmology, and agricultural know-how from which we still have much to learn today.

There I saw the things brought to the Emperor from the new land of gold ... and I have never seen anything in my whole life that has cheered my heart as much as these objects. In them I found wonderful artistic work and admired the subtle genius of the men from these strange lands.

ALBRECHT DÜRER, EXAMINING THE OBJECTS SENT BY HERNÁN CORTÉS FROM MEXICO TO HOLY ROMAN EMPEROR CHARLES V

General:

The Ancient Americas: Art from Sacred Landscapes (1992) edited by Richard F Townsend. A fascinating and beautifully illustrated collection of essays ranging from the southwestern USA to Bolivia, addressing the ways in which pre-Columbian art mediates between man and nature.

Central America:

The Gods and Symbols of Ancient Mexico and the Maya (1993) by Mary Miller and Karl Taube. The beginner's ABC guide to the Mesoamerican pantheon. This illustrated dictionary is packed full of up-to-date information and makes it easy to cross-reference subjects and themes.

The Blood of Kings: Dynasty and Ritual in Maya Art (1986) by Linda Schele and Mary Ellen Miller. Documents the breakthroughs made by Mayan epigraphers in interpreting the significance of ritual bloodletting performed to celebrate dynastic accession. Not for the faint-hearted!

Maya Cosmos: Three Thousand Years on the Shaman's Path (1993) by David Friedel, Linda Schele, and Joy Parker. An exuberant synthesis of new thinking on many aspects of Maya cosmology and creation myths.

Scribes, Warriors and Kings: The City of Copán and the Ancient Maya (1991) by William L Fash. Summarizes recent archaeological work at the site of one of the most powerful Classic Maya cities.

Teotihuacan: City of the Gods (1993) edited by Kathleen Berrin and Esther Pasztory. A well-illustrated, scholarly but readable introduction to the singular nature of this great highland metropolis – one of the six largest cities in the world in its hey-day during the early centuries AD.

South America:

The Incas and Their Ancestors (1992) by Michael E Moseley. The best recent introductory survey of the Andean cultures of Peru for the general reader.

Chavín and the Origins of Andean Civilization (1992) by Richard L Burger. A meticulous study of Chavín culture, the first widespread art style in the Andes, focusing on one of the principal cult centres – Chavín de Huántar.

Ceramics of Ancient Peru (1992) by Christopher B Donnan. An attractive and accessible visual guide to the vibrant pottery styles and technology of the best-known Andean cultures.

Inca Civilization in Cuzco (1990) by R Tom Zuidema. A demanding but rewarding concise guide to fundamental aspects of Inca social organization.

The Tiwanaku: Portrait of an Andean Civilization (1993) by Alan L Kolata. An overview of the capital and ceremonial centre lying at the heart of the pre-Inca Tiwanaku Empire, spectacularly located at an altitude of 3,600 m/12,000 ft on the Bolivian Altiplano.

LATIN AMERICA UNTIL INDEPENDENCE
Joseph Harrison

The 'discovery' and conquest of the New World by Spain and Portugal, followed by the destruction of the great pre-Columbian civilizations of the Aztecs and the Incas, has attracted a considerable amount of scholarship. There is a good deal of literature also on the administration of the two empires and the attempts at 'enlightened' reform at the end of the 18th century, as well as on the nature of the various independence movements. Above all, in recent years *The Cambridge History of Latin America* (1984), volumes 1 and 2 edited by Leslie Bethell, offers unrivalled coverage of such topics as the Spanish and Portuguese conquests of Latin America, the effect of conquest upon Indian society, Africans in Spanish-American colonial society, economic organizations, political organization, the church, population, intellectual and cultural life.

I and my companions suffer from a disease of the heart that can be cured only by gold.

HERNÁN CORTÉS

The European Discovery of America (1971,1974) two volumes by Samuel Elliot Morrison. Contains enormous detail on the early voyages of discovery, ships, crews, methods of navigation, and life at sea. The work is thoroughly researched by a naval authority.

The Spanish Conquistadores (1963) by F A Kirkpatrick. Provides an excellent overall view of the conquest of Spanish America.

The Vision of the Vanquished (1976) by Nathan Wachtal. A brilliant polemical account which analyses the ideological impact of the conquest of Peru and the destruction of Inca society by the Spaniards.

Early Latin America: A History of Colonial Spanish America and Brazil (1983) by James Lockhart and Stuart B Schwartz. An excellent outline account which concentrates on social factors and ethnic relations in the New World.

The Spanish Empire in America (1947) by C H Haring. Remains an invaluable survey of governmental institutions in Spanish America.

The Colonial Background of Modern Brazil (1967) by Caio Prado Jr. A fascinating survey by a distinguished Marxist historian.

Masters and Slaves: A Study in the Development of Brazilian Civilization (1956) by Gilberto Freyre. A classic work which looks at the multiracial origins of Brazilian society and the role of slavery.

The Independence of Latin America (1987) edited by Leslie Bethell. Analyses the breakdown and overthrow of Spanish and Portuguese colonial rule during the first quarter of the 19th century. There are individual chapters on the origins of Spanish American independence, the independence of Mexico and Central America, the independence of Brazil and international politics and Latin American independence.

The Spanish-American Revolutions, 1808–26 (1973) by John Lynch. Remains the best outline survey of the various phases of the independence movement in Spanish America.

LATIN AMERICA SINCE INDEPENDENCE
Joseph Harrison

There is an extensive literature on the history of the subcontinent since its independence from Spain and Portugal during the early 19th century. Above all readers are referred to the invaluable multivolume *Cambridge History of Latin America* (1984) edited by Leslie Bethell. These volumes contain many excellent essays by specialist scholars. The series has now been reissued in paperback form with volumes on specific countries. The region has acquired great fame for its revolutionary upheavals, military strongmen, and repressive regimes. US involvement in the subcontinent, particularly since the end of the 19th century, has also left a bitter legacy of anti-Americanism in many countries, not least in Central America and Cuba.

A people that loves freedom will in the end be free.

SIMÓN BOLÍVAR

Modern Latin America (1992) by Thomas E Smith and Peter E Skidmore. A comprehensive and tidily written volume, strong on interpretation, aimed mainly at the American undergraduate market.

Dependency and Development in Latin America (1969; translated 1979) by Fernando Henrique Cardoso and Enzo Faletto. The classic formulation of dependency analysis which has dominated much of the writing on the subcontinent in recent times.

Spanish America after Independence c. 1820–c 1870 (1987) edited by Leslie Bethell. Offers general surveys on economy, society, politics and ideology in Spanish America during the half-century after independence, followed by a series of case studies on individual countries.

Latin America: Economy and Society, 1870–1930 (1989) edited by Leslie Bethell. Outlines the Golden Age of export-led growth during the period 1870–1914, the arrival of the Great Depression in 1929, population growth, the rise of mass immigration, especially in Argentina and Brazil, the impact of capitalist penetration in the countryside, urbanization, the evolution of political and social ideas, and the role of the Catholic church.

Brazil: Empire and Republic, 1822–1930 (1989) edited by Leslie Bethell. Includes five chapters on the economic, social and political history of Brazil from independence in 1822 down to the revolution of 1930. The persistence of slavery until the end of the 1880s receives ample treatment.

Argentina Since Independence (1993) edited by Leslie Bethell. Deals with the economic, social, and political history of that country in the period since independence from Spain. Peronismo and the Falklands War of 1982 are well covered.

Mexico Since Independence (1991) edited by Leslie Bethell. Contains six chapters on the economic, social, and political history of the country, including works on the Porfiriato (1867–1910), the Mexican revolution (1910–20) and the rise and fall of Cardenismo (1930–46).

Chile Since Independence (1993) edited by Leslie Bethell. Offers four chapters covering the economic, social, and political history of Chile after 1830. The Allende regime (1970–73) and the military dictatorship of General Pinochet which followed are nicely set in context.

Central America Since Independence (1991) edited by Leslie Bethell. Provides general chapters on the region covering the periods 1821–70, 1870–1930, and 1930 to present, followed by chapters on each of the five Central American republics – Guatemala, El Salvador, Honduras, Nicaragua, and Costa Rica.

Cuba: A Short History (1993) edited by Leslie Bethell. Outlines the history of the island since the mid-18th century. It deals with the persistence of slavery until the end of the 1880s, independence from Spain after the Spanish-American War of 1898, the growing political and economic dependency of Cuba on the USA, the corrupt Batista regime, and the impact of the Castroite revolution of 1959.

CONTRIBUTORS

Brian Aldiss, a prolific author, anthologist and critic, is one of the leading figures in the development of the British New Wave which brought greater sophistication of style, characterization, and theme to science fiction. His works include *Hothouse* (1962), *The Malacia Tapestry* (1976) and the epic *Helliconia* trilogy, written in the early 1980s. *The Detached Retina*, a collection of essays and articles on science fiction, appeared in 1994.

David Anderson is a senior lecturer in history at the School of Oriental and African Studies, University of London. He is author of *Eroding the Commons* (1996), and has edited a number of books, including *Conservation in Africa* (1987), *The Ecology of Survival* (1988), *Policing and Decolonization* (1992), and *Revealing Prophets* (1995).

Alain Anderton is a teacher and lecturer. He has written a wide range of textbooks and other educational materials in the field of economics and business studies.

Burjor Avari teaches Indian history and promotes Indian studies at the Manchester Metropolitan University.

Paul Bahn is a freelance writer, translator, and broadcaster of archaeology. In addition to about 300 papers, reviews and articles, he is the author of *Pyrenean Prehistory* (1984), *The Shell Guide to British Archaeology* (with Jacquetta Hawkes) (1986), *Ancient Places* (with Glyn Daniel) (1987), *Images of the Ice Age* (with Jean Vertut) (1988), *The Bluffer's Guide to Archaeology* (1989), *Easter Island, Earth Island* (with John Flenley) (1992), and *Mammoths* (with Adrian Lister) (1994). He is currently writing *The Cambridge Illustrated History of Prehistoric Art* for Cambridge University Press.

Edward Barratt graduated from Cambridge University and is working as a freelance historian.

Simon Baskett is head of history at Cherwell School in Oxford and acts as a consultant for a number of educational publishers. He has lived and worked in Spain and has travelled widely in the Iberian peninsula.

Ian F A Bell is professor of American literature in the University of Keele. His most recent book is *Henry James & the Past. Readings into Time* (1991).

Malcolm Bradbury is professor emeritus of American studies at the University of East Anglia, Norwich. He is also a novelist – author of *Eating People is Wrong* (1959), *The History Man* (1975), *Rates of Exchange* (1983), Booker shortlist, *Doctor Criminale* (1992), and other works – and a prolific writer of TV screenplays. Among his many works of criticism are *Modernism* (1976), *An Introduction to American Studies* (1981), *The Modern American Novel* (1985), *The Modern British Novel* (1993), and *Dangerous Pilgrimages: Trans-Atlantic Mythologies and the Novel* (1995).

Elizabeth Breuilly is a member of ICOREC and has co-written several books on religion both for schools and for the popular adult market. ICOREC is a multifaith, multicultural consultancy engaged in promoting greater understanding and appreciation of the different faiths and cultures of the world. Activities include producing multifaith educational material for primary- and secondary-school publishers, working with organizations such as the World Wide Fund for Nature and the New Economics Foundation, and organizing international events.

Ruth Brown teaches at the University of Sussex. She has published on various aspects of New Zealand literature, culture, economics, and politics.

Bill Bryson is an American-born journalist and writer. Among his books on language are *Made in America, Mother Tongue,* and *The Penguin Dictionary of Troublesome Words.*

Anthony Burton is a professional writer who has concentrated on industrial and transport history. His works include *Remains of a Revolution* (1975), *Our Industrial Past* (1983), *The Canal Builders* (1972), *The Railway Builders,* and *The Rise and Fall of British Shipbuilding* (1994). He has also written and presented the television series *The Past At Work* (1980) and *The Rise and Fall of King Cotton* (1984).

Michael Carrithers is an anthropologist who now teaches at the University of Durham. He has written extensively on Buddhism, following three years' research among the forest monks of Sri Lanka. He has also written *Why Humans Have Cultures: Explaining Anthropology and Social Diversity,* and believes that the same spirit of generous and compassionate open-mindedness that informs Buddhism also shines through the work of anthropology.

David Cesarani is professor of modern Jewish studies at Manchester University. He edited *The Final Solution. Origins and Implementation* (1994), and is the author of *Justice Delayed* (1992), a study of how Britain became a refuge for Nazi collaborators. He was formerly director of the Wiener Library, Britain's largest collection of books and documents on the Holocaust.

Mary Cobbett works for the Centre for Alternative Technology, an internationally renowned education centre promoting ideas and information on technologies that support rather than damage the environment.

Anthony Clare is medical director of St Patrick's Hospital and clinical professor of psychiatry at Trinity College, Dublin. He is best known for his Radio Four series *In the Psychiatrist's Chair* (1982) and *All in the Mind* (1988), and his TV series *Motives* (1983). His publications include *Psychiatry in Dissent* (1976), *Psychological Disorders in General Practice* (1979), *Let's Talk About Me* (with S Thompson) (1981), *Social Work and Primary Health Care* (1982), *Psychiatry and General Practice* (1982), *In the Psychiatrist's Chair* (1984), *Lovelaw* (1986), and *Depression and How to Survive It* (with S Milligan) (1993).

David Crystal works from his home in Holyhead, Wales, as a writer, editor, lecturer, and broadcaster. Formerly professor of linguistics at the University of Reading, he now has an honorary affiliation to the University of Wales, Bangor. These days he divides his time between work on language and work on general reference publishing. He has written over 40 books in the field of language, including *Rediscover Grammar, The English Language,* and *The Cambridge Encyclopedia of Language.* He is also the editor of the general reference book *The Cambridge Encyclopedia,* and of the other encyclopedias in the Cambridge University Press family.

Stephanie Dalley is fellow in Assyriology at the Oriental Institute and senior research fellow at Somerville College, University of Oxford. She has copied and edited cuneiform texts from several excavations in Iraq, Syria, and Jordan, and has written more popular works including *Mari and Karana: Two Old Babylonian Cities* (1984). She has solved the problem of the Hanging Gardens of Babylon. A major work, *Babylonian Legacies,* is scheduled for publication.

Richard Dawkins is a reader in zoology at Oxford University and a fellow of New College. He is the author of various books, including *The Selfish Gene* (1976), *The*

Extended Phenotype (1982), and *River Out of Eden* (1995). He gave the Royal Institution Christmas Lectures for Children in 1991–92 and is a frequent broadcaster and writer in newspapers on scientific matters.

Denis Derbyshire has taught government in further and higher education and examined it for the University of London. His books include *An Introduction to Public Administration* (1979) and *The Business of Government* (1987). He is coauthor of *Politics in Britain: from Callaghan to Thatcher* (1990), *Political Systems of the World* (1989), and *World Political Systems* (1991).

Ian D Derbyshire is coauthor of *Politics in Britain: from Callaghan to Thatcher* (1990) and *Political Systems of the World* (1989), and author and editor of W & R Chambers Political Spotlights series, including volumes on Britain, China, France, Germany, Ireland, the Soviet Union, and the USA.

Colin Dexter graduated from Cambridge in 1953. He spent his years wholly in education until his retirement in 1988, first teaching Greek and Latin, then moving to Oxford in 1966 to work for the University Exam Board. His mystery novels follow the adventures of the beer-drinking, Eton-educated Detective Inspector Morse. His first novel, *Last Bus to Woodstock*, was published in 1975, and in addition to winning the Gold Dagger Award for *The Wench is Dead* (1989), Dexter has also been awarded Silver Daggers by the Crime Writers' Association for *Service of All the Dead* (1979) and *The Dead of Jericho* (1981). His other mysteries include *Last Seen Wearing* (1976), *The Silent World of Nicholas Quinn* (1977), *The Riddle of the Third Mile*, *The Secret Annexe 3* (1986), *The Jewel that Was Ours* (1991), and *The Way through the Woods* (1992). The Inspector Morse novels have, with large success, been translated for the small screen in ITV's series starring John Thaw.

Rosamund Diamond is an architect who practises, teaches, and writes about architecture. She teaches in the School of Architecture at Oxford Brookes University and has taught at University College and the Architectural Association, London; Bath University; and in the USA at Harvard and Columbia universities. She is an editor of the architectural periodical *9H*. She has edited various publications, including *Reality and Project: Four British Architects* (with Wilfried Wang) (1991), *From City to Detail: Diener & Diener* (1992), and *9H number 9: On Continuity*.

Dougal Dixon gained two degrees in geology at the University of St Andrews in Fife and has spent his working life in publishing. As well as editing encyclopedias and contributing to science magazines, he has had over 50 books published, mostly on earth sciences and dinosaurs. His most famous are *After Man, A Zoology of the Future* (1981), *Time Exposure* (1984), and *Dougal Dixon's Dinosaurs* (1993).

Nigel Dudley is a consultant ecologist and writer who has worked for many environmental organizations, governments, local governments, international organizations, and publishers. For the last few years he has co-directed Equilibrium Consultants with Sue Stolton, and worked closely with Elm Farm Research Centre in England. Previously, he was director of the Soil Association. He travels widely, and is based in Machynlleth, Wales.

Deborah Eade worked for eight years in Mexico both for several nongovernmental local development organizations and as Oxfam's deputy regional representative for Mexico and Central America 1984–90. She is editor of *Development in Practice*, a quarterly journal of policy and practice for the international development community; and with Suzanne Williams, is coauthor of *The Oxfam Handbook of Development and Relief*

(1995). She has written and published on a range of development issues, and has been a consultant to the Ford Foundation, the International Federation of Red Cross and Red Crescent Societies, the United Nations High Commission for Refugees, the United Nations Research Institute for Social Development, and the World Health Organization.

Paul Eggleton is head of the Termite Research Group at the Natural History Museum, London. He coedited the book *Phylogenetics and Ecology* (1994) and is senior editor of the journal *Systematic Entomology*.

Hans Eysenck is now retired after 50 years of work at the Institute of Psychiatry, University of London. He obtained his BA, PhD, and DSc degrees at University College, London, and has published over 1,000 articles and 75 books. His research has been mainly in the areas of personality, intelligence, behaviour therapy, social attitudes, behavioural genetics, and experimental aesthetics. He is at present conducting research on the psychophysiology of intelligence, and on the relationship between personality and cancer and coronary heart disease.

David Fallows is a reader in music at the University of Manchester, a chevalier in the Ordre des Arts et des Lettres, and the author of many books and articles about medieval music, including *Dufay* (1982) and *Chansonnier de Jean de Montchenu* (1991). He is also active as a broadcaster and a newspaper reviewer.

M R D Foot, an army officer from 1939 to 1945, taught at Oxford for 12 years, was professor of modern history at Manchester for six, and has written, among other books, *SOE in France* (1968), *Resistance* (1977), and *Art and War* (1990).

Edward Fox was born in New York in 1958. He studied English at Cambridge University and Middle Eastern languages and cultures at Columbia University. He now lives in London, where he works as a freelance journalist. His book *Obscure Kingdoms: Journeys to Distant Royal Courts* was published by Penguin in 1995. He is currently working on a book on the Palestinians.

Colin Garden is manager of the Intermediate Technology Bookshop in London. Intermediate Technology is an international development agency and registered charity which works with rural communities in Africa, Asia, and South America.

Derek Gjertsen was educated at the universities of Leeds and Oxford. He taught philosophy and the history of science at the University of Ghana from 1960 until 1980 and is currently a research fellow in the Department of Philosophy, Liverpool University. He is the author of *The Classics of Science, The Newton Handbook*, and *Science and Philosophy*.

John Gribbin is a visiting fellow in astronomy at the University of Sussex. His many books include *In the Beginning* (1993), *In Search of the Edge of Time* (1992), *Companion to the Cosmos* (1996), and *Time and Space* (with Mary Gribbin) (1994). He also makes radio programmes on scientific topics, including the fate of Schrödinger's kittens.

Paul Griffiths has written novels, librettos, and several books on music, especially 20th-century music. He is a regular contributor to the *New Yorker*.

Wendy M Grossman, founder of the *Skeptic* magazine, is a freelance writer specializing in science and technology.

Simon Hall is an editor specializing in popular and academic history. He has a postgraduate degree in English and European history of the 12th and 13th centuries from King's College, London.

Oliver Harris is a lecturer in American literature at the Department of American Studies, Keele University. He is the editor of *The Letters of William S Burroughs, 1945–1959* (1993).

Joseph Harrison is senior lecturer in economic history at Manchester University.

Martin Henig is visiting research lecturer in Roman archaeology and art, Oxford, and honorary editor of the British Archaeological Association. He is the author of a number of books, including, apart from *Religion in Roman Britain* (1984) and *The Art of Roman Britain* (1995), a catalogue of *Classical Gems in the Fitzwilliam Museum, Cambridge* (1994) and *Roman Sculpture from the Cotswold Region* (1993).

Jacqueline Herald writes and lectures on the theory and history of dress and textiles within art and design schools of the London Institute and at the Textile Conservation Centre, Hampton Court. She is author of *Renaissance Dress in Italy* (1981), *Fashions of a Decade: 1920s* (1991), *Fashions of a Decade: 1970s* (1992), *World Crafts* (1992), and of forthcoming histories of Indian textiles and of men's fashion.

Chris Holdsworth is the editor of *The Journal of the Anthropological Society of Oxford*. He recently received his DPhil from Oxford University and is preparing for publication his thesis about the revolution in anthropological thought that occurred in the 1920s. He also teaches anthropology at the Centre for Community and Continuing Education at Goldsmith's College, London.

Mawil Izzi Dien was born in Iraq and educated there and in Britain. He taught for many years in Saudi Arabia and now lectures in Islamic studies at the University of Wales, Lampeter. His specialist interests include Islamic law and culture, and the relationship between religion and the conservation of the natural environment.

Guy Julier, currently head of critical and contextual studies in design at Leeds Metropolitan University, is the author of *New Spanish Design* and the *Thames and Hudson Encyclopedia of Twentieth Century Design and Designers*. He is also a contributor to *Modernism in Design* and to various professional and academic design journals.

Kadiatu Kanneh is lecturer in English at the School of English and American Studies, University of Sussex. She has contributed essays to many books; for example, *Sisters Under the Skin: A Politics of Heterosexuality* in *Heterosexuality: A Feminism and Psychology Reader* (1993) edited by S Wilkinson and C Kitzinger; *What Is African Literature? Ethnography and Criticism* in *Writing and Africa* (1995) edited by P Hyland and Mpalive-Hangson Msiska; and *The Difficult Politics of Wigs and Veils: Feminism and the Colonial Body* in *The Post-Colonial Studies Reader* (1995) edited by Ashcroft, Griffiths, and Tiffin.

Stanley Kauffmann has been the film critic of the *New Republic* since 1958 and has published six collections of film criticism. He has also taught film and drama at several universities; currently he is at Adelphi University.

Roz Kaveney is a writer, reviewer, anthologist, and civil-liberties activist who lives and works in London.

Sandra Knapp and Bob Press are both research scientists in the Department of Botany at the Natural History Museum, London. Sandy Knapp is an expert on the family Solanaceae worldwide and on tropical botany; she is editor of *Flora Mesoamericana*. Bob Press specializes in plants from Europe and the Atlantic Islands; he has published a variety of popular guides to European and medicinal plants.

Susanne Lahusen is a lecturer for dance and dance history at the Laban Centre for Movement and Dance and at the London School of Contemporary Dance. She coauthored *Schrifttanz–Dance in the Weimar Republic* (with Valerie Preston-Dunlop) (1990) and has published extensively on the history of modern dance.

James Le Fanu is a graduate of Cambridge University, a general practitioner in London, and medical columnist of the *Sunday Telegraph*; he is also a weekly contributor to the *Times* and the *Daily Telegraphy*. He is author of *Health Wise*; *Eat Your Heart Out: the Fallacy of the Healthy Diet*, an intelligent guide for the over-60's; and *Environmental Alarums: a Medical Audit of Environmental Damage to Human Health*. He has also contributed articles to edited books and journals including *Health, Lifestyle and Environment: Countering the Panic*, published by the Social Affairs Unit and the Manhattan Institute.

L B Lewis studied Chinese in China in the mid-1980s. She has taught English to Chinese students and introductory Chinese to English-speaking students. Now based in Oxford, she works as an editor of a publishing company. She has contributed her first-hand knowledge of China to a series of books on world geography and written a simplified outline of Chinese history for a children's book.

Graham Ley has lectured on ancient literature and society in London University and in the University of Auckland, New Zealand. He currently lives and teaches in Cambridge, and is the author of *A Short Introduction to the Ancient Greek Theatre* (1991).

Andrew Linzey is a member of the Faculty of Theology at the University of Oxford. He holds the world's first post in the theological and ethical aspects of animal welfare – the IFAW Senior Research Fellowship at Mansfield College, Oxford. He is also special professor of theology in the University of Nottingham. He has written or edited 14 books on theology and ethics, including some pioneering works on the moral status of animals: *Animal Rights* (1976), *Animals and Ethics* (1980), *Christianity and the Rights of Animals* (1987), *Animals and Christianity: A Book of Readings* (1989), *Political Theory and Animal Rights* (1990), and *Animal Theology* (1994). He is editor with Paul Clarke of the Routledge *Dictionary of Ethics, Theology and Society* (1995).

David Lowe is the Monash lecturer in American politics at the Sir Robert Menzies Centre for Australian Studies, University of London. He has published a number of works on Australia in world affairs and recently edited a collection titled *Immigration and Integration: Australia and Britain* (1995).

Alison Lurie is an American novelist, academic, and critic. Her novels include *The Nowhere City* (1965), *The War Between the Tates* (1974), *Only Children* (1979), and *Foreign Affairs* (1984), for which she received a Pulitzer Prize. She has written several books for children and a study of children's literature, *Don't Tell the Grown-Ups* (1990).

T J Lustig teaches literature in the Department of American Studies at Keele University. He is the author of *Henry James and the Ghostly* (1995) and of a novel, *Doubled Up* (1990).

Helen M Macbeth is principal lecturer in anthropology in the Anthropology Unit at Oxford Brookes University. She teaches biological anthropology, but regularly includes sociocultural information. She is interested in the role that cultural factors play in biological processes: her recent research work has been in the Cerdanya Valley, E Pyrenees, studying the effect of the Franco-Spanish border on marriage patterns (therefore genetic models) and food habits (therefore nutrition), thereby integrating social, genetic, and nongenetic biological information towards understanding human population biology. She is European chair of the International Commission on the Anthropology of Food (IUAES), and editor of *Social Biology and Human Affairs*.

Colin McEwan is assistant keeper at the Museum of Mankind, London. He curated the recently opened Mexican Gallery in the British Museum at Bloomsbury (*Ancient Mexico in the British Museum* 1994) and has published articles on diverse themes in Andean archaeology. He directs the Agua Blanca Archaeological Project in Ecuador, which has pioneered a community-based approach to the investigation of the past, mindful of the environmental and social needs of the present.

Peter Martland is preceptor in history at Corpus Christi College, Cambridge, where he teaches British economic and social history. He is currently writing a book to mark the centenary of EMI Music Ltd.

David Maw researches medieval music in the University of Oxford and is a lecturer at the Queen's College.

Bob Moore is senior lecturer in modern history at Manchester Metropolitan University and has published on Dutch and German history in the 20th century. He is currently writing a book on the persecution of the Jews in the Netherlands during World War II.

Patrick Moore, the astronomer, writer, and broadcaster, has been the presenter of the BBC television series *The Sky at Night* since 1968. His immense enthusiasm and his ability to explain the most abstruse aspects of astronomy clearly and vividly make him an outstanding science popularizer. His many books include *Atlas of the Universe* (1970), *The Amateur Astronomer* (1970), *Guide to the Planets* (1976), and *Can You Speak Venusian?* (1977).

Charles Shaar Murray has written and broadcast on popular music and related topics since 1970, appearing in publications ranging from *NME*, *OZ*, *Mojo*, and *Q* to *New Statesman*, the *Daily Telegraph*, and *Vogue*. Modesty forbids him from nominating his own *Crosstown Traffic: Jimi Hendrix and Postwar Pop* (1989) – for which he received a Ralph J Gleason Music Book Award from the publishers of *Rolling Stone – Shots from the Hip* (1991), or *Blues on CD: The Essential Guide* (1993), but he'd still like you to know that they exist. He is currently working on a biography of blues singer John Lee Hooker.

Chris Murray is a freelance editor and writer working in Oxford. He specializes in reference and art history, and is presently editing an encyclopedia of French art and writing a study of the art critic Roger Fry.

Frederick J Newmeyer is professor and chair of the Department of Linguistics at the University of Washington, Seattle. He is author and editor of a large number of books, including *Linguistic Theory in America* (1980), *Grammatical Theory: Its Limits and its Possibilities* (1983), *The Politics of Linguistics* (1986), and the four volume *Linguistics: The Cambridge Survey* (1988).

Julia Neuberger is a rabbi who lectures in Bible at Leo Baeck College, London. She is chancellor of the University of Ulster, writes about Judaism and about health care, and broadcasts frequently.

Maureen O'Connor is a freelance journalist who was the first editor of the *Guardian's* education pages and now writes for the *Observer*, the *Independent*, and *The Times Education Supplement*.

Marina Oliver was chair of the Romantic Novelists' Association 1991–93. She has published over 30 historical novels. Her latest are sagas set in the first decades of this century: *The Cobweb Cage* (1994), *The Glowing Hours* (1995), and *The Golden Road* (1996).

Derek Parker is the author of some 40 books, including biographies of Lord Byron and John Donne; he coedited the *Selected Letters* of Edith Sitwell. He is the editor of the magazine *The Author*.

Gordon L J Paterson is a senior researcher in the Department of Zoology at the Natural History Museum, London. He studies communities of animals which live on the deep-sea floor and has published many scientific papers on their ecology and distribution.

Chris Pellant lectures in higher and further education. He has written many articles, including *Recent advances in meteorology* and *Changes in the climate since the ice age*. His books include *Earthscope* (1985), which contains much material on studying the Earth's weather from space, *Rocks, Minerals, and Fossils of the World* (1990), and *Rocks and Minerals* (1992). His photographs of earth-science phenomena have been published in books and periodicals worldwide.

Geraldine Pinch teaches Egyptology for the Oriental Studies Faculty at Cambridge University. She is the author of various works, including *Votive Offerings to Hathor* (1993), *Magic in Ancient Egypt* (1994), and *The Private Life of the Ancient Egyptians* in *Civilizations of the Ancient Near East* (1995).

Alan Brian Pippard was educated at Cambridge where, after wartime research on the development of radar, he obtained his PhD in 1947. He has remained at Cambridge ever since, serving as Plummer professor of physics 1960–71, Cavendish professor 1971–82, and is now professor emeritus. He served as president of the Institute of Physics 1974–76, and has received several awards in recognition of his work: the Hughes Medal of the Royal Society 1959, the Holweck Medal 1961, the Dannie-Heinemann Prize 1969, and the Gunthrie Prize 1970. His publications include *Elements of Classical Thermodynamics* (1957), *Dynamics of Conduction Electrons* (1962), *Forces and Particles* (1972), *The Physics of Vibration* (1978, 1983), *Response and Stability* (1985), and *Magnetoresistance* (1989).

Roy Porter, of the Wellcome Institute for the History of Medicine, London, is a well-known scientific historian and broadcaster. He is the author of *English Society in the Eighteenth Century* (1982) and *A Social History of Madness* (1987), and has edited *The Faber Book of Madness* (1991) and *London: A Social History* (1994).

Robert Prys-Jones is Head of the Bird Group at the Natural History Museum, Tring, in charge of the national bird collections. He has studied birds in diverse environments from polar regions to the tropics, including five years spent lecturing at the University of Cape Town, and has published on a wide array of ornithological topics.

Martyn Rady is lecturer in Central European History at the School of Slavonic and East European Studies, University of London. His publications include *Medieval Buda* (1985), *France: Renaissance, Religion and Recovery* (1988), *Emperor Charles V* (1988), *Romania in Turmoil: A Contemporary History* (1992), *The Netherlands 1550–1650: From Revolt to Independence* (1987), and contributions to *Cultural Atlas of the Renaissance* (1993) and *The Everyman Companion to East European Literature* (1993).

Glyn Redworth studied history at Cambridge and then at Oxford, where he wrote a doctoral thesis on Tudor history. He is the author of *In Defence of the Church Catholic: the life of Stephen Gardiner* (1990) and of a Historical Association pamphlet on the background to Ferdinand and Isabella. His next book is on the short reign of King Philip the Brief of England 1554–58. He lectures at Maynooth College, in the National University of Ireland.

Brenda Richardson has taught English at university level full-time or part-time in England, Ireland, and America. Currently she is completing a feminist study of the women in Shakespearean tragedy.

Richard Rorty is university professor of the humanities at the University of Virginia. He is the author of *Philosophy and the Mirror of Nature* (1979), *Contingency, Irony and Solidarity* (1989), *Objectivity, Relativism and Truth* (1991), and *Essays on Heidegger and Others* (1991).

Brian Rosen is the research specialist on the palaeontology and biology of corals and reefs at the Natural History Museum, London, and part-time lecturer at Birkbeck College, University of London, where he teaches palaeontology. He is particularly interested in how communities and ecosystems change through time in response to global change, and in biogeography.

Simon Ross is currently head of geography at Berkhamsted School, Hertfordshire. He has written and edited several geography school textbooks, including *Hazard Geography* (1987), *The Challenge of the Natural Environment* (1989), and *Exploring Geography* (1991). He coauthored the *Hutchinson Geography Factfinder*, initiated and series-edited *GeoActive*, and is currently acting as a geography consultant to the BBC working on multimedia and computer projects.

Julian Rowe studied at the universities of Edinburgh, Indiana, and British Columbia. He worked for several years in cancer research, on the editorial board of *Nature*, and as a teacher. He is a full-time science writer, editor, and publisher and specializes in science for the nonspecialist and younger readers.

Paul Rowntree read philosophy at the University of Newcastle-upon-Tyne and at Oriel College, Oxford. He has been a local-government officer and a management consultant with a leading City firm. Currently a freelance writer and researcher, he contributes the philosophy entries to the *Hutchinson Encyclopedia*.

Jack Schofield is computer editor of the *Guardian*, which he joined after editing *Practical Computing*, an early microcomputer magazine. He is the author of the hopelessly outdated *Guardian Guide to Microcomputing* (1985), and in the dark days BC (Before Computing) produced a number of books about photography. Oh, darkroom days, actually.

Darrell Siebert works in the Department of Zoology at the Natural History Museum, London, where he specializes in the taxonomy and evolution of freshwater fishes of Southeast Asia.

Robert C Solomon is Quincy Lee centennial professor of philosophy at the University of Texas at Austin and the author of *The Passions* (1976), *In the Spirit of Hegel* (1983), *About Love* (1988), *From Hegel to Existentialism* (1988), *Continental Philosophy Since 1750* (1988), *Ethics and Excellence* (1991), and *A Passion for Justice* (1995).

Susan Sontag is the author of three novels, *The Benefactor* (1963), *Death Kit* (1967), and *The Volcano Lover* (1992); a volume of short stories, *I, etcetera* (1978); a play, *Alice in Bed* (1993); and five books of essays, including *Illness as Metaphor* (1978), *Under the Sign of Saturn* (1980), and *AIDS and Its Metaphors* (1989). Her *On Photography* won the National Book Critics Circle Prize for criticism in 1978. Ms Sontag's books are translated into 23 languages.

Francesca Speight graduated in educational philosophy and history of art in 1980. She worked in publishing before taking up private tutoring.

Joe Staines is a freelance consultant editor in arts and travel.

Gloria Steinem is an American writer and feminist organizer who is consulting editor of *Ms*, the feminist magazine she cofounded in 1972. She is also president of Voters for Choice, a bipartisan political action committee, and a founder of the National Women's Political Caucus, the Ms Foundation for Women, and the National Coalition of Labor Union Women. Her most recent book, *Moving Beyond Words*, is a collection of six essays ranging from a satirical look at Freud to a futuristic look at revaluing economics.

Ian Stewart of the University of Warwick's Mathematics Institute, is a professional research mathematician who also writes for the general public and appears on radio and TV. His books include *Does God Play Dice?* (1989), *Fearful Symmetry* (1992), *The Collapse of Chaos* (1994), and *Nature's Numbers* (1995). He writes the Mathematical Recreations column for *Scientific American* and is mathematics consultant to *New Scientist*.

John Stewart is senior lecturer in British political history in the School of Humanities, Oxford Brookes University. He researches and writes on 20th-century British social policy and teaches courses on, among other things, the meaning and nature of history.

Anthony Storr is an honorary fellow of the Royal College of Psychiatrists, a fellow of the Royal College of Physicians, a fellow of the Royal Society of Literature, and an emeritus fellow of Green College, Oxford. His books include *The Dynamics of Creation* (1972); *Solitude* (1989); *Churchill's Black Dog, Kafka's Mice, and Other Phenomena of the Human Mind* (1989); and *Music and the Mind: An Adventure into Consciousness* (1995).

Chris Stringer of the Natural History Museum, London, is a palaeoanthropologist specializing in the later stages of human evolution. He coauthored *In Search of the Neanderthals* with Clive Gamble, and *African Exodus* with Robin McKie (for publication 1996).

Christine Sutton is with the Department of Physics at Oxford University. She is the author of several nontechnical books on particle physics, including *The Particle Connection* (1984) and *Spaceship Neutrino* (1992), and contributes regularly to *New Scientist*.

Doron Swade is senior curator of computing and information technology at the Science Museum in London. He has authored a variety of articles on the history of computing and curatorship, as well as two books, one on Charles Babbage and his calculating engines, the other (coauthored) on the computer age.

Peter Tallack studied medicine and genetics at the University of London and is now on the editorial staff of the science journal *Nature*.

Anthony Thwaite has published 12 books of poems, most recently *The Dust of the World* (1994). Apart from this, for the past 40 years he has earned his living teaching English literature (in Japan, Libya, England, and the USA), and as a literary editor, reviewer, broadcaster, and publisher.

Claire Tomalin is a writer and journalist, former literary editor of the *New Statesman* and the London *Sunday Times*. She is the author of several biographies, among them *The Life and Death of Mary Wollstonecraft* (1974), *Katherine Mansfield: A Secret Life* (1987), *The Invisible Woman: The Story of Nelly Ternan and Charles Dickens* (1990), and *Mrs Jordan's Profession* (1994).

Mark Tully is the chief of the BBC Delhi Bureau and has been reporting from India for over 20 years. In addition to his award-winning journalism he is the author of *Amritsar: Mrs Gandhi's Last Battle* (1985), *Salem House* (1986), *From Raj to Rajiv* (1988), and *No Fullstops in India* (1991). He wrote and presented a five-part BBC Radio Four series on which his book *From Raj to Rajiv* is based. His TV films, all for the BBC, include *Morarji Desai: Prime Minister of India* (1978), *Ruins of the Raj* (1990), and *Bangladesh, Addicted to Aid* (1991).

Veronica Voiels is senior lecturer in the Department of Religious Education in the Faculty of Education and Community Studies at Manchester Metropolitan University. She is also principal examiner in religious education for GCSE and A-level Hinduism.

Andrew Ward is a freelance writer who has written, or co-written, more than 20 books on sport. He has recently completed *Kicking and Screaming: An Oral History of Football in England* (with Rogan Taylor).

Toshio Watanabe is professor in history of art and design at Chelsea College of Art and Design, the London Institute. He is the author of *Turner's Watercolour and Drawings* (1978), *Paul Klee* (1981), *High Victorian Japonisme* (1991), and coeditor of *Japan and Britain: An Aesthetic Dialogue 1850–1930* (1991).

Stephen Webster, a teacher at the King Alfred School, Hampstead, divides his time between teaching and writing. His most recent publications are *Me and My Body*, *Inside My House*, and the play *Marking Time*.

Alan Williams graduated with a BSc degree from Leeds University and subsequently obtained a PhD working on the chemistry of oxygenated radicals. He currently holds the Livesey Chair of Fuel and Combustion Science and has been head of the Department of Fuel and Energy since 1973. He is author or co-author of over 260 papers on combustion, pyrolysis, and general fuel matters. He is a member of the Government Energy Advisory Panel, a member of the Energy Panel of the Technology Foresight Committee, and a member of the Advisory Committee on Coal Research (DTI). He was awarded a CBE in 1995.

Trevor I Williams has for a number of years edited the international scientific review *Endeavour*, recording the progress of modern science and technology, and is also a recognized authority on the history of science and technology. He was joint editor of the eight-volume *History of Technology* (1954–84) and author of *A Short History of Twentieth-Century Technology* (1982). He has a particular interest in scientific biography and has written lives of two Nobel laureates, Lord Florey and Sir Robert Robinson.

Roy Willis, a social anthropologist, has expounded his own theory of a myth and its relation to the history of an African people in *A State in the Making* (1981). He is also author of *Man and Beast* (1974) and *There Was a Certain Man* (1978) and has edited *Societies at Peace* 1989 and *Signifying Animals* (1990).

Nigel Wright is the chair of the British Section of Amnesty International.

THE OXFAM LITERACY FUND

Literacy opens up a new world of opportunity and is a necessary foundation for sustainable development.

Over one billion adults in the world cannot read or write. Education is a basic human right, and for most people the main cause of illiteracy is poverty. For women particularly, illiteracy can be a sign of the lack of social and educational opportunities. Oxfam's support for literacy work is part of an integrated approach to development. Reading, writing, and numeracy play an essential role in the provision of such things as health care, income generation, social development, education, and agricultural improvements. Literacy is also a way into the world of the imagination, a way of sustaining culture and communicating over generations.

The Oxfam Literacy Appeal aims to establish a link between those who work with books in the UK and Oxfam's project funding overseas. *Best Books* is contributing to this appeal by donating royalties from the book to the Fund. This book owes its very existence to the many contributors who gave generously of their time and expertise in support of this appeal.

OXFAM

The international family of Oxfam organizations works with poor people and their organizations in over 70 countries. Oxfam believes that all people have basic rights: to earn a living, and to have food, shelter, health care, and education. Oxfam provides relief in emergencies, and gives long-term support to people struggling to build a better life for themselves and their families.

Literacy programmes have been run successfully in many hundreds of projects supported by Oxfam UK and Ireland, including literacy and numeracy training in Brazilian Amazonia, and a radio literacy programme in India. A rural workers' union in Honduras was so successful that it gained government recognition as an educational institution. As well as programmes run by small local organizations, Oxfam has also supported national campaigns, such as those in Namibia and Burkina Faso.

To find out more about Oxfam, write to us:

In England:
OXFAM, 274 Banbury Road, Oxford OX2 7DZ

In Ireland:
OXFAM, 19 Clanwilliam Terrace, Dublin 2

and
OXFAM, 52-4 Dublin Road, Belfast BT2 7HN

In Scotland:
OXFAM, 5th floor, Fleming House, 134 Renfrew St, Glasgow G3 6ST

In Wales:
OXFAM, 46-8 Station Road, Llanishen, Cardiff CF4 5LU

In Australia:
Community Aid Abroad, 156 George St, Fitzroy, Victoria 3065

In Belgium:
OXFAM Belgique, 39 rue du Conseil, Bruxelles 1050

In the Netherlands:
NOVIB, Amaliastraat 7, 2514 JC, The Hague

In Canada:
OXFAM Canada, 294 Albert St, Suite 300, Ottawa, Ontario K1P 6E6

In Hong Kong:
OXFAM Hong Kong, Ground floor 3B, June Garden, 28 Tung Chau St, Tai Kok Tsui, Kowloon

In New Zealand:
OXFAM New Zealand, Room 101 La Gonda House, 203 Karangahape Rd, Auckland 1

In Quebec:
OXFAM Quebec, 2330 rue Notre-Dame Ouest, Bureau 200, Montreal, Quebec H3J 1N4

In the USA:
OXFAM America, 25 West Street, Boston MA 02111-1206